UTSA Libraries

Macroeconomic Policy in a Developing Country:
The Chilean Experience

CONTRIBUTIONS TO ECONOMIC ANALYSIS

109

Honorary Editor

J. TINBERGEN

Editors

D. W. JORGENSON

J. WAELBROECK

NORTH-HOLLAND PUBLISHING COMPANY
AMSTERDAM · NEW YORK · OXFORD

MACROECONOMIC POLICY IN A DEVELOPING COUNTRY

The Chilean Experience

JERE R. BEHRMAN

University of Pennsylvania

1977

NORTH-HOLLAND PUBLISHING COMPANY
AMSTERDAM · NEW YORK · OXFORD

ISBN North-Holland for this series 0 7204 3100 x
ISBN North-Holland for this volume 0 7204 0548 3

PUBLISHERS:

NORTH-HOLLAND PUBLISHING COMPANY
AMSTERDAM · NEW YORK · OXFORD

DISTRIBUTORS FOR THE U.S.A. AND CANADA:

ELSEVIER NORTH-HOLLAND, INC.
52 VANDERBILT AVENUE
NEW YORK, N.Y. 10017

Library of Congress Cataloging in Publication Data

Behrman, Jere R.
Macroeconomic policy in a developing country.
(Contributions to economic analysis; 109)
Bibliography: p. 305

1. Chile – Economic policy. 2. Fiscal policy – Chile.
3. Monetary policy – Chile.
I. Title. II. Series.

HC192.B33   339.5'0983   76-45447
ISBN 0-7204-0548-3

PRINTED IN THE NETHERLANDS

Introduction to the series

This series consists of a number of hitherto unpublished studies, which are introduced by the editors in the belief that they represent fresh contributions to economic science.

The term *economic analysis* as used in the title of the series has been adopted because it covers both the activities of the theoretical economist and the research worker.

Although the analytical methods used by the various contributors are not the same, they are nevertheless conditioned by the common origin of their studies, namely theoretical problems encountered in practical research. Since for this reason, business cycle research and national accounting, research work on behalf of economic policy, and problems of planning are the main sources of the subjects dealt with, they necessarily determine the manner of approach adopted by the authors. Their methods tend to be 'practical' in the sense of not being too far remote from application to actual economic conditions. In addition they are quantitative rather than qualitative.

It is the hope of the editors that the publication of these studies will help to stimulate the exchange of scientific information and to reinforce international cooperation in the field of economics.

THE EDITORS

Contents

Acknowledgments

I have been involved in this and in related studies of the Chilean economy for over seven years. Not surprisingly, the list of contributing individuals and organizations to whom I am indebted is a long one. Among individuals, special thanks are due to Ricardo Lira who worked with me as a research assistant both in Santiago and in Philadelphia and to Nancy Blossom who contributed substantially in the computer programming and data processing stages. Considerable thanks also are due to a large group of economists with whom I worked or who provided suggestions while I was in Chile: Edmar Bacha, Juan de la Barra, Hollis Chenery, Peter Clark, Richard Eckaus, Alejandro Foxley, Eduardo García, Jorge García, Everett Hagen, Arnold Harberger, Ana Maria Jul, Christian Ossa, Paul N. Rosenstein-Rodan, and Lance Taylor – all of whom were associated with the Oficina de Planificacíon Nacional (ODEPLAN), the Center for International Studies of the Massachusetts Institute of Technology, and the Ford Foundation project in 1967–1970; Jorge Cauas, Ricardo Ffrench-Davis, and Carlos Massad of the Central Bank, Teresa Jeanneret, Joseph Ramos, and John Strasma of the University of Chile, and Sergio de la Cuadra of the Catholic University. A number of the same individuals provided assistance in the United States, as did F. Gerard Adams, Lawrence Klein, Joze Mencinger, James McCabe, Almarin Phillips, Robert Pollak, Robert Rasche, and Oskar Rufatt at the University of Pennsylvania, Markos Mamalakis of the Latin American Studies Center at the University of Wisconsin–Milwaukee, Hans Bergendorf of the Development Research Center of the International Bank for Reconstruction and Development, and Jagdish Bhagwati, Carlos Diaz Alejandro, Charles Frank, Anne Krueger, and Hal Lary of the National Bureau of Economic Research project on Foreign Trade Regimes and Economic Development. Furthermore, Sara Nunn, Andia Brown, Margo Richardson, Florence Barrow, Eileen Sannini, Deborah

Wilkenfeld, and the Wharton Duplication Center under the guidance of Anna-May Busch provided essential bibliographical, secretarial, and organizational services.

Among organizations, special thanks are due to the Ford Foundation in Santiago and a Ford Faculty Fellowship in Economics in 1971–1972, the Center for International Studies of the Massachusetts Institute of Technology, the University of Pennsylvania, the Development Research Center of the International Bank for Reconstruction and Development, the National Bureau of Economic Research Project on Foreign Trade Regimes and Economic Development (financed by the Agency for International Development), and the National Science Foundation under grant GS-36459. Finally, I would like to thank the National Bureau of Economic Research for permission to reproduce all or part of tables 2.1, 2.1, 4.5, 4.7, 5.1, 5.2, 5.3 and 6.2 from Behrman (1975b), and *Econometrica* for permission to reproduce tables 4.2 and 4.3 and fig. 4.1 and 4.2 from Behrman (1972a). The usual disclaimer of responsibility, of course, applies to all of these individuals and organizations.

University of Pennsylvania,   JERE R. BEHRMAN
Philadelphia, Pennsylvania,
November 1975

List of tables

List of figures

List of abbreviations used in the study

AID   Agency for International Development of the United States government.

ALALC   Associación Latinoamericana de Libre Comercio (see LAFTA).

CAP   Companía Acero de Pacífico (Pacific Steel Company).

CES   Constant elasticity of substitution (production function).

CIAP   Comite Interamericano de Alianza para el Progreso (Inter-American Committee of the Alliance for Progress).

CODELCO   Corporación del Cobre (Copper Corporation).

CORFO   Corporación del Fomento (Development Corporation).

CORVI   Corporación de Vivienda (Housing Corporation).

DEC   Dirección de Estadística y Censos (Statistics and Census Department).

ECLA   Economic Commission for Latin American.

ENAP   Empresa Nacional de Petróleo (National Petroleum Enterprise).

ENDESA   Empresa Nacional de Electricidad SA (National Electrical Enterprise).

EER   Effective exchange rate. The number of units of local currency actually paid or received for a one-dollar international transaction. Surcharges, tariffs, the implicit interest foregone on guarantee deposits, and any other charges against purchases of goods and services abroad are included, as are rebates, the value of import replenishment rights, and other incentives to earn foreign exchange for sales of goods and services abroad.

GDP	Gross domestic product.
GNP	Gross national product.
IBRD	International Bank for Reconstruction and Development.
IMF	International Monetary Fund.
ITR	Implicit tariff rate. The ratio of the domestic price (net of normal distribution costs) minus the cif import price to the cif import price in local currency.
LAFTA	Latin American Free Trade Area (see ALALC).
LME	London Metal Exchange.
NBER	National Bureau of Economic Research.
NER	Nominal exchange rate. The official parity for a transaction.
ODEPLAN	Oficina de Planificación Nacional (National Planning Office).
PLD EER	Price-level-deflated effective exchange rate. The *EER* deflated by the domestic price index.
PLD EER(PI)	The *PLD EER* adjusted for the premium received by importers due to scarcity rents on import privileges.
PLD NER	Price-level-deflated nominal exchange rate. The *NER* deflated by the domestic price index.
SOQUIM	Sociedad Química y Minera de Chile, SA (Chemical and Mining Company of Chile).
UNCTAD	United Nations Conference on Trade and Development.

Principal dates and historical events in Chile

1536   Spanish discovery of Chile by Diego de Almagro.

1810–1818   Wars of Independence from Spain.

1865–1866   War with Spain.

1879–1883   War of the Pacific; Chile defeated Peru and Bolivia and became the owner of rich nitrate and copper deposits.

1891   Civil War; President José Manuel Balmaceda killed.

1920–1924   Presidency of Arturo Alessandri; initiation of substantial social legislation; creation of Central Bank; resignation of Alessandri.

1925   Revolution; reinstatement of Alessandri, approval of new constitution; abdication of Alessandri; election of Ermiliano Figueroa Larraín as president.

1927   Resignation of Figueroa Larraín, election of Carlos Ibañez del Campo as president.

1931   Catastrophic impact of Great Depression; abandonment of convertibility; resignation of Ibañez; establishment of restrictive foreign economic regimes; succession of governments and great political instability.

1932–1938   Reestablishment of political and economic order under President Arturo Alessandri (now more conservative than in 1920s).

1939   First year of Popular Front government under President Pedro Agiurre Cerda; major earthquake; creation of CORFO.

1941   President Agiurre died.

1942   Juan Antonio Ríos elected president; copper price fixed at 12¢ per pound by agreement with United States government as part of war effort.

1946   President Ríos died; Gabriel González Videla elected president with considerable support from leftist parties; fixed price of copper terminated.

1947	Government towards right; Communist Party outlawed; diplomatic relations with the USSR broken.
1950	United States unilaterally fixed copper price because of Korean conflict.
1951	Washington Treaty signed after strong Chilean outrage.
1952	Chilean copper-sales monopoly started; Ibañez elected again to presidency.
1955	*Nuevo Trato* (new deal) legislated for large-scale copper mining, political and economic situation disintegrated considerably; Felipe Herrera made Minister of Finance; Klein–Saks consulting firm contracted for aid in stabilization program.
1956	Ibañez–Klein–Saks stabilization-cum-liberalization program initiated.
1958	Jorge Alessandri Rodríguez elected president.
1959	Alessandri stabilization-cum-liberalization program commenced.
1960	Major earthquake in south.
1962	Stabilization-cum-liberalization effort abandoned.
1964	Eduardo Frei Montalva elected president.
1965	Frei stabilization-cum-liberalization effort began; sliding-peg exchange rate policy adopted; foreign debt renegotiated.
1966	Chileanization of Kennecott's copper holdings.
1967	Collapse of stabilization attempt.
1969	Nationalization of Anaconda's copper holdings.
1970	Abandonment of sliding-peg exchange rate policy; Salvador Allende Gossens elected president as head of Popular Unity Coalition.
1971	Complete nationalization of large-scale copper mining; intensified quantitative restrictions.
1972	Foreign debt renegotiation.
1973	Military coup in which President Allende was killed.

PART I

INTRODUCTION

CHAPTER 1

Overview and summary

This is an empirical study of the economic structure and of the impact of macroeconomic policies during the postwar period in the case of a particular developing economy – Chile. Ch. 2 provides historical and institutional perspective. Sectoral relationships on the nine-sector level of aggregation are estimated and their partial-equilibrium implications are discussed in the chs. 3–6 of Part II. Then they are combined into a complete-system model with which policy alternatives are simulated in Part III.

1.1. Motivation for this study

Why is such an investigation of interest? The answers to this question are many.

(1) The Chilean experience itself is of considerable importance because it has been fundamental in inspiring some of the most significant analysis of development problems by economists from developing nations (e.g. secular deteriorations in the terms of trade, 'structuralism', and 'dependence'[1]) and because it has included a wide range of macroeconomic policy objectives and tools under governments with substantially varying political philosophies (ch. 2). A better understanding of that experience is valuable in itself.

---

[1]For discussions of the hypothesized secular deterioration in the terms of trade of many developing countries, see Habeler (1961), Kindleberger (1956), Morgan (1959) and Prebisch (1959). In regard to structuralism, see Baer (1967), Campos de Olivereira (1964), Corbo (1971), Edel (1969), Pazos (1972), Prebisch (1961), Seers (1963), Sierra (1969), Sunkel (1958), and Wachter (1974). The seminal study on dependence is Sunkel (1967).

(2) Our ignorance of the structures of developing economies is enormous. Data inadequacies abound. Much analysis is based, perhaps quite inappropriately, on the transplantation of assumptions about functional forms and parameter values from developed to developing economies or from one developing country to another. This in-depth statistical investigation of Chile, in addition to adding considerably to our knowledge of that particular economy, may be helpful in regard to other developing nations.

(3) The main frameworks for macroeconomic policy analysis and policy recommendations for the developing economies in the postwar period have been provided by Harrod–Domar aggregate-growth models, Lewis–Fei–Ranis labor-surplus models, Leontief fixed-coefficient models, static and dynamic linear-programming models and Chenery two-gap models[2]. Assumptions which are generally made in the construction of these models include: (i) that the degree of capacity utilization, the rate of inflation, and the extent of aggregate demand are not important considerations; (ii) that the financial constraints on government and central bank behavior (and, thus, the entire fiscal–monetary–income–international policy–inflation nexus) safely can be ignored; and (iii) that short-run flexibility is extremely limited because elasticities of substitution are practically zero because short-run price responses are very low, and because any responses which do occur are distributed over long time periods. The resulting models usually include only real phenomena and are characterized by supply bottlenecks due to either foreign exchange or capital constraints. The present study tests most of the above-mentioned assumptions, both in partial and complete model contexts.

(4) The programming models (in the development of which the greatest resources have probably been expanded), moreover, max-imize a global objective function which leads to that exploration of the question 'What *could* happen if socially optimal readjustment of the economy occurred in response to policy changes?' rather than 'What *would* happen if independent economic units which make up the economy followed their traditional behavioral patterns in re-

[2]Examples (and basic sources) include Adelman and Thorbecke (1966), Blitzer et al. (1975), Cabezón (1969), Chenery and Strout (1966), Clark and Foxley (1970, 1973), Eckaus and Parikh (1968), Fei and Ranis (1964), Lewis (1954), Manne (1974), UNECAFE (1960), and UNCTAD (1968).

sponse to such changes?'[3] In determining the impact of macroeconomic policies, of course, it is the latter question which is of primary interest – and on which the present study focuses.

(5) Although the models mentioned above have ignored short-run stabilization issues, these concerns have long been of substantial policy interest in a number of developing countries, especially those with a history of high inflation (including Chile). The participants in the 'structuralist–monetarist' controversy in Latin America, for example, for years have focused on the relation between short-run stabilization and long-run development[4]. The worldwide inflation of the early 1970s has increased interest in short-run issues. Even the strongest advocates of supply-oriented, capital-and-foreign-exchange-constrained macroanalysis of the developing economies, moreover, seem to be having second thoughts about the wisdom of excluding short-run stabilization features from their models[5]. The complete system model of Part III of this study incorporates a large number of these short-run considerations.

(6) Because of this growing interest in stabilization and other short-run problems, a large number of Keynesian-based national-income-determination models have recently been constructed and utilized for the developing economies[6]. All too often, however, the

[3] 'Socially optimal' is used here not to imply that externalities are incorporated, but to mean that which maximizes the objective function given the constraints imposed by the model itself, starting and terminal conditions, and exogenous variables. Some limited aspects of behavioral responses, of course, are incorporated in these studies, such as the sectoral pattern of income elasticities for private consumption.

[4] See the references in the note 1 in this chapter.

[5] In their recent survey of the state of the art regarding the use of economy-wise models for developing countries, for example, Blitzer et al. (1975) do not even include a chapter on macroeconomic income-determination models. Throughout their book, however, there are frequent references to the need to add short-run features to the models which they are discussing (e.g. price responses, capacity-utilization determination, aggregate-demand-related policies).

[6] For examples for developing economies in Latin America, see Albertelli (1967), Barraza-Allande (1968), Barraza-Allande and Solis (1974), Behrman (1975e), Behrman and Klein (1970), Bello (1969), Beltran (1973), Beltran and Klein (1974), Cerboni (1975), Corbo (1971, 1974), Davila (1966), Deprano and Nugent (1966), Durán and Solís (1975), Dutta and Su (1969), Escuela National de Economía (1970), Fletcher (1965), Geithmann (1964), Gomez (1968), Gupta (1974), Harris (1970), Hernandez (1974), Iton (1968), Kelso (1973), Khan (1974), Lawrsen (1967), Lira (1975), Liu and De Vries (1969), Manhertz (1971), Marwah (1969), Marzouk (1969), Maneshi and Reynolds (1964), Molina and Mellor (1974), Montemayor (1974), Monterio (1971), Naranjo-Villalobos (1972 and 1974), Nugent (1965, 1974), Pandit (1971), Perez-Castillo (1963), Pujol (1969), Reinafarje and Yepez (1972), SIECA (1973), Slooten (1968), Stahl

structures of these models have been transplanted from aggregate-demand models of developed economies with little or no adjustments for the special conditions in the developing countries[7]. Numerous shortcomings in the resulting specifications are quite common: (i) National income is determined by aggregate demand, with no testing of the existence of possible capacity constraints due to the stock of capital and labor or the supply of foreign exchange. (ii) Aggregation is so great that there is no possibility of capturing the impact of policies on relative prices even though development economists like Hansen (1973) have maintained that policies in developing nations are primarily reflected in altered relative prices and Wachter (1974) has demonstrated that differing speeds of adjustment of relative prices may result in 'structural' inflation. The possible importance of intersectoral flows, moreover, is lost by the high level of aggregation. (iii) No attempt is made to explore the role of human capital despite the growing emphasis on its significance. (iv) Underemployed or surplus labor and dualism in the labor market are not incorporated. (v) The role of social overhead capital, long emphasized by such leading development economists as Rosenstein-Rodan (1961), is not investigated. (vi) The significance of the foreign sector as a source of non-competitive intermediate imports and of capital goods, as well as of a significant proportion of government revenues, is not well presented. (vii) The degree of endogeneity of fiscal and monetary variables is ignored, with the result that policy options are overstated. (viii) The importance – due to fragmented and poorly functioning capital markets – of direct flows and of retained earnings in the real investment process is not explored. (ix) The possible impact of quantitative restrictions, which are widely utilized in some developing nations, is not examined. (x) Disequilib-

---

(1965), Stavrou and Arboleda (1975), Steed (1969), Stewart (1966), Sutton (1968), Taylor (1969), Thorbecke (1969), Thorbecke and Condos (1966), Tintner et al. (1970), Tintner et al. (1970), United Nations (1964), UNCTAD (1968, 1973), and von Rijckeghem (1965a, 1965b, and 1969). Beltran (1974) summarizes the features of a number of these Latin American models. Lau (1975) provides references for models for developing nations in other parts of the world.

[7]Behrman (1975c, 1975d) and Behrman and Hanson (1975, 1976) on a general level discuss a number of changes which must be made in current standard stabilization models for developing economies before they might be appropriate for developing economies.

rium phenomena are ignored[8]. In contrast to its predecessors, the present study attempts to deal with all of these problems.

1.2. *Major results of the study*

This study provides considerable knowledge about the structure of the postwar Chilean economy and about the impact of macroeconomic policy within that economy. Some of this knowledge might appropriately be generalized to other developing economies. The detailed results are so numerous that it is impossible to summarize all of them concisely here. The following points, however, capture the more general major implications.

(1) There is a great deal of heterogeneity across sectors in technological substitutabilities and in both the degree and the time path of behavioral responses to economic variables. Especially since so much of the direct policy impact is on relative prices, as Hansen (1973) emphasizes, greater aggregation might lead to quite misleading analysis. Indeed, if the available data permitted it, the even greater disaggregation advocated by Hansen might be desirable.

(2) Estimated sectoral elasticities of substitution between capital and labor range from 0.0 to 0.9. The adjustment periods for substitution between primary factors are fairly long in several cases in which the long-run elasticities are high. For most sectors in the short and medium runs, therefore, the results provide some support for the assumption of limited flexibility which underlies Eckaus' (1955) technological explanation of the existence of under- or unemployed labor, the structuralist analysis of inflation, and the use of fixed coefficients in input–output based models.

Limited flexibility, however, is not the same as no flexibility. Some primary factor substitution apparently is possible in response to relative price changes. The sectors in which substitution is greatest in the short and medium runs, moreover, are not those

---

[8]Many of the studies cited in footnote 6 attempt to account for one or two of these features. Nevertheless, the list of shortcomings in any specific study is generally quite large. For example, the major previous study of Chile, Corbo (1974), does worry about the endogeneity of the money supply and does include supply constraints, but does not avoid many of the other shortcomings listed in the text. Note 1 in ch. 7 below provides a brief critique of this study. For a more extensive review see Behrman (1976).

which are generally thought to serve as the predominant absorbers of surplus labor (i.e. services, construction, agriculture, and government). Instead, it is relatively high in manufacturing and mining. Under the assumptions that labor is homogeneous and overabundant at inflexible wages and that capital is constraining production, therefore, society might benefit from wage subsidies (or other inducements) for sectors like manufacturing and mining in which labor has a relatively high marginal productivity so that they absorb surplus labor instead of the traditional sectors.

The same pattern of elasticities across sectors also suggests that the aggregate elasticity of substitution between capital and labor may grow and result in more overall flexibility if the government succeeds in its apparent policy of expanding the importance of manufacturing and mining[9]. Nevertheless, the aggregate Chilean elasticity of substitution between capital and labor is likely to remain substantially below one. Such a value may constrain growth if the rates of increase of the primary factors differ significantly. Under neoclassical assumptions, such a value also implies that the relatively quickly growing primary factor will decrease its share of the national product. According to the fragmentary evidence available, in fact, the faster growing factor – capital – has experienced a relative secular decline in its factor share.

(3) Estimated sectoral real physical capital investment functions suggest that the postwar Chilean experience has been substantially consistent with the putty–putty type of investment behavior model which has been used for the developed mixed-capitalist economies. Determinants of Chilean investment include real replacement needs, neoclassical considerations based on CES production functions, uncertainty, government financial investment, and, to a lesser extent, capacity utilization considerations and imports of machinery and equipment. These partial-equilibrium results imply that government policies can induce greater real physical investment, particularly in the key sector of manufacturing, by larger government financial investment and by increasing the price of output relative to the price of capital services through reductions in the cost of capital or in the effective direct business tax rate, through increases in

[9]This statement is contrary in spirit to that which Nerlove (1967) makes about shifts towards manufacturing because he assumes that the elasticities of substitution between capital and labor are high in primary as compared to secondary and tertiary industries.

depreciation allowances or investment tax credits, and through changes in foreign trade policy. Government fiscal and monetary policies which increase the degree of capacity utilization and reduce uncertainty may also result in greater real physical capital investment in some sectors.

(4) No significant role for human capital can be identified, despite extensive efforts. This failure may reflect the fact that the available data permit the representation of the stock of human capital only on an economy-wide level and only under strong assumptions about the returns to education being measured by earnings differentials[10]. Future research on a less aggregative level and with a more satisfactory measure of human capital might indicate a more important role. The present study, however, does not provide support for those who emphasize the significance of this factor.

(5) Substantial excess capacity has existed in the Chilean economy during the post-war period. The utilization of this excess capacity could have resulted in a significant increase both in the level and in the growth rate of the national product. Partial-equilibrium determinants of sectoral capacity utilization include product and factor prices, the state of economic activity, the quantity of credit, public infrastructure development, taxes, anticipated inflation, and the availability of imported inputs and of imported competitive products. The widespread response to market conditions (including the state of aggregate demand) suggests that markets do play an important allocative role in the short run[11]. Therefore policies should not distort the signals transmitted by these markets under the false assumption that they will have no effect on allocation. Policies that distort market conditions may be justified, but the government should not ignore the resource allocation costs. Also, for short- and medium-term policy, recommendations based on fixed capital coefficients and full capacity utilization assumptions (such as in the Harrod–Domar and Chenery models) may be misleading because of the existence of unutilized capacity in addition to the possibility of substitution among factors.

---

[10]Behrman and Taubman (1975, 1976a, and 1976b) and Taubman (1975) present estimates which suggest that conventional measurements of the returns to education are biased upwards by a factor of 2 or 3 because of the failure to control for differences in genetics and home environments.

[11]Paragraph (3) above suggests that markets also play an important allocative role in the long run.

(6) Partial-equilibrium estimates of import functions (by end use) and of export functions (by production sectors) indicate significant responses in a number of cases to relative prices (adjusted to incorporate the price-related effects of foreign trade policies), uncertainty, quantitative restrictions, demand and production.

The implied price responses suggest that the Chilean policy of maintaining a secularly increasingly overvalued exchange rate exacerbated substantially balance of payments difficulties[12]. For example, the 63% drop in the *PLD NER* (price-level-deflated nominal exchange rate) between 1946 and 1972 and the estimated elasticities, *ceteris paribus*, imply increases in imports of 57% for secondary consumption goods, 88% for transportation related investment goods, 18% for intermediate goods and 50% for services and drops in exports of 100% from industry, 50% from small- and medium-scale mining, 32% from agriculture, 19% from large-scale mining, and 13% for exports from services. These results also suggest that the foreign-sector regimes increased dependence on the traditional exports (i.e. those from large-scale mining) despite a number of stated intentions to encourage diversification.

The response to uncertainty in relative prices is widespread, although not generally large in magnitude. This pattern implies that there was a significant, but not substantial, payoff to the sliding-peg exchange rate policy of 1965–1970.

The impact of quantitative restrictions on imports is pervasive and large. They apparently are the only effective direct policy instruments, in fact, for habitual and durable consumption goods and for machinery and equipment imports. From examination of the partial-equilibrium estimates, the intensification of quantitative restrictions seems to favor non-durable consumption goods over consumption and investment durables and to favor goods over services.

Domestic demand and credit availability variables affect a number of import categories. Production affects most export categories. These responses point to the need to integrate the foreign sector functions into a general-equilibrium framework.

(7) The major determinant of savings is the appropriate net income variables. The marginal propensities increase from a range

---

[12]Behrman (1975a and 1975b) explores in detail Chilean exchange rate policy and other foreign sector policies.

of 0.04 to 0.38 for households and non-profit institutions, to 0.55 to 0.63 for businesses and to 0.67 to 0.73 for the government. Income shifts from households to businesses within the private sector and from the private sector to the public sector consequently would tend to increase savings. For households, shifts from the rest of the economy to agriculture and from non-wage to wage income tend to increase savings. Higher inflation also results in some forced savings by this sector. For households and businesses, real monetary balances in excess of desired levels reduce savings. For all three sectors there is some evidence that foreign savings at least partially substitute for domestic savings[13]. Thus, increased aid or private capital inflows may in part go to higher consumption.

(8) The major direct determinant of the rate of change of sectoral product and factor prices is the rate of change of the money supply, with its impact distributed over a number of periods and with some evidence of overshooting in the Diz (1966) sense. Growth in the money supply, in turn, primarily reflects the size of the government deficit financed internally and foreign exchange movements, with some modifications due to changes in Central Bank policy variables and in behavioral responses of commercial banks and of the public. In substantial part, hence, the money supply is a passive transmitter of inflationary pressure, as the structuralists have argued. Because of the lags in the price determination process, moreover, stemming inflation is quite difficult unless expectations about future price movements can be lowered drastically.

Non-monetary factors, however, also significantly affect prices. Cost-push factors operating through intermediate input and unit labor costs are more important in transmitting overall inflationary pressures (including those which arise from the role of expectations in the wage bargaining process) than previous studies, such as Harberger (1963), have maintained. Real changes in per capita GDP (and other indices of current activity), in labor productivities, in demands (final and intermediate) facing sectors relative to capacity, and in the distribution of factoral income and of sectoral product have significant effects. Foreign-sector policies, both price-related (i.e. exchange rates, taxes, prior deposits) and quantitative, are pervasive in their impact.

---

[13]Weisskopf (1972), among others, makes this hypothesis. Papanek (1972, 1973) provides criticism.

(9) One important implication of the partial-equilibrium results summarized in the above points is that the price system is playing to some degree a role which could lead to greater efficiency. Sector-specific prices reflect sector-specific costs and capacity utilization considerations. Hence, signals are given at least in the right directions, assuming that any countervailing externalities are not completely offsetting. Both capacity-utilization and capacity-creation decisions respond significantly to these prices. Possibilities for increased capacity utilization and for factor substitution do exist.

To ignore the role of the price system and these other characteristics when conducting analysis and giving policy prescriptions, therefore, may be costly in terms of forgoing the use of some policy tools, overemphasizing the role of 'key factors', and creating incentives for misallocations. And yet the dominant macroeconomic frameworks utilized for analysis of development problems for the most part do assume that these factors can be ignored [see (3) in section 1.1]. More explicitly in the Chilean case, ODEPLAN (Oficina de Planificación Nacional, National Economics Planning Office) has utilized relative rigid fixed-capital-coefficient and/or foreign-exchange-saving gap models as the basis for planning and prediction[14]. Policy tools have included price ceilings, quantitative restrictions on international trade and on credit, and multiple exchange rates at overvalued levels.

(10) This study also demonstrates that it is possible to model at least some developing economies in ways which reflect their special characteristics [see paragraph (6) in section 1.1.] Data limitations obviously constrain such an effort, but not nearly as much as the earlier studies referred to in note 6 (p. 5) might suggest.

(11) The complete system simulations suggest that simple textbook macromodels often are poor predictors of many of the short- and medium-run effects of exogenous changes. This is so because of substantial induced responses in government and bank behavior, considerable compositional changes, differing time patterns of responses across variables, non-linearities, and important simultaneous and lagged feedbacks.

(12) The complete system results suggest that policies can have significant impact. Fiscal, monetary, and foreign sector policies can

---

[14]For example, see Harberger and Selowsky (1966) or ODEPLAN (1970b).

have quite substantial effects on most areas of policy concern, although relatively less so on capacity expansion. Incomes policies have less potency. Fiscal policies have a greater impact on real capacity utilization than do the other alternatives.

(13) In some respects the complete model results support some of the prevailing beliefs concerning Chilean policy choices. Despite fairly high partial-equilibrium price elasticities, for example, the complete model balance of payments responses to devaluation are quite limited. Prices are increased significantly, with a negative inflationary impact and with a largely neutralizing effect on trade movements. Because of the stickiness of wages and of tax collections, the resulting inflation shifts resources away from labor and from the government. Liberalization leads to immediate stagnation, although subsequently reversals occur. Overvaluation does have the effects desired by various governments of inducing shifts from agriculture and mining to manufacturing. For balance of payments objectives alone, quantitative restrictions may be more effective than exchange rate adjustments.

(14) In other respects, however, the simulations illustrate ways in which historical policies have caused results opposite to those intended. The historical foreign sector policy choices, for example, have discouraged most of all the very non-traditional exports which various governments have claimed they wanted to expand. The intensification of quantitative restrictions on imports, moreover, not only does not limit primarily the 'postponable' durable imports, but also reduces exports – which exacerbates the foreign exchange shortages. Policies adopted to improve the distribution of income from the point of view of labor often increase regressivity among laborers.

(15) All in all, the complete model analysis suggest that the lot of a policymaker in such an economy is a very difficult one, a point which economists with such differing viewpoints as Friedman (1974) and Taylor (1974) have emphasized recently. Substantial trade-offs exist among various macroeconomic objectives (e.g. growth, distribution, nominal and real stability, resource allocation and structural change, and foreign economic position), so priorities must be established. As is noted above, simple textbook models and partial equilibrium analysis often are misleading predictors of the magnitude and even of the direction of short- and medium-run effects. Policy tools are limited by such realities as the absence of an

integreted capital market. Lags and indirect effects almost undoub-
tedly preclude successful 'fine-tuning' of the economy.

(16) The partial equilibrium and complete-model results of this
study do not exclusively support one side or the other in the
structuralist–monetarist controversy. In contrast to the structuralist
position, evidence is found for significant sectoral flexibility and
price responsiveness – even in agriculture. In support of the structuralist position, relative price changes are important in the inflationary process, the money supply is largely passive and limits overall
policy impact, and certain characteristics of the overall structure
(e.g. price expectations) would have to be changed before most
macroeconomic policies had large aggregate effects.

(17) The analysis also suggests – although quite tentatively – that
efforts at gradual change are liable to fail because political momentum probably will not last long enough for the benefits to be
perceived. The 'stop-and-go' history of stabilization policies in the
past two decades has created a real cynicism about the maintenance
of any economic program. Within this context, perhaps only abrupt
changes have much probability of altering expectations so that
sufficiently rapid success is attained.

CHAPTER 2

Three major postwar Chilean stabilization attempts

In the postwar period the Chilean economy has had a number of major macroeconomic goals: (1) stabilization in nominal and in real terms, (2) structural change and resource reallocation among sectors, (3) redistribution of income and of the control over resources, (4) growth; and (5) establishment of greater national control over the economy in general and over the foreign sector in particular.

As ch. 8 explores, trade-offs exist among these aims. Quite frequently in the past three decades the very high inflation has led to *prima facie* preoccupation with nominal stabilization, apparently at the cost of the attainment of some of the other objectives. A primary component of all of the major economic programs has been price stabilization. This chapter focuses upon the major stabilization programs in order to provide a framework for the subsequent analysis. Emphasis is placed on the three major stabilization attempts of the 1950s and 1960s since only limited information is available about the efforts of the 1970s.

Tables 2.1 and 2.2 give mean values and selected annual values for periods relating to the major stabilization episodes[1]. Variables are included for each of the five areas of major macroeconomic policy goals which are listed above. Based on this and on other relevant data, the sections below consider the stabilization efforts with emphasis on three questions. (1) What was the background for the attempt? (2) What was the nature of the overall economic program? (3) What were the results?

---

[1]Throughout this chapter, unless otherwise noted, all references to variables are to variables in table 2.1.

Table 2.1

Arithmetic means for major characteristics of the Chilean economy during stabilization attempts and other periods, 1940–1970.[a]

Variables	1940–1946	1947–1951	1952–1955	1956–1958	1959–1961	1962–1964	1965–1970
1. Cyclical variables							
1.1. Nominal terms							
1.1.1. Rate of change of *GDP* deflator (%)	15.1	20.8	47.8	37.6	19.3	35.4	31.7
1.1.2. Income velocity (annual)	8.56	9.54	10.54	12.77	13.03	12.13	11.70
1.2. Real terms							
1.2.1. Capacity utilization for *GDP*	0.93	0.90	0.91	0.90	0.92	0.96	0.95
1.2.2. Unemployment rate in Santiago in June					0.072[b]	0.053	0.062
1.3. Monetary policy-related variables							
1.3.1. Rate of change of money supply (%)	21.2[c]	20.7	45.3	35.8	26.2	35.2	43.2
1.3.2. Rate of growth of credit to public sector (%)	9.1[c]	19.0	64.4	46.7	74.4	51.1	35.5[d]
1.3.3. Marginal reserve requirement for demand deposits (%)	20	20	20	20	79.2	62	71.5
1.4. Fiscal policy-related variables							
1.4.1. Government current expenditures/*GDP*	0.08	0.09	0.10	0.10	0.10	0.10	0.10
1.4.2. Government savings/total savings	0.30	0.22	0.13	0.18	0.28	0.24	0.44
1.4.3. Government investment/total investment	0.44	0.45	0.56	0.48	0.38	0.35	0.45[d]
1.4.4. Government deficit/*GDP*	0.01	–0.00	0.02	0.02	0.04	0.04	0.02
1.4.5. Taxes/*GNP*	0.14	0.15	0.16	0.18	0.21	0.20	0.24
2. Resource allocation and structural change							
2.1. Composition of *GDP*							
2.1.1. Production sectors							
2.1.1.1. Agriculture	0.15	0.14	0.12	0.13	0.13	0.11	0.11
2.1.1.2. Mining	0.10	0.08	0.06	0.04	0.07	0.07	0.06
2.1.1.3. Industry	0.18	0.21	0.22	0.21	0.19	0.19	0.19
2.1.2. Final demand							
2.1.2.1. Private consumption	0.77	0.79	0.79	0.80	0.80	0.77	0.76
2.1.2.2. Investment in structures and equipment	0.08	0.10	0.10	0.10	0.11	0.13	0.11
2.2. Agricultural deflator/*GDP* deflator	0.98	1.01	1.14	0.99	0.94	0.92	1.06

3. Income distribution							
3.1. Average wage/consumption deflator (1965 = 1.0)[e]	0.57	0.67	0.74	0.77	0.78	0.92	1.12
3.2. Wage share of *GDP*[f]	0.58	0.64	0.63	0.63	0.60	0.64	0.67
4. Rates of growth in real terms (%)							
4.1. *GDP* per capita	2.2	1.2	0.9	1.4	1.2	1.6	2.5
4.2. Industrial *GDP*	7.5	6.3	6.8	-1.4	2.8	4.9	5.1
4.3. Agricultural *GDP*	1.2	0.9	1.7	10.7	-2.9	0.7	2.9
4.4. Investment in structures and equipment	7.0	3.8	4.6	2.7	15.1	2.6	4.0
4.5. Marginal gross capital/output ratio[g]	2.7	3.3	3.1	2.8	3.1	3.4	2.4
5. Foreign sector							
5.1. Prices							
5.1.1. Price-level-deflated nominal exchange rate (27/1/59 = 1.00)[h]	1.53	0.79	0.61	0.79	0.77	0.73	0.69
5.1.2. 1960 dollars/escudo	31.0	14.7	4.78	1.44	0.95	0.58	0.15
5.1.3. Free or black market rate/national accounts rate[i]	1.11	1.70	2.66	1.44	1.01	1.70	1.55
5.1.4. Effective exchange rates/national accounts rate[i]							
5.1.4.1. Consumption goods (1965 = 1.00)	0.99	1.27	1.49	1.06	0.99	1.03	0.96
5.1.4.2. Investment goods (1965 = 1.00)	1.25	1.24	1.30	0.96	0.97	1.01	0.96
5.1.5. Terms of trade							
5.1.5.1. Export unit value/import unit value (1965 = 1.00)	0.66	0.68	0.91	0.89	0.86	0.94	1.18[i]
5.1.5.2. Copper returns export unit value/import unit value[p]	1.39	1.93	2.65	1.93			
5.1.6. Import premium rate[l]	0.76[m]	0.73	1.43	0.87	0.58	0.58	0.50
5.1.7. Price-level-deflated effective exchange rate	4.42	4.42	3.35	4.29	4.30	4.00	3.60
5.2. Quantities							
5.2.1. Import good composition							
5.2.1.1. Consumption	0.35	0.31	0.30	0.30	0.33	0.35	.32/.16[n]
5.2.1.2. Investment	0.15	0.24	0.27	0.37	0.35	0.35	.33/.36[n]
5.2.1.3. Intermediate	0.50	0.35	0.43	0.34	0.32	0.30	.34/.44[n]
5.2.2. Imports/total supply							
5.2.2.1. Consumption	0.04	0.03	0.03	0.03	0.04	0.05	.04/.02[m]
5.2.2.2. Investment	0.16	0.19	0.24	0.32	0.37	0.36	.32/.40[n]
5.2.3. Export good composition							
5.2.3.1. Agriculture	0.13	0.13	0.09	0.09	0.08	0.08	0.04
5.2.3.2. Mining	0.79	0.80	0.81	0.83	0.84	0.85	0.86

Table 2.1 (continued)

Variables	1940–1946	1947–1951	1952–1955	1956–1958	1959–1961	1962–1964	1965–1970
5.2.3.3. Industry	0.07	0.07	0.09	0.08	0.08	0.06	0.10
5.2.4. Percentage rates of growth							
5.2.4.1. Import value (in constant United States dollars)	6.3	12.7	3.8	4.3	6.1	-1.8	6.0
5.2.4.2. Export value (in constant United States dollars)	6.2	12.8	7.0	-5.5	7.3	7.2	11.0
5.2.5. Chilean trade statistics/those of major trading partners							
5.2.5.1. Imports recorded by Chile/exports recorded by others		1.21°	1.36	1.17	1.15	1.20	1.07
5.2.5.2. Exports recorded by Chile/imports recorded by others		0.95°	1.00	0.98	0.94	0.92	0.95
5.2.6. Balance of payments (in 10⁶ 1958 United States dollars)							
5.2.6.1. Goods and services		-50.1	-5.6	-81.7	-163.0	-179.9	-77.0
5.2.6.1.1. Merchandise		20.7	56.3	-5.6	-71.0	-74.4	97.7
5.2.6.1.1.1. Exports		392.2	475.2	429.8	442.8	485.1	770.8
5.2.6.1.1.2. Imports		371.5	418.9	434.9	513.8	559.5	680.5
5.2.6.1.2. Services		-70.8	-61.9	-76.1	-92.0	-105.5	-174.7
5.2.6.1.2.1. Freight and other transportation		3.6	9.0	6.4	4.0	3.5	14.2[d]
5.2.6.1.2.2. Travel		0.6	-0.8	-7.8	-21.5	-8.8	-1.3[d]
5.2.6.1.2.3. Investment income		-77.1	-67.8	-71.4	-67.1	-89.0	-158.0
5.2.6.2. Unrequited transfers		1.1	-0.1	19.6	38.2	9.6	27.9
5.2.6.2.1. Private		0.9	-1.4	5.3	10.1	5.0	5.0[d]
5.2.6.2.2. Central government		0.2	1.3	14.3	28.2	4.6	9.4[d]
5.2.6.3. Capital and monetary gold		46.0	10.9	70.1	129.1	168.9	72.9
5.2.6.3.1. Nonmonetary sectors		39.9	18.6	37.4	82.6	143.9	145.9
5.2.6.3.1.1. Direct investment		22.0	16.8	42.8	43.7	-2.4	1.0[d]
5.2.6.3.1.1.1. Large-scale mining companies		13.0	9.2	20.7	-2.9	-18.7	-2.6[d]
5.2.6.3.1.2. Other private long-term		-0.3	-0.3	8.8	23.5	48.5	51.3[d]
5.2.6.3.1.3. Other private short-term		1.1	-1.2	-8.6	16.0	6.6	18.6[d]
5.2.6.3.1.4. Central government		17.0	3.4	-5.4	-0.6	91.3	82.1[d]
5.2.6.3.2. Monetary sectors		6.1	-5.6	32.7	46.4	24.9	-73.0
5.2.7. Other							

5.2.7.1. Index of quantitative restrictions	0.94	0.95	0.98	0.96	0.92	0.96	0.95[d]
5.2.7.2. Index of export capacity to import (1965 = 1.00)[b]	0.47	0.48	0.62	0.65	0.71	0.85	1.23[j]
5.2.7.3. Net foreign reserves held by banking system (10^6 US $)[a]	7.0[a]	89.1[a]	79.1	29.9	−60.0	−246.	−17.0[b]
5.2.7.4. Foreign debt at year end/exports for year				1.20[rs]	1.31[s]	2.52	2.41
5.2.7.5. Taxes related to foreign trade/total taxes	0.37[f]	0.35[c]	0.29[a]	0.21[t]	0.21[t]	0.21[c]	0.18[c]
5.2.7.6. Imports/*GDP*	0.09	0.09	0.09	0.10	0.12	0.12	0.13
5.2.7.7. Exports/*GDP*	0.19	0.15	0.11	0.12	0.12	0.13	0.12[d]
5.2.7.8. Import taxes/import value	0.22	0.24	0.22	0.17	0.20	0.21	0.17[d]

[a] Appendix A gives the sources of all variables with the following exceptions. The United States deflators and indices used in variables 5.1.2, 5.1.4.1, 5.1.4.2, and 5.2.7 are from the Council of Economic Advisors (1972); variable 5.1.2 is from Hurtado (1966) for 1940–1960 and from Ffrench-Davis (1971) for 1960–1969; variable 5.1.2 for 1970 and all balance of payments variables (5.2.6) are from table 8.1 in Behrman (1975b); variable 5.1.6 is from table A.1 in Behrman (1975b); variables 5.2.5.1 and 5.2.5.2 are calculated from data in IMF and IBRD (1953–1972); variable 5.2.7.2 is from Ffrench-Davis (1971) for 1952–1969; variables 5.2.7.5. and 5.2.7.6 are based on data from Humud (1969); and variable 1.2.2 is from Instituto de Economía (1958–1971).

[b] 1960–1961 only.

[c] 1941–1946 only.

[d] 1965–1969 only.

[e] The secular trend in the labor force is used in this series instead of actual employment data (which does not exist for the whole country over a long time period) which means that this series understates the wage level when employment is high relative to when unemployment is low.

[f] This series includes self-employed individuals.

[g] This variable is not in rate of growth terms, but is defined as the ratio of gross value of investment in structures and equipment within a period to the change in real *GDP* over the same period.

[h] The base for this variable is 27 January 1959 because Instituto de Economía (1963) and Leftwich (1966) suggest that, given the trade regime then in operation, the rate was very close to equilibrium at that time.

[i] The national accounts exchange rate is a weighted average of the various nominal exchange rates in use. It is used by CORFO and by ODEPLAN in the preparation of the national accounts.

[j] 1965–1966.

[k] The returned export unit value is the unit price of copper exports by large-scale mining adjusted for the proportion which stays in Chile due to taxes and local purchases (often at unfavorable exchange rates from the point of view of the owners of large-scale mining). The base year is 1925. See Reynolds (1965).

Table 2.1 (continued)

^lThe import premium rate is the average premium on competitive and non-competitive imports. For both of these categories of imports this rate is equal to (1.0 + implicit tariff rate)/effective exchange rate − 1.0.

^m1946 only.

ⁿFirst number is for 1965–1966 and is comparable with numbers for earlier years. Number after slash for 1967–1970 is not comparable with numbers for pre-1967 years.

^o1948–1951 only.

^pThis index is the value of exports divided by the unit value of imports.

^q1940–1946, 1947–1951, and 1952–1969 data apparently are not comparable.

^rPublic debt plus government guaranteed private debt.

^sThis ratio is for the end of the phase, *not* the average during the phase.

^tNumerator includes import taxes, implicit taxes on local cost of production for large-scale mining, and direct taxes on large-scale mining. Denominator includes all taxes (including social security system taxes).

Table 2.2
Selected indicators of internal and external Chilean economic situations in years preceding stabilization attempts and in first and last years of stabilization episodes[a].

Variables	1955	Ibañez		Allessandri		1964	Frei	
		1956	1958	1959	1961		1965	1970
	(1)	(2)	(3)	(4)	(5)	(6)	(7)	(8)
Internal situation								
1. Rate of change of GDP deflator (%)	75.6	58.3	26.2	40.6	7.9	47.2	28.2	34.3
2. Capacity utilization rate for GDP	0.89	0.88	0.91	0.90	0.93	0.90	0.93	0.96
3. Rate of change of money supply	61.6	44.4	27.7	30.1	25.7	40.4	54.4	65.9
4. Income velocity	11.3	12.7	13.0	13.8	11.9	412.4	11.1	11.1
5. Government deficit/GDP	0.02	0.02	0.03	0.03	0.04	0.04	0.04	0.00
6. Average wage/consumption deflator (1965 = 1.0)	0.74	0.78	0.80	0.72	0.84	0.96	1.00	1.09
7. Wage share of GDP	0.63	0.66	0.63	0.57	0.63	0.65	0.65	0.66
8. Rate of growth of real GDP per capita	-1.1	-1.3	0.2	-2.0	0.8	0.4	4.8	-0.9
External situation								
9. PLD EER for goods imports	2.90	3.62	4.37	4.61	4.02	3.65	3.85	3.35
10. Ratio of PLD EERs for nongoods transactions to goods	2.53	1.27	1.30	0.85	0.81	1.17	1.01	1.19
11. Black market/national accounts NERs	3.12	1.50	1.54	1.01	1.01	1.96	1.65	1.93
12. Ratio of high to low subsectoral PLD EER (PI)s	12.43	8.06	3.97	4.06	3.55	4.02	3.51	5.41
13. PLD EER(PI)s for imports relative to exports	1.35	1.34	1.90	1.71	1.67	1.65	1.47	1.09
14. Average import premium rate	2.04	1.32	0.64	0.51	0.62	0.69	0.57	0.47
15. Chilean trade statistics/those of major trading partners								
15.1. Imports recorded by Chile/exports recorded by others	1.44	1.05	1.36	1.35	1.06	1.27	0.98	1.17
15.2. Exports recorded by Chile/imports recorded by others	0.99	1.02	0.96	0.96	0.95	0.92	0.90	0.99
16. Net balance of payments (10^6 1958 dollars)								
16.1. Goods and services	27.0	-25.9	-107.1	-42.2	-288.6	-131.4	-46.9	-66.2
16.2. Capital to non-monetary sectors	-0.8	21.8	34.3	42.6	163.4	135.0	81.2	110.0
16.3. Capital and gold to monetary sectors	-35.0	2.6	22.3	-28.2	124.5	-20.2	-49.6	-67.3
17. Net foreign reserves held by banking system (10^6 dollars)	100.6	88.6	-13.4	12.0	-164.8	-238.7	-182.9	300.0

[a]Table 2.1 gives sources.

2.1. Ibañez–Klein–Saks program of 1956–1958

2.1.1. Background[2]

The world view of Chilean policymakers for the quarter century prior to the Ibañez–Klein–Saks stabilization program of 1956 was strongly conditioned by reactions to the impact of the Great Depression on the Chilean economy[3]. That impact, indeed, had been great. The Great Depression began to affect Chile in 1930. The resulting substantial immediate change in the overall economic situation is clear from the following observations. In 1930 the capacity to import fell 28%[4], the real value of imports fell 13%, capacity utilization fell 11%, real mining product fell 27% (with declines of 32 and 47%, respectively, in copper and nitrate physical production and of 25% in nitrate employment), and per capita real *GDP* fell 14%. Sectoral increases in real product per capita occurred only in agriculture and in government. Due, in Hirschman's (1963, p. 179) words, to 'misguided stubbornness in defending the gold standard', monetary policy was contractionary because of a 29% decline in gold reserves. Credit was restricted, wholesale prices

[2]Basic sources for the description of the Chilean economy in the pre-1956 quarter century include Baerresen (1966), Ballesteros and Davis (1963), Banco Central (1953b–1956b), Behrman (1975a, 1975b), Cohen (1960), Ellsworth (1945), Ffrench-Davis (1971), Hirschman (1963), Hurtado (1966), IMF (1950b–1957b), Instituto de Economía (1956 and 1963), Jeanneret (1971), Jul (1969), Lagos Escobar (1966), Leftwich (1966), Líbano (1970), Mamalakis (1965, 1967a, 1967b, 1969, 1971a, and 1971b), Marshall (1957), Mikesell (1971), Moran (1970), Muñoz (1968), Pinto (1962), and Senado, Oficina de Informaciones (1971).

[3]During this quarter century Chile also was headed by a fairly wide range of governments. One immediate result of the catastrophe due to the Great Depression was a short period of political instability. The violent economic contraction in mid-1931 gave opponents of what Hirschman (1963, p. 179) refers to as General Carlos Ibañez del Campo's 'thinly veiled military dictatorship' an opportunity to force Ibañez to resign on 26 July 1931. Fifteen months of instability followed, including the '100 days of Socialism' in 1932 under Carlos Davila. In October 1932, Arturo Alessandri was elected with support from the right to head a new government which succeeded in restoring political and economic stability. Near the end of 1938 a Popular Front government was elected under Pedro Aguirre Cerda, who was succeeded (after his death in 1941) by Juan Antonio Ríos. In 1946 Gabriel Gonzalez Videla was elected with considerable support from the left, but during the six years of his administration, the government moved substantially to the right. In 1952 Ibañez again was elected as an independent candidate who, it was widely hoped, would be a strong man capable of eliminating internal instability. Ibañez served through the end of this quarter century and through the liberalization attempt of 1956–1958.

[4]The 1929 capacity to import level, in fact, was not attained again until 1966.

declined 13.4%, the real Central Bank interest rate increased 3.4%, and the NER[5] was maintained constant. The only anticyclical policy of significance was an increase of 10% in real government production financed by foreign borrowing[6].

The extensive negative effect of the Great Depression on the Chilean economy in 1930 was intensified even further in 1931 and 1932. By the latter year, in comparison with 1929, the export capacity to import was 18%, the real value of imports was 13%, nitrate production was 23%, nitrate employment was 15%, copper production was 32%, capacity utilization was 55%, and per capita *GDP* was 49%[7].

Even granted that 1929 was a boom year for the Chilean economy and whether or not the League of Nations' assertion that, of all countries, Chile was the worst hit by the Great Depression is correct, such declines merit the characterization of catastrophic. The whole decade of the 1930s was a period of recovery. That the recovery was only partial is indicated by the following observations about 1939: real per capita *GDP* was 76% of the 1930 level and 66% of the peak 1929 level, and the value of exports in constant United States dollars was 53% of the 1930 level and 29% of the peak 1920 level. In some dimensions, especially in the foreign trade sector, pre-depression levels of economic activity were not regained for three or four decades.

For the purposes of this study the most important reaction to the Great Depression was the change in the prevailing economic philosophy and policy from liberalism to restrictionism and, somewhat more slowly, to interventionism. Tremendous frustration resulted from too much *dependencia* on the external sector[8]. In

[5]*NER* is the nominal exchange rate. This and other abbreviations are given in the table of definitions at the front of the book.

[6]More detailed discussions of the Chilean economy in the 1930s are given in Cohen (1960), Ellsworth (1945), Hirschman (1963), Marshall (1957), and Pinto (1962). Sources for the data utilized in this description are given in Behrman (1975b, section 1.3).

[7]If Mamalakis (1971b, p. 40) is correct in his claim that the Ballesteros and Davis (1963) estimates used for the *GDP* calculation are biased downward before 1929 and upward thereafter by the failure to include services which were highly related to foreign trade activity, then the actual decline in real per capita product was greater than 51%. On the other hand, independent CEPAL estimates for 1929–1932 reported in Mamalakis (1965, p. 384) imply a smaller decline of 32% in real per capita product. In any case, that the decline was considerable is incontestable.

[8]Moran (1970) presents an interesting discussion of *dependencia* in regard to Chilean decisions concerning large-scale copper mining in recent decades.

hopes of reducing that dependence and the associated vulnerability, acceleration of internal industrial development was desired. Restrictive policies, especially for the foreign sector, were seen as the most effective means of encouraging domestic industry, reducing dependence on the foreign sector, and conserving scarce foreign exchange. Previous tendencies towards restrictionism were accelerated abruptly with the imposition of quite restrictive policies in 1931. These were maintained, albeit with numerous modifications, for the next quarter century. For the foreign sector, for example, there was a switch from the major pre-Great Depression policy tools of a unified exchange rate and indirect taxes on foreign trade to multiple exchange rates, a myriad of indirect taxes and surcharges on imports, direct taxes on the major export producers, licensing, quotas, permitted and prohibited lists, special regimes for exports and imports, explicit and implicit subsidies, tax rebates, bilateral and compensation agreements, and regulations concerning direct investment and related flows and capital movements[9].

In addition to the Great Depression, two other events had substantial effects on the Chilean economy. First, the Popular Front government, elected near the end of 1938, expanded substantially government regulation and intervention in the economy. CORFO (Corporacíon de Fomento, a quasi-public development corporation established in 1939), for example, controlled or influenced a high proportion of financial and real investment[10]. Under subsequent governments the increased regulation and interventionism was generally maintained, although particular forms which it took were modified.

Second, exports – and thus total aggregate demand and the command over external resources – continued to be determined primarily by the situation in international mineral markets. For the half-century before the Great Depression nitrates had been the most important Chilean export, but in the 1930s copper regained its position as the dominant export – a position which has been maintained to the present[11]. Fluctuations in the international copper

[9]For an extensive discussion of the nature of these policies and of their effects, see Behrman (1975b).
[10]Mamalakis (1969) gives a history of CORFO's development and activities.
[11]In 1960–1970, for example, copper accounted for 81% of the value of exports from mining and 70% of the value of total merchandise exports. Nitrates, in contrast, represented only 5% of the value of total merchandise exports.

market, thus, had substantial effects on the Chilean economy –
intensified in part by the disequilibrium exchange control system
which the government maintained (Behrman, 1975a; 1975b). Chile
benefited from the copper market booms associated with the Second
World War and the Korean War[12], but suffered from the depressed
copper market before and after these wars.

Table 2.1 summarizes the major features of the Chilean economy
for the decade and a half before the 1956 stabilization attempt, by
means of three subperiods: the Second World War related years of
1940–1946, the years of 1952–1955 which immediately preceded the
stabilization attempt, and the 1947–1951 years between these two
subperiods[13]. The evidence relating to each of the five areas of
macroeconomic policy goals is now discussed in turn.

2.1.1.1. Cyclical variables

In nominal terms the mean percentage annual rate of change of the
GDP deflator indicates a secular increase in inflation from 8.5% for
the 1930s to 15.1, 20.8, and 47.8%, respectively, for the three
subperiods included in table 2.1 (variable 1.1.1). Not surprisingly, as
the cost of holding real monetary balances increased, the income
velocity of money also rose secularly (variable 1.1.2). The mean rate
of change of the nominal money supply (M_1) was of the same order
of magnitude as that for prices in the 1947–1951 and 1952–1955
periods, although somewhat higher during the Second World War
years (variable 1.3.1). Luders (1970) estimates that somewhat over a
third of monetary emissions originated in Central Bank foreign
exchange and gold operations in 1940–1946, but less than a twentieth
so originated in the next two periods[14]. Instead financing the growing
public sector deficit became an ever more important cause of such
emission, especially in 1952–1955 (variables 1.3.2 and 1.4.4). In

---

[12]These benefits were limited, however, by the agreement between the Chilean and
United States governments to fix the price of copper at 12¢ per pound between 1942
and 1946 and the unilateral establishment by the United States of a price of 24.5¢ per
pound in June 1950, modified by the Washington Treaty of May 1951 which was in
effect until February 1952. For details, see Behrman (1975b, sections 4.2.1 and
7.1.2.3).

[13]The 1930s are not included in this table since many of these data are not available
for years before 1940, the first year covered by the national accounts. That data which
is available for the 1930s is summarized in Behrman (1975b, table A.1).

[14]Prior to the Great Depression, in contrast, Luders estimates that monetary
emissions were almost entirely related to Central Bank foreign exchange and gold
operations.

addition, inflation was probably partially imported due to international price increases during the Second World War, the immediate postwar period, and the Korean conflict, although at other times internal price changes far outpaced external ones[15].

In real terms the capacity utilization index suggests an increase from an all-time low in the 1930s to an average level for 1940–1946 which was exceeded only after 1962 among the periods included in table 2.1 (variable 1.2.1). In the postwar period, a decline occurred to depths second only to those in the 1930s, with some recovery on the average in 1952–1955. In part, this pattern reflects the shifts in demands in international markets: the copper market booms due to the Second World War and the Korean conflict and the market declines due to the Great Depression and the European and United States recessions in the late 1940s and mid-1950s[16]. Changes in internal aggregate demand due to government fiscal policies also *prima facie* had a role. The postwar trough, for example, was associated with contractionary fiscal policies (variable 1.4.4).

2.1.1.2. Resource allocation and structural change

The secular shifts in resources among production sectors were out of agriculture (despite an apparent increase in the terms of trade for this sector) and out of mining (although the relative share of this sector in *GDP* increased during the Second World War in comparison to the 1930s). Resources were shifted into manufacturing and into services. The mean share of manufacturing in *GDP* of 11% in 1928–1930, for example, had doubled by 1952–1955[17]. Manufacturing grew fast, not only relative to the other sectors during the same time

---

[15]Unit import values in foreign currency and the imported component of the wholesale price index, respectively, rose at mean annual rates of 15.2 and 38.8% over the 1940–1946 period, and in 1947 and 1951 substantial increases occurred in the unit value of both imports – 23.6 and 16.8% – and of exports – 31.4 and 26.5%.

[16]Behrman (1975b) concludes that the impact of such shifts was exacerbated by Chilean attempts to maintain a disequilibrium system with an overvalued exchange rate.

[17]The share of industry in the labor force, however, hit a peak of 19.7% in 1952 and thereafter declined. The subsequent failure of industry to increase its relative absorption of the labor force despite the continuance of internal and external policies favorable to this sector in the view of Mamalakis (1971b, pp. 214–217, 370–371), raises serious doubts about the structuralist characterization of Chilean industrialization as being relatively successful given the apparent overall economic objectives of the country.

period, but also relative to its own performance in subsequent periods[18].

More careful examination of manufacturing suggests that at least initially the shift of resources into this sector reflected considerable import substitution. According to Muñoz (1968, p. 82), import substitution accounted for 73% of real industrial growth in the 1927–1937/38 period as compared with a Chenary normal value of 17%. On a more disaggregated nine-subsector level, import substitution was particularly important for clothing and shoes, non-metallic minerals, metal products, leather and rubber products and textiles, and only for wood products was Chilean import substitution in this period less than Chenery's normal value. However, for the 1937/38–1952/53 period Muñoz's estimate of the coefficient of import substitution is only 15% as compared to a Chenery normal value of 19%, although the Chenery normal values were still exceeded substantially for textiles, non-metallic minerals, and metal products and exceeded slightly for clothing and shoes and wood products[19]. On the basis of the drop in the estimated coefficient of import substitution between these two periods, de Castro and de la Cuadra (1971, p. 4) and Mamalakis (1971b, p. 371) conclude that import substitution declined drastically after 1939[20].

In addition to the concentration of manufacturing import substitution (at least in the relative sense) in the early part of this period, also noteworthy was the apparent importance of intermediate products in addition to final consumer products in the import substitution process. On an intersectoral level the resource shifts seem to have been consistent with the goal of closing somewhat the

[18]Behrman (1975b, table A.2) reports a significantly non-zero increase of 1.2% in the growth rate of manufacturing for the years 1940–1955 as compared to the entire 1940–1965 period. Other significantly non-zero deviations for 1940–1955 from the longer-run sectoral growth rate are − 2.4% for mining, − 1.4% for construction, and 1.4% for the government.

[19]Among manufacturing sub-sectors, in fact, import desubstitution occurred in the 1937/38–1952/53 period for food, drink and tobacco, paper and printing, and leather and rubber, according to Muñoz (1968, p. 85).

[20]The Instituto de Economía (1963, pp. 2, 9) suggests that substantial import substitution occurred due to import supply shortages in the Second World War. Substantial import substitution may have occurred in the Second World War and the subsequent subperiods in an *absolute* sense without being inconsistent with the *relative* estimates of Muñoz, given that the rate of growth of industrial product was two to three times as high in 1940–1955 as it was in 1931–1939.

Chilean economy and reducing the vulnerability of the economy to foreign sector fluctuations through a reduction in dependence on mining exports and an increase in domestic industry. The intrasectoral shift towards industrial intermediate goods import substitution was also consistent with this aim, although the apparent import desubstitution in agricultural products and in capital goods (variable 5.2.2.2 in table 2.1) implied greater dependence on the foreign sector.

The international economic policy regime played a strong role in inducing most of these shifts by providing the barriers behind which industrial import substitution occurred (although the increasingly overvalued exchange rate offset many of the price-related barriers), by limiting the inducement for the expansion of mining, and by channelling foreign reserves for import substitution through CORFO. Of course, domestic policies also played an important role in the structure of incentives for import substitution. For example, the shift from production to sales taxes introduced by law 11575 of 14 August 1954 implied an increase in effective protection since the production tax had been basically on goods produced by domestic industry.

2.1.1.3. Distribution of income and of control over resources

In respect to the factoral distribution of income, the position of labor apparently improved secularly, at least as measured by the real wage and by the labor share in *GDP* (variables 3.1 and 3.2 in table 2.1)[21]. Some policies were directed towards such an end: favorable policies for the imports of consumptive goods of prime necessities, the indexing of basic wages (i.e. the *sueldo vital*), and the discrimination (although declining) against imported relatively capital-intensive technology. In other respects, however, policies were partially offsetting. The lowest income classes probably did not benefit much from import preferences; the exchange rate policy for large-scale copper mining[22] and the CORFO foreign-currency-

---

[21]If the information were readily available the division of labor into blue and white collar groups would be useful and might reveal differential results since social legislation clearly favored the latter group. For the 1940–1950 period, for which the data are available, however, Marshall (1957, pp. 190–192) reports that changes in income distribution between these two groups were not statistically significant.

[22]Consider large-scale copper mining. Under the assumptions of a constant elasticity of substitution production function, given output, given price, and long-run tendencies to adjust to marginal productivities, the ratio of labor that would have been employed in large-scale mining in long-run equilibrium L' under different labor

backed loan policy both encouraged the use of very capital-intensive technologies[23]; in general, neither the large private gains which could be attained by obtaining special exemptions from policies nor the large import premia (variable 5.1.6) were captured by the laboring class; and a number of policies attempted to turn the terms of trade against agriculture, in which sector large numbers of relatively poorly paid laborers earned their livelihood.

The distribution of income and of the control over resources has other dimensions in addition to the distribution of factor shares. In respect to regional distribution, policies continued to cause transfers from mining in the north (although the second largest copper mine, El Teniente is not far from Santiago) and agriculture in the south to the center where most expenses related to the operation of the regime occurred, where most government revenues were spent, and where most imports were utilized. Special import regimes for remote areas at either end of the nation, however, caused a relatively small counter flow in the opposite direction (Behrman, 1975b, subsection 4.1.5.1). In respect to sectoral income distribution, as is noted above, the regime favored industry and government (and possibly other services) at the expense of mining and, to a lesser extent, agriculture. In respect to the international distribution

---

prices PL', to those actually employed in long-run equilibrium L under actual prices PL, depends on the elasticity of substitution between capital and labor σ in the following way: $L'/L = (PL/PL')^{\sigma}$. On the basis of Reynolds' (1965, p. 284) implicit estimate that PL/PL' equalled 2.03 and the estimate in Behrman (1972a) that σ equals 0.51, under these assumptions the long-run equilibrium labor force in large-scale mining would have been 44% larger had the exchange rate discrimination not affected the dollar cost of labor. If PL/PL' is assumed to be the ratio of the general exchange rate to the special large-scale mining exchange rate in 1954 (although the former clearly was undervalued) and other assumptions are maintained the same, the long-run equilibrium labor force in large-scale mining would have been 590% larger. With the option of increasing output, even larger employment would have resulted. Such calculations should not be taken literally, but they do suggest that the employment effects of the discriminatory exchange rate policy may have been quite considerable.

[23] According to Mamalakis (1971b, pp. 565–587) loans from CORFO to enterprises in domestic currency but backed by hard currencies were repaid in domestic currency at less than their original hard currency equivalent value because of the negative real interest rates used (with a subsidy in this case apparently from transfers from the central government). For one example of the effect on employment, the relative share of the labor force decreased after 1945 in the most rapidly growing industrial subsector, basic metals, because of the capital-intensive nature of the CORFO-financed steel company (CAP) operations.

of income, despite the increasing and very high implicit and explicit tax rate on large-scale copper mining, the regime allowed quite substantial outflows of investment income (variable 5.2.6.1.2.3) and apparently high rates of return on foreign investment[24]. In respect to the intertemporal distribution of the use of resources, as is discussed below, policies apparently favored current over future consumption, but in declining degrees over time. Finally, in respect to public versus private control over resources, the Great Depression resulted in an initial relative decline in public sector command over resources because of the evaporation of nitrate tax revenues and foreign capital inflows to the government. Subsequently, the government secularly increased its relative command over resources for current and investment expenditures partly through expanded internal taxation (variables 1.4.1–5). Relative government savings declined secularly at the same time, however, thereby adding to inflationary pressures through increased deficits, especially in the last years of this period.

2.1.1.4. Economic growth
Growth in real *GDP* per capita varied substantially from subperiod to subperiod from a low mean of − 1.1% per year in 1931–1939 (due almost entirely to the initial fall) to a high mean of 2.2% in 1940–1946 (the highest value of variable 4.1 for all pre-1965 periods and subperiods included in table 2.1), with secularly declining mean growth rates in the last two subperiods[25]. The secular decline in the overall growth rate persisted into the last subperiod, in fact, despite some recovery in that subperiod from the immediate postwar trough in both agriculture and industry (variables 4.2 and 4.3) because of more than offsetting falls in the growth rates of the rest of the economy. This secular decline continued into this last subperiod, moreover, despite an increase in the rate of growth of investment in

[24]For example, based on estimates by Moran (1970, p. 343), the mean annual profit rates (defined by net profits/book value) for 1945–1955 for the foreign-owned operations at the largest two Chilean copper mines were 33.7 and 28.4% (although the former drops to 11.5% if a disputed $94 000 000 1913 carryover is included in the book value).
[25]The increase in the growth rate in 1940–1946 as the terms of trade declined and the decrease in the growth rate in 1947–1955 as the terms of trade increased perhaps should suggest caution for those who propose simple causal models between the terms of trade and economic growth in economies such as Chile's (variables 4.1 and 5.1.5.1).

structures and equipment and a decrease in the marginal gross capital–output ratio (variables 4.4 and 4.5). This last observation points to the importance of factors additional to capital accumulation in the growth process.

Government policies had a number of effects on the growth process. The impact on real domestic savings, for example, probably was positive due to the shift of resources to the government with its relatively high marginal propensity to save, to the induced shift out of agriculture to which real household savings seemed to have responded positively, and to the low real cost of foreign exchange to which real business savings seemed to have responded inversely (subsection 5.1.1 below). Some counter tendencies also may have existed due to an inverse response to quantitative restrictions (as reflected in the real black market rate) in real household savings and to the general substitution of foreign for domestic savings.

Chilean economic policies apparently also had some positive influence on investment. The declining discrimination against capital goods imports resulted in a shift in import composition towards investment goods which presumably made possible increased investment (variables 5.1.4.1–2, 5.2.1.2, and 5.2.2.2). Furthermore, CORFO helped to establish a favorable investment climate, focused attention on the importance of imported machinery and equipment, made possible more systematic analysis of the Chilean economy by its data collection and processing efforts, probably increased foreign capital inflows, and made possible large-scale investment projects under Chilean control[26].

On the other hand, the regime had quite possible offsetting negative impacts on investment. Quantitative restrictions were applied with most force on capital imports at times of balance of payments crises (Behrman, 1975b, ch. 6). The increasing relative dependence on imported capital equipment implied that total investment was increasingly vulnerable to balance of payments crises (variable 5.2.2.2)[27]. Policies towards large-scale copper mining probably discouraged investment in that subsector[28]. Mamalakis (1971b,

[26]Mamalakis (1971b, p. 571) also emphasizes the first three of these benefits from CORFO.

[27]Of course, considerations of comparative advantage probably would suggest considerable dependence on foreign sources for machinery and equipment.

[28]Behrman (1975b, subsections 4.2.1 and 7.1.2.3) summarizes these policies and their impact and gives references to other more extensive studies thereof.

pp. 565–587), moreover, suggests that due to other scarcities (e.g. skilled labor, foreign exchange, and the deterioration of local capital markets once inflation increased) CORFO investment may have largely replaced rather than supplemented other investment. Finally, the resource allocation shifts described above may have only altered, but not increased real capacity and in many cases may have resulted in lost growth possibilities due to increased inefficiencies[29].

The impact of policies on other growth determinants is much more speculative. However, to the extent that technology was embodied in capital one might hypothesize that the shift towards capital imports implied that the regime became less discriminatory against new technology over time. On the other hand the very existence of the increasing quantitative restrictions presumably meant that entrepreneurship and trained labor was increasingly devoted to high private, but low social, return operations in attempts to circumvent (or maintain, from the government side) the policies themselves.

2.1.1.5. External position [30]

The disastrous deterioration in her foreign markets had a catastrophic impact on the Chilean economy in the early 1930s, as is

---

[29]Over the period labor intended to shift out of agriculture and mining and into construction, industry (at least until 1952) and services. For most of the period, mining was an above-average and industry was a below-average labor productivity sector. Under the assumption that the intersectoral pattern of average labor productivities reflected the intersectoral pattern of marginal labor productivities (discussed below) shifts from mining to industry quite possibly were inefficient. Within industry under similar assumptions the subsectoral data presented in Muñoz (1968, pp. 57, 61) also suggests inefficient shifts (e.g. in the 1930s out of food, drinks, and tobacco and into paper and non-metallic metals and in the 1950s out of food, beverages, tobacco, paper, chemicals, and basic metals and into textiles, clothing and non-metallic metals). Moreover, shifts of trained labor, both in the government and in the private sector, apparently occurred in order to operate and to deal with the expanding quantitative control systems.

Under the assumption of sectoral constant elasticity of substitution production functions with constant returns to scale, the marginal product of labor *MPL* is related to the average product of labor *APL* by the following expression: $MPL = (b\,APL)^{1/\sigma}$, where σ is the elasticity of substitution and b depends on the state of technology and other parameters of the production function. On the basis of the estimates of the sectoral elasticities of substitution and other relevant parameters presented for agriculture, mining and industry in Behrman (1972a) the same ordering among these three sectors holds for marginal as for average labor productivities. Such a calculation must be viewed with a certain amount of caution, however, since it depends crucially on the magnitude of the constant term in the original estimates.

[30]Behrman (1975a and 1975b) examines the foreign sector in great detail.

suggested above. In desperation, the government resorted to substantial quantitative restrictions on the foreign sector. After the early 1940s the Chilean currency was secularly more overvalued even though the Chilean terms of trade were secularly improving (variables 5.1.1, 5.1.2, 5.1.7, and 5.5.5.1–2). Because of pessimism about the efficacy of devaluation in resolving the balance of payments crisis without inordinate domestic costs, the government secularly turned more and more to a complex system of quantitative restrictions to regulate foreign transactions, with very high overvaluation and import premiums for those allowed to import being part of the results (variables 5.1.3, 5.1.4.1–2, 5.1.6, 5.2.5.1, and 5.2.7.1). Over this same period cyclical attempts were made to liberalize and reform the control system, but they failed rapidly because of the basic disequilibrium nature of the system. The net result was a very complex set of regulatory policies, with fluctuations in the degree of restrictionism depending in large part on the state of export markets or of net capital imports.

The composition of trade also shifted secularly, in part as the result of the policy regime. Import substitution led to relative declines in consumption goods and intermediate goods (variables 5.2.1.1–3). The overvalued exchange rate discouraged the expansion of non-traditional agricultural and industrial exports, so mining became ever more dominant as a source of exports, and overall exports did not keep pace with *GNP* (variables 5.2.3.1–3 and 5.2.7.7). In part because of the restrictions on imports and the disincentives for exports, but also because of conscious efforts to develop alternative domestic sources, taxes related to foreign trade as a percentage of total taxes dropped substantially (variable 5.2.7.5).

2.1.1.6. Immediate prelude to the stabilization program [31]
The greatly deteriorating internal situation near the end of this period should be clear from the following considerations. In 1954 and 1955 real per capita *GDP* decreased by 4%, capacity utilization fell to an average of 0.89 (the lowest level since the mid-1930s), real wages fell to 17% below the historically high 1953 level, annual

---

[31] Data underlying the quantitative statements in this subsection are from the sources indicated in table 2.1. Table 2.2 gives some of this data for 1955. For further descriptions of the economic conditions in these years see Cohen (1960, pp. 23–24), Ffrench-Davis (1971, p. 160), and Hirschman (1963, pp. 199–292).

strikes and labour conflicts increased by an average of 25% above
the previously all-time high 1953 level, and the mean annual increase
in the *GDP* deflator was 71.7%. In 1954 a major blue collar strike
took place in May, and a state of siege was declared in September.
In 1955, three different Ministers of Finance held office in the first
half of the year, a general strike occurred in July, the long-silent
Central Bank issued a report on the inflation which recommended
forceful anti-inflationary measures in July, and rumors of a military-
backed suspension of the Constitution abounded.

In the external sector, in contrast, the immediate situation was
relatively favorable in many respects. The mean capacity to import
increased 29%. The mean deficit on the goods and services account
was the smallest in absolute value in the postwar period. In 1954 and
1955, furthermore, net foreign loans in constant dollars to the
Chilean government increased rapidly. In 1955 exports and imports
in constant dollars rose 18.4 and 11.0%, and the terms of trade were
the most favorable since 1937.

But the *PLD NER* declined to the lowest level in 1908–1970
because devaluation lagged behind inflation. The resulting high
demand for foreign exchange was augmented by capital flight due to
internal instability. Exchange control, therefore, was intensified to a
postwar high. The average black market to legal exchange rate
reached 2.66, a level not exceeded before 1971. The International
Monetary Fund was pressing for reform of the Chilean international
economic policy regime[32]. Net credits available to Chile from the
IMF declined.

2.1.2. The Ibañez–Klein–Saks stabilization and liberalization program

Because of the rapidly deteriorating internal situation, in mid-1955
the government hired the Washington-based Klein–Saks consulting
firm to advise in the formulation of a stabilization program[33]. In

---

[32]Pinto (1960) analyzes the role of the IMF in influencing Chilean policy.

[33]Hirschman (1963, p. 202) reports that the Klein–Saks firm was contacted on the
urging of and through the intermediation of Augustin Edwards (publisher of *El
Mercurio*, the most influential Chilean newspaper) and that Klein–Saks was selected
because of their previous success in 1949 in Peru, their reputed good connections
with Washington, and their availability. Ffrench-Davis (1971, p. 10) suggests that their
known orthodox, if not rightist, approach to economics, also may have been
important.

September 1955, the Klein–Saks mission arrived and Oscar Herrera became Minister of Finance. In late 1955 an informal coalition was formed by Herrera, the Klein–Saks mission and the parliamentary majority. The stabilization program developed was substantially the same as the earlier Felipe Herrera, Jorge Pratt (both former Ministers of Finance), and Central Bank proposals (except for the prior deposits on imports which Ecuador had been using since 1953), although the program became strongly identified with the Klein–Saks mission. Whatever the contribution of the mission to the program formulation, Hirschman (1963, pp. 203–204, 209) suggests that it performed useful immediate functions by giving Herrera a breathing space in which to build alliances for the 1956 wage readjustment battle and by acting as a binding agent (and scapegoat) for the Ibañistas, Conservatives, and Liberals in the government who did not want formal ties. (Hirschman also suggests that the longer-run implication of the latter role was negative in that the relevant competing groups were able to evade their basic responsibilities of hammering out workable solutions in direct discussions.)

The stabilization program met with initial internal success as law 12006 of January 1956 was passed to eliminate automatic wage readjustments, to limit the 1956 readjustment to 50% of the increase in the cost of living index of the previous year, to limit the maximum increase in any controlled price to 40%, and (in order to soften the impact on labor) to establish a minimum wage for industrial workers at 37% of the white collar minimum wage and to increase family allowances substantially for government employees and blue collar workers. Four days later a general strike fizzled out, probably partially due to strike fatigue.

Shortly thereafter, the government instituted a major liberalization in the international economic policy regime[34]. It unified considerably the exchange rate system, announced several major devaluations, established a system of indirect controls through prior deposits on imports at specified rates ranging from 0 to 10 000% for 30–90 days, replaced the previous system of specific quotas of foreign exchange budgeting and of import licensing by a list of

[34]Although most of the policies listed below were liberalizing there were some changes in the other direction. For example, a number of new special foreign sector regimes were established or old regimes modified in this period, which probably resulted in increased restrictiveness in order to favor particular industries or particular isolated regions. See Behrman (1975b) or Jeanneret (1971).

permitted imports which any economic entity could import freely upon payment of duties, taxes, and the prior deposit without licenses (except for a few items which required a certificate of necessity from the Ministry of Economics), and allowed a large number of bilateral, compensation, and barter agreements to expire. The year 1956 also was the first full year of operation of the *Nuevo Trato* (new treatment), agreed upon between the Chilean government and the foreign-owned large-scale copper companies in May 1955. With this agreement both parties hoped to eliminate some of the negative features of the previous regime[35]. The *Nuevo Trato* was a considerable rationalization and liberalization of the treatment of large-scale copper and was to be the basic law governing such treatment for at least a decade[36].

2.1.3. The results of the Ibañez–Klein–Saks program

Consideration of the five areas of major macroeconomic policy goals indicates that in many respects, especially initially, the program met with success.

---

[35]From the point of view of the companies the previous regime greatly limited the control of their operations, reduced the returns from their investments, and made maintenance of market shares difficult (especially for Anaconda). From the point of view of the Chilean government, negative features included the decline in Chile's share of world copper production from 20.2% in 1934 to 19.2% in 1944–1946 to 11.8% for 1953–1954; the decline in net returned value of 16.7% over the 1953–1954 period because of reduced sales; the decline in the real linkages of large-scale mining to the rest of the economy due to the substitution of capital for labor, of highly skilled (and often foreign) labor paid in dollars for less skilled Chilean labor paid in pesos; and imported intermediate inputs for domestic inputs, because even when the peso costs for local factors of quality comparable to foreign factors were quite low, the dollar costs were quite high as a result of the exchange rate discrimination.

Major features of the *Nuevo Trato* were: (i) all previous charges were replaced by a single direct tax on profits; (ii) the basic tax rate was to be 50% with up to a 25% surtax which was an inverse function of quantities and which became zero when production reached approximately 190% of the 1949–1953 levels (or 140% of previous peak levels); (iii) the limit on depreciation allowances was increased from 5 to 20% of the value of plant and equipment; (iv) exchange rate discrimination against large-scale copper mining was ended; and (v) the government copper corporation (Corporación del Cobre, CODELCO) was established with the somewhat vague role of creating national expertise regarding copper, controlling exports and quantities, encouraging the use of local factors of production, and preparing statistics.

[36]Behrman (1975b) provides much more detail on the changes in foreign sector policies.

2.1.3.1. Cyclical variables

The mean rate of change of prices dropped from 47.8% for 1952–1955 to 37.6% for 1956–1958 (variable 1.1.1), with annual declines from 58.3% in 1956 to 28.3% in 1957 to 26.2% in 1958. Apparently, inflationary expectations, at least initially, we reduced by the imposition of the program. Specific measures in the program also helped reduce inflation (e.g. the shift to external financing of more of the government debt, the absorption of credit through the imposition of prior import deposits, the increased supply of imports, and the reduction of wage readjustments)[37]. The mean income velocity, perhaps somewhat surprisingly, increased (variable 1.1.2). This suggests that inflationary expectations may have remained quite high on the average despite the decline in the measured rate of change of prices[38]. The mean rate of change of the nominal money supply (M_1) was about the same percentage as that for prices (variable 1.3.1). Luders (1970), however, estimates that the sources of monetary emission changed substantially from the 1952–1955 averages with a large increase in the share due to foreign exchange operations (to 25.7% of the total), a small decrease in the share due to Central Bank operations with the public sector (37.3%), and a larger decrease in the share due to Central Bank credit to the private sector (30.4%). These shifts reflected the partial opening up of the economy, the increased availability of foreign credits, the attempt to finance the continuing large public sector debt (variable 1.4.4) more externally and the attempt to limit internal private credit expansion.

The mean capacity utilization rate increased above the 1954 and 1955 levels, although it declined slightly below the 1952–1955

---

[37]Rising external prices did not have major direct roles in the still relatively high internal price increases. The mean annual rates of increase for the unit values of imports and exports, respectively, were 0.8 and −6.2%. Nevertheless, the imported component of the wholesale price index did increase quite substantially (about 30%) relative to the overall index, because the relative unification of exchange rate treatment resulted in rather large effective devaluations for some of the 'essential' imports (e.g. sugar, coffee, and Paraguayan tea) which previously had been more favored and which had disproportionately large weights in this index. Likewise the changes in the regime resulted in relatively large increases for export- and mining-related price indices due to the reduction of discrimination against key products therein.

[38]An alternative hypothesis is that the official data vastly overstate the actual decline in inflation since they reflect with considerable weight the price movements for some items for which government price ceilings were imposed. The effectiveness of such ceilings, however, is far from clear.

average (variable 1.2.1). Critics of the stabilization program have focused on this decline. Even though they probably overstate the extent to which the economy was stagnant, it is clear that the general lessening of restrictions did not result in an immediate boom as some of the proponents of liberalization had hoped. Section 4.3 suggests that the increased competition from imported supplies due to reduced quantitative restrictions in the international economic policy regime had a significant role in the reduction of capacity utilization rates in some sectors. The actual decline in real *GDP* in industry (variable 4.2), the previously most protected sector, may reflect that this sector least of all could compete with the increased imports and imply that previous resource allocation to this sector had often been inefficient.

2.1.3.2. Resource allocation and structural change
Percentage shares in *GDP* of mining and industry declined to averages of 4 and 21, respectively. Those of agriculture and all other sectors increased to means of 13 and 62% (variables 2.1.1.1–3)[39]. Such shifts in part reflected the impact of the changed international economic regime, as has been suggested above for industry. Crosson (1970) gives the same explanation for agriculture – despite the declining relative agriculture price (variable 2.2) – due to the increased availability of modern and largely imported agricultural inputs during these years. The relative decline in mining occurred, however, despite the substantially more favorable treatment due to the *Nuevo Trato* (although in part this decline reflects the treatment of price changes in the national accounts).

2.1.3.3. Distribution of income and of control over resources
As is noted above, a major plank in the program was to limit cost-of-living adjustments for labor in order to break the cost–price–inflationary expectations spiral. As is also noted, unutilized capacity – and therefore probably unemployment – also rose. The movement towards a more unified exchange rate system, furthermore also worked in some sense to the detriment of labor because exchange rates for a number of consumption necessities were

---

[39]Behrman (1975b, table A.2) presents estimates that indicate that the sectoral exponential growth rates in real *GDP* for 1956–1958 were significantly higher than for the entire 1940–1965 period in agriculture and significantly lower in mining and services (although only at the 20% level of significance in the latter case).

increased relatively greatly. On the basis of such observations some commentators, such as Ffrench-Davis (1971, p. 20), Instituto de Economía (1963, p. 71) and Sierra (1969, p. 51), claim that labor suffered substantially from this stabilization program.

In fact, real wage rates and the wage share of national product (variables 3.1 and 3.2) did not return to the previous peak 1953 values. In the first year of the program (variables 6 and 7 in table 2.2) and on the average, however, both indicators at least equalled the mean for the 1952–1955 subperiod, and the former probably increased significantly. Moreover, government policies resulted in other possible benefits to labor, such as the increased inducement to hire labor in large-scale mining because of the end of discriminatory exchange rate treatment against local costs of production or the reduction in import premia going to non-labor classes (variable 5.1.6). Such evidence is not conclusive, but it does raise questions about the conventional Chilean wisdom concerning the negative effects from the point of view of labor of this program on the factoral distribution of income.

In other facets of control over income and over resources, effects can also be identified. In the intersectoral dimension, as is suggested above, policy changes probably resulted in shifts out of industry and into agriculture. In the interregional dimension, an associated shift away from concentration in the Santiago–Valparaiso area probably occurred. In the international dimension the analysis in Behrman (1975b, subsection 7.1.2.3) suggests that the *Nuevo Trato* may have resulted in an increased income transfer abroad[40]. In the intertemporal dimension the present generation apparently was favored relative to future generations by the increased foreign debt and the relatively great reduction in the effective exchange rate for consumption goods (variables 5.1.4.1–2). In any case, the share of private consumption in *GDP* increased (variable 2.2.1). Finally, in respect to private versus public control over resources, the decline in import taxes relative to import value (offset in part by the relative

---

[40]Therefore, Moran (1970, p. 93) characterizes the *Nuevo Trato* as being more of a new deal for the foreign owners of large-scale copper mining than for Chile. Nevertheless Moran's (1970, p. 343) calculation of profit rates (i.e. net profit divided by book value) do not indicate such a sharp change. For the biggest mine his rates dropped from an average of 33.7% for 1945–1955 to 19.3% for 1956–1958 (or, if an unrecorded $94 000 000 claim from 1913 is included in the book value, increased from 11.5 to 12.0%). For the second biggest mine the rates increased from 28.4 to 36.6%.

increase in imports), the decline in taxes related to foreign trade relative to total taxes (variables 5.2.7.5 and 5.2.7.8), and the decline in favoritism towards government imports all suggest a shift towards the private sector. The relatively increased government access to domestic bank credit and to foreign capital may have been partially counteracting. In any case, the government role in the economy increased in some important respects, as is suggested by the increased ratio of taxes to total product (variable 1.4.5).

2.1.3.4. Economic growth
The mean annual rate of growth of real per capita *GDP* in 1956–1958 (variable 4.1) increased to 1.4%, the highest average since the Second World War, because of the large increase in 1957 after three consecutive years of decline in real per capita product. Such an increase is somewhat surprising in the light of the general characterization by the structuralist school and others (e.g. Edel, 1969, p. 86; Instituto de Economía, 1963, p. 75; and Mamalakis 1971b, p. 164) of this period as being a very stagnant one due to the stabilization program. Ffrench-Davis (1971, p. 245) therefore suggests that the national accounts must be overestimated for 1957 (although he is not specific in his evidence, nor is he clear as to whether he thinks the rate of growth is also underestimated in the national accounts in 1956 or 1958 or in some other year because of what he considers to be an error). Without specific evidence to the contrary, however, it seems reasonable to conclude that significant real growth did occur in this period despite the claims of many critics of the stabilization program[41], but it is also relevant to note that as a result of such growth, the level of per capita real *GDP* only returned to about that of 1953.

Changes in government policies had mixed effects on the growth rate. Subsection 5.1.1 below suggests that the impact on domestic savings must have been positive in the case of household savings due to the lowered real black market exchange rate and the shift of relative product towards agriculture. But a substantial negative impact must have occurred due to the increased foreign savings, the shift of resources away from the government with its high marginal propensity to save and the negative reaction in real business savings to the higher real cost of foreign exchange.

[41]Sierra (1969, p. 64) is an exception in that he criticizes the stabilization program from a structuralist's viewpoint, but also concludes that growth occurred in 1957.

The impact on real investment must have been positive. The substantial increase in capital imports apparently resulted in highly productive investment (as measured by the marginal capital output ratio), and capital inflows increased substantially (variables 4.5, 5.2.1.2, 5.2.6.3.1.1–2). Moreover, reduced discrimination (both positive and negative) for imported capital must have resulted in more efficient primary factor allocations. Thus, substantial growth occurred despite a decline in the rate of growth of overall investment (variable 4.4)[42] and despite the relative disincentives for investment in industry.

Finally, the changes in the policies must have had additional positive impacts on growth that are very difficult to quantify. For example, more embodied technology was imported with machinery and equipment, and the incentives to utilize skilled manpower in attempts to bypass (or maintain, from the government side) quantitative controls were lessened substantially.

2.1.3.5. External position

All of the available indices suggest that on the average the foreign sector was liberalized substantially and overvaluation was reduced. The *PLD NER* rose 30%, the *PLD EER* rose 28%, the import premium rate fell 44%, the ratio of the black market *NER* to the national accounts *NER* dropped 46%, and the Ffrench-Davis quantitative restrictions index and the degree of overinvoicing both declined (variables 5.1.1, 5.1.3, 5.1.6, 5.1.7, 5.2.5.1 and 5.2.7.1). Imports grew so much more rapidly than exports, however, that the mean deficit on the goods and services account in 1958 dollars increased from $-5\,600\,000$ to $-81\,700\,000$ (variable 5.2.6.1). This enlarged deficit was partially offset by mean increases in net unrequited transfers from $-100\,000$ to $19\,000\,000$ 1958 dollars (largely due to foreign official support for the stabilization effort) and in net non-monetary capital inflows from $18\,600\,000$ to $37\,400\,000$ 1958 dollars (variables 5.2.6.2 and 5.2.6.3.1). But mean net monetary capital and gold movements also increased from $-5\,600\,000$ to $32\,700\,000$ 1958 dollars (variable 5.2.6.3.2), which placed growing pressure on the dwindling foreign exchange re-

---

[42]The decline in the rate of growth of real investment and in the marginal capital output ratio both partially reflect the reduction in construction activity (i.e. housing investment fell over 21% per year) because of the relatively tight credit conditions and the end of the almost hyperinflation-inspired building boom.

serves. Among the causes of this pressure were a reduction in export value due to a decline in the terms of trade which reflected recessionary conditions in foreign markets (variable 5.1.5.1), increased demand for foreign exchange for imports due to the decline in the *PLD NER* after the fixing of *NER*s at constant levels in mid-1957, and a shift towards foreign financing of the government deficit. Available foreign credit lines were used up, international reserves dropped (variable 5.2.7.3), and total public sector foreign debt increased 56% to $392000000. As a result of the pressure on foreign exchange reserves, exchange controls were intensified in the last half of this period, although probably not to the 1955 level.

2.2. Alessandri stabilization program of 1959–1961[43]

2.2.1. Background

In most major facets of the economy the performance on average during 1956–1958 was better than for years immediately prior to the Ibañez–Klein–Saks stabilization attempt. The original momentum, however, was not maintained. After some initial successes, a number of setbacks occurred. Herrera was replaced as Minister of Finance in August 1956. Parliament refused to pass basic tax reform legislation. Rumors of graft and corruption increased (especially in respect to the operation of the special regime in the department of Arica). Students demonstrating against increases in bus fares clashed with troops, and 18 deaths and over 500 injuries resulted in April 1957. A poor harvest in 1957 caused relatively rapid increases in food prices. Government fiscal deficit problems were not solved (variables 5 in table 2.2). By the time of the 1958 departure of the Klein–Saks mission, the rate of growth per capita had declined almost to zero, a large deficit was being run on the balance of goods

---

[43]Basic sources for this section include Banco Central (1959–1961b), Behrman (1975a and 1975b), Bradford (1970, pp. 55–56), de Castro and de la Cuadra (1971, pp. 34–35), CORFO (1963), *The Economist* Intelligence Unit (1960–1961), Edel (1969, p. 88), Ffrench-Davis (1971, pp. 27, 33, 72–81, 125–133, 172–178, 253, 262, 273), Gunder-Frank (1972, pp. 7–10), Hirschman (1963, pp. 210, 218–220), Instituto de Economía (1963, pp. 78–88, 139–140, 203–206, 229, 230), Jeanneret (1971, pp. 150, 350–362), Jco (1970, pp. 4–8), Jul (1969, pp. 70–93), Leftwich (1966, pp. 408–411), Líbano (1970, p. 727), Mamalakis (1971b, p. 554), Mikesell (1971, p. 374), Senado, Oficina de Informaciones (1971, pp. 22, 48, 52, 54), and Sierra (1969, pp. 72–90, 153).

and services, the level of net foreign reserves held by the banking system was very low, and the black market *NER* was rising relative to the legal *NER*s (variables 8, 11, 16.1, and 17). Although the mean rates of inflation and unutilized capacity for 1958 were relatively low in comparison with recent historical experience, both were increasing within the year. The government lost much of its effectiveness. In the presidential election of late 1958, relatively conservative Jorge Alessandri with a plurality of only 31%, narrowly defeated the Socialist candidate, Salvador Allende Gossens.

2.2.2. The Alessandri stabilization and liberalization program

The new government took office in late 1958. Roberto Vergara was Minister of Finance, Economics, and Mining, posts which he maintained until September 1960. In part to avoid identification with the discredited Ibañez–Klein–Saks program of three years earlier, no formal document describing the Allessandri–Vergara stabilization and liberalization program was released. Despite the lack of an explicitly defined program, however, there was clearly an economic program designed to revitalize the economy and to achieve price stabilization through increased supplies induced by liberalized internal and external policies. In comparison with the stabilization attempt of the previous period, the Alessandri–Vergara effort placed less emphasis on price stability *per se* and more emphasis on economic vitalization[44], although the underlying assumptions about the benefits of liberalization remained the same. After allowing several months of adjustments to the December 1958–January 1959 devaluations of 25.4% and the 1959 wage readjustment of from 22 to 27% (with an increase in the *sueldo vital* of 36.7%), the government began to pursue its goals in earnest in April 1959. This stabilization–activation–liberalization attempt dominated the Chilean economic picture through 1961.

In contrast to the preceding attempt, under the Alessandri program the foreign sector was to play not an auxiliary role, but a major role by providing inflows of capital, competition for domestic industries, an increased supply of goods, and a symbol of the

[44]Of course the 1959 effort was initiated in a period in which price increases were substantially below the 70–80% range in which the 1956 stabilization effort was started, which may explain the difference in the degree of preoccupation with price stability in the two efforts.

stability of the economy. In an attempt to enable the foreign sector to play such roles, considerable liberalization and rationalization was introduced so that the foreign economic policy regime became the most liberal one which Chile has had in the 45 years since the start of the Great Depression.

Exchange control was reduced by granting the right to deal in all classes of foreign exchange and monetary instruments to commercial banks in January 1959. The Central Bank was given more control over exchange movements than it had had since 1931 by the incorporation of the Foreign Exchange Commission into it in April 1960. The exchange rates were devalued substantially initially[45], and subsequently they were unified at a fixed nominal rate until the end of 1961. In April 1959 tax immunities were established for capital repatriated from abroad to buy tax-exempt dollar bonds, and the establishment of foreign currency deposits was facilitated. Soon thereafter banks were granted the authority to make loans expressed in terms of foreign currency and to pay interest on foreign currency time deposits. In September 1959 legal delays in selling foreign exchange to importers were reduced substantially, and in May 1961 they were eliminated. In April 1959 the government introduced an additional tax (*impuesto adicional*) payable in dollars of from 2 to 200% of the cif value in six categories to gradually replace the prior deposit system. Over the same period prior deposits were reduced, made payable in dollars and then in treasury bonds, and finally eliminated in November 1961. Licensing was no longer required for permitted imports, and the list of permitted imports was expanded considerably in April 1959 and effectively made almost all-inclusive in December of that year. Bilateral, compensation and barter agreements, generally, were allowed to expire. In April 1959 more liberal depreciation allowances for tax purposes were introduced for large-scale mining by permitting readjustment of asset values in conformity with changes in the cost-of-living index. Other foreign investment was encouraged by special provisions in April 1959 and April 1960, which allowed numerous tax exemptions for particular industries defined to be in the national interest, as well as the possibility of many specific presidential decree privileges and guarantees covering such matters as future taxation, depreciation

---

[45]Instituto de Economía (1963, p. 203) and Leftwich (1966, p. 407) suggest that, given the trade regime in operation at the time, after the devaluation of 27 January 1959, the rate was close to equilibrium.

allowances, withdrawal of capital, remittances of profits, etc. for ten years (and in special cases, 20 years)[46].

Some counter tendencies existed. For example, special regimes were expanded, especially for specific industries, so that by 1961 they covered over 40% of Chilean imports in value. Due to the general liberalization, however, the exemptions given by those regimes probably were of relatively less importance than in earlier periods. In any case, such counter movements were dominated by the general liberalizing and rationalizing changes[47].

2.2.3. The results of the Alessandri program

Once again, in many respects this stabilization program at least initially apparently met with considerable success.

2.2.3.1. Cyclical variables

In respect to fluctuations in nominal terms, the rate of inflation declined steadily from 40.6% in 1959 to 9.5% in 1960 to 7.9% in 1961, with the latter two years representing the lowest inflationary rates since before the Second World War (variable 1.1.1). The international economic policy regime contributed to this deceleration of inflation by allowing substantial external financing of government deficits, by increasing real supplies through greater imports, by reducing oligopolistic returns to importers[48], by the contractive influence on the money supply of the loss of international reserves, and by the dampening effect of the reduction in quantitative resolutions on many prices (see ch. 6 below). The mean rates of increase of the unit values of imports and exports, respectively, of − 2.2 and 2.9% imply at worst a fairly neutral direct impact of the

---

[46]Also during this period Chile signed the Treaty of Montevideo which instituted the Latin American Free Trade Area (LAFTA) in February 1960. The signatories agreed gradually to eliminate all barriers to intraregional trade over a 12-year period. In December 1961 Chile announced the national import list with special provisions for LAFTA countries.

[47]Once again Behrman (1975b) provides a much more extensive examination of foreign sector policies in this period.

[48]The imported component of the wholesale price index declined relative to the overall index by a mean annual average of 5.3% due to the increasing overvaluation and increasing trade liberalization. However, the largest decrease occurred in 1959 in which year a devaluation of about 25% was also completed, a phenomenon which the Instituto de Economía (1963, p. 85) claims reflects the reduction of oligopolistic returns to the previously more limited number of importers.

Chilean price level of international price movements. The sharp decline in domestic price changes occurred despite enlarged governments deficits (variable 1.4.4), the partial financing of which caused considerable expansion of the money supply (variables 1.3.1–2) even though foreign loans also were used. The high monetary expansion, together with the exhaustion of foreign reserves (variable 5.2.7.3), led to expectations of an eventual resurgence of inflation and an increased income velocity of money (variable 1.1.2).

In regard to the real component of cyclical fluctuations, the capacity utilization index (variable 1.2.1) suggests a definite increase in the utilization of Chile's real economic potential in this period despite the increased competition from the foreign sector due to liberalization which seemed to have affected utilization rates negatively in the previous period. Neither this rate, nor the employment rate (variable 1.2.2), however, were as high as in the 1960s and early 1970s.

2.2.3.2. Resource allocation and structural change

Intersectoral resource shifts apparently occurred from industry into the other sectors. In respect to sector of origin of real *GDP*, the agricultural share remained at about 13%, the mining share increased for the first time since the start of the Second World War to 7%, the industrial share continued its decline to 19%, and the rest of the economy share declined slightly to 61% (variables 2.1.1.1–3)[49]. Behrman (1975b, table A.2) presents estimates which suggest that significant period-coincident deviations from the secular exponential growth rates for 1940–1965 occurred in 1959–1961 with a positive sign for agriculture[50] and a negative sign for industry. The rate of

---

[49]Over the longer period between the 1952 and 1960 censuses, shifts of labor occurred out of the 'goods' sectors and into 'service' sectors (especially construction and government): agriculture (31.2–29.6%), mining (4.9–4.5%), industry (19.7–18.2%), construction (4.7–6.7%), government (7.6–8.8%), and all services including government plus construction (44.2–47.7%). (If construction is included with the goods sector the shift towards services was from 39.5 to 41.0%.) This relative shift away from goods production has been a matter of some preoccupation to a number of Chilean observers of the economy. Note that this shift occurred despite considerable overall liberalization and reduction in inflation between the two census years (although both restrictionism and inflation first increased substantially until the end of 1955 and also increased somewhat in 1958).

[50]Note that due to the very high agricultural real *GDP* in 1958, within the 1959–1961 period agricultural product actually declined somewhat, despite the significant period-coincident positive deviation in the growth rate for this sector (see variable 4.3). In part, this decline may have reflected the impact of the great 1960 earthquake.

growth of industrial real *GDP* did become positive again in 1960 after two years of negative values, but over the phase averaged only 2.8% and by the end of 1961 the level of industrial real *GDP* was still 7.0% below that for 1957. These intersectoral shifts are consistent with the expected impacts of the changes in the international economic policy regime in that such changes reduced favoritism for industry[51] and reduced the need for a large service sector to operate and to deal with the international trade regime mechanisms[52].

On the subsector level the physical production of copper and iron continued to increase, while that of nitrates continued to decline in mining; the shares of tobacco, clothing, furniture, and wood declined in industry (despite relatively high protection for the first three of these subsectors in 1961 according to the estimates in Behrman, 1975b, table 5.1); and the share of construction particularly increased among the other sectors. Alterations in the international economic regime seem to have been important for these intrasectoral changes, especially within the industrial sector. For many industrial subsectors on the two-digit level (except textiles, paper, tobacco and non-metallic products) substantial declines in the nominal protection from international competition occurred during this phase because of trade liberalization. However, there is no significant correlation between the degree to which customs barriers were reduced over the period among industrial subsectors and the rates of growth of production between 1958 and 1961[53]. Also of note is that even near the end of this liberalizing phase in 1961, the estimates presented in Behrman (1975b, table 5.3) suggest that considerable variance remained in the degree of resource allocation incentives and of resource misallocation costs among industrial and primary subsectors. These same estimates suggest, moreover, that if a correction were made for overvaluation, the level of nominal or effective protection for many subsectors was not particularly high (negative, probably, in a number of cases). Thus, the heightened

[51]Note that for both consumption goods and investment goods import desubstitution occurred in the gross sense in that imports increased relative to domestic product (variables 5.2.2.1–2).

[52]But see footnote 49 in respect to this point.

[53]The subsectoral industrial increases in production in 1958–1961 are based on data in Muñoz (1968, p. 161). The subsectoral industrial change in custom barriers for 1958–1961 are based on calculations of Sergio de la Cuadra in Hachette (1966, p. 59). The correlation between these two data sets is 0.15, which is not significantly non-zero at standard significance levels.

import competition due to the increasingly overvalued currency may have been more important than the dismantling of the exchange control system and its various quantitative restrictions in explaining the relative stagnation in 1959–1961 of a number of industrial subsectors.

2.2.3.3. Distribution of income and of control over resources

In the factoral and class dimensions, the net impact of policy changes may have been progressive due to the elimination of oligopolistic returns to importers, the reduction of wage differentials by the previously described resource allocation shifts[54], the incidence of increased import taxes on the middle- and upper-class users of imported 'non-necessities'[55], the increased employment associated with higher capacity utilization, the relative reduction in consumer goods prices (variables 5.1.4.1–2), and the increased real wage (variable 3.1). On the other hand, the direct benefits of the expansion of non-essential imports probably accrued primarily to the middle- and upper-income classes. Moreover, mean real wages increased only very slightly and the mean labor share of *GDP* fell 3.0% in comparison with the previous period[56], although both indices increased steadily within the years 1959–1961 from the low 1959 values (variables 3.1–2 and variables 6 and 7 in table 2.2).

In the other facets of the control over income and over resources effects also can be identified. In the intersectoral dimension the changes in the regime allowed continued relative shifts out of industry, although the interregional shifts away from the Santiago–Valparaíso nucleus of the previous period may have been reversed due to the increased commercial activity related to the liberalized regime. In the international dimension the analysis below suggests

[54]In particular wages increased relatively in previously low relative wage sectors such as construction and commerce (the latter in part due to increased commercial activity related to expanded foreign trade).

[55]Ffrench-Davis (1971, p. 36) and Sierra (1969, p. 89) claim that the tax system became more regressive in this period because of the increase in indirect taxes from 44.4 to 49.1% of the total. However, most of the increase occurred in the import taxes in a manner in which the burden probably was borne largely by middle- and upper-income classes.

[56]Neither of these variables nor the substantial increase in strikes and labor conflicts seem to support Sierra's (1969, p. 88) statement that labor benefited more in the Alessandri stabilization attempt than in the previous Ibañez stabilization attempt (although the reduction in unemployment and the increase in investment in human capital under Alessandri may lead one to agree with Sierra).

that in an immediate sense the changes in the regime resulted in an increased Chilean command over resources[57], although at the cost of loss of longer-run control to foreigners. In the intertemporal dimension the present generation again was favored relative to future generations by the increased foreign debt, the relative decline in the effective exchange rate for consumption goods, the increase in the consumption share of import goods, and the maintenance of the consumption share of *GDP* at the historically high levels of the previous period (variables 2.1.2.1, 5.1.4.1–2, 5.2.1.1, 5.2.7.3, and 5.2.7.4).

Finally, in respect to private versus public control over resources, the changes in the policy regime led to a definite shift towards the public sector by allowing relatively increased government access to foreign capital sources and by increasing substantially the share of import taxes in total taxes from 8.8% in the previous phase to 12.4% in this period due to the establishment and expansion of the additional tax, the overall increase in imports, and the shift in composition of imports towards relatively highly taxed 'non-essentials' (variables 5.2.4.1, 5.2.6.1.1.2, and 5.2.7.9). Despite this increase, however, the share of all taxes related to foreign trade in total taxes remained about the same at 21% because direct taxes on large-scale mining declined substantially due to the previously described somewhat depressed conditions in the world copper market (variable 5.2.7.5). Even so, taxes were increasing relatively rapidly in comparison to overall product as is indicated by the increase in the ratio of total taxes to *GDP* from a mean of 18% in the previous period to a mean of 21% in this one (variable 3.3.4)[58].

2.2.3.4. Economic growth
The mean annual rate of growth of real per capita *GDP* declined slightly to 1.2% (variable 4.1). Given the much greater emphasis on revitalizing the economy in this period than in the previous one, the

---

[57]Despite the net outflow of direct investment in large-scale mining (variable 5.2.6.3.1.1), the profit rates (i.e. net profits/book value) according to Moran (1970, p. 383) dropped from 19.3 to 14.3% (or from 12.0 to 10.1% if the disputed 1913 claim is included in the book values) and from 36.6 to 28.3% for the two dominant copper mines.

[58]The increased tax revenues and increased deficit apparently were largely related to increased debt payments and transfer payments (especially in the social security system, but also related to earthquake relief as the government current expenditures remained about constant relative to *GDP*, and government direct and financial investment declined somewhat relative to *GDP* – variables 1.4.1-4).

failure to accelerate growth represented at least partial frustration of the attainment of a major economic goal.

Changes in the policy regime of this period apparently affected both savings and investment. Based on the estimates in subsection 5.1.1 below, the impact of such changes on domestic savings were mixed. Domestic savings were apparently increased, *ceteris paribus*, due to the shift in resources to the government with its relatively high marginal propensity to save, the lowered real black market exchange rate in the case of household savings, and the lowered real cost of foreign exchange in the case of business savings. On the other hand, domestic savings were decreased, *ceteris paribus*, due to the increased foreign savings.

The mean annual rate of growth of real investment increased to an all-time high of 15.1% despite a substantial decline in 1959[59] and the mean share of investment in structures and equipment in *GDP* increased to the highest level since at least before the Second World War and probably since before the Great Depression (variables 2.2.2 and 4.4)[60]. The changed policy regime, in net, probably contributed

[59]Hirschman (1963, p. 219) claims that investment sagged somewhat in 1960 which opened the government to criticisms from the left and from the structuralists, but the national accounts indicate that record 29.5% increase in real investment occurred in that year.

[60]That higher growth in real product or in real capacity did not occur despite this high rate of increase in real investment apparently was in part due to the May 1960 earthquake. *Picks' Currency Yearbook* (1965, p. 116) reports the loss to have been $500000000 and about 5% of production capacity, but the negative effects of this natural calamity were somewhat offset by the increased international resources made available as a result. Another factor underlying the low growth rates was a shift in composition of investment towards government public works projects with long gestation periods and towards housing, which together resulted in a mean annual rate of increase in real *GDP* from construction of 8.2%. Housing investment, for example, increased at mean annual rates of 32.7% at least partially due to a number of policy changes: (1) decree law of 31 July 1959 established exemptions from taxes on contracts and budgets, from income tax on income received from housing, from real estate taxes, and from 50% of sales and transfer taxes for 10–20 years for housing of 35–140 square meters in size (with the length of the exemption being inverse to the size); (2) by the same decree law, the government Housing Corporation (Corporación de Vivienda, CORVI) which had been founded in 1953 was reorganized, integrated with a technical department and eight pension plans, and assigned new functions, including direct operations in respect to expropriation and urgent construction, promotion of housing using the resources of the pension plans, and administration and control of the Housing Plan (*Plan Habitacional*, which included fiscal and pension plan resources and a system of readjustable deposits in the State Bank with the right of the depositor to obtain home mortgages); (3) decree law 205 of 5 April 1960 allowed the establishment of private savings and loan associations to facilitate financing housing; (4) decree law 326 of 6 April 1960 legitimized housing cooperatives under CORVI supervision.

to this increased investment through attracting capital from abroad by the stabilization-cum-liberalization program in general and by specific inducements discussed above, such as the changed policies for direct foreign investment and the establishment of dollar deposits and loans[61]. Moreover, the changed structure of effective protection probably tended to induce more efficient investments[62]. Finally, the changes in the regime presumably continued to allow the importation of technology embodied in imported machinery and equipment[63] and to reduce the use of skilled manpower to operate and to deal with the regime itself.

2.2.3.5. *External position*

All of the available indices suggest that the 1959–1961 period was the most liberal in respect to the foreign sector of the 45 years since the Great Depression. The mean ratio of the black market *NER* to the average of all legal *NER*s was almost 1.00 (variable 5.1.3). The mean index of quantitative restrictions fell to the lowest level of any period after 1940 (variable 5.2.7.1). The mean import premium rate and the mean degree of overinvoicing dropped to their lowest levels in the immediate two postwar decades. Because of the large initial devaluation and the imposition of the additional tax, the average *PLD NER* dropped but slightly and the average *PLD EER* actually

[61]Also CORFO published a ten-year economic plan in 1961 (with characteristics such as an annual rate of growth in real *GDP* of 5.5%, an increase in the share of investment in *GDP* to 18%, a shift in the composition of investment towards human capital and towards agriculture and mining, and reforms in agriculture, in the social security system, and in the tax system) which had minimal explicit policy recommendations and which probably had little direct impact on internal allocation decisions. On the other hand, it may have served to raise the general consciousness concerning economic development, as a basis for discussions with international agencies about external financial needs and may have induced greater availability of external financing.

[62]For example, in the discussion of resource allocation above, relative shifts out of relatively high domestic resource cost subsectors such as footwear and clothing and furniture are noted (see also Behrman, 1975b, table 5.3). On the other hand, the shift out of tobacco also noted was not out of a high domestic resource cost subsector. Under the assumptions discussed above, moreover, the shifts of labor out of mining and into construction and into the government probably were inefficient. On the subsectoral level for industry under the same assumptions, furthermore, the substantial shift of labor which Muñoz (1968, p. 57) reports into basic metals to make the most important industrial subsector employer with 24.8% of the labor force in 1961 probably was inefficient (although the equally substantial shift out of clothing probably was efficient).

[63]Note that although the share of capital imports in total imports declined slightly, the absolute level of such imports increased because of the large increase in total imports (variables 5.2.1.3 and 5.2.4.1).

increased somewhat (variables 5.1.1 and 5.1.7). Due to the policy of maintaining a fixed *NER* after the initial devaluations, together with the continuing liberalization and inflation (although the latter was declining), the exchange rate became increasingly overvalued within the period.

The value of merchandise exports in constant dollars increased in 1959 and 1960, but declined in 1961, with the result that the mean value was 3% above that of the previous period and the export to *GDP* ratio increased to 12% (variables 5.2.4.2, 5.2.6.1.1.2, and 5.2.7.7). Nevertheless, the mean value of merchandise exports in constant dollars still was almost 7% below that of the 1952–1955 subperiod. The composition of export goods was dominated even more by mining with an average share of 84% (variables 5.2.3.1–3), and within mining in 1960 and 1961 copper alone accounted for 83% of the export value. With the possible exception of iron ore (which in 1960 and 1961 accounted for 10.2% of the value of mineral exports) and the growing importance of small and medium mining relative to large-scale mining (in 1960 and 1961 the former accounted for 20.2% of copper and iron export values) export diversification by *any* product related measure decreased.

A major factor conditioning Chilean export performance in this period was the somewhat depressed international copper market due to recessionary conditions in some of the major destinations which resulted in a further decline in the Chilean terms of trade, although not down to the levels of the 1950s (variable 5.1.5.1). The United States producers' price for copper, for example, although almost 13% above the 1957–1958 level, averaged almost 26% below the 1956 peak (the London Metal Exchange price followed the same pattern during this period).

The Chilean international economic policy regime, however, also apparently had some significant impact on exports in this phase. On the positive side, exports may have increased due to greater certainty concerning future exchange rate policy (see subsection 5.2.2.1 for statistical evidence of such a response), copper exports in physical terms increased over 14% and finally surpassed the previous peak 1942–1944 levels partially due to the investment of the previous period, and the returns to Chile from large-scale copper mining increased 12.0%. On the negative side, the fixed *NER* policy resulted in a decline of 34% in the mean value of the escudo in constant dollars and of 3% in the cost of foreign exchange in 1960 escudos (variables 5.1.1–2), with results which more than offset the meager export promotion attempts given the fairly substantial export price elasticities (especially for non-traditional export goods) presented below in subsection 5.2.2.1[64].

The increased liberalization and the increasingly overvalued exchange rate[65] induced an accelerated growth in merchandise imports. The mean value in constant dollars increased by over 18% from that of the previous period, and the ratio of total imports to *GDP* increased to the highest level since the 1930s (variables 5.2.4.1, 5.2.6.1.1.2, and 5.2.7.6). Behrman (1975b, table A.2) estimates that in terms of constant escudos, total imports increased from 9.8% below the 1940–1965 secular trend for 1959 to 7% above in 1961. The estimates in the same table also indicate that during this period (except for in 1959) total and service imports had the highest exponential growth rates for the entire 1940–1965 period. The liberalization of imports also induced changes in the composition of imports. As the effective exchange rates for consumption decreased relative to that for investment goods, the average composition of import goods shifted from investment (although an intraperiod shift towards investment occurred) and from intermediate to consumption goods (variables 5.1.4.1–2, 5.2.1.1–3).

The more rapid increase of the value of merchandise imports than of exports, together with a large increase in imports of travel services which more than offset a small decline in net outflows due to investment income, resulted in a doubling of the mean deficit in goods and services on the current account (variables 5.2.6.1, 5.2.6.1.1–2, and 5.2.6.1.2.2). Net transfers also approximately doubled on the average (although they declined by over half in 1961 relative to 1960), apparently again largely due to the approval of the stabilization–liberalization program by other governments and by international organizations, and therefore continued to offset over a fifth of the deficit for goods and services (variables 5.2.6.2).

Over three-fourths of the substantially increased deficit in goods and services again were covered by changes in the capital and

[64]The average exchange rate declined from 79.9 to 68.4% of the parity rate between 1959 and 1961 (based on a 1950 ECLA estimate adjusted by the change in the Chilean cost of living index relative to the change in the United States gross national product deflator) according to CIAP.

[65]See subsection 5.2.1.1 for evidence of widespread statistically significant responses to both of these changes in the international economic regime.

monetary gold account. Net private capital inflows continued to equal about half of the deficit in goods and services, but in this period such inflows exceeded the absolute value of the net outflows of investment income and differed substantially in composition from those of the previous period (variables 5.2.6.3.1, 5.2.6.3.1–3). Apparently because of perceived favorable changes in the overall environment for foreign investors and because of the specific inducements for foreign non-large-scale mining direct investment described above, the mean net level of such investment more than doubled from that of the previous period (variables 5.2.6.3.1.1–5.2.6.3.1.1.1). For similar reasons, including the establishment of dollar accounts in the Chilean banking system, net private capital inflows increased from almost nothing in the previous period to almost the level of net direct investment in this period (variables 5.2.6.3.1.2–3).

Partially offsetting these substantial increases, however, was a sharp drop in direct investment in large-scale mining. For example, in large-scale copper mining gross investment declined by 17.6% from the level of the previous period, gross investment minus amortization declined by 87.8%, the ratio of gross investment to after tax profits declined from 89.7 to 52.0%, and the ratio of gross investment to after-tax profits plus amortization declined from 72.7 to 36.1%. For total large-scale mining net direct investment in constant 1958 dollars declined from an average of $20700000 in the previous period to $2900000 in this period (variable 5.2.6.3.1.1.1). Thus, it would be difficult to argue that the *Nuevo Trato* continued to induce substantial new investment in this period, or that the general liberalization of the international economic regime had much positive impact on new investment in large-scale mining. In fact, new company investment plans were shelved in 1960 and 1961 reputedly because the government would not agree to a 20-year guarantee against changes in the tax rates and against expropriation. On the contrary, in late 1961 after an impasse had been reached, two special surtaxes totaling 13.0% on the profits of large-scale mining were passed and the Socialist Party introduced a bill (which was not passed) to nationalize large-scale mining with a payment of $209000000 in the form of 3% 30-year bonds.

Capital and monetary gold flows to the banking system and to government institutions also changed in composition during this phase. Such net inflows to the central government increased somewhat, but remained slightly negative (variable 5.2.6.3.1.4). Mean annual net inflows to commercial banks increased substantially from 2 600 000 to 13 400 000 1958 dollars. Mean annual net inflows to the Central Bank reflected almost tripled use of IMF credit and an almost 50% increase in loans received, partially offset by a substantial negative change in the IMF reserve positions. These changes in capital and monetary gold flows to the banking system and to the government reflected not so much changes in kind as extensions in degree of two major alterations noted above in respect to the previous period. First, the supply of foreign capital increased substantially due to the decreases in the rate of inflation, the apparent political stability under a right of center democratically elected government, the liberalization of the foreign economic regime, the response to the earthquake of May 1960, the existence of a CORFO economic plan, and the starting of the Alliance for Progress. Second, the demand for such foreign capital increased substantially due to the effects of the increasingly overvalued exchange rate on imports and exports noted above and due to the continued practice of financing the increasing government deficits largely externally in order to avoid generating internal inflationary pressures[66]. As a result the public sector debt in foreign currency increased 101% to a level of $788 000 000 by the end of the period, total Chilean debt in foreign currency (not including direct private credits, nor deferred payment import credits for which data are not available) increased 81.7% to a level of $954 000 000 or 183% of exports of 22% of *GDP* (at the official exchange rate) in 1961, and net international reserves held by the banking system plummeted to a new low of − $164 800 000 at the end of 1961 (also see variables 1.2.7.3 and 1.2.7.4).

[66]The government had hoped that such dependence on external financing would be transitory. Relative success was had in obtaining some tax changes (e.g. law 13305 of April 1959 extended sales taxes to several necessities previously exempted, established the additional tax on imports, created a tax on the assessed value of dwellings, eliminated the taxes on foreign currency, checks and interest, increased the legal penalties for tax evasion, increased the interest charge on tax payments in arrears to 3% per month, effectively created new revenue sources by consolidating public operations into a single account (*Cuenta Unica Fiscal*) and established government dollar bonds and treasury dollar bills with tax exempt interest; and law 14171 of October 1961 increased the tax rate on real estate by 0.5%, increased the tax rate on profits 5% to a level of 38%, and instituted a forced savings plan with 1% of wages and 20% of the profits of large-scale mining). Nevertheless, government revenues lagged behind government expenditures partially due to slower than hoped for growth, and the government deficit increased to all-time highs (variable 1.4.4).

2.3. Frei stabilization program of 1965–1970[67]

2.3.1. Background

The Alessandri stabilization attempt of 1959–1961 terminated with a balance of payments crisis at the end of 1961. In December of that year the Central Bank liquid reserves were down to the equivalent of approximately ten days of imports, a considerable number of import applications were still pending, and the Central Bank could not borrow further from abroad because of the substantial foreign debt noted above. On 27 December 1961, the Central Bank revoked all authority to deal in foreign exchange and established temporary prohibitive 10000% prior deposits on all imports. Foreign exchange reserves and the national foreign credit standing were exhausted due to the failure to control the government deficit and to the maintenance of a substantially and increasingly overvalued exchange rate with a liberal trade regime. The Alessandri stabilization and liberalization attempt thus came to an end, with an abrupt reversion to restrictionism interventionism, and shortly thereafter, inflation[68]. The next three years were characterized even less than 1959–1961 by a systematic overall economic program. Instead, piecemeal policies led to a generally more complicated and restrictive system.

The general performance of the economy in 1962–1964, neverthe-

[67]Basic sources for this section include Bacha and Taylor (1973), Banco Central (1966a–1969a, 1962b–1971b, 1967c, 1967d, 1968c, 1969c, 1969d, 1970c, 1970d, n.d.c, n.d.d), Cauas (1970, 1972), Corbo (1974), CORFO (1968, 1970), de Castro and de la Cuadra (1971), de la Cruz (1967), *The Economist* Intelligence Unit (1962–1970), Ffrench-Davis (1971), Ffrench-Davis and Carrasco (1969), Griffin (1969), Gunder-Frank (1972, pp. 11–16), Instituto de Economía (1963, pp. 87–88, 241–243), IMF (1969a, 1961b–1971b), Jeanneret (1971, pp. 140, 150), Joo (1970), Jul (1969, pp. 48–49, 95–147), Leftwich (1966, pp. 411–413), Levinson and de Onis (1970, pp. 157–158), Líbano (1970, pp. 727–728), Mamalakis (1971b, pp. 165, 554), Mikesell (1971, pp. 374–386), Ministerio de Relaciones Exteriores (1970), Moran (1970), *Picks' Currency Yearbook* (1961–1970), Senado, Oficina de Informaciones (1971, pp. 22, 48–54), and Sierra (1969).

[68]Although anticipated in some quarters, these events were not foreseen by all observers. For example, apparently late in 1961 Hirschman (1963, p. 220), after approving of the appointment of Luis Escobar (a representative of the structuralist school who had been Dean of the Faculty of Economics at the University of Chile) as Minister of Economics in August 1961 and noting that the government had a majority in both houses and had the assurance of long-run assistance from the Alliance for Progress, concluded: 'Hence, the chances for improving the performance of the Chilean economy in various structural ways while keeping the traditional scourge (i.e. inflation) under control looked more promising than they had for a long time'.

less, was in some respects satisfactory. The mean rate of growth of real *GDP* was the highest since the Second World War (variable 4.1). The mean rate of capacity utilization was the highest among all the periods and subperiods and subperiods in 1940–1970 (variable 1.2.1). However, problems were present. The mean annual rate of change of prices increased to 35.4% (variable 1.1.1), with levels recorded in 1963 and 1964 (variable 1 in table 2.2) that were exceeded in the Chilean experience only in the almost hyperinflations of 1954–1956 and 1972–1975. The relatively high mean rate of growth, moreover, was due almost entirely to 1962. On a per capita basis, the economy almost stagnated in real terms in 1963 and 1964 (variable 8 in table 2.2).

Inflation outpaced even the rather substantial devaluations, so the *PLD NER* fell another 5% (variable 5.1.1). The increased inducement to import was restrained by the reintroduction of a multiple exchange rate system with quantitative restrictions and prior import deposits. The mean ratio of the black market *NER* to the average of the legal *NER*s rose to 1.70 (5.1.3), which provides one index of the increased exchange control. Bacha and Taylor (1973, p. 144) estimate that the degree of overvaluation averaged 47% in 1962–1964.

The export capacity to import increased about 20% (variable 5.2.7.2) because of an improvement of almost 10% in the terms of trade (variable 5.1.5.1) and an expansion in the physical quantity of copper exports. Even though exports grew more rapidly than imports, however, the mean net deficit on the goods and services account rose to its largest value in the postwar period, primarily because of the large augmentation in net factor payments abroad (variables 5.2.6.1 and 5.2.6.1.2.3). Mean net unrequited transfers fell, but mean net non-monetary capital inflows increased substantially because of the highest mean net inflow of loans to the central government recorded in any post-Second World War period (variable 5.2.6.3.1.4). As one result, mean net monetary capital and gold movements fell by almost half from the previous period (variable 5.2.6.3.2). As another result, foreign debt by the end of 1964 had risen to \$1 896 000 000 – 178% of the export value or 36.1% of the *GDP* for that year.

The increasing stagnation and increasing inflation reinforced the perception that the government had lost direction. The presidential campaign of 1964 featured two candidates who promised to provide substantial new directions and commitments for Chile: Eduardo

Frei Montalva, a Christian Democrat, and Salvador Allende Gossens, once again the leftist coalition candidate. Frei won the election by a substantial margin, and his government assumed office later that year.

2.3.2. The Frei stabilization and liberalization program

The new government had as its goals substantial changes in the economic, political and social fabric of the country. Among the major objectives were (1) increases in the rates of economic growth through higher capacity utilization and capacity expansion[69]; (2) gradual programmed price stabilization; (3) redistribution of income and of political power towards the lower economic classes; (4) increased national control over the national destiny and the elimination of balance of payments problems by changing the nature of control over Chilean mineral resources, by increasing the capacity to export both traditional and non-traditional products, and by increasing domestic production in 'dynamic' sectors; and (5) structural changes including agrarian, social security, educational, constitutional, housing, tax, governmental and (later) industrial organization reforms and popular promotion (*promoción popular*) of wider participation in decisionmaking.

These broad objectives had firm roots in the structuralist analysis of the Chilean economy. Price stabilization was included as one of the major objectives for the third time in a decade, but was not given priority over all other aims.

Although resistance was substantial on a number of issues, initially the new government had a number of successes in moving towards these objectives. The very existence of a government with definite goals and broad domestic and international support created expectations which led to higher capacity utilization and greater growth. The gradual price stabilization program appeared successful for most of the first two years, through a combination of monetary, fiscal, incomes, and price control policies (see Cauas, 1970). Foreign sector liberalization was initiated almost immediately with the

[69]In a comparative sense, Chilean economic growth had not been particularly high for some time. According to unpublished 1970 UNCTAD calculations, for the 1950–1965 period among 45 developing countries, Chile ranked 29th in terms of per capita real *GDP* increases. For the 1960–1965 period among 56 countries, Chile ranked 38th.

introduction of a sliding-peg *NER* policy in early 1965. Negotiations with the large-scale copper companies about expanding capacity and increasing Chilean participation were commenced immediately after the election. In 1966 large-scale mining was 'Chileanized' (with 51% Chilean ownership of the second largest mine and 25% ownership of several smaller mines), and a program initiated which was scheduled to increase capacity by 65% in the next six years[70]. Legislative proposals for parliamentary consideration were developed for tax reform, agrarian reform, and other structural changes.

Subsequently, as the post-election euphoria wore off, attempts at structural changes through legislation or negotiation appeared stalemated, frustrations continued, and price stabilization appeared to be failing, such successes were less. Political support declined, both inside and outside of the Christian Democratic Party. Preoccupation with short-run problems related to price stability and capacity utilization increased. In the view of structuralist observers such as Sierra (1969, pp. 122, 154), the government changed from a basically structuralist view to an orthodox view concerning the appropriate policies.

In late 1967, as part of a renewed effort at price stabilization, the government proposed legislation which included a compulsory savings plan for 1968 wage increases exceeding 10% and a suspension of strike rights (together with increased taxes, price controls, requirements that companies reinvest or buy government bonds with at least 66% of their profits, and encouragement for profit sharing and increased worker participation in management). In reaction to such proposals a general strike was called in December 1967. The political parties of the left coalesced against the government, and political support from the right also declined in opposition to the features of the program which would limit the freedom of business and in opposition to other government programs such as agrarian reform. Raul Saez replaced Sergio Molina as Minister of Finance and several months later Andres Zaldivar replaced Saez in the same post. Finally, the government effort was defeated after months of acrimonious debate. Instead an increase of 21.9% in the *sueldo vital* was approved. The broad political support which Frei earlier had enjoyed was further reduced. In the March 1968 elections

[70]Behrman (1975b, subsection 4.2.1) provides details about changes in policy towards large-scale mining.

the Christian Democrats received only 31% of the vote and lost its majority in the Chamber of Deputies. Some of the redistributional aims among the labor force seemed to have been abandoned. The death knell was sounded for further price stabilization attempts under the Frei administration. After this debacle some significant programs continued and some significant modifications were made, but evidence of overall governmental coordination was even less and the government seemed to lose substantial control over internal policy decisions[71].

For foreign sector, as opposed to domestic, policies, the time pattern of reforms lagged substantially. The first three or four years were characterized by cyclical attempts at rationalization and liberalization, together with significant expansion of Chilean control over copper exports. As is noted above, the sliding-peg exchange rate system was introduced in 1965, and the 'Chileanization' of large-scale copper mining occurred in 1966. Also in 1966 the price of Chilean copper was set equal to the London Metal Exchange price, which in this period exceeded substantially the former reference, the United States producers' price. During these first years, however, foreign exchange shortages also resulted in the institution of some more restrictive foreign sector policies. Examples include the 'added additional tax' of late 1964, the allocation system with quotas by custom categories used in 1965 and early 1966, and the extension of time delays before receiving foreign exchange.

In the last two or three years, attempts to reform and to liberalize the foreign sector increased substantially, and control over copper was expanded further. The difference in timing in comparison to internal reform attempts primarily reflected Chile's improving foreign exchange position within the period due, in substantial part, to the booming international copper market[72]. Perhaps also of some importance was the concentration of the efforts of a number of talented individuals in the Central Bank on reforming the foreign

---

[71]For extensive descriptions and analysis of overall economic policy and events under the Frei government see Bradford (1970), Cauas (1970 and 1972), The *Economist* Intelligence Unit (1964–1970), Ffrench-Davis (1971), Gunder-Frank (1972), Levinson and de Onis (1970, pp. 234–239), Mamalakis (1971b, pp. 167–173) and Sierra (1969).

[72]Due in part to the Vietnam War, the mean United States producers' copper price in 1965–1970 exceeded that for 1962–1964 by 39%, and the mean London Metal Exchange copper price in 1965–1970 exceeded that for 1962–1964 by 77%. Therefore, the Chilean terms of trade improved substantially (variable 5.1.5.1).

economic sector after hopes for the reforms in other areas had been frustrated. In any case, movements were made towards a unified exchange rate system, the abolition of prior deposits on imports, the elimination of special regimes and exceptions, the rationalization of price controls on foreign trade through the adoption in 1967 of a new tariff law to replace the 1928 code, the development of incentives for non-traditional exports, the discouragement of speculative capital movements through taxes, the extension of Chilean control over copper by the nationalization of the largest mine, and regional integration within the Andean Group. These reform efforts continued until 1970 when they were stopped, if not reversed in some cases, by events relating to the presidential election in September of that year[73].

2.3.3. The results of the Frei program

As in the proceeding two cases, this attempt initially met with some significant successes. Also parallel to the earlier efforts, momentum could not be maintained in most dimensions. As noted above, internal efforts at reform petered out with the failure of the proposed stabilization legislation for 1968. External reforms accelerated, however, in the last years of the Frei presidency.

2.3.3.1. Cyclical variables

In respect to price stability, the mean rate of inflation was significantly below that of the 1952–1955, 1956–1958, and 1962–1964 periods (variable 1.1.1). It did not, however, approach the 1959–1961 average level. Within this period, moreover, it increased in the last three or four years after an initial decline. The drop in the mean income velocity to the lowest level since before 1956 (variable 1.1.2), however, suggests that inflationary expectations may have been reduced below those of the previous two stabilization efforts even if the actual rate of inflation was higher than in the Alessandri attempt.

The initial reduction in inflation, the fall on the average in inflation, and the apparent decline in inflationary expectations reflected at least some success in government policies. Of substantial importance was the substantial increase in taxes relative to

[73]Behrman (1975a and 1975b) provide an extensive analysis of foreign sector policies during this period.

product due to improved collections and increased tax rates, and the accompanying considerable decline of the government deficit (variables 1.4.4 and 1.4.5). Changes in foreign sector policies also probably reduced inflationary pressures, *ceteris paribus*, by expanding supplies through increased imports, by decreasing quantitative restrictions and the associated import premium rates (variables 5.1.3, 5.1.6, and 5.2.7.1), by the impact on prices of maintaining an overvalued exchange rate, and by generally reducing the costs of importing due to tariffs, prior import deposits, and delays in receiving foreign exchange after initial import applications had been filed (although these delays were first increased in 1965 and then shortened). Changes in the monetary system, such as the increase in marginal reserve rates (variable 1.3.3) and the elimination of float, also tended to work in the same direction.

Nevertheless, the monetary supply expanded quite quickly. The mean average increase of 43.2% (variable 1.3.1) was almost as high as during 1952–1955 and significantly higher than in any other previous period or subperiod. In contrast to the four previous periods, however, internal bank credit to the public sector was not expanded as rapidly as the money supply (variables 1.3.1 and 1.3.2). Instead, much more important in the monetary expansion were increases in foreign reserves (see below) and increases in credit to the private sector as part of the attempt to stimulate economic activity.

In regard to the real component of cyclical fluctuations, the capacity utilization index and the Santiago unemployment rate both suggest a decrease in the average utilization of Chile's short-run potential (variables 1.2.1 and 1.2.2). Nevertheless, the average values of these variables imply greater success in inducing fuller utilization in capacity during this effort than during the previous Ibañez and Alessandri attempts. The year-by-year figures indicate, moreover, that initially capacity utilization was quite high, but that subsequently it declined considerably. The estimates in table 4.7 below suggest that the decline in utilization in many sectors may have been related to increased competitive imports as quantitative restrictions were reduced.

2.3.3.2. Resource allocation and structural change
Intersectoral resource shifts apparently occurred from agriculture and mining slightly to industry, but more to all other sectors, as is

suggested by the changed sectoral shares in real *GDP* (variables 2.1.1.1–3). Due to the long gestation period involved, of course, such a measure does not reflect the substantial shift into mining after 1967 because of the investment program associated with the Chileanization policy.

The examination of subsector nominal and effective protection rates in Behrman (1975b, section 5.2) suggests that both the level in 1967 and the change between 1961 and 1967 in nominal protection rates were associated positively with: (a) the degree of industrial concentration (and therefore with the degree of organized political power?); (b) the degree of previous dynamitism; and (c) the relative importance of the subsector in providing capital. The changes in effective protection rates over the same period indicate somewhat of a shift away from the traditional 'easy' import substitution – industrial subsectors towards intermediate industrial subsectors. Both the nominal and the effective protection rate estimates suggest that after a correction for overvaluation is made the 1967 levels of protection in reality were not so high as *prima facie* they appeared. Both the nominal and the effective protection rates also imply relatively high protection for manufacturing as opposed to primary (especially the traditional mineral exporting) sectors and for import substitution as opposed to export promotion. Furthermore, they imply no significant reduction in the substantial variance across subsectors in comparison with earlier estimates.

Thus, these estimates imply some success of the changes in policy regime in the attainment of goals such as the inducement of greater efficiency by the possible reduction in overvaluation-adjusted protection and the establishment of inducements for intraindustrial shifts from the traditional 'easy' import substitution industries (which had been relatively protected for at least four decades, if not since the tariff legislation of 1897) to the more dynamic intermediate goods industries. On the other hand, the desired shift towards favoring capital imports apparently did not occur, exports continued to be discriminated against despite the special regime for export promotion[74], and the inducements for inefficient resource allocation remained in that subsectoral variances apparently were not re-

---

[74]Selowsky (1970, p. 12) estimates that the resource cost of a marginal dollar earned by exports was two-thirds of one earned by import substitution in 1969.

duced[75]. Some further headway in the attainment of the government's stated aims may have been made during the increasing liberalization of the last years of this period, but there is no evidence of particular successes in these respects in the patterns of relative effective exchange rates through 1970 which Behrman (1975b, table 5.2) presents.

2.3.3.3. Distribution of income and of control over resources

In the factoral and class dimension, progressive impacts were numerous. The shift away from the use of fiscal bonds for prior deposits in late 1964 eliminated the previous high scarcity rents for the relatively wealthy owners thereof. The reduction of the discrimination against agriculture in the protection structure aided in the initial increase of wages in this relatively low-wage sector. The demand for labor increased in large-scale mining due to the end of exchange rate discrimination against this sector and due to the expanded investment program therein. A tax on wealth was introduced. Mass education and health programs were expanded. Oligopolistic returns in some of the traditionally relatively protected industrial subsectors were reduced. Generally changes in protection across subsectors were associated with improved positions for labor.

Regressive impacts, however, also occurred. Increased foreign

[75]An extreme case of inefficiency due to the international economic regime was the restriction of the automobile industry to Arica in northern Chile by the special regime for that area (although this restriction was not introduced in this period, it was maintained initially therein). Johnson (1967) describes the state of this industry as of 1965, notes the considerable problems of seasonality due to the difficulties of obtaining both domestic and foreign imputs in combination with the pressure to produce before the end of each calendar year so that the annually increasing national component requirements could be met, and estimates that the trade-off between local resources used and the dollars saved was as high at 4 to 1 at the official rate or 2.4 to 1 at the black market rate (although he suggests that the elimination of extraordinary rents might lower these estimates somewhat).

Ffrench-Davis (1971, p. 95) suggests that the export drawback program also encouraged inefficiency by giving larger drawbacks to more costly operations. If the drawback rates in fact were based on tax incidence, the basis for this claim is not clear. However, if the establishment of rate levels reflected in part political pressures (such as Jul, 1969, suggests for many of the covered products) then Ffrench-Davis may be right. de Castro and de la Cuadra (1971, pp. 36–37) also criticize the drawback program for not encouraging efficient producers across commodities due to disparities in rates, and for being more subject to uncertainty than a devaluation because the policy might be changed at any time (although in the Chilean context exchange rate policy also seems to be subject to sudden changes).

competition from imports, mentioned above, caused general downward pressure on employment. Subsidies were reduced on certain mass-consumption imported necessities. The reduction or removal of restrictions on imported luxuries benefited mostly the middle- or upper-income classes. The distributive aspects of certain policies favored vested economic interests such as the drawbacks for SOQUIM (the nitrate company) and for the one-time cement exports to Argentina and Brazil.

The net effect of total government policies apparently was progressive. Real wages and the wage share of *GDP* both increased to the highest mean totals recorded among post-1940 periods and subperiods (variables 3.1 and 3.2).

In other facets of the control over income and over resources, effects also can be identified. In the intersectoral dimension the regime encouraged shifts into agriculture (although, on net, the flows were still out), mining, and the banking and commerce part of services (although shifts also occurred out of services due to the reduced restrictiveness of the regime). In the interregional dimension, shifts into the central nucleus continued to be encouraged. In the international dimension, although the regime allowed large net outflows of investment income (variable 5.2.6.1.2.3), the changes in the policy towards large-scale mining probably resulted in a shift from foreigners to Chile because of the resulting large Chilean participation in the returns from the copper boom[76]. In the intertemporal dimension policy changes had a mixed impact. The decline in the relative effective exchange rate for consumption versus investment goods seemed to favor the present generation (variables 5.1.4.1–2). The reduction in the relative level of the foreign debt seemed to favor future generations (variable 5.2.4.7). The stable composition of import goods in respect to consumption and investment shares seemed to reflect no basic change in this dimension (variables 5.2.1.1–3).

[76]However ECLA (1970, pp. 152–153) suggests the opposite conclusion for 1965–1968 before the surtax on copper prices was effective because the percentage of large-scale copper mining gross value returned to Chile declined from an average of 76.4 in 1962–1964 to 74.8 in 1965–1968, in part because of the abolishment of the 5 and 8% additional taxes. The ECLA analysis does not seem to consider, on the other hand, that some of this reduction in the percentage returned value reflects the fixed-cost nature of a substantial proportion of the legal costs of production which implies a lower percentage returned value *ceteris paribus* when prices increase as in the 1965–1968 period. After the imposition of the surtax in 1969, the ECLA estimate for the percentage returned value is 80.4.

Finally, in respect to private versus public control over resources, the change in credit composition mentioned above and the reduced import barriers resulted in some shift towards the private sector. Nevertheless, the net impact was clearly a shift towards the public sector because of the increased government revenues and increased direct control from the changes in policy towards large-scale mining, the change from fiscal bonds to domestic currency for prior import deposits in late 1964, the increased government revenues due to the increased level of imports, general tax reforms, and, at least initially, an increased relative access of the public sector to imports. Due to these and other changes in government policy, the total role of the government in the economy increased substantially in this period (variables 1.4.1–5).

2.3.3.4. Economic growth

The mean annual rate of growth of real per capita increased to 2.5%, the highest level for any of the period or subperiods in 1908–1970 (variable 4.1)[77,78].

On the basis of the estimates discussed below in section 5.1.1, the impact on domestic savings of changes in Chilean policies were positive due to: (a) the shift in resources to the government with its high marginal propensity to save; (b) the inverse impact of the decreased foreign savings; (c) the positive impact on the reduced cost of foreign exchange on business savings; and (d) the positive impact of reduced quantitative restrictions on household savings (variables 1.4.2, 1.4.5, 5.1.3, 5.1.7, and 5.2.7.1).

The net impact of changes in policies on investment in structures and equipment was also positive because of: (a) the expansion of large-scale mining subsequent to the start of Chileanization; (b) the inducements for greater relative efficiency in investments (which may account in part for the substantially reduced marginal capital output ratio, variable 4.5); and (c) the freeing of skilled manpower from operating and dealing with the control system. These more

---

[77]Within the period this growth rate varied substantially with large increases in 1965 and 1966, a decline to a negative value in 1967, and subsequent moderate increases thereafter except for a slight decline in 1970 – which was probably related to the political uncertainty in that presidential election year.

[78]Behrman (1975b, table A.1) gives average growth rates for periods between 1908 and 1940.

than offset the slight (and apparently originally unintended) increase in discrimination against investment imports (variables 5.1.4.1–2 and 5.2.1.2).

2.3.3.5. External position
Most available indices suggest that 1965–1970 on the average was second only to 1959–1961 among post-Great Depression periods in terms of liberalizing and rationalizing the foreign sector policy regime. The mean ratio of the black market *NER* to the average of all legal *NER* rates fell to 1.55, second lowest among post-1940 periods (variable 5.1.3)[79]. The index of quantitative restrictions dropped to the second lowest value among post-Second World War periods (variable 5.2.7.1). The mean import premium rate, the mean degree of overinvoicing, and the spread among sectoral effective exchange rates all dropped to their lowest levels among post-Second World War periods (variables 5.1.6 and 5.2.5.1; variable 12 in table 2.2). Within the 1965–1970 period, as is noted several times above, moreover, reforms in foreign sector policies accelerated in the last two or three years.

The sliding-peg exchange rate policy supposedly was to result in an increase in the real exchange rate of 2% per year in order to lessen overvaluation, discourage imports, and encourage exports. In fact, however, the mean *PLD NER* fell 6.5% and the mean *PLD EER* dropped 10% (variables 5.1.1 and 5.1.7). The impact of the various policy changes, together with world market conditions, on exports, imports, and other foreign account items is now considered.

The value of total exports in constant dollars increased at a mean annual rate of 11%, and the mean value of merchandise exports in constant dollars increased 59% over that of the previous period (variables 5.2.4.2 and 5.2.6.1.1.2). The major factor in this substantially increased export value was the world copper market boom, due in part to the Vietnam War. Because of this boom the mean United States copper producers' price exceeded that of 1962–1964 by 77%, and the Chilean terms of trade improved substantially

---

[79]This average value includes a quite high ratio for 1970 of 1.93 (variable 11 in table 2.2). The high value for this year occurred despite considerable liberalization of trade flows because of capital flight associated with the presidential election in September and increased restrictions after the new government took power later that year.

(variable 5.1.5.1)[80]. The mean exports in physical terms for copper did increase in this period, but only by about 10%, and the mean share of Chile in world copper production continued to decline from 13.5% in 1962–1964 to 12.3% in 1965–1969.

In respect to the sectoral origin of Chilean good exports, both mining and industry increased to the largest mean shares (and, of course, agriculture decreased to the smallest) among the post-1940 periods (variables 5.2.3.1–3). Within mining exports, moreover, the mean share of copper increased 76% in 1962–1964 to 85% in this period.

The effects of the changes in the international economic policy regime on exports were substantial. On the positive side, most important of all were the changes in price, tax, surtax, and government participation policies in large-scale copper mining. These enabled Chile to participate quite substantially in the returns from the copper market boom (in sharp contrast to the Second World War and early Korean conflict years). They resulted in mean annual returned earnings in current dollars to Chile from large-scale copper mining for 1965–1969 more than 80% above that of 1962–1964. This increased inflow, as is suggested above, probably was the single most important factor in permitting continuing liberalization over the six years of this period[81]. Other positive effects included the positive responses to the declining degree of overvaluation in the first three years of the period, to the special regime for exports and to the reduced uncertainty due to the sliding-peg exchange rate policy (see subsection 5.2.2 for evidence of significant responses to such changes[82]. Moreover the very fact of some resolution of the

[80]The mean ratio of real exports to real *GDP* in constant escudos actually decreased in this period, because once a correction is made for changing relative export prices, exports did not increase as rapidly as other products (variable 5.2.7.7). For a comparison of 1963–1966 with 1950–1953 Balassa (1971, pp. 41–42) reports related results for Chilean major exports (the sum of copper, iron, and nitrates) and for minor exports. The substantial increases in the markets and in the prices (for the former) were offset in large by a deterioration in Chile's competitive position (as measured by a decline in market shares).

[81]The Chilean export capacity to import (variable 5.2.7.2) increased to the highest level in more than 40 years at the start of this period.

[82]Ffrench-Davis and Carrasco (1969) claim that the success of the sliding-peg exchange rate policy was reflected in the surplus of $325 000 000 in the balance of payments for 1965–1968 ($186 000 000 of which would have occurred in their view primarily due to this policy had the price of copper been a 'normal' 40 ¢ per pound) and in the decline in the average annual increment to the national external debt from

controversy over control of large-scale copper mining probably resulted in more short-run output than would have a continuation of the uncertainty and dissatisfaction of previous periods (although this resolution did not occur so quickly in this period).

The major negative impact once again was due to the maintenance of a substantially overvalued exchange rate in the light of evidence of a substantial export response to the exchange rate level, and despite official recognition of this impact and initially successful attempts to reduce the discrepancy between the actual and the equilibrium exchange rates. The developments in the non-traditional exports are suggestive in this context. For example, the average value of industrial exports in constant dollars for 1965–1966 (during which time the degree of overvaluation was decreasing according to the Bacha and Taylor (1973) estimates) *exceeded* by 28% the average value for 1967–1970, despite the favorable changes in the special regime for exports which came into effect at the start of the latter subperiod. For most products which benefited from the changed special regime for exports, the percentage export drawbacks were never sufficient to offset the degree of overvaluation. Even for those few products with drawback rates near or at the maximum of 30%, probably only in 1968 was the overvaluation offset by this policy.

Due to the increasing liberalization of the regime the mean annual rate of growth of the constant dollar value of imports increased to 6%, the mean share of real imports relative to real *GDP* increased to 13% (the highest mean since the 1930s), and the mean value of merchandise imports in constant dollars increased 20% above that for 1962–1964 (variables 5.2.4.1, 5.2.6.1.1.2, and 5.2.7.6). The mean effective exchange rates for consumption and investment relative to

about $200000000 in 1959–1964 to about $65000000 in 1965–1968. A number of qualifications, however, should be made. These two indices are not independent. It is hard to judge the effects of this one policy in isolation (although that such improvements occurred despite the, on net, probably general liberalizing trend in other features of the international regime at the same time would seem to provide further support for Ffrench-Davis and Carrasco's positive evaluation). The use of a 'normal' price of copper of 40¢ may substantially underestimate the extent to which the copper boom accounted for the improvements, since the LME copper price for 1965–1968 averaged 59.0 ¢ per pound as compared to an average of only 30.7¢ per pound for the 1957–1964 period (with only the price for 1964 above 31.1¢ per pound). These authors do not consider the apparent subsequent increase in the degree of overvaluation. Thus, the degree of actual improvements due to this policy probably is overstated by Ffrench-Davis and Carrasco, despite the appealing arguments which they present on its behalf.

the national accounts exchange rate both declined to post-1940 lows (variables 5.2.4.1–2). Although the somewhat greater relative decline for consumption goods may have reflected relatively improved terms for consumption imports, the average division of import value among consumption, investment and intermediate imports remained about the same (variables 5.2.1.1–3). Nevertheless, within the period the consumption and capital shares increased monotonically.

The impact of the changes in the international economic policy regime were several: (a) the inducement of greater imports through the maintenance of an overvalued exchange rate and the reduction in certain import-related costs (such as the prior deposits and, for capital imports, tariffs); (b) the allowance of greater imports through the reduction of quantitative restrictions; and (c) the inducement of the within-period shift towards capital imports and, to a lesser extent, towards consumer goods imports by specific policy alternations which particularly favored the former and by reductions in the degree of quantitative restrictions which also relatively favored the former (see subsection 5.2.1).

In 1965 and early 1966, as is noted above, a relatively restrictive import policy was followed because of foreign exchange shortages and pending foreign debt payment renegotiations. All import applications in a month for a given category were rejected automatically if applications in that category exceeded by more than 5% the average import levvel of the past 12 months in the same category. As a result, the constant dollar value of merchandise imports for 1965 was 14% below the next lowest value during this period, and also was below the value for 1964. Behrman (1975b, ch. 6) discusses a number of distortions induced by this rationing procedure. Some of these negative effects were perceived by the relevant authorities. Once the immediate crisis had passed with the renegotiation of foreign debt payments, this system was abandoned. The constant dollar value of merchandise imports increased over 20% in 1966.

The relatively rapid acceleration in export value in comparison with import value resulted in a mean annual surplus of almost 100000000 1958 dollars on the merchandise account (variable 5.2.6.1.1). But a substantial part of the mean 172400000 1958 dollar annual increase on the merchandise account was offset by a mean 77% increase in net outflows for investment income, so the mean deficit on the goods and services account decreased (in absolute value) a little over 100000000 1958 dollars to − 77100000 1958 dollars (variables 5.2.6.1 and 5.2.6.1.2.3). This mean deficit was the smallest in absolute value since the 1952–1955 subperiod. A little less than one-fifth of it was offset by mean net transfers, which increased by 50% (due to a more than doubling of those to the government) although they remained substantially below the 1956–1961 averages (variables 5.2.6.2 and 5.2.6.2.2). The remaining four-fifths were offset by substantially smaller net movements on the capital and non-monetary gold account than had been required in the previous two periods.

The mean level of private non-monetary sector capital inflows in constant dollars increased by 35% and was almost 90% of the mean deficit on the goods and services account (variable 5.2.6.3.1). Mean net foreign investment in large-scale mining companies remained negative for the third consecutive period, but at a much smaller absolute level than in the previous period (variable 5.2.6.3.1.1.1). In fact the Chileanization program resulted in a reversal of this flow from a mean outflow of $-36\,100\,000$ 1958 dollars in 1965–1966 to a mean inflow of $19\,600\,000$ 1958 dollars in 1967–1969. Moreover the Chileanization program also resulted in a mean increase of $40\,800\,000$ 1958 dollars in the other private long-term capital inflows between these two subperiods and probably in additional increases in net capital inflows to the Chilean government (variables 5.2.6.3.1.2 and 5.2.6.3.1.4). From the point of view of capital inflows, therefore, the change in policy towards large-scale copper mining would seem to have been a success. Behrman (1975b, subsection 7.1.2.3) provides a more extensive evaluation of this policy towards large-scale mining.

Mean net foreign direct investment, excluding large-scale mining, decreased from $16\,300\,000$ constant 1958 dollars in 1962–1964 to $3\,600\,000$ for 1965–1969 (variable 5.2.6.3.1.1 minus variable 5.2.6.3.1.1.1). Mean net other private long-term capital inflows (still excluding large-scale mining) decreased from an average of $48\,500\,000$ 1958 dollars in 1962–1964 to $26\,700\,000$ for 1965–1969 (variable 5.2.6.3.1.2). Thus, changes in the international economic policy regime apparently did not induce large net inflows of private long-term capital except into large-scale mining. Mean net inflows of private short-term capital, in contrast, almost tripled (variable 5.2.6.3.1.3)[83]. In part, this increase may reflect the success of some

[83]However the mean absolute magnitude of the error and omission item was over three-fourths of that of mean short-term capital movements and the sign was opposite. If, as is sometimes hypothesized, this error and omission item represented largely unrecorded short-term capital movements, then the mean total net short-term capital flow may have even decreased from the level of 1962–1964.

changes in the regime such as the reduction in *ad valorem* duties on capital imports in proportion to the length of foreign credit terms obtained by the importer. On the other hand, this increase may mean that the attempt to limit speculative and potentially destabilizing short-term capital movements by tax policy on foreign exchange transactions in the brokers' market was not very effective.

Mean net capital and monetary gold credit entries for the banking system and the central government declined from 116 000 000 1958 dollars in 1962–1964 to 7 900 000 1958 dollars in 1965–1969 (variables 5.2.6.3.1.4 and 5.2.6.3.2). The major net credit item in this part of the accounts was the entry for the net loans received by the central government, but even the mean value of this term declined by 7% in constant dollar terms due to increasing repayments of past loans over the phase. This decline may be surprising given changes in the regime which would seem to have made Chile more attractive to the traditional donors[84], given the above-mentioned inflows associated with changes in the large-scale mining policy, and given the initiation of credit agreements with the USSR in 1967. However, such considerations relate primarily to the supply of potential official foreign inflows. In fact, there was a strong desire to reduce dependence on foreign capital and to reduce the external debt. The decline in net inflows to the government reflected the partial attainment of such aims, made possible by the returns from the copper boom. The changes in the capital and monetary gold flows for the monetary sector from a mean of 24 900 000 1958 dollars in 1962–1964 to a mean of −74 200 000 1958 dollars in 1965–1969 presumably reflect the same considerations (variable 5.2.6.3.2). Also because of the returns from the copper boom, net international reserves held by the banking system increased to the highest level in at least two decades at $219 800 000 at the end of 1969 and the accumulation of Chilean debt in foreign currency decelerated at least in the early years of the Frei administration (variables 5.2.7.3–4). Nevertheless, by the end of 1969 the foreign debt was estimated to be over $2 800 000 000 (and over $3 000 000 000 a year later). Although in a relative sense this debt fell slightly to 248% of the export value and to 27.2% of *GDP* (at the national accounts

---

[84]Including not only economic policy changes, but also political changes in that Frei and the Christian Democrats were widely touted as viable alternatives to Castroism or militarism in Latin America.

exchange rate), the average annual exponential increase between 1964 and 1969 was 7.3%. The composition of this debt shifted further towards the public sector with an increase of almost 82% to account for 79% of the total at the end of 1969. Finally, the obligations renegotiated in 1965 implied considerable obligations due in 1970 and thereafter.

2.3.4. Termination of the Frei program

Although the Frei government had some important initial accomplishments in regard to its internal objectives and some significant subsequent achievements in regard to the foreign sector, it was not sufficiently successful in one of its most basic aims – the maintenance of sufficient unity and backing in the party and in the population in general to enable it to continue with its programs under the successor to Frei[85]. In the presidential election of September 1970, the Christian Democratic candidate, Radomiro Tomic, finished a distant third. The contest was between groups further to the left and to the right. Salvador Allende, the Popular Unity candidate (a coalition of the Communist, Socialist, Radical, and several minor parties), narrowly defeated former president Alessandri (thus reversing the results of the 1958 election).

According to Américo Zorrilla (1970, p. 1477), the first Minister of Finance in the Allende government, the central long-run aim of the new government was 'to transform the ... economic structure, terminating the power of foreign and domestic monopolistic capital and of the *latifundia*, in order to initiate the construction of socialism'[86]. Related medium- and long-run goals included: (1) the redirection of benefits of the economy more to lower- and middle-income classes; (2) the development of an extensive multilevel planning system with wide participation; (3) the reduction of external dependence in all of its possible forms; and (4) the establishment of a new ownership structure for the means of production – state

[85]The Chilean constitution precluded the possibility of Frei running again for President in 1970.

[86]In addition to Zorrilla (1970), sources on which this summary of the objectives of the Allende government is based include Allende (1971), Cauas (1972, pp. 46–56), CORFO (1970–1973), Gunder-Frank (1972, pp. 16–18), Hobsbaum (1971, pp. 23–32), ODEPLAN (1970a, 1970b), Pisciotta (1971, pp. 236–237), Vuskovic (1971, pp. 385–399).

(basic natural resources, large monopolies, banks, foreign commerce, and other strategic activities for development), mixed (parts of the industrial, fishing, mining, and trade sectors), and private. The government proposed to move towards these goals gradually and constitutionally in 'the Chilean way', not by extralegal means.

To broaden support for the long-run attempt to transform society, the government recognized that some short-run successes were essential. The components of short-run policy, as outlined in the 1971 plan, were the following:

(1) The revitalization of the economy by reducing uncertainty through the use of guaranteed production contracts with the state and by increasing aggregate demand through increased exports, a substantial redistribution of income, and a large increase in government expenditures on public works, housing and human capital.

(2) The constraint of inflation by strict price controls, by freezing the *NER* and by increasing supplies from domestic production (due to increased capacity utilization) and from imports (financed through expanded exports and the available international reserves).

(3) The redistribution of income to the lower and middle classes by a minimum readjustment of wages and salaries of 100% of past price increases (and larger adjustments for lower wages and salaries) in combination with reduced inflation, by increased lower-income housing, by increased human-capital investment (especially in education and in health), by increased employment, by reductions in returns to national and foreign higher-income groups through the nationalization of key subsectors in the economy, by accelerated agrarian reform, and by the democratization of the distribution of credit.

(4) The redistribution of control over resources from the private to the public sector in hopes of providing the basis for planned 'harmonized and balanced growth' which favored the lower and middle classes by the expansion of the planning apparatus and by the extension of the state area in the productive sector.

(5) The initiation of structural reform which would lay the basis for high long-run growth and the transformation to socialism by the accelerated investment of public-sector enterprises[87], by the enlargement of the state area in the economy, and by the acceleration of agrarian reform.

[87]Such investment, however, would have a lower imported component than previously in order to reduce external dependence.

(6) The expansion of state activities in all aspects of international economic interchange by the reintroduction of a very restrictive regime in order to reduce foreign dependence of all types and to utilize the foreign sector in the pursuit of the other aims mentioned above.

In 1971 in a number of important general respects the performance of the economy was quite positive. Capacity utilization rose to a very high level. Unemployment dropped substantially[88]. The rate of change of prices fell to 26.4%. The rate of growth of per capita real product of 3.3% exceeded the means for all of the periods and subperiods in table 2.1.

In the same year the new government also succeeded in several ways in its aims of transforming ownership relations and of extending state control. With unanimous legislative support, Chile completely nationalized large-scale copper mining, which previously had been subject to considerable foreign control[89]. The state extended its direct control over a number of other formerly foreign- and domestic-owned enterprises, including most private banks. The government accelerated agrarian reform. Exchange control increased and the public-sector share in approved import registration rose from 34% to 44% in 1971 (and to 65% in the first eight months of 1972).

Some of these short-term gains, however, were purchased at not insubstantial long-term costs in four respects.

(1) The high growth in 1971 reflected more higher capacity utilization due to the expansion of current consumption than it did an increase in productive capacity. In 1971 real capital investment increased only 1% and it declined to 82.3 and 82.5% of the 1971 level in 1972 and 1973, respectively[90]. Per capita *GDP* actually fell -2.6 and -1.7%, respectively, in 1972 and 1973.

(2) The decline in the rate of change of prices in 1971 occurred despite a 121% increase in the money supply because of greater supplies of goods from domestic production and imports, more

---

[88]June 1972 unemployment had dropped further to a level of 3.7%.

[89]Before the Chileanization and nationalization policies of the previous period, large-scale copper mining had been entirely foreign-owned. The Frei policies, however, had given substantial ownership to Chile.

[90]de Castro (1972, p. 45) suggests that actual investment under the Allende government is overestimated in the national accounts because much of the construction investment was done by the government and measured at factor costs and thus overvalued in real terms due to the very high rate of increase of wages.

extensive price controls, the maintenance of a fixed *NER*, and an upward shift in the demand for real monetary balances resulting from income redistribution and changed expectations. Given the augmentation of the money supply and of labor payments, these measures could not suppress inflation for long. In late 1971 price increases began to accelerate. For 1972 and 1973, respectively, the *GDP* deflator rose 86.8 and 521.1%. Even by Chilean standards, such rates are extraordinary! Black markets flourished for many commodities.

(3) Real exports fell 2% in 1971, 15% in 1972, and 4.6% in 1973. These drops reflected policy changes which discouraged non-traditional exports, the slump in the world copper market[91] and the failure of Chilean production to reach planned levels (e.g. in 1971 production was less than 80% of that planned for the year). In part because of the United States' reaction to the terms of the copper nationalization, net unrequited transfers in constant dollars also fell and net non-monetary movements in constant dollars plummeted. At the same time, real imports remained stable in 1971, fell 4.5% in 1972, but increased 20.1% in 1973. The deficit on the current account in real terms about doubled in 1971 and increased by about another half in 1972 and 1973. As a result, international reserves held by the banking system fell by over $300 000 000 in 1971 and continued to fall thereafter. Net monetary capital and gold outflows in constant dollars reached a post-Second World War high, and a severe foreign exchange shortage existed by the end of 1971. Therefore, the escudo was devalued by 30% in December 1971 and by 58% in August 1972, exchange control became much more restrictive, and the large foreign debt obligations were renegotiated in 1972[92]. Nevertheless, the country continued to be on the verge of foreign exchange crises.

[91]To provide some perspective, however, the 1971 and 1972 copper prices still were higher than that received for any year before 1965 and, according to Cauas (1972, p. 42), were higher than the price which had been used in 1970 in the Central Bank in its projections for 1971.

[92]The Allende government inherited $3 000 000 000 of foreign debts with amortization and interest payments of $433 000 000 due in 1971, $409 000 000 due in 1972, $410 000 000 due in 1973 and $388 000 000 due in 1974. In April 1972 the Paris Club (the United States and ten other major creditors) recommended the adoption of a new payments program over an eight-year period, including a two-year grace period on 70% of the Chilean debts which were due between 1 November 1971 and 31 December 1972. The creditors promised to study 'with good will' the refinancing of those debt payments due in 1973, but no agreement on further rescheduling had been reached by the end of the Allende government.

(4) The attempt to transform the power and ownership relations of society caused considerable politicalization and polarization in Chilean society. Foreign interests helped to exacerbate political instability. In 1972 martial law had to be invoked several times, and the economy ground to a halt in October because of a 25-day work stoppage by the Truck Owners' Association (supported by many business and professional groups) which was terminated after the government added three military members to the cabinet. Internal instabilities increased in 1973. Copper mines went on strike in May. An attempted military coup was squashed on 29 June 1973. Truckers, businessmen, and professionals again struck. On 11 September Allende was killed in a military coup.

A military junta assumed power, with General Pinochet the strongest individual in the ruling group. The new government has as its basic aim the reversal of the changes of the previous governments and the eradication of the power base of the left. Civil rights and the constitution were suspended. Repression was widespread. By many indices the economic situation deteriorated significantly. Despite substantial efforts, inflation continued at rates measured in 100s of percentage points per year and unemployment soared, lower-class real income fell drastically. Through 1975 such problems continued to be major.

This book does not attempt to investigate the events of the 1970s in Chile for two reasons: (1) The data are much less satisfactory after 1970. (2) Because of the two attempts to radically change the structure of the economy and the substantial polarization of society, it does not seem reasonable to assume that the economic structure remained sufficiently unchanged so that the 1970s can be combined with the preceding years in time series econometric analysis. Nevertheless, the analysis below should give some general insights into the nature of the functioning of the Chilean economy in the 1970s, as well as that of other developing economies.

PART II

PARTIAL-EQUILIBRIUM
RELATIONS

CHAPTER 3

Government policy variables

Part II of this book considers partial-equilibrium estimates of structural relations on the sectoral level for the postwar Chilean economy. This chapter examines government variables. One section each is devoted to fiscal, monetary, foreign sector, and income policies. The next three chapters explore aspects of supply (capacity production functions, physical capital investment, the distribution of labor, and capacity utilization), demand (consumption, savings, inventory investment, imports, and exports), and prices (final product, labor, intermediate inputs, capital costs, aggregate demand deflators and others).

These investigations are of considerable interest in themselves because of what they reveal about the structure of the Chilean economy and what light they shed on the questions raised in section 1.1. The estimates also are integrated into the complete system model of Part III below. For more perspective about how the various components fit together, see Part III – especially section 7.1.

A major characteristic of government policies which comes out of the considerations of this chapter is that they are definitely limited in their scope for discretionary action. Many government expenditures are previously committed or are related to politically sensitive government employment. Government revenues depend not only on legal tax rates, but also on activity levels and the degree of compliance, which in turn reflects expectations concerning inflation and foreign exchange costs. Because of foreign exchange movements and compulsory credit for the fiscal sector, the size of the monetary base is largely outside the control of the Central Bank. Even for a given monetary base the behavior of commercial banks and of the non-banking public limits the extent to which the Central

Bank can alter the money supply through its reserve, interest, discount and other policies. When there is an export boom or sufficient foreign exchange reserves, some discretion exists in the choice of exchange rates and other foreign sector policies. This latitude is limited, however, especially since a preference has predominated for a disequilibrium, overvalued exchange rate. Attempts to maintain overvalued rates eventually end in foreign exchange crises and unavoidable pressures for policy changes.

A second characteristic is that, even though the degree of exogeneity is limited, there are a fairly large number of policy tools. Perhaps of greater significance, the impact of these policy instruments, as the next three chapters discuss, is quite heterogeneous across sectors.

Before preceding to the analysis underlying these points, some general comments about the data base and estimation procedures utilized throughout Part II are useful.

Most of the relationships are estimated on the basis of annual data for the 1945–1965 period. Annual data are utilized for the following three reasons: (1) Much of the data, especially the national accounts data, are available only on an annual basis. (2) Responses of interest are those of more than very transitory impact such as might dominate with shorter observation periods. (3) Strong seasonal patterns exist due to the timing of agricultural production and to the timing of annual wage (and related price) readjustments. The 1945–1965 period is used because a consistent set of national accounts does not exist before 1940 nor after 1965[1]; the existence both of lagged responses and of a possibly altered structure for the Second World War years suggests the necessity and/or wisdom of dropping the 1940–1944 observations; and the switch to the Brussels nomenclature associated with the adoption of the new tariff law at the start of 1967 was also associated with a widespread reclassification of all international trade data with the result that foreign sector series consistent with earlier definitions are not available in many cases after 1966.

For critiques of the basic Chilean data see Ballesteros and Davis (1963), Eckaus (1967a and 1967b), Ffrench-Davis (1971), Mamalakis

[1]Estimates based on CORFO definitions are available for 1940–1965, and estimates based on ODEPLAN definitions are available starting in 1960. For a comparison of the two sets of estimates, see appendix A.

(1967a, 1967b and 1971b), Muñoz (1968), Sierra (1969), and Torres (1969). Much of the criticism is focused on the nature of the price indices which have such a crucial role because of the high rate of inflation (variable 2.1 in table 2.1). Therefore, Ffrench-Davis presents alternative price indices with more realistic weights for the underlying components and a correction for the probable underestimate in the official series for the rate of change of housing prices. I have calculated correlation coefficients between the revised Ffrench-Davis series and the original estimates for consumer, wholesale, and general price indices (and some components thereof) over the 1952–1969 period. That in no case a correlation less than 0.97 is obtained is somewhat reassuring for users of the official data – at least in respect to one of the most commonly claimed biases in the data. For further consideration of the data, including a listing of sources, see appendix A.

The estimation technique primarily used for the estimated relationships is ordinary least squares (although in some cases non-linear maximum likelihood procedures are utilized for autocorrelated error structures or non-linear functions). The expected returns of adopting more sophisticated methods are less than the expected costs of doing so given the nature of the data, some questions about the robustness of alternative estimators, and the opportunity costs of sophistication in estimation procedure in terms of exploring various model structures. Lags due to adjustments and to the formation of expectations are represented by simple lagged values or by the Hall and Sutch (1969) flexible distributed lag without a 'tail'. With the tail constrained to zero, the Hall–Sutch technique is formally identical to the Almon technique, except that only the right-hand tail is constrained to zero and that the various terms included in the procedure represent coefficients of the linear, quadratic, cubic, and/or quartic terms in the lag polynomial.

3.1. Fiscal policy

Table 3.1 presents some of the basic characteristics over the 1945–1965 sample period of the major components of government expenditures and revenues: the mean percentage of each component relative to *GDP*, the average percentage composition of taxes, the mean percentage growth rate in real terms, and a measure of

Table 3.1

Important characteristics of major components of Chilean government expenditures and revenues, 1945–1965[a].

Item	Mean percentage of		Mean percentage growth rate in real terms	Standard deviation from secular trend as percentage of mean in nominal terms
	GDP	Total taxes		
	(1)	(2)	(3)	(4)
Expenditures				
Current consumption	9.6		5.5	26.1
Direct and indirect investment	4.6		2.7	28.5
Subsidies	1.5		−10.2	27.6
Net transfers	5.2		14.0	43.4
Revenues				
Taxes	17.9	100	8.6	20.1
direct taxes	9.7	53.8	8.9	22.3
business	2.9	16.4	11.1	26.0
large-scale mining	1.8	10.3	11.9	29.5
other	1.1	6.1	11.5	30.3
personal	1.2	6.8	9.1	88.4
social security – employers	3.8	21.0	12.1	26.5
social security – workers	1.7	9.5	7.0	20.8
indirect taxes	8.3	46.4	8.5	19.5
imports	2.3	12.9	8.1	25.2
production	1.5	8.5	−0.4	26.9
sales	1.6	8.8	51.8	96.5
legal acts	0.5	2.9	13.3	54.5
services	1.1	5.9	4.5	42.8
other	1.3	7.4	19.5	17.6
Income from property and enterprises	0.8		31.6	48.1
Savings on current account	2.8		47.2	82.5
Savings on fiscal account	−3.6		−7.2	26.4

[a]Appendix A gives the underlying data sources.

fluctuations – the standard deviation around the secular trend relative to the mean.

3.1.1. Government expenditures

Total government expenditures averaged over a fifth of *GDP*. The major components have been current consumption (9.6% of *GDP* over the sample), net transfers (5.2%), direct and indirect investment (4.6%), and subsidies (1.5%). A fairly considerable shift in composition occurred from subsidies to net transfers and, to a lesser extent, from direct and indirect investment to current consumption. Total real expenditures and the two largest components thereof grew faster in real terms than the 4.2% average annual growth rate for real *GDP* (column 3 in table 3.1). Net transfers, by far the fastest-growing component, also fluctuated much more than the others (column 4 in table 3.1). Current consumption varied slightly less than direct and indirect investment and subsidies, but not substantially so. For the foreign sector, investment-related expenditures have been subjected to *much* larger variations than consumption expenditures because the former have been considered relatively postponable at times of crises by the government (section 5.2 and Behrman, 1975a and 1975b). For government expenditures, the same sharp distinction between variations in consumption and in investment does not seem to have existed.

3.1.1.1. Government current consumption expenditure
This is often assumed to be directly policy determined in macroeconometric models. In the Chilean experience – and in that of many other countries – the government does not have much short-run discretionary power over these expenditures because of existing commitments (such as to government employees) which can be changed quickly often only at a large political cost. Therefore in the complete system model of Part III below government current consumption behavior generally is endogenous[2]. The estimated relationship is discussed together with the other included consumption–savings relationships below in subsection 5.1.1. The major determinant of real government consumption and savings is

[2]For some simulations, however, this variable is considered to be a policy instrument and exogenized.

real government revenues. There also is some evidence of a significant substitution between government and foreign savings.

3.1.1.2. Net transfers from the government

These also are endogenous in the complete system model of Part III. They directly affect the level of disposable income and therefore private consumption and savings decisions. To limit multicollinearity and heteroskedasticity, the dependent variable in the underlying regression is the average effective net transfer rate (i.e. the ratio of net transfers to income)[3]:

$$NTR/Y = (0.00138 + 0.00227D1)\,TIME - 0.0394D2$$
$$\quad\quad (2.1) \quad\quad (5.0) \quad\quad\quad\quad (4.3)$$
$$\quad\quad [0.1] \quad\quad [0.3] \quad\quad\quad\quad [-0.3]$$

$$\quad\quad - 0.00310(PLD\ NER^{BM} - PLD\ NER) + 0.0696,$$
$$\quad\quad\quad (2.2) \quad\quad\quad\quad\quad\quad\quad\quad\quad\quad (6.1)$$
$$\quad\quad\quad [-0.1]$$

$$\tag{3.1}$$

$$\bar{R}^2 = 0.92, \quad SE = 0.0070, \quad DW = 2.5, \quad 1948\text{--}1965,$$

where NTR/Y is the ratio of net transfers from the government to national income. $D1$ is a dummy variable with a value of one for 1948–1958 and of zero thereafter; $D2$ is a dummy variable with a value of one for 1948–1959 and of zero thereafter; $TIME$ is a time trend with a value of one in 1945; and $PLD\ NER^{BM} - PLD\ NER$ is the difference in price-level-deflated nominal exchange rates between the black market and the legal market(s). In relationship (3.1) the average effective net transfer rate is posited to depend on two considerations.

(1) Numerous legislative changes have altered the coverage in the sample period. To explicitly summarize these changes in one legal transfer rate is beyond the scope of this study because of substantial data problems. Instead, the time trend is a proxy for the secular upward change in these rates. Additive and multiplicative dummy

---

[3]Throughout this study, regressions are presented with the absolute values of t-statistics in parentheses beneath the point estimates and the elasticities at the point of sample means in brackets below the t-statistics. $\bar{R}^2$ is the coefficient of determination. SE is the standard error of estimate. DW is the Durbin–Watson statistic. ρ is the first order auto-correlation coefficient as estimated by the Cochrane–Orcutt scanning method.

variables represent other changes in the legal rates. Relationship (3.1) indicates that there was a significantly non-zero secular trend in the effective average net transfer rate of about 0.37% per year in 1948 through 1958 and of about 0.14% per year thereafter. The base effective average net transfer rate (i.e. the constant adjusted for additive dummy variables), however, was 3% for 1948 through 1959 and 7% thereafter. Although secular the growth rate was significantly higher before 1959 than after, therefore, the largest upward discontinuity was due to the legal changes which became effective near the end of that year.

(2) At times of budgetary crises both internal and external, the government reputedly has effectively reduced net transfer payments by increasing delays in processing and administering the relevant programs. Given the high inflationary rates (variable 2.1 in table 2.1), delays in nominal transfers can result in not insubstantial reductions in real transfers. The situation in the black market for foreign exchange is a useful indicator – although far from perfect – of these and other economic crises[4]. The coefficient of the real discrepancy between the black market and legal exchange rates in relationship (3.1) in fact is significantly non-zero and negative. The estimates, thus, provide some support for the hypothesized government behavior.

3.1.1.3. Direct and indirect government investment

This is much more under government discretionary control than are government current consumption and net transfers – at least in nominal terms. Revenues do not provide a tight constraint on these expenditures because the Central Bank is required to provide credit to the government if necessary (section 3.2). Within the complete system model, therefore, direct and indirect investment in nominal terms is an exogenous government policy instrument. The real value of this item, however, depends on the endogenously determined deflator for real physical capital investment (subsection 6.3.2). In a number of sectors there is evidence of a significantly non-zero response in real physical capital investment decisions to the real value of this variable (subsection 4.2.2).

---

[4]Subsection 6.3.3 further considers the black market exchange rate.

3.1.1.4. Government subsidies to business

These are less than a third of the magnitude of the three expenditure categories already discussed and declined relatively over the sample period (columns 1 and 3 in table 3.1). In the general-equilibrium model below this item is exogenously determined in real terms. The econometric explorations reported in sections 4.3 and 6.1 below reveal no evidence of a significant impact of these subsidies on sectoral capacity utilization or price determination.

3.1.2. Government revenues [5]

Total government revenues averaged slightly less than a fifth of *GDP*. Total government expenditures averaged somewhat more than a fifth of *GDP*. The mean deficit on fiscal account was 3.6% of *GDP*.

The major source of revenues has been taxes. Over the sample period they averaged over 95% of the total. Income from property and enterprises made up most of the remainder – 4%.

Both of these components (and, of course, total revenue) grew in real terms faster than the 4.2% rate for real *GDP* during the sample. The differential growth rates imply a slight shift from taxes to net income from property and enterprises in terms of relative contributions.

Income from property and enterprises was relatively volatile due to two factors. (1) This is a net concept. Therefore, small variations in either revenues or costs may imply large relative variations in the difference. (2) During the sample the government altered substantially its ownership of some major enterprises (e.g. the sale of much of its interest in CAP, the steel complex).

Total tax revenues, in contrast, were much less volatile than other revenue sources and than the major expenditure components. This observation raises some doubt about the structuralist claim that variations in foreign trade have caused large fluctuations in government tax revenues and thus have increased instabilities in government expenditures.

On a more disaggregated level, direct taxes averaged 53.8% of total taxes and increased slightly more rapidly (and with slightly

---

[5]Table 3.1 provides the data which underlie the comments in the first part of this subsection.

greater fluctuations) than indirect taxes. On an even more disaggregated level, the ordering of the various tax sources over the sample is employers' social security taxes (a mean of 21% of total taxes), import taxes (12.9%), large-scale mining direct taxes (10.3%), workers' social security taxes (9.5%), sales taxes (8.8%), production taxes (8.5%), indirect taxes not otherwise classified (7.4%), personal direct taxes (6.8%), business direct taxes – excluding large-scale mining (6.1%), service taxes (5.9%) and legal acts taxes (2.9%).

The substantial importance of the social security system is quite noticeable. Almost a third of taxes were for social security during the sample. The employers' social security taxes, moreover, grew faster than any other component of direct taxes. Chs. 4 and 6 indicate that these taxes have significant effects on short- and long-run allocation decisions and on price and wage levels.

Other direct taxes on domestic activities (i.e. direct personal taxes and direct business taxes excluding those on large-scale mining) averaged 12.9% of total taxes during 1945–1965. Chs. 4 and 5 below indicate that these taxes have had significant effects on the private consumption–savings decisions and on short- and long-run allocation decisions (especially in sectors other than mining). These taxes grew slightly relative to overall taxes, but also were relatively volatile (especially the direct personal taxes). The limited dependence on such taxes as compared with more developed economies is a frequently encountered phenomenon in developing economies for several reasons: (1) accounting systems are less well developed; (2) indirect taxes (especially in the foreign sector) are (or at least thought to be) more easily administered and collected; (3) strong vested interests resist income taxes; and (4) withholding systems only recently have become more widespread.

Foreign sector related taxes (i.e. import taxes plus direct taxes on large-scale mining) accounted for almost a quarter of taxes during the sample period. Chs. 4, 5, and 6 below suggest that such taxes have had significant impact on short- and long-run allocation decisions in mining, on imports, and on domestic price levels. Direct taxes on large-scale mining increased relatively rapidly (second only to employers' social security taxes among direct taxes). Import taxes increased somewhat less quickly than overall taxes because of a tendency towards reducing foreign sector barriers in the last decade of the sample period (sections 1.4, 4.1.1, 5.1, 13.1, and 13.2 in Behrman, 1975b). Foreign sector-related taxes thus have been important, but not nearly so much so as earlier in Chilean history (or as in many other developing economies). In 1908–1927, for example, taxes related to foreign trade were 83% of total taxes (Behrman, 1975b, table A1)[6,7]! In part this reduced dependence reflected a conscious attempt to turn inward after the catastrophic impact of the Great Depression. It also was partially due to the reduced exports caused by the maintenance of an overvalued exchange rate in a disequilibrium system (section 5.2 below; Behrman, 1975b, ch. 7).

Finally, note that not only has the dependence on foreign-sector-related taxes been less than sometimes seems to be suggested, but these tax sources have not been particularly volatile. Relative fluctuations were less during the sample period for direct taxes on large-scale mining than for other direct business taxes and direct personal taxes. Likewise, relative fluctuations were less for import taxes than for four of the five other categories of indirect taxes.

The most important domestic indirect taxes on the average during the sample period were those on production and sales. In the 1950s there was a conscious shift from the former to the latter, which explains their relative growth rates (and much of the measured volatility of the sales tax). Among the remaining domestic indirect taxes those of legal acts and the miscellaneous category increased relatively rapidly during the sample in comparison to those on services. But both the indirect taxes on legal acts and on services fluctuated considerably from the secular trend in part because of many legal changes.

3.1.2.1. Tax functions
In most macroeconomic models total tax collections or effective tax rates are assumed to be exogenously determined by government policy. For the Chilean experience and for many other developing economies the assumptions underlying such procedures are too strong. The government simply does not have that much control over taxes. It can establish legal rates, but effective rates often are

---

[6]The major source of such taxes for the half century after the War of the Pacific in 1879–1882 was the export tax on nitrates. After the international market for natural nitrates evaporated in the Great Depression, however, no significant export taxes were retained.

[7]The analysis in Behrman (1975b, section 1.2) suggests that even in this earlier era of tremendous dependence on export taxes in particular and the foreign sector in general, evidence of the importation of instabilities is much less compelling than many structuralists and others have argued.

much different.

For the complete system econometric model of Part III below, therefore, taxes are endogenous. Table 3.2 presents the regression estimates utilized for each of the 11 tax categories mentioned above. In each case the dependent variable is the average effective tax rate in order to limit problems with multi-collinearity and heteroskedasticity. Examination of this table suggests that the underlying general specification is consistent to a varying degree with the variations in the effective tax rates. In 8 of the 11 cases the coefficient of determination implies that the specification is consistent with at least threequarters of the variance in the dependent variable. The three exceptions are direct personal income taxes, import taxes, and other indirect taxes. With the exception again of direct personal income taxes for which an autocorrelation coefficient estimate is included because of the lags in payment, problems of autocorrelation do not seem to be serious.

The major variables included in these relationships are related to those discussed above in regard to net government transfers.

(1) Numerous changes in legal tax rates were enacted during the sample period. For the social security taxes, time series of legal rates are readily available. For import taxes the Ffrench-Davis (1971) index of foreign sector restrictionism may serve as an adequate proxy. For the other taxes time trends and additive and multiplicative dummy variables are used, because to construct indices based on the legal changes presents data problems the resolution of which is beyond the scope of this study. Of course, these indices, especially the time trends, may represent other phenomena – such as changes in voluntary compliance or in effectiveness of the tax collection system. Therefore, these variables are included in the social security and import tax functions in addition to the other functions mentioned above.

For the social security effective tax rates, the legal tax rates do not have significantly non-zero coefficients even at the 15% level. This result highlights the above-mentioned inadequacy of using the legal tax rates as an exogenous policy instrument which, when applied to the appropriate base, gives tax collections. In these two cases sufficient changes occurred in the coverage of the tax[8] and the

[8]In principle, one could define the base so that it reflected the change in legal coverage. In fact, this would entail costs of data collection beyond the scope of this study.

Table 3.2
Average effective tax rate functions for major Chilean taxes, 1945–1965[a].

Dependent variable: tax relative to base	Time	Legal change dummy variable	Time* legal change dummy variable	Rate of inflation	Exchange rate/ GDP deflator	Constant	$\bar{R}^2$ / SE / DW
Employer social security contribution/wage income	0.00315 (12.6) [0.6]		0.000624[b] (2.7) [0.1]		0.00946 (3.2) [0.5]	-0.0105 (1.0)[m]	0.91 / 0.0054 / 1.9
Employee social security contribution/wage income	0.000239 (1.7)[f] [0.1]		-0.00111[d] (3.8) [-0.1]		-0.000431[e] (1.2)[c] [-0.0]	0.0267 (10.4)	0.77 / 0.0020 / 2.3
Direct personal income tax/(income–employer SS contributions)[g]			0.0001[d] (1.4)[f] [0.0]	-0.01 (1.6)[f] [-0.2]		0.0158 (8.6)	0.16 / 0.0028 / 1.7
Business tax except for large-scale mining/profit	0.00282 (7.7) [0.7]			-0.0284 (2.3) [-0.2]	-0.00820 (1.5)[f] [-0.5]	0.0549 (2.7)	0.77 / 0.00802 / 2.6
Direct tax on large-scale mining/(GDP from mining–legal cost of product with latter estimated at exchange rate for large-scale mining)[b][h]	0.238[i] (1.5) [0.3]	-0.280[j] (3.4) [-0.2]	0.0211[k] (1.9) [0.2]			0.395 (15.1)	0.81 / 0.0741 / 2.3
Sales tax/GDP	0.00198 (63.8) [1.2]		-0.00164[l] (17.7) [-0.2]				0.99 / 0.0017 / 1.6
Import tax/imports	-0.00327 (3.0) [-0.2]			-0.126 (3.5) [-0.2]	-0.0386 (2.4) [-0.6]	0.418 (6.9)	0.56 / 0.0235 / 1.7

Production tax/GDP	−0.00441 (3.8) [−0.4]	0.00353^m (2.7) [0.1]	0.00127^l (9.0) [0.3]		0.143 (7.6)	0.97 0.0014 2.0
Legal tax/GDP		−0.00479^h (4.9) [−0.4]	0.000282^n (2.5) [0.2]	−0.000318^e (1.8) [−0.1]	0.00750 (20.2)	0.80 0.0008 1.9
Tax on services/GDP	−0.000892 (7.1) [−1.2]	−0.0112^h (14.6) [−0.6]	0.000610^n (3.4) [0.0]		0.0246 (11.4)	0.80 0.0010 2.1
Other taxes/GDP	0.000555 (3.8) [0.1]				0.00625 (3.2)	0.44 0.0032 1.8

[a] Beneath the point estimates in parentheses are the absolute values of the t-statistics, each of which is significantly non-zero at 5% level unless otherwise noted. Beneath the t-values in brackets are the elasticities at the point of sample means. Appendix A gives the data sources.
[b] Dummy variable has value of 1.0 in 1945–1961, 0.0 otherwise.
[c] Significantly non-zero at the 15% level.
[d] Dummy variable has value of 1.0 in 1955, 1956, 1959, 1960, 1965.
[e] Difference between *PLD NER* for black market and for legal exchange rate(s).
[f] Significantly non-zero at the 10% level.
[g] First-order autocorrelation coefficients of 0.409 estimated by Cochrane–Orcutt scanning procedure.
[h] 1948–1965.
[i] Not time trend but dummy variable has value of 1.0 in 1945–1957, 0.0 otherwise.
[j] Dummy variable has value of 1.0 for 1945–1955, 0.0 otherwise.
[k] Dummy variable has value of 1.0 for 1945–1957, 0.0 otherwise.
[l] Dummy variable has value of 1.0 for 1945–1954, 0.0 otherwise.
[m] Dummy variable has value of 1.0 for 1945–1953, 0.0 otherwise.
[n] Dummy variable has value of 1.0 for 1945–1955, 0.0 otherwise.

degree of compliance that the variance in the effective tax rate is
more consistent with the secular trend and the dummy variables
than with the variance in the legal tax rates.

For import taxes the index of foreign sector quantitative restrictions also does not have a coefficient estimate which is significantly
non-zero at the 15% level. This result may reflect the cancelling out
of two opposing tendencies. (1) When quantitative restrictions were
increased, tariffs also were sometimes raised to help create even
greater barriers between the foreign market and the domestic
economy[9]. (2) Quantitative restrictions generally tended to be applied more strongly to luxuries (non-essentials) and durables with
high tariff rates. Increases in these restrictions thus caused a
compositional change which lowered the aggregate effective tariff
rate.

An alternative explanation for the lack of a significant coefficient
for quantitative restrictions in the import tax function also comes to
mind. Quantitative restrictions tend to be highest when the Chilean
currency was most over-valued and the *PLD NER* was lowest.
Therefore, the first alternative mentioned in the previous paragraph
actually dominated, but multicollinearity between the quantitative
restrictions index and the *PLD NER* (discussed below) precludes
identification of the separate contribution of the quantitative restrictions index.

The secular trend and/or the dummy variables, in contrast to the
social security legal tax rates and the foreign sector quantitative
restrictions index, have significantly non-zero coefficients for almost
every tax category. Seven of the categories have significantly
positive secular trends for a substantial part of the sample: direct
taxes on large-scale mining, employers' social security contribution,
direct taxes on business other than large-scale mining, sales taxes,
other indirect taxes, employees' social security contribution, and
legal acts taxes. One category does not have significantly non-zero
coefficients for the secular trends: direct personal income taxes.
Three categories have significantly negative trends: production
taxes, service taxes, and import taxes. Legal alterations and changes
in effect collection rates thus resulted in shifts towards higher
effective rates for direct taxes generally (although not towards direct

---

[9]Of course, if tariffs and other price-related measures had been increased sufficiently, there would have been no need to intensify quantitative restrictions.

personal income taxes) and for sales and miscellaneous indirect taxes.

The relatively rapid increase in effective tax rates for large-scale mining[10], however, terminated once the *Nuevo Trato* (New Deal) for large-scale mining of 1955 became effective. At that point there was a significant downward shift of 28% in this average effective rate, with no significantly non-zero secular trend thereafter[11].

For import taxes the negative secular trend originates in the secular tendency towards liberalization over the sample period (Behrman, 1975a and 1975b). For production taxes the negative trend after 1954 and the significant additive dummy variable before then (as well as the significant increase in the secular trend for sales taxes after 1954) are due to the shift from production to sales taxes at that time. For taxes on both legal acts and services, finally, changes in 1957 resulted in a twisting of the effective tax schedule so that the base thereafter was higher, but the secular trend lower.

(2) During the sample most tax schedules were denominated in nominal terms. Given the high rate of inflation (variable 2.1 in table 2.1), therefore, a strong incentive existed to delay tax payments in order to reduce their real value. The estimates in table 3.2 suggest that such reductions were significant in at least three cases: direct personal taxes, direct taxes on business other than large-scale mining, and import taxes. In each case a 10% increase in inflation resulted in a 2% reduction in the effective average tax rate.

(3) The situation in the foreign exchange market, as represented by the real cost of foreign exchange at the legal rate(s) or the real discrepancy between the black market and the legal rate(s), may also have affected tax compliance. The *a priori* sign expected on the exchange rate market variable is ambiguous. A high real cost of foreign exchange means that the cost of tax evasion for purposes of capital flight is high, which would lead to expect a positive relation. On the other hand, a low real cost of foreign exchange or a large real discrepancy between the black market and legal rates may lead to expectations of imminent changes in exchange rate policy, an

---

[10]This rapidly growing effective rate partially reflected increasing exchange rate discrimination for the legal costs of production in this sector (section 3.3).

[11]Behrman (1975b, subsections 4.2.1, 7.1.2.3) describes the *Nuevo Trato* in detail and concludes that the short-run impact of this legislation was probably negative from the Chilean point of view. The long-run effects are more difficult to evaluate, but may also have been negative.

advantage in tax evasion for immediate capital flight, and an inverse relation. For five of the tax categories included in table 3.2, one of these two effects dominates so that the relevant coefficient is significantly non-zero: employers' and employees' social security taxes, business taxes (excluding large-scale mining), import taxes, and legal acts taxes. For all but the first of these categories the relevant point estimate is negative, which implies that the expectational effect dominates.

Net government income from properties and enterprises. As is discussed above, this variable is the difference between two flows, both of which changed considerably during the sample period because of shifts in government ownership. On the average over the sample, the net revenue from this source was less than that from all but one of the 11 tax categories included in table 3.2 (column 1 in table 3.1). Because this has not been a very important revenue source and because specification of the determinants of the underlying flows would be so difficult, in the complete system model of Part III below net government revenues from properties and enterprises in real terms are simply assumed to vary with the level of overall *GDP*:

$$NGIPE = 0.00873 GDP,$$
$$(30.6) \tag{3.2}$$
$$\bar{R}^2 = 0.97, \quad SE = 8.6, \quad DW = 1.5, \quad 1945-1965,$$

where *NGIPE* is the net government income from properties and enterprises in real terms. This relationship at least picks up most of the variance in this revenue source over the sample period.

3.2. Monetary policy [12]

In many macroeconometric models the money supply is considered to be an exogenous policy variable. Such treatment would be quite inappropriate in the Chilean case. The Central Bank has been able to effect the size of the money supply at the margin through its loans, interest rate ceilings, quantitative restrictions on credit expansion, rediscount policy, and average and marginal reserve rates on

---

[12] A broad definition of monetary policy would include exchange rate determination and other foreign sector operations. In this section, focus is on the domestic aspects of monetary policies. Section 3.3 considers the foreign sector.

demand and time deposits[13]. Such control, however, has been far from complete. The behavior of commercial banks and of the private sector have altered the size of the money supply. More importantly, the Central Bank has not really been independent of the fiscal sector needs. On the contrary, it has been generally required to accommodate those needs. Given the persistent fiscal deficits (table 3.1), these needs have been quite considerable and growing. Banking system credit to the public sector, in fact, increased in the sample period at an annual average rate of 44.8% in nominal terms – or 15.2% in real terms (table 3.3)[14]. Furthermore, the locus of decision-making power in regard to many foreign sector aspects of monetary policy has often been outside of the Central Bank. Thus changes in both the fiscal situation and in foreign reserves have had substantial impact on the money supply independent of any desired policy of the Central Bank[15].

Table 3.3 summarizes some of the major characteristics of various domestic monetary variables over the 1945–1965 sample period: means, means relative to *GDP*, mean growth rates, and the standard deviation around the secular trend relative to the mean (a measure of volatility). That part of the following discussion pertaining to the behavior of components of the money supply during the sample period is based on this table.

The supply of the *monetary base* (*MONB*) is the sum of Central Bank international reserves (*IRCB*) in domestic terms, Central Bank credit (*LCB*) and other net terms (*MONBO*):

$$MONB = MONB_{-1} + EXRAT^* \Delta IRCB + \Delta LCB + \Delta MONBO,$$
$$(3.3)$$

where *EXRAT* is the exchange rate. The demand for (or the use of) the monetary base consists of the demand of commercial banks for net free (excess) reserves (*NFR*) and required reserves (*RES–NFR*)

---

[13]As in most developing economies, the size of the bond market has been so small that open market operations have not been very effective. The Chilean bond market has not only been small, but it probably shrank during the sample period because of the high inflation.

[14]Banking system credit to the private sector, in contrast, increased at an average annual rate of only 31% in nominal terms and 1.4% in real terms.

[15]Wachter (1974) investigates the independence of the Chilean money supply in a somewhat different framework. She applies a Sims test to see if there is statistical support for one-way causality between the money supply and the price level. She rejects one-way causality in both directions and thus concludes that the money supply is endogenously determined within a simultaneous system.

Table 3.3
Selected characteristics of Chilean monetary variables, 1945–1965[a].

	Mean	Mean percentage of nominal GDP	Mean percentage growth rate	Standard deviation from secular trend as percentage of mean
Monetary base	227	7.3	34.7	20.6
Money supply	323	10.4	33.4	22.5
Currency	170	5.5	32.5	19.8
Demand deposits	153	4.9	34.5	26.5
Time deposits	41	1.3	34.8	78.3
Reserves	56.7	1.8	19.6	240
Net free reserves	10.2	0.3	4.0	1643
Total credit	506	16.3	34.6	52.0
credit to public sector	143	4.6	44.8	63.6
credit to private sector	363	11.7	31.0	44.8
central Bank credit	551	17.8	35.7	72.2
interest rate	13.2		2.6	8.9
reserve requirements				
demand deposits – average	20.0		0.0	0.0
– marginal	36.9		5.0	31.6
time deposits – average	8.0		0.0	0.0
– marginal	29.1		9.5	95.2
Annual income velocity	9.6		2.3	

[a]Appendix A gives the sources. For the first 11 variables the means are in millions of escudos. For the interest and reserve rates the means are in percentages.

and the demand of the non-bank public for currency (*CUR*). Over the sample the monetary base grew at a mean annual rate of 34.7% in nominal terms or 5.1% in real terms. A major source of this growth was the government deficit, which averaged 3.6% of *GDP* (column 1 in table 3.1)[16]. This growth was not particularly volatile, in comparison at least to the other monetary variables.

3.2.1. Net free reserves

These reflect the response of commercial banks to the environment in which they operate, including Central Bank policies. Over the sample period, net free reserves grew slightly in nominal terms, primarily because rediscount policy was tightened up substantially after 1955. Because of inflation, however, the opportunity cost of

[16]Luders (1970) examines the sources of growth in the monetary base in some detail for the first part of the sample period.

holding excess reserves generally was high. Therefore they averaged near zero, although with considerable fluctuations. Relationship (3.4) is used to represent the behavior of net free reserves held by the commercial banks in the complete system model of Part III:

$$NFR/PGDP = 0.685(DD/PGDP) - 108.5R - 1780.R^2[PGDP]$$
$$(3.9) \qquad\qquad (4.7) \qquad (5.4)$$
$$+ (-1103 + 66.7 TIME)REDIS$$
$$(5.6) \quad (4.7)$$
$$- 0.857(NFR/PGDP_{-1}) + 1537,$$
$$(5.6) \qquad\qquad (3.9) \qquad\qquad (3.4)$$

$$\bar{R}^2 = 0.82, \qquad SE = 58.2, \qquad DW = 2.0, \qquad 1945-1965,$$

where $PGDP$ is the deflator for GDP; DD are demand deposits; R is the bank interest rate; $R^2[PGDP]$ is a distributed lag of the rates of change of the GDP deflator squared with quadratic weights of 0.32, 0.30, 0.24 and 0.14 for years 0 through -3; $TIME$ is a time trend with a value of one in 1945; $REDIS$ is a dummy variable with a value of one for 1945 through 1955 and zero thereafter; and other variables are defined above[17].

On an overall level this relationship appears satisfactory. The posited adjustment (or, overadjustment) response to reserve needs,

[17]Relationship (3.4) does not include reserves for time deposits. Within the complete system model of Part III there is also included the following relationships which include the impact of time deposits:

$$\frac{NER'}{PGDP} = 3.62 \frac{DD/PGDP}{(DD/PGDP)_{-1}} - 72.1R - 3759R1[PGDP]$$
$$(1.5) \qquad\qquad (2.8) \qquad (2.3)$$
$$+(-833 + 60.1 TIME)REDIS$$
$$(4.1) \quad (3.8)$$
$$+ 11.6 TIME*SB - 0.732\left(\frac{NFR'}{PGDP}\right)_{-1} + 1019, \qquad (3.4')$$
$$(1.5) \qquad\qquad (4.4) \qquad\qquad (2.6)$$

$$\bar{R}^2 = 0.61, \qquad SE = 66.1, \qquad DW = 2.6, \qquad 1945-1965,$$

where NFR' are net free reserves including the impact of time deposits; $R1[PGDP]$ is the same as $R[PGDP]$ except that the weights are linear (0.40, 0.30, 0.20, 0.10) instead of quadratic; SB is a dummy variable with a value of one in 1945 through 1953 and zero thereafter; and the other variables are defined in the text. The general interpretation of relationship (3.4') is the same as that of relationship (3.3), although the parameter values differ and marginal instead of average demand deposits have a significantly non-zero coefficient. In addition, the point estimate of the dummy variable for the pre-State Bank (SB) period suggests that net free reserves were larger before the establishment of that institution.

opportunity costs, and rediscount policy is consistent with 82% of the variance in the dependent variable.

The first right-side term is the size of demand deposits in real terms. Its inclusion reflects a precautionary motive for keeping excess reserves to cover obligations in case demand deposits are suddenly withdrawn. The point estimate implies that for every extra escudo of potential demand for reserves by holders of demand deposits, Chilean commercial banks kept 0.685 escudos in excess reserves. This high marginal rate suggests quite conservative behavior.

The next two right-hand-side terms in relationship (3.4) relate to the opportunity costs of holding excess reserves. The significantly negative point estimates imply that the commercial banks behaved rationally by reducing such holdings when interest rates or expected inflation (as represented by a distributed lag of past inflation) increased.

The next two coefficients refer to the changes in rediscount policy, especially near the end of 1955. The estimates suggest that this policy was secularly becoming more restrictive until that time, and became substantially more so after 1955 with the initiation of the Ibañez–Klein–Saks stabilization program (section 2.1). In contrast, there is no evidence of a significantly non-zero response in the net free reserves held by commercial banks to the structural change in the banking system which accompanied the creation of the State Bank (Banco del Estado) in 1953[18].

3.2.2. Total reserves (RES)

These equal net free reserves plus required reserves. Required reserves are defined by average and marginal reserve rates for demand deposits. Relationship (3.5) therefore defines total reserves:

$$RES = NFR + RRDDM * \Delta DD + RRDDA_{-1} * DD_{-1}. \qquad (3.5)$$

Over the sample period total reserves grew at a rate of 19.6% per year in nominal terms, with considerable fluctuations around the secular trend (although not as much as for net free reserves)[19].

---

[18]But see note 17.

[19]If time deposits are also considered (see note 17) then the average and marginal reserve requirements for time deposits must be added to relationship (3.5) analogously to the requirements for demand deposits.

The *demand for currency* held by the non-bank public and the *demand for demand deposits* depend on the total nominal money supply (narrowly defined, *MONS*) and the division of that supply between currency and demand deposits. The ratio of currency to demand deposits averaged 1.12 in 1945–1965, as compared to a value of 0.26 for the United States in 1947–1965. The much higher level for Chile reflects the lesser development (both in regard to the banking system and in regard to per capita income) and the impact of inflation (see below). Over the sample period currency held by the non-bank public grew at an annual average rate of 32.5% and demand deposits grew at an annual average rate of 34.5%. In real per capita terms the former stayed about constant, and the latter increased by about 2% per year. Relative to *GDP*, both declined somewhat. As *GDP* grew, therefore, some shift occurred from currency to demand deposits. This compositional change is the one normally experienced with economic growth. However, holdings of neither asset grew as fast as *GDP* because of the high opportunity cost of holding real balances given the rapid inflation. Finally, note that currency holdings deviated relatively little from the secular trend in comparison to the other monetary aggregates, including demand deposits.

Relationship (3.6) is an estimate of the determinants of division of the money supply between currency and demand deposits:

$$CUR/DD = 1.28L1[GDP] - 0.266L2[GDP^2] - 0.0300R$$
$$\quad\quad (2.6) \quad\quad\quad\quad (2.7) \quad\quad\quad\quad (2.1)$$
$$+ 3.05R1[PGDP] + 0.649R2[PGDP^2]$$
$$\quad (2.4) \quad\quad\quad\quad (2.0)$$
$$+ 0.0498(EXRAT/PGDP) - 0.212SB + 1.97, \quad (3.6)$$
$$\quad (2.1) \quad\quad\quad\quad\quad\quad (3.4) \quad\quad (9.0)$$
$$\bar{R}^2 = 0.87, \quad SE = 0.0524, \quad DW = 2.6, \quad 1945\text{–}1965.$$

where $L1$ and $L2$ are lag operators over four periods with linear and quadratic rates; and all other variables are as defined above.

On an overall level this relationship seems to be reasonably successful. It is consistent with 87% of the variance in the dependent variable. There are no significant problems of serial correlation. There is no significantly non-zero evidence of adjustment to desired levels of this ratio taking longer than a year.

The first two right-hand side terms refer to the effect of real *GDP* on this division between monetary assets. A polynomial distributed lag represents permanent income effects. The estimates imply a quadratic pattern with a sufficiently large weight on the second-order term so that the net effect is always negative for the *GDP* values in the sample. As *GDP* increases, therefore, the net effect is increasingly to induce relative shifts from currency to demand deposits.

The next four right-hand-side terms refer to opportunity costs. The estimates imply that there is a significantly non-zero relative shift from the non-interest-bearing asset as interest rates increase[20]. They also imply an increasing relative shift away from demand deposits as inflationary expectations (as represented by a quadratic distributed lag of past inflationary experience) increase. Inflation not only discourages the holding of real money balances, therefore, it also induces compositional changes from demand deposits to currency. The point estimates further suggest that increases in the *PLD NER* also have significantly non-zero effects in the same direction. The movements towards currency with higher inflationary expectations and with higher foreign exchange costs both may reflect a common desire to reduce the possibility of tracing illegal behavior – tax evasion in the first case and capital flight in the second.

The last variable with a significantly non-zero coefficient estimate is the dummy variable for the creation of the State Bank in 1953. The point estimate implies that this structural change in the banking system increased the ratio of currency to demand deposits. Such a result is somewhat surprising. *A priori*, I would have anticipated that this change would have had the opposite effect.

The *time deposits* held by the non-bank public averaged slightly over a quarter of demand deposits. In the United States in 1947–1965, for a point of comparison, time deposits were 62% of demand deposits. The lower ratio in Chile reflects the less extensive development of the banking system and the higher relative opportunity costs of holding this asset since the interest rate paid thereon usually was less than the rate of inflation. Over the sample period, time deposits increased slightly relative to demand deposits, but – like demand deposits – not relative to *GDP*. Time deposits

[20]Interest is paid on demand deposits in Chile.

were much more volatile, however, than either currency or demand deposits.

Time deposits relative to the money supply (narrowly defined) are hypothesized to depend on determinants similar to those discussed above for other monetary assets:

$$TD/MONS = 0.0066R - 0.537R1[PGDP]$$
$$(2.9) \qquad (1.6)$$
$$+ 0.0117(EXRAT/PGDP) + 0.0275\$DEP$$
$$(2.3) \qquad\qquad\qquad (2.4)$$
$$+ 0.736(TD/MONS)_{-1} - 0.0937, \qquad\qquad (3.7)$$
$$(10.1) \qquad\qquad (2.8)$$

$$\bar{R}^2 = 0.95, \qquad SE = 0.0132, \qquad DW = 2.6, \qquad 1945{-}1965,$$

where $\$DEP$ is a dummy variable for the introduction of dollar deposits in 1959–1961 (section 2.2); and all other variables are as defined above.

This relationship, once again, seems to be rather successful. It is consistent with 95% of the sample-period variance in the dependent variable. In contrast to relationship (3.6), however, in this case a fairly slow adjustment process is implied by the significantly non-zero and substantial coefficient of the lagged dependent variable. Also in contrast, there is no evidence of a significantly non-zero income response for the decision about holding time deposits versus other more narrowly defined monetary assets. The opportunity–cost variables, on the other hand, do have significant roles. Higher interest rates and real foreign exchange costs induce relative shifts into time deposits, although inflationary expectations induce shifts out (and probably into currency). Institutional changes, finally, also have had a significant role. The existence of the option of holding time deposits in dollars during 1959–1961 (section 2.2), to be more explicit, increased the long-run ratio of time deposits to the money supply by over 10%.

The *money supply*, narrowly defined, averaged 10.4% of *GDP* over the 1945–1965 sample. The mean implied annual income velocity was 9.6, as compared to 3.2 for the United States in 1947–1965. The higher Chilean velocity, once again, reflects the same two factors mentioned above: a less-developed monetary system and a very inflationary experience. Because of the latter, the money supply grew more slowly than nominal *GDP* so that annual income velocity increased at an average annual secular rate of 2.3% with fairly substantial fluctuations. In other words, desired real balances declined because of the high and secularly increasing (although not monotonically increasing) opportunity cost due to inflation. Attempts to reduce undesired balances thus were accompanied by pressure on prices. Section 6.1 below further explores the nature of this pressure on the determination of prices through the incorporation of the derivative of the demand for real money balances in the price determination relationships.

The money supply is defined to be the sum of currency held by the non-bank public and demand deposits:

$$MONS = DD + CUR = DD + MONB - RES. \tag{3.8}$$

The money supply thus reflects all of the considerations underlying relationships (3.2–3.6) above. Independent of Central Bank domestic policy, the monetary base may be altered by obligatory loans to the fiscal sector and by changes in international reserves. For a given monetary base, behavioral relationships for commercial bank reserves and for the non-bank-public asset composition determine the magnitude of the money supply. Within limits, the Central Bank can affect the size of the money supply by changing average and marginal required reserve rates, rediscount policy, interest rates (or ceilings thereon[21]), and restrictions on foreign exchange deposits. Marginal required reserve rates for demand deposits, for example, ranged from 20.0 to 87.5% during the sample. Through such instruments, chs. 4, 5, and 6 suggest that the Central Bank can have some direct impact on prices and direct and indirect impact (through prices) on capacity creation and utilization and on the components of final demand. The extent to which the Central Bank has discretion in determining the size of the money supply, however, is definitely limited by the constraints under which it acts.

---

[21]Bank interest rates generally have been close to or at the ceilings set by the Central Bank because the ceilings have been low relative to actual inflation rates (and, presumably, relative to expected inflation rates). Therefore, the interest rate is treated as an exogenous variable in the complete system model of Part III below and the impact of quantity of credit is explored in chs. 4, 5, and 6 since credit rationing may have been a factor.

3.3. Foreign sector policies[22]

Import substitution has been a major goal of Chilean foreign sector policy at least since the 1897 tariff law. The catastrophic impact of the Great Depression on the Chilean economy, however, resulted in a quantum increase in the restrictiveness of foreign sector policies. No other course was judged to be possible at the time. The experience of the 1930s led to some general attitudes which shaped the evaluation of policy possibilities in the 1945–1965 sample period and thereafter: export pessimism and a desire to establish greater domestic control over the national economic destiny, even at the cost of foregoing possibly considerable static comparative advantage.

In the decades after the Second World War a disequilibrium system with an overvalued *NER* prevailed because of the above-mentioned attitudes and the perceived negative impact of devaluation on income distribution, inflation, and the cost of imported capital goods. The intensity of exchange control, however, varied considerably. The system, in combination with external stimuli, generated cycles in the degree of complexity and restrictiveness. Subsequent to devaluation and rationalization, *ad hoc* changes of greater specificity were made with increasing frequency because of the perception of unintended side effects of quantitative restrictions, the attempt by the government to use such restrictions for a multitude of reasons additional to managing the balance of payments, and the growing overvaluation due to the internal inflation. In each cycle the government resisted formal devaluation for some time because of the above-mentioned perceived negative effects. For a short period of time the government was able to continue with increasingly overvalued *NER*s despite the disequilibrium pressures. Before long, however, the pressures for at least partial adjustment proved to be irresistible. Inflation was high enough so that, despite accelerated *ad hoc* changes in the international economic policy regime devaluation of the *NER*s to new fixed rates (generally accompanied by considerable rationalization and some liberalization) could not be avoided. From that point the cycle began again. Even when the

---

[22]This section draws heavily upon the extensive consideration of these policies and of their impact in Behrman (1975a, 1975b).

government operated a sliding-peg *NER* policy, moreover, the *NER*s were left overvalued so that the cycle was only moderated, but not eliminated.

The remainder of this section considers the major instruments of the foreign sector policy regimes during the sample period. As is suggested above, of course, the government had discretionary use of these tools only in the short run.

3.3.1. Exchange rates

Except for during 1959–1961, Chile had a multiple exchange rate system throughout the sample period. Three major legal *NER*s are included in the complete system model of Part III below as exogenous policy instruments: the brokers' rate for services, the large-scale mining rate for the payment of domestic costs of production in large-scale mining, and the national accounts rate for all other legal transactions. The black market rate also is included in the model, but is endogenously determined (subsection 6.3.3). Although a large number of other rates also existed at times (for details see Behrman, 1975b, ch. 3; and Baerrensen, 1966), these four rates capture the major features of Chilean *NER* policy. They have direct impact on domestic prices, capacity creation and utilization decisions, savings and tax compliance decisions (section 3.1 and chs. 4–6).

During the sample period (and before and after) the cyclical disequilibrium system mentioned above prevailed. Repeatedly, *NER*s were devalued and then maintained constant at the new level[23]. At the start of the Alessandri government in 1959–1961 (and also at the start of the Allende government in 1970–1971), for example, constant *NER*s were cited frequently by officials as symbols of stability. Even if the initial devaluation in a cycle was to an equilibrium level, however, the internal inflation caused the associated *PLD NER*s to decline quickly. Therefore, a disequilibrium situation soon developed. The results usually included a loss in

---

[23]When official devaluations were not announced, however, *de facto* devaluations were sometimes implemented by switching items partially or entirely from one *NER* to another in the multiple exchange rate system instead of actually changing the *NER*s. Only in 1959–1961 did a unified exchange rate exclude this possibility.

reserves, an increase in restrictiveness, and an eventual *de facto* devaluation (thus beginning another cycle).

The secular trend in the overall mean *PLD NER* was downward at an exponential average of over 5% per year for over three decades, including the sample period. For example, the special *PLD NER* used for the legal costs of production for large-scale copper mining, for varying quotas of the returns from most other exports and for government imports, in 1956 was only 2% of the 1939 value. In the 32 years after 1940, in fact, in only five years did the weighted average of all legal *PLD NERs* increase. The value for 1972 was less than one-sixth of the value for 1940. Even during the sliding-peg experience of 1965–1970, at the end of the sample period, the weighted average of all legal *PLD NERs* fell a total of 8% (in contrast to the intended increase of 2% per year). The steady and substantial decline vastly outpaced the long-run expansion of Chilean control over foreign exchange through exports and capital inflows. Therefore, the *NER* was overvalued more and more in a long-run sense, although export booms and capital inflows sometimes masked this disequilibrium in the short run. As a result, exports were discouraged and imports were encouraged (section 5.2).

The dispersion among legal *NERs* sometimes was quite considerable. For example, the ratio of the gold *NER* to the special *NER* was 9.8 in 1953. In general, such variances were reduced on the average during liberalization attempts (but not eliminated except in 1959–1961). The *NER* for domestic costs of large-scale mining generally was most disadvantageous. The legal *NER* used for invisibles (i.e. the broker rate) usually was less advantageous than that for goods and was increased substantially relative to the *NERs* for goods at times of exchange shortages and extensive exchange control.

The ratio of the black market *NER* to the weighted average of all legal *NERs* ranged from about 1.0 in 1959–1961 to 2.95 in 1954[24]. Generally, the black market *PLD NER* moved inversely with the overall average of legal *PLD NERs*. This negative correlation reflects that exchange control (and therefore demand in the black market) was less when the legal *PLD NERs* were higher.

[24]This ratio was higher at times under the Allende government after the sample period. In 1972, for example, it averaged 10.

3.3.2. Supporting policies for imports

A large number of price-related and quantitative policies were used to supplement *NER* policy in the control of the magnitude and composition of imports: tariffs and related indirect taxes, quotas, licenses, foreign exchange budgets, permitted lists, time constraints regarding foreign exchange cover for imports, prior deposits on imports, special regimes (for geographical regions, particular industries, or government agencies), and bilateral, compensation, and barter agreements. Owing to the attempt to maintain a disequilibrium system with an overvalued exchange rate, cyclical fluctuations occurred in the extent of restrictiveness and in the degree of complexity. When favorable external conditions prevailed and the exchange rate(s) was not too far below the long-run equilibrium level, the import control system was relatively simple. After external conditions deteriorated and the *PLD NER* declined due to inflation with a fixed *NER*, the system was made much more complex and restrictive in response to *ex ante* balance of payments deficits.

Because of this pattern, a number of policy tools which were initially introduced to liberalize and rationalize the system, were subsequently altered in their basic character and used to make the system more restrictive and specific. The prior deposit system on imports, for example, was initiated in 1956 with liberalizing and rationalizing intents. As the liberalization attempt faltered in 1957 and 1958, however, prior deposits were made higher in order to limit imports, and more varied in order to discriminate more among them. Therefore, in the next liberalization attempt, the additional tax was imposed to replace the prior deposit system. When that liberalization attempt failed, prior deposits were reinstituted and the additional tax was maintained. Next, the added additional tax was introduced with the same intent, but eventually prior deposits, the additional tax rate, and the added additional tax were all in effect.

The large number of tools, often applied in *ad hoc* and very specific ways, caused large import premia for the recipients of import privileges and quite high, but variable, import barriers. The dispersion in such barriers was very substantial across production sectors and subsectors and across end-use classifications. Movements in the effect of policies on these categories were not highly correlated over time. Nevertheless, generally the regimes tended to favor manufacturing over agriculture over mining, the traditional 'easy' import-substituting industries which had received high protection since the 19th century over intermediate-goods producing ones, import substitution over export promotion, and goods imports over non-goods international transactions. In times of foreign exchange crises, restrictions were increased most severely on non-goods transactions and on investment-goods imports. These restrictions resulted in a clear trade-off between short-run balance of payments needs and long-run growth objectives. Variations for intermediate goods, on the other hand, were relatively low. This implies some success of attempts not to disrupt operation of existing capacity through erratic changes in the availability of imported inputs.

Within the complete model econometric analysis of Part III below, price-related supporting import policies are represented by the average *ad valorem*-equivalent nominal tariff rate (discussed in subsection 3.1.2) and the import prior deposit cost rate. The former incorporates all of the taxes and exemptions. The latter reflects the levels of required deposits, the required time period, and opportunity costs. After they were introduced in 1956, in fact, the prior deposits were the major price-related tool for imports. At times of foreign exchange crises they were raised to prohibitory levels on many items and their structure altered to favor certain mass-consumption necessities. During more liberalized periods the prior deposit system was gradually eliminated – only to be reinstated abruptly with the abandonment of the liberalization effort.

Within the complete model, quantitative policies on imports (or pressures for such policies) are represented by the Ffrench-Davis (1971) quantitative restrictions index, ratios of aggregate internal prices to *EER*s, and variables which relate to the short-run availability of foreign exchange (such as the export capacity to import and the net foreign exchange reserves of the banking system).

3.3.3. *Supporting policies for exports*

The overall export regimes have not been as complicated as the import regimes because of the much greater concentration of toal export value among a few products.

Control over the most important export source – large-scale copper mining – shifted steadily (although not monotonically) from the foreign-owned copper companies and the United States government to the Chilean government. Important policies included special exchange rates, taxes, price agreements, and a sales monopoly. The secular shift in control culminated in the Chileanization and nationalization programs of the Frei and Allende governments after the end of the sample period.

For the first quarter-century after the Great Depression, Chilean *NER* policy towards large-scale mining included a curious combination of very unfavorable *NER*s for local costs and very favorable *NER*s for imported components. For that period and later until nationalization, moreover, returns on foreign-owned factors and amortization were practically unregulated.

Export promotion attempts for non-traditional exports accelerated near the end of the sample, but still had limited coverage and did not compensate for the disequilibrium *NER* policy. Much of the limited resources involved in such programs, moreover, subsidized industries for reasons other than their export potential.

Within the complete model of Part III below these policies are represented by a subsidy rate for non-traditional exports, quantitative restrictions indices for all exports (subsection 3.3.2), the legal cost of production for large-scale copper mining (i.e. domestic costs paid at an often very disadvantageous *NER*), direct taxes on large-scale mining (subsection 3.1.2), the use of the Chilean producers' price for copper starting in 1964, and dummy variables for such events as the maintenance of the Chilean copper sales monopoly in 1952–1954.

3.4. Income policies

For a number of recent Chilean governments a major policy goal has been to redistribute income and wealth. After the end of the sample period under the Allende government of 1970–1973, for example, a very important concern was the attempt to restructure the economy with such a goal in mind. During the sample period, however, such efforts were not so extensive. Tools for redistributing income basically were limited to taxes and transfers, generally ineffective price ceilings, foreign sector policies to favor certain mass-consumption items, geographical regions or industries, and minimum wage laws[25].

Most of these policies are discussed above. Minimum wages, however, have not yet been considered. Almost every year during the sample period minimum wages were readjusted upward. To represent these changes the *sueldo vital*, by far the most extensive legislated reference point for wages, is an exogenous policy instrument in the complete system model of Part III below. Dummy variables are also included for the unusual timing of the wage readjustment in 1960–1961, the introduction of an agricultural minimum wage in 1953, and the unification of agricultural and manufacturing minimum wages in 1965. Of course, all of these policy changes had their direct impact primarily on the determination of wages, but they also had effects on other variables such as the deflator for government current consumption expenditures (sections 6.2 and 6.3).

The *sueldo vital* increased at an average annual percentage rate of 28.6 over the sample. Since the *GDP* deflator and the consumer price index rose at average annual rates of 29.6 and 30.7%, respectively, in real terms the *sueldo vital* declined secularly at a rate of 1–2% per year. In comparison to overall average prices or wages, moreover, it fluctuated relatively greatly from the sectoral trend[26].

In debates about the size of the appropriate readjustment of the *sueldo vital* frequent reference was made to the rate of increase of the consumer price index for the previous year. At times, in fact, this latter increase was the legal standard for changes in the *sueldo vital*. These observations suggest that the *sueldo vital* might better be considered a recursive variable rather than an exogenous policy variable. A regression of the rate of change of the *sueldo vital* on the rate of change of the consumer price index permits exploration of

[25]These comments are not meant to suggest that the policies followed did not have substantial distributional impact. Foreign sector policies, for example, tended to favor certain long-protected industries, the recipients of import privileges, the owners of factors used in certain 'promoted' exports and the government bureaucracy, although they had mixed impact impact on the labor share (Behrman, 1975b, ch. 11). Generally, these effects, however, were only by products, but not the *stated* aims of policies.

[26]The ratio of the standard deviation from the secular trend to the mean was 22.2% for the *sueldo vital*, 19.2% for the *GDP* deflator, and 14.1% for average wages. Table 6.1 indicates, however, that some sectoral wages and prices were much more volatile.

this possibility:

$$R[SV] = 1.05 R[CPI_{-1}] - 34.1 IKS, \qquad\qquad (3.9)$$
$$(15.1) \qquad\quad (4.1)$$

$$\bar{R}^2 = 0.35, \qquad SE = 11.3, \qquad DW = 1.90, \qquad \rho = -0.399,$$
$$1945\text{--}1965,$$

where $R[SV]$ is the percentage rate of growth in the *sueldo vital*; $R[CPI_{-1}]$ is the percentage rate of growth in the consumer price index lagged one year; and *IKS* is a dummy variable with a value of one in 1956 and 1957 for the Ibañez–Klein–Saks stabilization program (section 2.1) and zero for other years. This relationship is consistent with only about a third of the variance in the dependent variable even when the special effects of the Ibañez–Klein–Saks program[27] and the negative autocorrelation to compensate for previous deviations are both incorporated. This result suggests that the readjustment in the *sueldo vital* was substantially determined by factors other than the lagged change in the consumer price index. In the simulations in Part III below, therefore, the *sueldo vital* is generally treated as an exogenous variable (although the option of utilizing relationship (3.9) is built into the simulation package).

---

[27]The significant and quite substantial coefficient of the Ibañez–Klein–Saks variable *prima facie* supports the frequent criticism of that program as being antilabor. The question of interest, however, is the impact on actual wages, not on the *sueldo vital*. Section 6.2 below suggests that the dependence of sectoral wages on the *sueldo vital* is significant in some cases, but is much less substantial and less widespread than is often hypothesized. Therefore, the appropriate conclusion may be that the Ibañez–Klein–Saks stabilization program intended to lower real wages and therefore legislated relatively small adjustments in the *sueldo vital*, but succeeded in this attempt only to a quite limited extent.

CHAPTER 4

Supply

Supply constraints are widely thought to be much more relatively important in the developing economies than in the developed ones. Many of the models referred to in paragraph (3) of section 1.1, in fact, include only supply considerations.

This chapter considers domestic[1] supply relationships for the Chilean economy on the nine-sector level which is utilized for most of the model in Part III. Table 4.1 gives the nine sectors and some of their salient features over the 1945–1965 sample period. Section 4.1 explores the determination of sectoral capacities of real value added. Section 4.2 examines the long-run allocation of primary factors among sectors. Section 4.3 investigates sectoral capacity utilization decisions.

4.1. Sectoral capacities of real value added and elasticities of substitution[2]

Column 1 of table 4.1 gives the mean distribution of capacity across sectors, and column 2 gives the mean percentage growth rates. Other services, manufacturing, and agriculture are the only sectors which averaged over 10% of total capacity. Government, transportation, mining and housing services all accounted for between 7.0 and 8.5%. Construction and utilities had 2.5 and 1.3%, respectively. Construction, housing services, utilities, government, and manufacturing all expanded in capacity more rapidly than the national

---

[1]Foreign sources are analyzed in ch. 5.
[2]The first part of this section draws heavily on material presented in Behrman (1972a).

Table 4.1

Sectoral supply characteristics of the Chilean economy, 1945–1965[a].

Sector	Mean percentage of total capacity	Mean percentage growth rate of capacity	Mean percentage of total labor force	Mean percentage growth rate of labor force	Mean labor productivity as percentage of total	Mean percentage growth rate of labor productivity	Mean percentage of total investment	Standard deviations as percentage mean for investment	Minimum percentage capacity utilization rates[b]	Mean percentage capacity utilization rate	Standard deviation in capacity utilization rate	Total unused capacity as percentage of mean real GDP	Mean percentage of total real GDP	Mean growth rate of real GDP
	1	2	3	4	5	6	7	8	9	10	11	12	13	14
Agriculture	12.2	1.8	30.9	0.5	41	1.9	5	46	88	95	5	100	12.6	2.4
Mining	7.4	2.2	4.7	0.3	147	2.9	4	70	53	86	15	320	6.9	3.2
Construction	2.5	7.2	6.1	6.0	41	1.8	c	c	80	93	8	136	2.5	7.8
Manufacturing	19.6	3.9	18.5	1.2	109	2.9	22	32	83	95	05	110	20.1	4.1
Transportation	7.7	3.4	5.0	3.0	146	1.8	20[d]	20[d]	71	88	11	269	7.3	4.8
Utilities	1.3	5.4	1.0	3.5	130	3.0	8	56	65	88	12	311	1.3	6.5
Housing services	7.1	6.6	0	0	0	0	33	22	75	91	9	229	7.0	7.4
Government	8.3	5.0	8.3	2.8	100	3.9	c	c	82	93	7	185	8.3	6.7
Other services	33.9	3.5	25.5	1.6	137	3.0	c	c	83	96	5	94	35.0	4.6
Total economy	100.	3.6	100.	1.6	100	2.6	100	33	88	93	1	145	100.	4.2

[a] Appendix A gives the sources of data which underlie the calculations for this table.

[b] For the trend-through-the-peaks capacity definition utilized (see section 4.3) the maximum capacity utilization rate for each sector is 100%. The range, therefore, is clear from this column.

[c] Sectoral investment data are not available for construction, government, and other services. For these three sectors aggregated together the entries for columns 7 and 8, respectively, are 8 and 95%.

[d] 1950–1965 only.

average. The rest of this section considers the technical determinants of these sectoral production capacities.

4.1.1. The model for the capacity of real value added

For each sector the capacity of real value added is defined by the
'trend-through-the-peaks' method (section 4.3). The underlying technology is assumed to include fixed coefficients for all intermediate
inputs and a CES production function with homogeneity of degree
one and with factor augmenting technological change for the
capacity of real value added[3]:

$$CV = [(E_L L)^{-\rho} + (E_K K)^{-\rho}]^{-1/\rho}, \tag{4.1}$$

where CV is the capacity of real value added; L is the secular trend
in the labor force; K is capital stock; E_L is the level of efficiency of
labor (assumed equal to $b\ e^{rt}$)[4]; E_K is the level of efficiency of capital
(assumed equal to $b'e^{r't}$); and t is a time trend. Under the
assumption that the value of the marginal product is equated to the
nominal wage, a relation can be derived which allows the estimation
of some of the key parameters without using the relatively shaky
capital stock and rate of return data:

$$\log \frac{CV}{L} = \frac{1}{1+\rho} \log \frac{W}{P} + \frac{\rho}{1+\rho} rt + \frac{\rho}{1+\rho} \log b, \tag{4.2}$$

where W is the nominal wage (including employers' social security
payments) and P is the nominal gross product price. Note that a
relation of exactly the same form would result if all the same
assumptions were made except that Hicks-neutral technological
change (i.e. $r = r'$) were assumed instead of factor augmenting
technological change[5]. Finally, eq. (4.2) is assumed to represent the
desired $\log(CV/L)$ towards which actual $\log(CV/L)$ adjusts in a
Koyck–Cagan–Nerlove process. Relation (4.3) thus is actually esti-

---

[3] David and van de Klundert (1965). The seminal article on CES production
functions, of course, is Arrow *et al.* (1961). For excellent and more recent relevant
discussions, see Brown (1966 and 1967) and Fisher (1969).
    [4] Considerable efforts to relate E_L to the stock of human capital estimates by
Harberger and Selowsky (1966) do not result in significant estimates.
    [5] In fact, the assumption of Hicks-neutral technological change is made below. The
possibility of factor augmentation is included in relation (4.1) to allow exploration of
the effects of changes in the stock of human quality (see note 4).

mated:

$$\log(CV/L) = (1 - \lambda) \log(CV/L)_{-1} + \lambda\sigma \log(W/P)$$
$$+ \lambda\sigma\rho rt + \lambda\sigma\rho \log b, \qquad (4.3)$$

where $\sigma = 1/(1 + \rho)$ is the elasticity of substitution between capital and labor and λ is the adjustment coefficient.

Because of the substantial inflation throughout the sample period (variable 2.1 in table 2.1), deflation of nominal value added is essential in order to avoid substantial upward biases in the estimates of the elasticity of substitution between capital and labor[6]. Because of the lack of information about intermediate inputs and prices, however, sectoral gross product price indices are used instead of true value-added deflators. The directions of biases so introduced are not clear, but in an economy with a history of inflation so continuous and so substantial as that which Chile has experienced it would seem worse not to deflate than to follow the above procedure. Independent of this question of the use of gross versus value-added deflators, biases may have resulted from the deflation process[7]. The fixed weights in the deflators used are based on years which are relatively early in the sample. If relatively large increases in the true weights are correlated with relatively declining prices because of relatively rapid supply expansions (and vice versa), the deflator used may overestimate the level of the true deflator more and more in the later years of the sample. Under such assumptions, the estimates of the elasticity of substitution are biased downward, as is now demonstrated with reference to relations (4.2a) and (4.2b)[8]:

$$\log(P' \cdot CV/P'' \cdot L) = \sigma \log(W/P'') + \sigma\rho \log b, \qquad (4.2a)$$

where P' is the true deflator (assumed to be identical for gross and net value); and P'' is the deflator actually used:

$$\log(P' \cdot CV/P'' \cdot L) = \sigma \log(W/P'') + \sigma\rho \log b$$
$$+ (1 - \sigma) \log(P'/P''). \qquad (4.2b)$$

[6]This statement is made under the assumption that the true elasticity of substitution is less than one and that the adjustment process is complete in one period (otherwise the estimates are not unbiased in any case because of the lagged dependent variable). See Nerlove (1967, pp. 73–74).

[7]I wish to thank James McCabe who suggested that this question merited exploration.

[8]Eq. (4.2a) is eq. (4.2) with the assumption that r equals zero.

If P' and P'' are not identical, then relation (4.2a) is estimated, but relation (4.2b) should be estimated. If the true elasticity of substitution between capital and labor is less than one, the coefficient of $\log(P'/P'')$ is positive. For all but one of the individual sectors, $\log(W/P'')$ is positively correlated with time[9]. Under the above assumptions $\log(P'/P'')$ is negatively correlated with time, and therefore the covariance between $\log(W/P'')$ and $\log(P'/P'')$ is negative. Thus, the bias, as is indicated in relation (4.4), is downward:

$$E[\text{est } \sigma - \sigma] = (1 - \sigma) \operatorname{cov} \frac{[\log(P'/P''), \log(W/P')]}{\operatorname{var}[\log(P'/P'')]}. \qquad (4.4)$$

Our final characteristic of the model is important and merits emphasis. An attempt has been made to abstract from short-run fluctuations and to concentrate upon the long-run structure. Therefore, the capacity of real value added is used instead of current real value added; the weighted average of wages to prices with lags of from one to five years[10] is used instead of the current wage–price ratio; and the possibility of long-run adjustment is included in relation (4.3). The reason for this emphasis on the long run are threefold. First, short-run labor data are not available except for the last few years of the sample. Second, the pressures for following the assumed competitive-like behavior would seem to be greater in the long run. Third, there is a need to abstract from transitory cyclical fluctuations in order to estimate the underlying structural relation of interest[11]. For example, assume that the true structural relation is

[9]The correlation coefficients between time and the logarithm of the weighted average of past wages to prices (see the next note) for the individual sectors in the same order as they appear in tables 4.1 and 4.2 (excluding housing services) are 0.92, 0.06, 0.81, 0.66, 0.58, -0.09, 0.85, and 0.52.

[10]The weights of the various lagged values of this variable are estimated for each sector by a maximum-likelihood scanning procedure. The pattern of such lags is geometric for lags of from two to five years (i.e. δ for two years, $\delta(1-\delta)$ for three years, etc.) with a residual weight for one year so that the sum of the weights equals one (i.e., $1 - \delta \sum_{i=1}^{4}(1-\delta)^{i-1}$), and zero for all other lags. This weighting scheme allows somewhat more flexibility than the usual geometric pattern in that the maximum weight can be for a lag of one or of two years, but still only one parameter is estimated. Because of the use of this maximum-likelihood estimating procedure the statistics and significance tests included in table 4.2 are asymptotic.

[11]The transitory components in the determination of the rate of change of prices and possibly of wages, for example, apparently are considerable in magnitude and in duration. See Behrman (1971a and 1973c), Behrman and García (1973), and ch. 6 below.

given by relation (4.2c) (in which r is assumed to be zero once again), but that the current values of the logarithm of real value added and of the logarithm of real wages are related to the respective structural values as is indicated in relation (4.2d), so that relation (4.2c) is actually estimated:

$$\log(V/L)^* = \delta \log(W/P)^* + \text{constant}, \tag{4.2c}$$

where $(V/L)^*$ is the true long-run value added per laborer and $(W/P)^*$ is the true long-run wage relative to product price;

$$\log(V/L) = \log(V/L)^* + v, \qquad \log(W/P) = \log(W/P)^* + u, \tag{4.2d}$$

where V/L is the current observed real value per laborer, W/P is the current observed wage relative to the product price, and u and v are transitory components in the respective relations;

$$\log(V/L) = \alpha \log(W/P) + \text{constant} + w, \tag{4.2e}$$

where $w = v - \sigma u$.

These assumptions lead to the classical 'errors in variables' problem (Johnston, 1963, pp. 148–176). Even if u and v are assumed to be mutually and serially independent with constant variances, and also to be independent of $\log(V/L)^*$ and $\log(W/P)$, the full assumptions necessary for the application of ordinary least squares to relation (4.2e) are not met because w is not independent of $\log(W/P)$. The estimate of σ is biased and inconsistent (in the probability limit an underestimate is obtained). In an attempt to minimize such biases and inconsistencies, therefore, the variables have been defined so as to approximate $\log(V/L)^*$ and $\log(W/P)^*$ instead of the current values thereof.

Given the estimates of λ, ρ, σ, and r from relation (4.3), the remaining parameters in relation (4.1) are estimated by a non-linear maximum likelihood procedure (Goldfeld *et al.*, 1966).

4.1.2. *Sectoral estimates of the elasticity of substitution and of the capacity production functions*

Time series estimates of relation (4.3) are made for all of the nine sectors listed in the introduction to this chapter except for housing (in which case there are no data on the labor input). In the case of government, the price index of the service sector is used to

Table 4.2

Estimates of relations from CES production functions for capacity of real value added in six Chilean sectors, 1945–1965[a].

Sector	$\log(CV/L)_{-1}$	$\log E(W/P)$	Time	Constant	$\bar{R}^2$ SE	F	σ (long run)	r	δ
	1	2	3	4	5	6	7	8	9
Agriculture	0.579 (3.58)	0.129 (2.26)		1.38 (2.63)	0.89 0.037	78.8	0.31		0.94
Mining		0.508 (6.07)	0.0137 (8.66)	5.10 (19.0)	0.85 0.044	59.1	0.51	0.028	0.16
Manufacturing	0.735 (6.82)	0.201 (3.03)	0.0040 (1.53)	1.53 (1.93)	0.99 0.014	933.5	0.76	0.017	0.35
Utilities		0.321 (6.42)		6.12 (37.1)	0.67 0.107	41.2	0.32		0.00
Services		0.088 (2.30)	0.0193 (16.6)	4.75 (86.4)	0.95 0.029	201.0	0.09	0.019	0.00
Government	0.860 (22.2)	0.125 (2.30)		1.07 (3.26)	0.96 0.029	252.2	0.89		0.24

[a]Data sources are given in appendix A. Under each point estimate in the estimated relationship is the t-value. All t-values are significantly non-zero at the five percent level, except for the coefficient of time in manufacturing which is significantly non-zero at the 10% level. r is consistent with Hicks-neutral or labor augmenting technological change and is related to the expectations of the wage-price ratio in column 2 (see footnote 10 on page 117 and fig. 4.1).

represent the product price because, of course, no market price is available. The direction of biases so introduced is not clear (but at least the general inflationary trend is removed), nor is the degree of distortion due to the assumption that the government behaves like a marginal cost pricer in the long run evident. Table 4.2 summarizes estimates for six sectors. Estimates for construction and transportation indicate that the elasticities of substitution between capital and labor are not significantly non-zero even at the 25% level. Under the assumption that capital is the constraining factor in the production of real value added, estimates of a semi-Cobb–Douglas function are obtained for transportation and for housing services (for which there are no recorded labor inputs). For construction, the other sector for which no significant estimate of the elasticity of substitution between capital and labor is obtained, the lack of data on investment precludes following a similar procedure. Under the assumption that labor is the constraining factor in the production of real value added, however, estimates of a semi-Cobb–Douglas function are obtained for construction and, once again, for transportation. Table 4.3 presents all of the semi-Cobb–Douglas estimates. Table 4.4 gives the non-linear maximum-likelihood estimates of relation (1) for the sectors for which investment series are available and for which table 4.2 implies non-zero substitution possibilities between capital and labor[12].

[12]Included is the sum of construction, government and services, which accounts for the residual investment (i.e. the total minus that going explicitly to other sectors). In the complete model of Part III below increments in the total capacity for these three sectors from table 4.4 are divided among them on the basis of distributed lag adjustments to their respective capacity utilization rates and relative shares in GDP:

construction: $CV = 0.944CV_{-1} + (-0.219 + 3.88S + 1.04S_{-1})\Delta CV^* + 33.8,$
$\qquad\qquad\quad$ (15.8) $\qquad$ (2.2) $\quad$ (1.9) $\quad$ (1.4) $\qquad\qquad$ (2.1)
$\qquad\qquad\quad \bar{R}^2 = 0.99, \qquad SE = 18.0, \qquad DW = 1.4, \qquad 1945\text{–}1965;$

services: $\qquad CV = 0.99CV_{-1} + (0.932U)\Delta CV^* - 50.2,$
$\qquad\qquad\quad$ (137) $\qquad$ (16.0) $\qquad\quad$ (1.4)
$\qquad\qquad\quad \bar{R}^2 = 0.999, \quad SE = 33.0, \qquad DW = 1.6, \qquad 1945\text{–}1965;$

government: $CV = 0.965CV_{-1} + (0.564S)\Delta CV^* + 71.6,$
$\qquad\qquad\quad$ (44.4) $\qquad$ (2.0) $\qquad\quad$ (2.8)
$\qquad\qquad\quad \bar{R}^2 = 0.99, \qquad SE = 30.4, \qquad DW = 1.1, \qquad 1945\text{–}1965;$

where CV is the capacity of real value added for the sector of interest, S is the ratio of the GDP of the sector of interest relative to the GDP for the three residual sectors, ΔCV^* is the first difference of the capacity of real value added for the three sectors combined, and U is a distributed lag of capacity utilization rates in the sector of interest with weights of 0.4 for the current year and 0.3, 0.2, and 0.1, respectively, for the three previous years.

Table 4.3

Estimates of 'semi-Cobb-Douglas' functions for capacity of real value added in construction, transportation, and housing services in Chile, 1945–1965[a].

Sector	$\log (CV)_{-1}$	$\log K$	$\log L$	Time	Constant	$\bar{R}^2$ SE	F	Rate of depreciation
Construction	0.599 (3.71)		0.446 (2.58)		0.219 (1.32)	0.99 0.0551	820	
Transportation[b]	0.380 (2.12)		0.662 (3.52)		1.254 (3.25)	0.99 0.0209	1420	
		0.398 (6.09)		0.017 (5.40)	3.731 (7.32)	0.996 0.011	1922	0.0385
Housing services	0.757 (8.73)	0.309 (2.53)			−0.975 (1.93)	0.99 0.053	1108	0.0367

[a] Data sources given in appendix A. Under each point estimate in parentheses is the absolute value of the t-statistic, all of which are significantly non-zero at the 5% level except for the constant term in the transportation sector (which is significantly non-zero at the 10% level). If labor is assumed to be the binding input (as for the first two estimates) the estimating equation is

$$\log CV = (1 - \lambda) \log CV_{-1} + a\lambda \, \log L + b\lambda \, \text{time} + \text{constant} + \text{disturbance}.$$

If real capital stock K is assumed to be the binding input (as for the last two estimates) the estimating equation is

$$\log CV = (1 - \lambda) \log CV_{-1} + a\lambda \, \log K + b + b\lambda \, \text{time} + \text{constant} + \text{disturbance},$$

where

$$K = K_{-1}(1 - d) + I_{-1},$$

where I is real investment and d is a constant depreciation rate (which was estimated in a maximum-likelihood scanning procedure).

[b] In the general-equilibrium model of Part III below, the real capacity of value added for transportation is given by the minimum of these two estimates under the assumption that there is no substitution possible between capital and labor.

Table 4.4

Maximum-likelihood estimates of sectoral CES capacity of real value added production functions, 1945–1965[a].

Sector	Coefficient of labor b	Coefficient of capital b'	Rate of Hicks-neutral technological change $r = r'$	ρ	Constant depreciation rate	Initial capital stock (in 10^3 1965 escudos)	$\bar{R}^2$ SE
	1	2	3	4	5	6	7
Agriculture	0.271 (43.0)	0.285 (4.9)	0.0	2.22	0.0333	62	0.58 171
Mining	0.827 (19.7)	0.50	0.028	0.96	0.0796	2980 (1.8)	0.56 100
Industry	0.956 (12.5)	0.305 (1.8)	0.017	0.315	0.0222	1700 (3.5)	0.98 86
Utilities	0.986 (32.2)	1.03 (3.3)	0.0	2.12	0.0263	82 (2.0)	0.86 23
Residual (construction, government and services)	1.07 (8.8)	3.32 (2.5)	0.0	0.73[b] (5.0)	0.0333	502 (4.3)	0.97 281

[a] Appendix A gives the data sources. The Goldfeld *et al.* (1966) maximum-likelihood procedure is used to estimate all of the parameters of relationship (4.1) for which t-values are indicated. The asymptotic t-values are under the point estimates (all of which are significantly non-zero at the 5% level). The parameters for which no t-value is given are set *a priori*. The rates of Hicks-neutral technological change and the ρ's (except for the residual sector) are constrained to equal those implied by the estimates in table 4.2. The initial capital stock in agriculture and the depreciation rates are from unpublished ODEPLAN sources.

[b] Implies an elasticity between capital and labor of 0.58.

The results presented in these tables may be summarized under four general observations.

(1) On an overall basis the models used appear to be reasonably satisfactory. The models are consistent with substantial portions of the variances in the dependent variables (although less so for agriculture and mining in table 4.4). The F-tests indicate that the relations are significantly non-zero at least at the 1% level.

(2) The results suggest that significantly non-zero exponential technological change occurred only in four sectors (in order of the estimated impact): mining, manufacturing, services, and transportation (if capital is the binding factor). As is noted above, one cannot distinguish in relation (4.3) between labor-augmenting and Hicks-neutral technological change (both of which are identical of course in the case of the semi-Cobb–Douglas form used for transportation). For mining, the sector for which by far the largest estimate of the coefficient of the time trend is obtained, however, the Chilean conventional wisdom suggests that this estimate probably includes substantial labor augmentation because the predominantly foreign-controlled (at least within the sample period) large mining companies reputedly paid relatively high wages and attempted to introduce labor-saving technology in a desire to limit the possibilities of politically sensitive labor conflicts occurring[13]. Also consistent with the Chilean conventional wisdom is the concentration of technological change in mining, industry, and transportation (although utilities might also be included in this category). The suggestion of relatively large technological change occurring in the service sector, however, is consistent neither with *a-priori* expectations nor with characterizations of the relative impact of technological change on services in other countries. This result may be a statistical fiction related to the relatively low estimate of the elasticity of substitution between capital and labor obtained for this sector and problems in the construction of the price index for services (see appendix A). To the extent that the time trend is better

[13] A labor-augmenting bias in technical change is a labor-saving innovation if, and only if, the elasticity of substitution between capital and labor is less than unity (see David and Van de Klundert, 1965, p. 362). The statement in the text is made under the assumption that this elasticity is less than one in the case of mining. This assumption is supported by the observation that the estimate of this coefficient in table 4.1 is significantly less than one at the 0.1% level. See Behrman (1971a) for some statistical evidence of the described behavior in mining.

correlated with the movements in the logarithm of the true ratio of
wages to prices than is the logarithm of the series actually used for
this ratio, for example, the surprisingly high and very significant
coefficient estimate of the time trend obtained in the service sector
may be representing movements in the logarithm of the true ratio.
Given the very heterogeneous composition of this sector, the
observed relative movements away from some low-skill occupations
(i.e. domestic service), and increases in the overall educational
levels, of course, the estimate may reflect true augmentation on the
average of labor in the service sector.

(3) The estimated adjustments vary across sectors in generally
reasonable patterns. In respect to the adjustment of the actual value
of the dependent variable towards the desired value thereof, the
sectors for which the adjustment coefficient is significantly less than
one (in order of increasing speed of adjustment) are government,
housing services, manufacturing, construction, agriculture, and
transportation (if labor is the binding factor). This ordering makes
some sense *a priori* in that the government is least subject to market
pressure for adjustment (although there are basic questions mentioned above in regard to the use of relation (4.3) for the government), housing services probably do adjust relatively slowly due to
long gestation periods in the financing and construction of homes,
and agricultural adjustments are limited by seasonal considerations.
The estimated slowness of the adjustment of industry in comparison
to agriculture, mining, utilities, and transportation, however, is
somewhat surprising. In respect to the adjustment in expectations of
the long-run wage–price ratio, the estimated patterns are illustrated
in fig. 4.1. For all sectors except agriculture and manufacturing the
estimated peak weight is for a lag of one year. Services and utilities
have complete adjustment after a one-year lag and – given the
nature of the overlap of the crop and calendar years – agriculture
has an adjustment which, effectively, is almost as rapid. Once again
the slowest adjusting sectors are the government and
manufacturing[14].

(4) The pattern of the estimates of the elasticities of substitution
across sectors suggest generally limited substitution possibilities

---

[14]These relative rates of speed of sectoral adjustment in regard to the capacity of
real value added seem to reflect generally the same patterns reported in Behrman
(1973c) for the adjustment of the rate of change of sectoral prices to the rate of
change of nominal money supply, real per capita income, and the exchange rate.

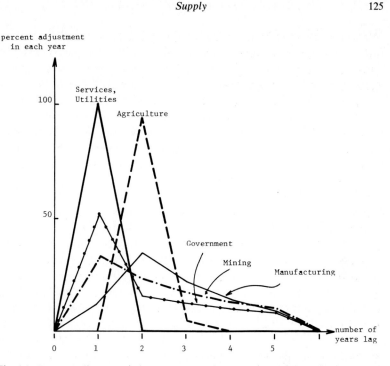

Fig. 4.1. Percent adjustment in long-run sectoral expectations of the ratio of wages to prices (based on the estimates of δ given in the last column of table 4.1 and the weighting procedure described in footnote 10).

even on this relatively aggregate level of estimation. In the short run, only mining among the six sectors included in table 4.2 (see column 3) has an estimate of this elasticity which is not significantly less than 0.50 at the 5% level, and only mining and utilities have estimates which are not significantly less than 0.40 at the same level[15]. The ordering of these short-run estimates (from highest to lowest) is as follows: mining, utilities, manufacturing, government, agriculture, and services. The ordering of the long-run estimates (column 7 in table 4.2) is government, manufacturing, mining, utilities, agriculture, and services[16]. Although this ordering bears no

[15]In no year in the sample, moreover, did the two sectors with relatively high estimated short-run elasticities of substitution account for as much as 10% of the total national capacity of real value added.

[16]The estimate for the combined residual sectors (i.e. construction, government and services) in table 4.4 would place them between manufacturing and mining in this ordering.

relation to the ordering of the sectors by their respective growth rates in the capacity of real value added over the sample, it is highly correlated with that for growth rates in the capacity of real value added per laborer over the sample[17]. Because of the adjustment process discussed above, the long-run elasticities of substitution are substantially greater than the short-run ones in the case of government, manufacturing, and agriculture. However, in order for this adjustment process to be 95% complete, nineteen, nine, and five years, respectively, must pass. Thus even in these three sectors, medium-term flexibility is limited.

How do the individual sector estimates compare with *a-priori* expectations or with other available estimates for developing economies? For agriculture, services, construction, and possibly government (in the short or medium run), the estimates for the Chilean elasticities of substitution are much lower than much of the discussion in the economic development literature seems to assume (alternative estimates, however, are not available)[18]. In part, this apparent discrepancy may only reflect a failure in many discussions to distinguish clearly between the degree of labor intensity and the degree of substitution possible between capital and labor. Also, in the relevant range of the production function for the relatively labor-intensive economies in much of the rest of the lesser-developed world, elasticities of substitution between capital and labor may be higher for these sectors (see fig. 4.2 for a possible isoquant). Nevertheless, these sectors are often characterized as residual sectors in respect that the absorption can occur only by driving the real wage down substantially or by accepting labor underemployment[19]. The literature on economic development suggests, however, that among the motivations for accepting such underemployment, paternalistic and familial obligations are relatively more important than in the case of labor hoarding in the developed economies.

---

[17]The ordering for the annual percentage growth rates in the capacity of real value added per laborer is as follows: manufacturing (2.6), government (2.1), services (2.1), mining (1.4), transportation (0.2), and construction (0.1). In an intramanufacturing sector study of Argentina, Katz (1969, p. 187) reports a similar correlation.

[18]One exception to this comment is McCabe's (1970) discussion of the Turkish construction industry in which he maintains that the elasticity of substitution is very low, at least between skilled labor and other factors.

[19]This section has tried to abstract from the cyclical component of such labor absorption by focusing on longer-run aspects of relation (4.3).

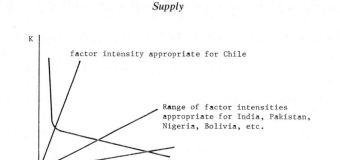

Fig. 4.2. Isoquant to illustrate possibilities of widely differing elasticities of substitution at various factor intensities.

For transportation, one might expect the elasticity of substitution to be lower the more this sector depends upon modern mechanical modes for which the elasticity of substitution between capital and labor is low. In the case of Chile such a dependence apparently is substantial, and no significantly non-zero estimate of the elasticity of interest could be obtained. I am aware of but one other estimate for such a sector in a developing country – McCabe's (1970) estimate for Turkey which is significantly non-zero, but very small (0.10–0.13) in the long run.

For utilities, substitution appears more possible than in the above sectors in respect to some components such as water distribution, but no more so in respect to other components such as electricity production and distribution. The estimate suggests that the existence of the former component results in a measured higher elasticity of substitution on the sector level of aggregation than in the case of the above sectors. No comparable estimates are available from other developing economies.

For mining and (at least in the long run) manufacturing, the Chilean estimates are somewhat high in comparison with *a-priori* expectations and with the other existing estimates for developing countries. Both of these sectors have large modern components in which largely imported technology is utilized and for which the elasticity of substitution between capital and labor has generally been assumed to be low relative to sectors such as agriculture and services. The estimates, however, suggest the opposite pattern. For mining, the only other available estimates are those presented by McCabe (1970) for Turkey, which are very small and generally not significantly non-zero. For Turkish manufacturing, McCabe gives some short-run estimates higher than the Chilean short-run estimate, but in none of these alternative aggregations or formulations is the long-run estimate nearly as high as that for Chile. For Argentine manufacturing (on both a sectoral and a more disaggregate level), Katz (1969, pp. 47–50, 59, 63–64) presents cross-section estimates which tend to be higher and time-series estimates which tend to be lower than the long-run Chilean estimate. Argentine time-series estimates on the sector level of aggregation, however, apparently are not significantly different from the short-run Chilean estimate (and, by the criterion used in this study, Katz's estimates are short-run estimates). For Peruvian manufacturing (on a more dis-aggregate level), Clague (1969) gives cross-section estimates which for the most part are lower than the long-run Chilean estimates. Because of the different approaches used in these other studies (e.g. the use of cross-section data, the use of more disaggregate data which would seem to lead to lower estimates in time-series analysis, and the failure to attempt to abstract from problems of transitory fluctuations which may lead to underestimates), placing great weight on these comparisons does not seem justified. To the present author, however, these comparisons do not suggest that obviously the order of magnitude of the Chilean estimates is very suspicious.

4.1.3. *The aggregate Chilean elasticity of substitution between capital and labor*

For some considerations the economy-wide elasticity of substitution between capital and labor is of interest. A (non-constant) national elasticity of substitution can be obtained by working with the production function which is the sum of all the estimated relations in table 4.4.

An alternative is to ignore the substantial aggregation problems and to estimate relation (4.3) on an economy-wide basis. The results of such a procedure, however, are not very satisfactory in the sense that the estimates are not robust under relatively minor specification changes. That the sectoral composition changed over the sample period suggests that one major problem with this procedure is the assumption of a CES function on the economy-wide level, since even if the sectoral functions are CES the economy-wide function is not, because sectoral growth rates have varied (column 2 in table

4.1). A relationship identical to relation (4.3) except that the constant elasticity of substitution is replaced by one with a linear time trend included, therefore is also explored. Although the results are more robust, they are not satisfactory because the time trend in the elasticity of substitution between capital and labor is sufficiently negative to make the elasticity itself negative by the end of the sample period. Although one could always think of alternative functional specifications to investigate, I decided that the expected returns from further exploration did not merit the effort given the data limitations and the apparent aggregation problems. If the problems encountered do originate in the aggregation in the small Chilean economy, then the attempts to estimate economy-wide production functions for much larger and apparently more diversified economies such as that of the United States are even more demanding in terms of the assumptions required.

As a final alternative in order to obtain a somewhat better idea of the order of magnitude of the Chilean aggregate elasticity of substitution between capital and labor, a weighted average (with the sectoral proportions of the capacity of real value added as weights) of the sectoral long-run elasticities is calculated. Given the relatively high estimate for industry and the government, and the general tendency for these sectors to increase their shares of value added as per capita income increases[20], *a-priori* one might expect some positive trend in such a weighted average. In fact, this weighted average ranges from 0.32 to 0.36, with its maximum value occurring relatively early in the sample period in 1952 because the steady increase in the government share is only supplemented to a limited extent by the very small relative increase in the industrial share, and eventually is offset by the decline in relative shares of mining and agriculture. In any case, the variations over time implied by this procedure are not substantial, and the result suggests a lower aggregate Chilean elasticity of substitution between capital and labor than has been estimated in the majority of the available attempts for the United States[21].

---

[20]Chenery and Taylor (1968) and Kuznets (1966).
[21]The estimates for the United States, however, have substantial variance. See Nerlove (1967, pp. 93–94).

4.1.4. Implications of the estimates

What insights in respect to the considerations listed in ch. 1 does this section provide?

(1) The estimates imply that the degree of flexibility in responses to changes such as occur in international markets is limited in the Chilean case. For some of the sectors for which long-run flexibility in respect to the substitution between capital and labor apparently is relatively great, moreover, effectively complete adjustment towards the long-run values may take five to ten years or even longer. The structuralist emphasis on limited flexibility, particularly in agriculture, is also given some support[22].

(2) The generally low values of the estimated elasticities of substitution together with the long adjustment periods in several cases provide support for Eckaus' (1955) technological (whether real or only incorrectly perceived due to imitation of more advanced economies) explanation of the existence of under or unemployed labor. In some sectors some substitution can occur, but substantial (and perhaps unlikely) relative wage changes may be required in order to absorb a large increment of laborers if competitive-like behavior is maintained. The results suggest, however, that the sectors which are generally thought to serve as the predominant absorbers of surplus labor are among those with the most limited estimated technical possibilities of substituting labor for capital (i.e. services and construction and – in the short and medium run – agriculture and government). On the other hand – and contrary to Clague's (1969) claim for Peru – manufacturing has a relatively high estimated capacity for such substitution. Under the assumptions that this labor is homogeneous[23] and overabundant at inflexible wages, and that capital is constraining production, society might benefit from wage subsidies (or other inducements) given to sectors such as industry and mining so that the sectors in which labor has a relatively high marginal productivity absorb the surplus instead of the traditional sectors in which labor has relatively low marginal productivity.

[22]Generally, however, Chilean agriculture does not seem to be as rigid as the structuralists assert. See Behrman (1973a).
[23]Within a linear programming framework Clark and Foxley (1970) explore some implications of the assumption of heterogeneous labor in the Chilean case. Yoon (1974) has some interesting results about the limited degree of substitution between skilled and unskilled labor on a cross-country basis.

(3) The results suggest that an assumed linear technology is not a tremendously distorting assumption for the substitution between capital and labor in most sectors. This assumption is brought into question most of all by these results, however, in the case of two sectors – mining and manufacturing – for which it has been least questioned traditionally. Of course it is possible that in these sectors the elasticities of substitution between capital and labor in reality are much smaller on the more disaggregate level at which many linear planning studies are conducted, but that changes in the mix among these more disaggregated components result in the relatively high estimates of this study.

(4) The results certainly imply that the aggregate Chilean elasticity of substitution between capital and labor is less than one so that, under neoclassical assumptions, the relatively quickly growing primary factor decreases its factor share. According to the fragmentary available evidence, over the sample the capital stock grew more quickly than the labor force, and the factor share of labor apparently indeed increased.

(5) The Chilean aggregate elasticity of substitution between capital and labor probably is relatively low, which may constrain growth if the rates of increase of the primary factors are substantially different. The relatively high estimate for manufacturing, however, suggests that more dynamic flexibility in this sense may be gained if the government succeeds in its apparent policy of encouraging the relative growth of this sector[24].

4.2. The long-run allocation of labor and capital among sectors

4.2.1. The secular distribution of the labor force

Table 4.1 gives the mean distribution among sectors and the mean growth rates for both labor and average labor productivity during the 1945–1965 sample period (columns 3–6). Almost three-quarters of the labor force was concentrated in three sectors – agriculture,

[24]This statement is contrary in spirit to that which Nerlove (1967, p. 57) makes about shifts towards manufacturing because he assumes that the elasticities of substitution between capital and labor are high in primary as compared to secondary and tertiary industries.

other services, and industry. None of these three sectors had mean labor force growth rates above the national average, however, so these two decades had some increase in the dispersion of the labor force. Construction was by far the most rapidly growing sectoral employer of labor.

The high average labor productivity sectors were mining, transportation, other services, and utilities. Manufacturing also was slightly above the national mean. Agriculture and construction were far below the overall average. With the exception of transportation and possibly of the government, relative changes in average labor productivity tended to increase the dispersion during the sample period – in contrast to the hypothesis of Kuznets (1966) and others about the narrowing of differentials among labor productivities with development. The associations between secular labor movements and either levels or changes in average labor productivities, finally, are not simple ones characterized by high zero-order correlations (e.g. the fastest-growing employer – construction – had the lowest mean level and rate of change in average labor productivity).

Within the model of Part III the sectoral distribution of labor is generally determined by the assumption of competitive-like behavior in the long run on the demand side. Therefore relation (4.3) is solved for each sector to obtain the secular labor force for that sector[25]. The secular labor supply is assumed to be exogenous[26]. Since agriculture and services are widely hypothesized to absorb surplus labor, any discrepancies between the total secular labor demand and the total labor supply are allocated to these two sectors (with the division of the residual between them determined by the relative size of their respective predicted labor demands)[27].

[25]Table 4.2 gives those estimates for six sectors. Table 4.3 gives the estimates for construction. There is no labor used in housing. The secular trend in the labor force in transportation is assumed to depend only on the capital stock in that sector, since there is no evidence of significant substitution between capital and labor in this case:

$$L = 0.995K + 129.3,$$
$$(6.1) \quad (9.0)$$
$$\bar{R}^2 = 0.998, \quad SE = 0.870, \quad DW = 1.1, \quad \rho = 0.95, \quad 1951–1965.$$

[26]In simulation 8.4.4, however, the size of the total labor force is endogenous.
[27]In simulation 8.4.5 manufacturing absorbs any surplus labor instead of agriculture and services.

4.2.2. *The secular distribution of the capital stock*

This is determined among sectors by sectoral real physical capital investment decisions and sectoral depreciation rates. Once investment is made in a particular sector, it is assumed not to be possible to shift the resulting capital stock to another sector.

The available data permit the exploration of Chilean investment behavior in the postwar period for six sectors: agriculture, mining, manufacturing, transportation, utilities, and housing. Table 4.1 gives the mean distribution of investment among sectors and the ratio of the standard deviation of investment to the mean within sectors for the sample period (columns 7 and 8). These data indicate that in order of the size of real gross physical capital investment the sectors were housing, manufacturing, transportation, utilities, agriculture, and mining. In order of the size of the standard deviation of real gross physical capital investment normalized by the means, the ordering is mining, utilities, agriculture, transportation, manufacturing, and housing. Thus, housing, manufacturing, and transportation have accounted for a substantial proportion (75% over the sample) of the total real gross physical capital investment, although at least in a relative sense the variances in the real gross physical capital investment in these three sectors have been small. For the foreign-controlled (at least during the sample) mining sector, in contrast, the relative fluctuations in real gross physical capital investment have been rather large.

Examination of columns 7 and 13 in table 4.1 suggests that in order of the gross (ignoring depreciation and obsolescence) incremental capital–output ratios over the sample, the sectors are utilities, housing, transportation, manufacturing, mining, and agriculture. Such an ordering is consistent with that usually assumed in the development literature (i.e. high incremental capital–output ratios in housing and in the social overhead areas). Finally, these same two columns indicate that the six sectors for which investment data are available have been much more dominant in total real gross physical capital investment (accounting for 92% of the total in the sample) than in total real product (accounting for 55% of the total in the sample). An examination of the determinants of real gross physical capital investment in these six sectors, therefore, is almost equivalent to an examination of the determinants of real gross physical capital investment in the Chilean economy, but is far from a determination of the total real productive capacity in the Chilean economy because of the large relatively non-capital-intensive construction, services, and government sectors. These last three sectors are combined in one category for the estimation of investment functions which are discussed below[28].

4.2.2.1. The model

Under general putty–putty assumptions[29], real gross physical capital investment is the sum of real net investment and real replacement investment:

$$I^G = I^N + I^R, \tag{4.5}$$

where I^G is the real gross physical capital investment, I^N is the real net physical capital investment, and I^R is the real replacement physical capital investment.

Real net physical capital investment is hypothesized to depend upon changes in the desired real physical capital stock with a distributed lag adjustment over $n + 1$ periods because of lags in the decision-making and implementation processes:

$$I^N = \sum_{i=0}^{n} a_i \Delta K_{t-i}^D, \tag{4.6}$$

where K^D is the desired real physical capital stock.

One would expect the sum of the weights in the lag adjustment to be one if any change desired real physical capital stock is eventually to result in net investment of exactly the same magnitude:

$$\sum_{i=0}^{n} a_i = 1. \tag{4.6a}$$

[28]In the model of Part III total investment in these three sectors is assumed to affect total production capacity (as given by the function in table 4.4). This aggregate capacity is then subdivided among the sectors by the distributed lag adjustments to capacity utilization and the relative share in *GDP* which are given in note 12 on p. 120.

[29]Behrman (1972b) gives earlier estimates of both 'putty–putty' and 'putty–clay' real sectoral investment functions for the Chilean economy. One conclusion of that study is that the putty–clay formulation is less satisfactory for this data base. I have also explored models dependent on liquidity, but the results are not of interest. Therefore this subsection reports only the putty–putty model estimates. For discussions of these underlying models, see Behrman (1972b), Bischoff (1969 and 1971), Coen (1968, 1969, and 1971), Eisner (1960, 1967, and 1969a and 1969b), Eisner and Nadiri (1968), Eisner and Strotz (1963), Fisher (1971), Hall and Jorgenson (1967, 1969, and 1971), Helliwell (1971), Jorgenson (1963, 1965 and 1971), Jorgenson and Siebert (1968), Jorgenson and Stephenson (1967a and 1967b), Klein (1974) and Klein and Taubman (1971).

The desired real physical capital stock is assumed to depend primarily on neoclassical investment behavior[30]. In contrast to the assumption of Jorgenson and his various collaborators, however, the underlying technology is not assumed to be only Cobb–Douglas. Instead, the more general assumption is made of a CES production function with constant returns to scale and with Hicks-neutral technological change[31]:

$$K^D = b(P/P_K)^\sigma V^{e^{r(\sigma-1)t}} \exp[r(\sigma-1)t], \qquad (4.7)$$

where P is the price of output; P_K is the price of capital services[32]; V is the real output (value-added); σ is the elasticity of substitution between capital and labor; r is the rate of Hicks-neutral exponential technological change; and b is the constant[33]. If the elasticity of substitution between capital and labor is one, this formulation reduces to that used by Jorgenson. If the elasticity of substitution between capital and labor is zero, this formulation reduces to the accelerator model used by Eisner and others[34]. In the present subsection this formulation is used with the elasticity of substitution and the rate of technological change constrained *ex ante* to the estimates given in section 4.2. Possible modifications of the desired capital stock due either to underutilization of capacity (section 4.3) or to variance in the product price relative to the overall price level (section 7.1) also explored by the addition of linear terms to represent such considerations:

$$K^D = b(P/P_K)^\sigma V \exp[r(\sigma-1)t] + c(V/CV) + dSD(P/P_{GDP}), \qquad (4.7a)$$

where CV is the capacity of real output (value-added), $SD(X)$ is the

[30]See the references to articles by Jorgenson and various collaborators in note 29.

[31]This is consistent with relation (4.1) above under the assumption that $r = r'$. Among the studies listed in note 29, Behrman (1972b), Bischoff (1969, 1971) and Coen (1968, 1969, 1971) start with the more general CES production function instead of the special Cobb–Douglas case.

[32]The price of capital services depends on the price of investment goods, the cost of capital, and the tax structure. See Jorgenson and Siebert (1968, p. 695). In the present study, capital gains are not included explicitly in the price of capital services, because the cost of capital series utilized better approximates the real than the nominal cost of capital and thus represents the general effect of inflation. The impact of sector-specific price deviations from the general inflation is included in the last term in relation (4.7a).

[33]The constant depends on the elasticity of substitution between capital and labor, the scale parameter γ which denotes the initial efficiency of the technology, and the capital intensity parameter δ: $b = \gamma^{\sigma-1}\delta^\sigma$.

[34]See the references in note 29 to articles by Eisner and various collaborators.

standard deviation of X over three periods $(t, t - 1, t - 2)$, and P_{GDP} is the deflator for *GDP*. If the degree of capacity utilization is relevant in the real desired capital decision, the coefficient of the first additional variable should be positive and significantly non-zero. If expectations of the standard deviation of product prices relative to the overall price level are relevant and are represented sufficiently well by the above formulation, and if risk aversion is predominant, the coefficient of the second additional variable should be negative and significantly non-zero. Finally, when relation (4.7a) is substituted back into relation (4.6), the possibility of differential patterns of lagged adjustment to the different components of the desired real physical capital stock is allowed in the estimates given below.

In the general putty–putty model real replacement physical capital investment is given according to two alternative considerations.

(1) If capital (and other factors) is really malleable (i.e. complete putty–putty), then it would seem to make no difference whether gross investment were for replacement or for net capital stock addition purposes. In either case the same range of alternatives would be available, and the formulation discussed above for real net physical capital investment would seem to be equally appropriate for real replacement physical capital investment. In such a case one could not distinguish between the determinants of net and of replacement real physical capital investment.

(2) If replacement options are limited due to fixed characteristics of surviving capital or of other factors in the same process (i.e. partial putty–putty or putty–putty in net investment but not in replacement investment), replacement needs may be determined directly by the depreciation of the existing real physical capital stock[35]. Due to lags in the decision-making and implementation processes, once again real replacement physical capital investment in any one period may depend on the needs so generated for several m periods (perhaps as modified by the state of technology for the period in which the real replacement physical capital investment actually occurs). Because of the very limited information available about the size of the capital stock at any point in time for the data cells of the present study, the capacity of real output (corrected for the state of technology at the time the investment occurs by the same factor as is included in

[35]This is the procedure generally followed by Jorgenson and his collaborators in the studies referred to in note 29.

relation (4.7) above) is used as a proxy for the real physical capital stock:

$$I^R = \left(\sum_{i=0}^{m} f_i CV_i \right) \exp\left[r(\sigma - 1)t\right].$$
(4.8)

For estimation purposes in this second alternative, relation (4.8) is substituted into relation (4.5) together with the appropriate representation of real net physical capital investment[36].

In addition to the net and replacement investment variables discussed to this point, two additional factors are sometimes hypothesized to affect Chilean investment decisions: (1) government real direct and financial investments (equal to 53% of total investment in 1945–1965), and (2) investment goods imports (equal to 28% of total investment in 1945–1965)[37]. Therefore, variables related to these factors are included as additive terms in the investment regressions.

4.2.2.2. *Sectoral investment estimates*
Table 4.5 presents estimates of the model of the previous subsection for the six sectors for which investment data is available. Relation (4.9) is a similar estimate for the residual category which includes construction, service and the government:

$$I^G = 0.487 I^G_{-1} + 0.0969\Delta(V_{-1}) - 526.R[P_{GDP}]$$
(4.9)
$$\qquad (3.8) \qquad (1.8) \qquad\qquad (3.5)$$
$$- 504.DUMMY + 0.216MK_{-1} - 3885.QRFD + 3609.,$$
$$\quad (6.9) \qquad\qquad (1.9) \qquad\qquad (3.5) \qquad\qquad (3.5)$$
$$\bar{R}^2 = 0.84, \qquad SE = 80.2, \qquad DW = 2.4, \qquad 1950–1965,$$

---

[36]The available data do not permit the separation of sectoral gross investment into replacement and net components. Therefore, this substitution is made so that gross investment can be used as the dependent variable.

Aggregate depreciation estimates are available in the national accounts. For the general-equilibrium model of Part III below the following relationship for aggregate depreciation is used:

$$D = 1.220D^* + 433, \qquad \bar{R}^2 = 0.54, \qquad SE = 225, \qquad DW = 2.3, \qquad 1945–1965,$$
$$\quad (4.9) \qquad (2.5)$$

where D is the aggregate depreciation in real terms; and D^* is the depreciation calculated on the basis of sectoral exponential depreciation rates and sectoral capital stocks (based, in turn, on the estimates in table 4.4).

[37]The proportion of total investment accounted for by imported machinery and equipment varies substantially across sectors (see the last column of the second part of table 6.6 below).

Table 4.5
Chilean real physical capital sectoral investment functions, 1945–1965[a].

Sector	Elasticity of substitution	Replacement investment[b]		Δ Desired capital stock[b]							Government direct and indirect real investment		Imported investment goods[c]		Constant	$\bar{R}^2$ SE DW
				Neoclassical term			Capacity utilization		Standard deviation of relative prices							
		1	2	1	2	3	1	2	1	2	0	1	0	1		
Agriculture	0.00[d]	140.0 (3.6)	−29.0 (3.6)	−12.8 (1.9)					0.875 (3.1)		0.0511 (3.9) [0.7]	0.0269 (1.9)	0.0404 (1.1)[e] [0.2]		−75.2 (1.8)	0.95 8.7 2.9
Mining	0.51	191.0 (1.9)		−94.6 (1.6)[f]	12.1 (1.3)[e]		−2.06 (1.9)	0.349 (1.5)[f]	6.21 (2.7)	−0.448 (3.2)					63.5 (8.6)	0.42 33.0 1.4
Industry	0.76	−461.0 (1.9)	89.6 (1.9)	−13.3 (1.5)[f]	0.573 (1.2)[e]				3.94 (1.6)[f]		0.224 (1.4)[f] [0.5]				−279.0 (1.9)	0.60 75.0 2.2
Transportation	0.00	−93.9 (2.6)							−10.9 (2.9)	2.76 (3.3)	0.0966 (1.2)[3] [0.3]	0.152* (2.3)			−700.0 (2.2)	0.92 42.0 2.4
Utilities	0.32				64.9 (2.1)	−15.4 (2.2)					0.0681 (4.2) [0.5]	0.148* (9.8)	0.0498 (1.8) [0.1]		25.0 (2.8)	0.97 12.0 1.6
Housing	0.00						5.38 (3.5)	−0.296 (3.5)			0.138* (2.7) [0.1]				491.0 (22.8)	0.54 78.0 1.9

[a] Appendix A gives the data sources. The absolute value of the t-statistics are given in parentheses beneath the point estimates. All point estimates are significantly non-zero at the 5% level unless otherwise noted. Long-run elasticities at the point of sample means are given in brackets for the variables for which the Hall–Sutch polynomial method is not used.

[b]The Hall–Sutch (1969) polynomial method with the tail constrained to zero is used for replacement investment and for change in desired capital stock variables (the numbers at the column heads refer to the degree of the relevant polynomials). The implied lag structures are as follows:

Lags	-0	-1	-2	-3	Σ
Agriculture:replacement					
neoclassical term	-0.0964	0.0147	0.0677	0.0629	0.0489
standard deviation	0.0512	0.0384	0.0256	0.0128	0.128
	-3.50	-2.63	-1.75	-0.875	-8.75
Mining:neoclassical term	-0.0248	0.0841	0.0762	0.0241	0.160
capacity utilization	265.	94.2	-6.9	-38.3	0.314
standard deviation	381.	957.	1265.	1035.	3637.
Industry:replacement	0.410	0.039	-0.153	-0.166	0.129
neoclassical term	0.0167	0.0039	-0.0054	-0.0079	0.0072
standard deviation	-15.8	-11.8	-7.89	-3.94	-39.4
Transportation:replacement	0.378	0.282	0.188	0.094	0.939
standard deviation	-0.68	-8.81	-11.4	-8.47	-29.4
Utilities:neoclassical term	-0.0513	-0.0019	0.0848	0.116	0.148
Housing:capacity utilization	-258.	251	532.	557.	1132.

[c]The numbers at the column heads refer to lags in the indicated variable.

[d]An elasticity of substitution of 0.31 actually was used, but in exploration of a putty–clay type hypothesis the neoclassical term was split into quantity and price components. Since the coefficients of the latter were not significantly non-zero even at the 25% level the price component was dropped. With only a quantity component the model reduced to what it would be with an elasticity of substitution equal to 0.0.

[e]Significantly non-zero at the 15% level.

[f]Significantly non-zero at the 10% level.

[g]Current-year value for 1960 onwards (included due to change in data definition for the government direct and indirect real investment).

where I^G is the real physical capital gross domestic investment in the residual sectors, V is the real *GDP* in the residual sectors, $R[P_{GDP}]$ is the rate of growth of the *GDP* deflator, *DUMMY* is a dummy variable for data definition problems in 1954 and 1959, *MK* is real capital goods imports, and *QRFD* is the Ffrench-Davis (1971) quantitative restrictions index for the foreign sector.

Examination of the results in table 4.5 and in relation 4.9 suggests that on an overall level the model is satisfactory. There is no evidence of serious problems of serial correlation, the coefficients generally have the *a-priori* anticipated signs (although in some cases the estimated lag structure includes some unexpected signs, especially at endpoints), and the corrected coefficients of determination indicate that the specification is quite consistent with variations in the dependent variable for utilities, agriculture, transportation, and the residual sectors – although less so for manufacturing and housing, and even less so for mining. Note that this ordering implies that the model is least consistent with investment decisions in the two relatively modern sectors of manufacturing and mining, and in housing. The quite limited success in mining probably reflects the special characteristics of that sector: the bilateral bargaining between the government and foreign-owned large-scale mining, the subsidization of small- and medium-scale mining, that the foreign owners of large-scale mining (at least Anaconda) reputedly operated so as to maintain their international market share independent of short- and medium-term fluctuations, and that for the foreign owners of large-scale mining the basic question was whether to expand capacity in Chile or elsewhere, the answer to which depended much more on expectations of political events than on the considerations embodied in the specification utilized[38]. The relatively limited success in housing probably also reflects the existence of special determinants in this sector, and particularly serious problems with the price indices for housing because of rent control.

The other features of these estimates are considered in the same order as discussed in subsection 4.2.2.1.

(1) Significant coefficients for some aspect of the change in the desired capital stock are obtained for every sector. Responses to the neoclassical term are significant in agriculture, mining, industry,

---

[38]For details concerning these characteristics, see Behrman (1975b, subsections 4.2.1 and 7.1.2.3).

utilities, and the residual category. Capacity utilization is important in mining and housing. Uncertainty affects investment decisions in agriculture, mining, industry and housing.

(2) 'Partial putty–putty' responses to replacement considerations are significant in agriculture, industry, transportation, and the residual category. For the other three sectors the results are consistent with a 'complete putty–putty' model in which there is sufficient flexibility so that no significant distinction can be made between the factors determining replacement investment and those influencing net investment.

(3) The results suggest that government direct and indirect investment has significantly non-zero and rather substantial effects in the infrastructure sectors of transportation, utilities, and housing, and in the goods-producing sectors of agriculture and industry. The implied distribution of government investment across sectors, with most overall emphasis on industry, but increased relative emphasis on infrastructure under Alessandri in the early 1960s, also seems consistent with the historical patterns of such investment.

(4) Imported investment goods have a significantly non-zero coefficient for the residual sectors (as does the quantitative-restrictions index), utilities, and agriculture (but only at the 15% level for the last of these). The evidence for a strong *direct* impact of the foreign sector on real physical capital investment in Chile through imports as hypothesized by Mamalakis (1971b) and others, thus seems weak[39,40]. The indirect effects through the price system and through capacity-utilization rates apparently have been more important.

4.2.2.3. *Implications of investment estimates*
Although questions have been raised recently about the widely assumed dominance of real physical capital stock investment in the economic development process, the importance of real physical capital stock as one of the major factors in development is still generally accepted. The question of what determines real physical capital investment behavior in developing countries, therefore, is a

---

[39]The evidence seems surprisingly weak given that the sectoral investment series are based in part on data for imported investment goods.

[40]Investment in mining, of course, has depended much more directly on the foreign sector than investment in other production sectors. See Behrman (1975b, subsections 4.2.1, 7.1.2.3, 8.2.1).

very important one. Estimates of real physical capital stock investment functions on the sectoral level for the postwar Chilean
experience imply that this experience has been substantially consistent with the putty–putty type of investment behavior models which
have been used for developed economies. Evidence has been
presented of the fairly widespread significance in Chilean real
investment behavior of real replacement needs, of neoclassical
considerations based on a CES production function, of higher
moments of the subjective probability function as represented by the
standard deviation of prices, of government direct and financial
investment, and, to a lesser extent, of capacity utilization considerations and of imported capital goods.

These partial-equilibrium results, therefore, suggest that government policies can induce increased real physical capital investment,
including that in the key sector of manufacturing, by increasing the
price of output relative to the price of capital services through
reductions in the cost of capital or in the effective direct business tax
rate, through increases in depreciation allowances or investment tax
credits, and through foreign sector policy. Direct and indirect
government investment also has widespread impact. Government
fiscal, monetary, and foreign sector policies which increase the
degree of capacity utilization and reduce uncertainty, moreover, may
result in increased real physical capital investment in various
sectors[41].

4.3. Sectoral capacity utilization determinants [42]

In the first two postwar decades the emphasis in development
literature and policy recommendations was on the creation of
capacity. Recently, growing attention has been paid to capacity
utilization rates, primarily because the utilization rates of something
like rated capacity in the manufacturing sectors of many developing
economies are substantially below the utilization rates for the

[41]At times in the past, however, some policies have worked in the opposite direction.
For example, Behrman (1975b) shows that the government treatment of investment
goods as postponable at times of foreign-exchange crises has resulted in more variance
(and therefore more uncertainty) in the relative price of investment goods than for any
other category.
[42]The first part of this section draws on material in Behrman (1973b).

developed economies[43]. The very procedure of comparing such utilization rates between less and more developed economies, however, seems to reflect the assumption that the really important constraint on production is the stock of physical capital (on which the rated capacity depends), and other currently binding constraints can be loosened relatively cheaply and should be loosened. But as Winston (1969) emphasizes in respect to the possibility of increasing rated capacity utilization through an increase in the number of shifts, the costs of loosening the non-physical capital constraints may be considerable at least in the short run[44].

The question of fluctuations in the degree of capacity utilization within these (short-run, at least) binding non-physical capital con- straints in developing countries is a question on which relatively little attention has been focused. The pervasive assumption in the develop- ment literature is that the benefits likely to be obtained from attention to fluctuations in the utilization of historically attained capacity are not sufficient to warrant the costs. Indeed, attention has been focused on physical capital accumulation, on removing non-physical capital constraints so that higher utilization of rated capacity can be attained, on 'big pushes', and on 'minimum critical efforts'[45]. This section focuses on the question of fluctuations in the degree of utilization of historically attained levels of production in the developing economy of postwar Chile in order to explore the empirical evidence relevant to these issues and to provide a critical component of the complete system model of Part III.

The 'trends-through-the-peaks' method[46] is used to define histori- cally attainable capacities of real *GDP* for the nine sectors included in table 4.1. This method of estimating capacity does take into account the non-physical capital considerations which historically have limited peak production to levels substantially below rated values. This method also has the advantage of not demanding nearly as extensive data as do most alternatives[47] and thus of being

[43]For example, see UNIDO (1969) and Winston (1969).
[44]Klein (1960, p. 274) makes the same point when he emphasizes that rated capacities refer to technical limitations and not to economic considerations.
[45]In addition to references cited in ch. 1, see Inada (1968), Leibenstein (1957), and Rao (1952).
[46]See Behrman (1973), Klein and Summers (1966), Phillips (1963), and the Phillips article in UNIDO (1969).
[47]Alternative measurements of capacity are discussed in the Phillips references cited in note 46.

applicable over a fairly long time period and of being applicable to sectors other than manufacturing. On the other hand, even for the purpose at hand, this method has several limitations.

(1) There is an aggregation problem, because even at a sectoral peak some components of a particular sector may not be operating at their peak level. For example, suppose that a given sector is composed of two components A and B that have full capacity outputs of 100 and 50, respectively, but whose time paths of utilization are not highly correlated, as is illustrated in fig. 4.3. The trends-through-the-peaks method of estimation of the level of capacity utilization for the sector, therefore, may be biased downward considerably, as is indicated in this figure, even though it would be fine for measuring the capacity of the components of the sector[48]. If the rates of utilization of the subcomponents of each sector are not more highly correlated than are the rates of utilization of the sectoral aggregates (see the discussion of table 4.6 below) this bias may be quite substantial[49].

(2) Even ignoring the aggregation problems, as Phillips (1963, p. 290) notes there is no reason to believe that every peak in the time

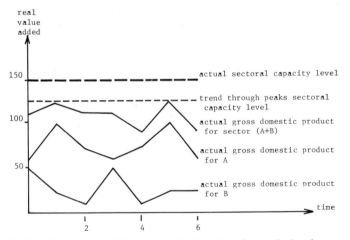

Fig. 4.3. Possible downward bias in trend through peaks methods of measuring capacity utilization due to aggregation problems.

---

[48]As should be clear, aggregation problems might lead to errors in the measurement of directions of trends of capacity levels and not only in the levels themselves.

[49]For further discussion of aspects of the aggregation problem in the use of such a procedure, see Summers (1968).

Table 4.6
Simple correlation coefficients among Chilean sectoral real *GDP* utilization rates over the 1945–1965 period[a].

	A	M	C	M	T	U	H	G	O	Total
Agriculture	1.00									
Mining	−0.20	1.00								
Construction	0.08	−0.21	1.00							
Manufacturing	0.02	−0.14	−0.04	1.00						
Transportation	0.14	−0.23	0.41	−0.13	1.00					
Utilities	0.09	−0.22	−0.12	0.54	0.00	1.00				
Housing services	−0.09	0.17	−0.38	0.31	0.09	0.53	1.00			
Government	−0.14	0.04	−0.08	0.24	−0.04	−0.03	0.22	1.00		
Other services	0.08	0.61	−0.10	−0.22	0.11	−0.24	0.23	0.27	1.00	
Total	0.19	0.52	−0.05	0.27	0.27	0.14	0.55	0.41	0.80	1.00

[a] Data sources are given in appendix A. A correlation coefficient with an absolute value of 0.42 or greater is significantly non-zero at the 5% level.

series necessarily reflects full capacity utilization in the sense desired. For example, suppose that the real capacity level is given by the dashed line in fig. 4.4, but that the trend-through-the-peaks measure of capacity is given by the dotted line because period five is wrongly thought to be a year of full capacity utilization by the appropriate criteria[50]. Once again a downward bias in the estimated level of capacity may result.

(3) In a somewhat different vein, efficiency implications of full capacity utilization so defined are not clear. In a world without external effects, production by each firm at the minimum point of its long-run average cost curve would be efficient, but (ignoring the aggregation problem) there is no reason for a specific relation to exist between full utilization as defined by the trend-through-the-peaks method and any particular point on long-run average cost curves.

These limitations – especially in regard to the probable downward bias in the estimation of the capacity levels – should be kept in mind in the discussion below.

Tables 4.1 (columns 9–14) and 4.6 summarize characteristics of

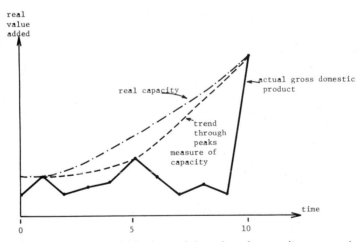

Fig. 4.4. Possible downward bias in trend through peaks capacity measure due to false identification of peak in period five with full utilization.

[50]Such a downward bias is especially liable to occur for periods near the end of the sample. In the case of the Wharton trends-through-the-peaks capacity utilization index for the United States, Summers (1968, pp. 31–32) finds that the estimate of the capacity level has been biased down near the end of the sample, but the estimates of changes in the utilization rates have not been so biased.

Chilean total and sectoral capacity utilization rates based on the trend-through-the-peaks method for annual data for the 1945–1965 period. On the global level the rates of utilization have ranged from 88 to 100% with a mean of 93% and a standard deviation of 1%. If capacity had been fully utilized at historically attainable levels, therefore, actual output could have been an average of 8% per year higher than it actually was. Or, alternatively, the foregone output over the 21 years was equal to the actual mean production of over 17 months (1.45 years). Given that these estimates of the output foregone probably are biased downwards, the benefits of fully utilizing the available capacity would have been considerable. Even ignoring the probable downward bias in this estimate of the benefits, the increased national product that could be obtained if capacity utilization were increased from its mean actual value of 0.93 to full utilization would be greater than the increase in national product that could be obtained if the same rate of capacity utilization were maintained and capacity expanded for two years at the mean annual exponential growth rate of capacity actually experienced over the period[51].

In the previous paragraph the once-and-for-all gains of an increase in the rate of capacity utilization are emphasized. But one should not conclude that the gains are limited to those of a once-and-for-all nature. A simple Harrod–Domar framework provides an example to the contrary. Within this framework an increase in the average rate of capacity utilization is like an increase in the marginal savings rate or a decrease in the marginal capital–output ratio in that it increases the equilibrium rate of growth permanently (Winston, 1969, pp. 2–3).

On the sectoral level, rates of capacity utilization have ranged much more than on the global level because the sectoral fluctuations have tended to cancel each other out. This tendency is reflected in the fact that only 3 of the 35 correlation coefficients in table 4.6 among the sectoral utilization rates are significantly non-zero at the 5% level[52]. This apparent independence among current sectoral rates of capacity utilization suggests that the conditions which cause underutilization of capacity vary considerably (at least in respect to lags) across sectors. This independence also suggests that an aggregate measure-

[51]The mean annual exponential growth rates of actual output and of capacity over the 1945–1965 period are 4.2 and 3.6%, respectively (table 4.1).
[52]The three exceptions are between mining and other services, between utilities and manufacturing, and between housing services and utilities.

ment of unused Chilean capacity calculated directly from the time series of aggregate product by the trend through the peaks method (such as Okun, 1962, uses for the United States) would substantially understate the actual unused capacity because of the counterbalancing sectoral fluctuations. Likewise, if Chilean subsectoral fluctuations in current rates of capacity utilization are nearly as independent as are the Chilean sectoral fluctuations in current rates of capacity utilization, then the present procedure understates substantially the extent of unused Chilean capacity. Of course, one would not expect as much independence on the more disaggregate subsectoral level because of greater homogeneity, but the possibility of significant downward bias in the estimates of unused capacity due to lack of complete correlation among subsectoral utilization rates should not be discounted too heavily.

In order of decreasing foregone product relative to capacity (and in order of the standard deviations of the rates of capacity utilization, except that government and construction are interchanged) the Chilean sectors rank as follows: mining, utilities, transportation, housing services, government, construction, manufacturing, agriculture, and other services (columns 10–12 in table 4.1). The first four sectors have had substantially more unutilized capacity than the national average, and the last three sectors have had substantially less. Several characteristics of the individual sectors and of this ordering merit mention.

(1) Mining is a somewhat unique sector in that almost all of Chile's exports originate therein, largely (at least during the sample period) under the control of a few foreign companies. Because the exchange rate has been overvalued for most of the period (Behrman, 1975b), the estimate given in table 4.1 probably underestimates the true resource cost to Chile of the substantial underutilization in this sector. Moreover, an alternative method of estimating rates of capacity utilization in this sector (based on the utilization of electric energy sources) suggests that the mean rate of utilization has been only 80% and the foregone production has been equal to five years of the mean actual production[53]. Most of the low rates of capacity utilization (as calculated by the trend-through-the-peaks method) underlying the

[53]This calculation is based on the extension of results for the dominant large-scale mining to all of the sector. The series of rates of capacity utilization so calculated, however, are not significantly correlated at the 5% level with the series calculated by the trend-through-the-peaks method.

low mean value for this sector occurred in the 1952–1958 period in which considerable uncertainty existed about the future course of relations between the Chilean government and the major mining companies[54]. To the extent that the uncertain nature of relations between the government and these companies did underlie the historically low utilization rates, one might expect higher utilization rates in the future because of the recent nationalization of the leading mining companies[55]. Of course, substantial fluctuations may still occur because of fluctuations in the international copper market. Moran (1970) suggests, moreover, that Chile may be more vulnerable to such variations in the international copper market in the future because her copper policies (including those related to pricing) have made her a much more marginal supplier.

(2) Three of the sectors in which fluctuations in capacity utilization are, in general, hypothesized to be relatively large, have had relatively limited fluctuations and relatively high mean levels of capacity utilization. The first of these three sectors is agriculture, for which fluctuations are generally thought to be large because of variations in natural conditions. The other two sectors are construction and manufacturing, in which fluctuations have been hypothesized to be relatively large because of relatively great sensitivity to variations in aggregate demand[56]. Of course, the recent upsurge in interest about the existence of unused capacity in the last of these three sectors, manufacturing, is based on the discrepancies between actual utilization and *rated* capacities, not historically attained levels of production[57].

(3) An examination of interindustry and final demand flows

[54]For details about the relations between the government and these mining companies, see Behrman (1975b, sections 3.2, 4.2.1, 7.1.2.3, 7.2.1). Mamalakis (1967a, 1971a), and Reynolds (1965).

[55]During the Allende presidency of 1970–1973, however, the utilization rate in large-scale mining was quite low in part because of the substantial politicization of the production process. See Behrman (1975b, subsections 4.2.1, 7.1.2.3) for more details.

[56]For an example in the case of another Latin-American country, see Lawrsen and Taylor (1968, p. 10).

[57]For evidence of this interest and measures of levels of capacity utilization in manufacturing in developing countries, see UNIDO (1969) and Winston (1969). For Chilean manufacturing ODEPLAN (1968) gives estimates for capacity utilization in 1964–1965, which (under the assumption of a proportional relation between the ODEPLAN estimates and the trend-through-the-peak estimates) imply a mean rate of capacity utilization in this sector of from 0.54 to 0.75. The underlying definition of capacity, however, is not clear.

indicates that there is limited support for Hirschman's (1962, p. 73) assertion that

'the risk of excess capacity is lowest when the project's output is widely spread as an input over many sectors (or regions) or when output goes overwhelmingly to final consumption demand; the risk is bigger the greater the concentration of the project's output in a few final consumers or on a few cells of the interindustry matrix.'

For agriculture, manufacturing, and other services, outputs are relatively widely distributed, but final consumption demand absorbs a fairly large share. All three of those sectors have high mean capacity utilization rates. On the other end of the spectrum as far as mean utilization rates are concerned, the output from mining is sold to a few (mostly foreign) buyers so that risks are relatively high due to this concentration. On the other hand, the results for utilities, transportation, and construction do not seem to support Hirschman's hypothesis. The outputs of utilities and transportation are fairly widespread among final and intermediate uses with substantial portions going to final consumer demand, and yet mean utilization rates are low. In contrast, output from construction is very concentrated in gross investment (which itself is usually considered quite volatile), and the mean utilization rate for construction is about the same as for the economy as a whole.

4.3.1. A model for the determination of capacity utilization

Relations (4.10) and (4.11) give the model used in this section. Relation (4.10) states that actual real *GDP* adjusts towards desired *GDP* in a geometric process:

$$V = V_{-1} + \gamma(V^d - V_{-1}) = (1 - \gamma)V_{-1} + \gamma V^d, \qquad (4.10)$$

where V is the actual real *GDP* and V^d is the desired real *GDP*. Relation (4.11) states that the desired real *GDP* is proportional to the capacity of real *GDP*:

$$V^d = \alpha CV, \qquad (4.11)$$

where CV is the capacity of real *GDP*. Substitution of relation (4.11) into (4.10) gives an expression for current real *GDP* in terms of its lagged value, the capacity of real *GDP*, the adjustment coefficient, and the proportionality factor. Section 4.1 discusses the determination of the capacity of real *GDP*. The question of primary interest for this section is what determines the proportionality factor or desired utilization rate (i.e. α).

The primary group of determinants discussed by most observers, e.g. UNIDO (1969), ODEPLAN (1968, p. 5), and Winston (1969, p. 4), relates to conditions in the relevant product and factor markets. Frequently mentioned possible causes of low utilization of capacity within this group include the fact that product prices are not remunerative, that demand is inadequate, that primary and inter-mediate inputs (especially imported ones) are not available or are too expensive, and that labor unrest disrupts normal functioning. In order to represent these considerations, the proportionality factor is hypothesized to be a linear function of a number of variables: the product price relative to the *GDP* deflator, the tax-adjusted product price relative to unit labor costs (i.e. wages adjusted for productivity and for employers' social security contributions), the tax-adjusted product price relative to intermediate input prices[58], aggregate demand conditions, the state of infrastructure development, imports of intermediate goods relative to *GDP*, total imports relative to *GDP*, and indices of quantitative restrictions and other foreign sector policies.

A second group of determinants frequently mentioned is the availability of short-term funds from bank credit or other sources. To represent this condition the proportionality factor is hypothes-ized to be a linear function of total credit from the banking system relative to total *GDP*.

A third group of determinants which merits consideration is related to various natural conditions. Of course, these conditions probably are most important in the case of agriculture, but other sectors – such as utilities (to the extent that hydroelectric electricity production and water distribution are important) – may also be affected. To represent these natural conditions the proportionality factors are hypothesized to be a linear function of indices related to rainfall and to the intensity of earthquakes.

4.3.2. Sectoral estimates of capacity utilization functions

Table 4.7 gives estimates of the relations discussed in subsection 4.3.1 for all of the sectors except for the government[59]. The government is excluded because the provision of government

[58]The last column in the first part of table 6.6 below gives the sectoral sources of intermediate inputs.

[59]Earlier estimates of Chilean sectoral capacity utilization determinants are in Behrman (1973b).

Table
Determinants of Chilean sectoral

Dependent variables sectoral real GDP	Each variable multiplied by					
	Domestic determinants					
	Relative product to input prices (tax adjusted)		Economic activity (current indicators index)	Credit relative to GDP^b	1960 earthquake dummy variable	Sector specific variables
Lag	0	1	0	0	0	0
Agriculture			0.190 (3.9) [0.1]			0.302^d (3.9) [0.1]
Mining	0.004^e (4.3) [0.3]	0.0305^f (2.6) [0.2]		1.58 (2.9) [0.1]		
Construction					−0.119 (2.4) [−0.1]	1.48^g (1.5)^h [0.1]
Manufacturing			0.305 (5.0) [0.2]			
Transportation		0.231^{k,f} (1.9) [0.2]	−4.08^l (7.0) [−1.4]			−12.9^m (5.7) [−1.3]
Utilities	0.00318^e (6.2) [0.4]	0.00119^{e,f} (3.6) [0.2]	0.367 (6.2) [0.3]			0.0357^n (6.9) [0.2]
Housing			0.216 (2.1) [0.1]	4.53 (4.8) [0.5]	0.176 (4.3) [0.0]	−5.35^m (4.3) [−0.5]
Services		0.00922^{p,f} (2.3) [0.2]		1.45 (4.0) [0.2]		

^{a}Beneath the point estimates in parentheses are the absolute values of the t-statistics. All point estimates are significantly non-zero at the 5% level unless otherwise noted. Beneath the t-statistics in brackets are the elasticities at the point of means. With this model, elasticities are identical for real GDP and for capacity utilization. Appendix A gives data sources.

^{b}Public credit only for mining, private credit only for housing, both for services.

^{c}Imports of habitual consumer goods relative to agricultural capacity for agriculture, intermediate imports relative to total GDP for mining, and lagged total imports relative to lagged total GDP for housing.

^{d}Sum of depreciated (at 3%) value of real government direct and indirect investment through past year relative to total real GDP.

^{e}Product price adjusted for direct and indirect taxes relative to unit labor costs including employers' social security contributions.

^{f}Lagged two periods.

4.7
capacity utilization, 1947–1965[a].

sectoral capacity of real *GDP*				Constant	$\bar{R}^2$ SE DW
	Foreign sector determinants				
Constant	Imports relative to product[c]	Ffrench-Davis quantitative restrictions index	Black market *NER* relative to nat. accounts *NER*		
	0	1	0		
0.913 (32.8) [1.0]	−1.10 (6.5) [−0.2]				0.96 47.4 1.8
1.59 (2.6) [1.8]	11.8 (3.1) [0.5]	−1.76 (2.8) [−2.0]			0.95 57.9 2.0
		0.882 (5.6) [0.9]		−25.8 (1.2)[i]	0.98 23.9 1.9
0.574 (7.5) [0.6]		0.0966[j] (2.0) [0.1]	0.0367 (2.6) [0.1]	222.1 (1.4)[h]	0.97 100.0 2.0
3.25 (7.6) [3.7]			−0.098 [−0.2] [−0.2]		0.96 2.5 2.5
0.235[o] (3.0)		0.135[j] (2.7) [0.2]		−26.9 (2.6)	0.98 6.4 2.6
	−1.50 (1.3)[i] [−0.2]	1.47 (9.4) [1.6]		−590. (4.1)	0.98 47.4 2.6
		0.715 (5.6) [0.7]		−941. (2.2)	0.94 286. 2.0

[a]Non-inventory investment relative to *GDP*.
[h]Significantly non-zero at the 10% level.
[i]Significantly non-zero at the 15% level.
[j]Domestic *GDP* deflator to United States *GDP* deflator adjusted for the average import tax rate and the average prior deposit rate.
[k]Product price adjusted for direct and indirect taxes relative to material inputs price index.
[l]Total inventory stock level relative to *GDP*.
[m]Average indirect tax rate.
[n]Rate of change of *GDP* deflator.
[o]Lagged dependent variable (*not* multiplied by sectoral capacity). For this sector the Durbin–Watson statistic is biased toward two.
[p]Product price adjusted for direct and indirect taxes relative to wage adjusted for employers' social security contribution.

services seems to be determined by factors much different from those posited above. The major characteristic of these estimates can be summarized under six general observations.

(1) On an overall level the results suggest that the underlying model is reasonably successful. The coefficients of determination indicate that the results are consistent with 0.94–0.98 of the variance in the dependent variable over the sample period. Evidence of considerable problems of autocorrelation does not appear. The signs of the significantly non-zero coefficient estimates generally are those anticipated *a priori.*

(2) Variations in sectoral real capacities underlie much of the fluctuations in real products, but the variations in the desired sectoral capacity-utilization rates also are quite important.

(3) Adjustment of actual towards desired *GDP* is quite quick. Only for utilities is there evidence that this adjustment takes more than one year. Even in the case of utilities, moreover, almost threequarters of the adjustment occurs within the first year.

(4) The results support the hypothesis that the conditions in the product and factor markets significantly influence the rates of capacity utilization and, therefore, real *GDP*. For half of the sectors (mining, transportation, utilities and services) there is evidence of some response to relative prices. The implied elasticities are all less than unitary and are quite low in transportation and other services. Nevertheless, the evidence of widespread significant responses to relative prices even at the sectoral level[60] is important because of the common assumption of the existence of effectively complete rigidities in the developing economies.

In addition to the response to relative prices, moreover, there is evidence of significant responses to overall aggregate demand conditions in five sectors (agriculture, manufacturing, transportation, utilities[61] and housing) and to aggregate investment in a sixth (construction)[62]. Positive significant responses are also recorded for the state of infrastructure development in agriculture, the availability of intermediate imports for mining, and the extent of foreign

[60]Because intrasectoral factory mobility may be greater, at least in some sectors (e.g. agriculture), than intersectoral factor mobility, one might expect to find higher elasticities at a more disaggregate level of analysis.

[61]For utilities there are significant responses to both the current activity index and the rate of inflation.

[62]For construction investment is obviously the most important component of aggregate demand.

sector quantitative restrictions[63] for construction, manufacturing, utilities, housing, and services. The last of these responses suggests that for a number of sectors foreign sector quantitative restrictions have induced greater capacity utilization by limiting competing imports. Negative significant responses are implied for the indirect tax rates for transportation and housing, the quantity of competing imports for agriculture and housing, and the extent of foreign sector quantitative restrictions for mining and transportation. The last of these inverse responses reflects the limitation of production by imported input shortages in two sectors which depend on critical intermediate imports.

The responses to various aspects of product and factor market conditions, thus, seems to be widespread and often substantial. Policies that are based on analysis which ignores such responses to market conditions may be quite misleading.

(5) For mining, housing, and services there is evidence of significant responses to the relative availability of short-term credit. The lack of a response in manufacturing, however, is somewhat surprising, given the importance that Chilean manufacturers seem to place on the availability of credit in informal explanations of the low rate of capacity utilization (see also ODEPLAN, 1968, p. 5). One might think that the cost, not the quantity of credit, would be an important consideration, but for much of the sample period the rate of inflation exceeded the nominal bank credit rates. Credit rationing, therefore, was accomplished by non-price means. In such a situation the desire for increased credit is understandable, but the results suggests that changes in the availability of credit apparently did not affect manufacturing utilization rates (whatever effects they may have had on income distribution or on other variables).

(6) The 1960 earthquake has a significant impact in construction and housing. However, in no sector – including agriculture – is there evidence of a significant response to the variables used to represent other natural conditions. This somewhat surprising result may only reflect the difficulties of constructing a good index[64]. Nevertheless, the model used is consistent with over 96% of the variance in

[63]The extent of these restrictions and other trade barriers is represented by the Ffrench-Davis (1971) index, the ratio of internal to external prices, and the ratio of the black market *NER* to the weighted average of all legal *NER*s.

[64]For more extensive attempts to construct an appropriate index, see Evans (1969) and Oury (1966).

agricultural real *GDP* without including any index of natural
conditions, and when any one of several alternative indices were
included, the apparent explanatory power of the model did not
improve.

4.3.3. Implications of capacity utilization estimates

Despite probable downward biases in the measurement procedure
used, on the bases of comparisons with historically attained levels of
output (and *not* with rated capacities) significant excess capacity
has existed in the Chilean economy during the postwar period. The
utilization of this excess capacity could have resulted in a substantial increase both in the level and in the growth rate of national
product[65]. The primary determinants of fluctuations in the rates of
sectoral capacity utilization in most sectors seem to be the conditions in factor and product markets (including the state of aggregate
demand). The policy conclusions that follow for the case of Chile
and for any other similar developing economies are as follows.

(1) Substantial gains may be obtained from increasing capacity
utilization by following appropriate market and anticyclical policies.
These gains may or may not warrant the cost of following the
necessary policies, but the possibility that the benefits do outweigh
the costs should not be rejected casually without further investigation.

(2) The widespread response to market conditions suggest that
markets do play an allocative role in such an economy. Policies
should not distort the signals transmitted by such markets under the
false assumption that they will have no significant effects on
allocation. Policies that distort the market conditions (e.g. the
Chilean price ceilings) *may* be justified, but the existence of costs in
terms of resource allocation should not be ignored.

(3) For short- and medium-term policy, recommendations based
on fixed capital coefficients and full capacity-utilization assumptions
(such as in the Harrod–Domar and Chenery models) may be
misleading, not only because of the probable importance of other
factors and the possibility of some substitution, but also because of
the existence of unutilized capacity.

---

[65]The results in table 4.5, moreover, suggests that at least in mining and housing,
investment responds to the degree of capacity utilization.

CHAPTER 5

Demand

Final demand is largely ignored in many models of developing economies because of the assumption that output is basically determined by supply constraints (see paragraph (3) in section 1.1). The existence of substantial excess capacity and the evidence of widespread significant responses to final demand in the determination of capacity utilization rates (section 4.3), however, suggest that the common misspecification due to the exclusion of demand considerations may be quite costly.

Chapters 3 and 4 discussed several important components of final demand: government current expenditures, taxes, money supply, and investment. This chapter investigates the remaining major variables. Section 5.1 considers the other domestic aggregates – savings and inventory changes. Section 5.2 explores foreign sector variables – imports, exports and net factor income from abroad.

5.1. Other domestic components of aggregate demand

5.1.1. Savings

These determine the availability of resources for capital accumulation. If the government could costlessly use fiscal policy to alter savings rates or if unlimited foreign savings were available, the amount of domestic savings would not constrain investment. Such conditions, however, have not predominated in recent Chilean history.

The available data permits the estimation of time-series savings–consumption functions for households and non-profit institutions (44% of gross savings in 1945–1965)[1], businesses (39%) and the government (20%)[2]. Table 5.1 presents alternatives for each of these categories. The model utilized hypothesizes that savings–consumption decisions depend basically on an appropriate income variable, with modifications due to a number of factors discussed below.

In terms of the degree of consistency with variations in the dependent variables or of apparent problems of serial correlation, all of the relations in table 5.1 seem to be reasonably satisfactory. However, substantial multicollinearity exists among a set of variables which includes per capita real monetary balances, the black market *PLD NER*, the inverse of the *GDP* deflator, net foreign savings, and the standard deviation of the *PLD EER*. Therefore, in all three cases alternatives with various subsets of those variables deleted are presented: (1) the combination of variables which maximizes the degree of consistency with the variance in the dependent variable; (2) the alternative which maximizes the degree of consistency with the variance in the dependent variable subject to the inclusion of real net foreign savings; and (3) for households and non-profit institutions, a third possibility for which the degree of consistency with the variance in the dependent variable is almost as great as in the first alternative, but in which per capita real monetary balances are included instead of the black market *PLD NER*. Because of the multicollinearity, of course, the coefficients of the variables among which it occurs must be interpreted with care.

The major determinant of real savings in each case is the net income variable: real disposable income for households, real after-tax non-wage income for businesses, and real government revenues for the government. The marginal savings propensities for these three groups vary substantially. After complete adjustment[3], the

---

[1] For households and non-profit institutions, the national accounts indicate a negative savings rate for every year in the 1960–1971 period. This characteristic presumably is more an artifact due to the residual nature of savings and a systematic overvaluation of depreciation than a reflection of reality. The estimates below are made under the assumption that such a measurement error is independent of the included variables. For further discussion of the netative savings estimates in the Chilean accounts, see Mamalakis (1967b) and ODEPLAN (1970a).

[2] Depreciation averaged 84% of gross savings.

[3] For households there is adjustment because of permanent income considerations. For the first year, the point estimate of the marginal propensity to save for households range from 0.61 to 0.75. Therefore, they are as high as for any other group if only the immediate impact is considered. This range also implies that impact multipliers are not very large because of the considerable leakage into savings.

point estimates range from 0.04 to 0.38 for households and non-profit institutions, 0.55 to 0.63 for businesses, and 0.67 to 0.73 for the government. Income shifts within the private sector to business and from the private sector to the government, thus, tend to increase real savings[4].

For households and non-profit institutions there is further evidence of a distributional impact on savings. Columns 11 and 12 indicate that shifts from non-wage to wage income and from the rest of the economy to agriculture would both increase savings. The former result, in particular, may be somewhat surprising[5]. If valid, the Chilean world is clearly not Kaldorian, and savings could not be increased by shifting income away from labor.

For the private sectors, real monetary balances in excess of desired levels might induce expenditures and therefore reduce savings. Desired real balances are not directly observable, but presumably depend on the level of after-tax real income and the cost of holding real balances. The major component of this cost is the expected rate of inflation[6].

Under the assumption that the expected rate of inflation is represented by a distributed lag of past price changes or by a distributed lag of *PLD EER*s, the estimates in table 5.1 provide some support for an inverse role of excess real monetary balances in the savings process. Consistent with this hypothesis, for both households and businesses the point estimates imply an elastic inverse response of savings to the level of actual balances, an inverse response to price expectations as represented by patterns of *PLD EER*s, and a positive response to after-tax real income[7].

The positive sign of the household saving response to the distributed lag of the rate of change of prices, in contrast, is not consistent with the real balance hypothesis. However, the sign of this response probably only reflects the relative inability of households to defend their share of the command over goods in the face of

[4]Under the Allende government, however, it is not clear that the government remained a relatively high marginal saver. In 1971, for example, real savings fell (and became negative, in fact) although real revenues rose.

[5]This result may reflect that a very wide definition of labor is used here (i.e. returns to self-employed proprietors are included in the wage share).

[6]Real interest rates *a priori* would seem to be much less important because of their small magnitude in comparison to expected inflation. No statistical evidence of their significance could be found.

[7]The effect of real income on desired real balances, however, cannot be disentangled from its direct impact on savings.

Real consumption–savings functions for Chilean households and

Dependent variable		Per capita real disposable income $Z1^b$	Rate of inflation		Per capita real monetary balances $Z1^b$	PLD NER for the black market
			$Z1^b$	$Z2^b$		
		(1)	(2)	(3)	(4)	(5)
Real per capita private consumption –	I	−0.623 (6.5) [0.6]	2.24 (6.9) [−0.0]	−0.418 (6.2)		13.6 (2.9) [0.0]
	II	−0.674 (5.8) [0.6]	2.32 (5.4) [−0.0]	−0.439 (4.8)	−9128. (2.0) [1.2]	
	III	−0.961 (24.6) [0.9]	1.94 (4.7) [−0.0]	−0.371 (4.4)		15.0 (2.3) [0.1]

		Real after tax non-wage income	PLD EER		Real monetary balances
			$Z1^b$	$Z2^b$	
Real business savings –	I	0.633 (13.4) [0.3]	26.0 (5.5) [−0.2]		−0.627 (5.1) [−1.5]
	II	0.554 (10.9) [0.3]	108.9 (2.4) [−0.2]	−18.9 (2.1)	−0.767 (4.4) [−1.9]

		Real government revenues
Real government consumption –	I	0.331 (11.0) [0.6]
	II	0.275 (7.0) [0.5]

ªThe absolute value of the t-statistics are given in parentheses beneath the point estimates. All point estimates are significantly non-zero at the 5% level unless otherwise noted. Long-run elasticities at the point of sample means are given in brackets beneath the t-statistics. Appendix A gives data sources.

Real per capita private consumption –	I	Income
		Rate of inflation
	II	Income
		Rate of inflation
		Monetary balances
	III	Income
Real business savings: real cost of foreign exchange adjusted for import taxes –	I	Rate of inflation
	II	
Real government consumption: real net foreign savings –	III	

ᶜSignificantly non-zero at the 10% level.
ᵈPer capita for real household and non-profit institution savings estimates.
ᵉSignificantly non-zero at the 15% level.

5.1
non-profit institutions, business, and the government, 1945–1965ᵃ.

Inverse of *GDP* deflator	Real foreign savings	Standard deviation		Non-wage income/ total income	Agric./ total *GDP*	Constant	$\bar{R}^2$ SE DW
		Rate of inflation	*PLD EER*				
(6)	(7)	(8)	(9)	(10)	(11)	(12)	(13)
−1.04 (4.9) [−0.0]		3.65 (3.7) [0.0]	−61.9 (1.6)ᶜ [−0.0]	508. (4.0) [0.1]	−2083. (4.0) [−0.2]	798. (3.8)	0.98 18.5 2.4
−1.11 (4.6) [−0.0]		4.75 (3.6) [0.0]	−72.0 (1.5)ᶜ [−0.0]	512. (3.5) [0.1]	−1841. (3.0) [−0.1]	572. (2.0)	0.98 20.9 2.5
	0.837ᵈ (4.3) [0.0]	2.0 (1.6)ᶜ [0.0]		790. (4.7) [0.1]	−591. (1.1)ᵉ [−0.0]		0.96 26.9 2.4

Inverse of *GDP* deflator	Real foreign savings					Constant	$\bar{R}^2$ SE DW
4.55 (4.7) [0.4]						644. (2.5)	0.94 89.9 2.1
	−0.178 (1.6)ᶜ [−0.0]					650. (2.0)	0.91 110. 2.4

Inverse of *GDP* deflator	Real foreign savings					Constant	$\bar{R}^2$ SE DW
		Z1ᵇ	Z2ᵇ	Z3ᵇ			
−0.667 (1.1)ᵉ [−0.0]						516. (4.9)	0.94 94.5 1.7
1.25 (1.2) [0.0]		0.400 (1.5) [0.1]	−0.252 (1.6)	0.0372 (1.4)		758. (4.8)	0.96 80. 2.2

ᵇThe Hall–Sutch (1969) polynomial method with the tail constrained to zero is used for this variable. Zi (i = 1 or 2) is the order of the polynomial. The implied lag structures are as follows:

Lags	−0	−1	−2	−3	Σ
	0.249	0.187	0.125	0.063	0.623
	−227.	−44.5	53.9	68.8	−148.
	0.270	0.202	0.135	0.067	0.674
	−225.	−37.4	62.9	75.4	−125.
	0.3651	0.2738	0.1826	0.093	0.9128
	0.385	0.288	0.192	0.096	0.961
	−183.	−25.7	−57.0	65.6	−85.8
	−10.4	−7.80	−5.20	−2.60	−26.0
	−13.3	−42.9	9.3	23.6	−23.3
	0.065	0.250	0.153	0.004	0.465

high inflation rates. Thus, they experience some forced savings.

Weisskopf (1972), among others, has hypothesized that foreign savings are at least partially substituted for domestic savings[8,9]. The last alternative for each of the three groups provides some support for this hypothesis. In one sense, in fact, the support is too strong because the total of the relevant coefficients implies that a permanent increase in real net foreign savings of one unit *ceteris paribus* results in a decrease in real net domestic savings of at least the same order of magnitude. If it were not for the problem of multicollinearity, therefore, one might conclude that in the Chilean case there is support for a rather extreme version of the foreign-savings-substitution hypothesis. However, given that the relevant coefficient estimates for the real private domestic savings functions are probably biased upward in absolute value due to the incorporation of part of the price and possibly of the real monetary balance effects, any deduction about at least the size of the substitution must be qualified. Nevertheless, the conclusion seems warranted that the impact of net real foreign savings on Chilean real domestic savings may be quite significant[10].

The final determinants of real savings behavior for which there is some evidence of statistically significant responses are in regard to uncertainty[11]. For household savings the point estimates suggest an inverse response to increased uncertainty in regard to inflation, but a direct response to higher uncertainty about *PLD EER*s. Neither of these effects, however, is very large.

These partial-equilibrium savings estimates thus suggest that the government policies discussed in ch. 3 have considerable impact on domestic savings behavior. Much of this impact is indirect, how-

[8]Papanek (1972 and 1973) presents a critique of this view.

[9]The two-gap model posits a different relation between domestic and foreign savings. Because of a lack of foreign exchange, savings may be frustrated at the margin.

[10]One point that is not touched upon in this subsection is that sheltered markets might induce added foreign savings to finance attractive investment. Evidence to explore this possibility is very difficult to obtain. In a related vein, however, Mamalakis (1971b) claims that CORFO investment largely replaced rather than supplemented other investment due to shortage of skilled labor and foreign exchange and the deterioration of local capital markets once inflation was high. The more important were the shortages of other factors, the less likely that restrictive regimes induced additional savings through this mechanism.

[11]Table 5.1 also gives an estimate for the coefficient of the inverse of the *GDP* deflator (column 6). This variable is included because the functions are initially specified in nominal terms, but then deflated in order to lessen multicollinearity and heteroskedasticity.

ever, so it is better explored in the context of the complete model of Part III.

5.1.2. Inventory

Data is available only on the total economy level for the sample period. Within the model of Part III inventories are treated in two alternative ways.

(1) For most simulations the change in inventories is defined to be the difference between supply (as determined by capacity, capacity utilization and import functions) and non-inventory demand (as determined by consumption, investment, and export functions). The change in inventories feeds back into other relationships by directly affecting prices, import and capacity utilization decisions (subsection 5.2.1 and sections 4.3 and 6.1).

(2) For some simulations a behavioral relationship is used in which inventory levels are assumed to adjust to a desired level which depends upon the expected level of production in the goods-producing sectors, opportunity costs as measured by the expected inflation, interest, and foreign exchange rates, and uncertainty due to variances in such rates[12]:

$$INV = 1.15GDP^{AMM} + 6.85Z1[GDP^{AMM}] - 1.16Z2[GDP^{AMM}]$$
$$(2.3) \qquad (1.7) \qquad (1.7)$$
$$[0.3]$$

$$- 49.0Z2[PGDP/PGDP] - 722SD[PLD\ EER]$$
$$(1.9) \qquad\qquad (3.4)$$
$$[0.6] \qquad\qquad [-1.2]$$

$$+ 0.417INV_{-1} + 2104, \qquad\qquad (5.1)$$
$$(2.2) \qquad (5.2)$$

$$\bar{R}^2 = 0.89, \quad SE = 132, \quad DW = 2.6, \quad 1945\text{--}1965,$$

			Lags		
	-0	-1	-2	-3	Σ
GDP^{AMM}	0.274	-0.310	0.026	0.129	0.119
$PGDP/PGDP$	1.958	1.469	0.979	0.490	4.896

[12]For this alternative total production is adjusted to be consistent with final demand.

where *INV* is the level of inventories in 1965 escudos, GDP^{AMM} is real *GDP* in the goods-producing sectors (i.e. agriculture, mining, and manufacturing), $Z1$ is the Hall–Sutch (1969) linear polynomial, $Z2$ is the Hall–Sutch quadratic polynomial, *PGDP/PGDP* is the rate of change in the *GDP* deflator, and *SD[PLD EER]* is the standard deviation over the past three years in the *PLD EER*.

This relationship is consistent with almost nine-tenths of the variance in the level of real inventories. The normal level of output in the goods-producing sector is an important determinant. The long-run elasticity of 0.3 with respect to this variable implies increasing returns to scale in holding inventories. Among the opportunity cost variables only the rate of inflation has a significantly non-zero coefficient estimate. In this case, the long-run elasticity of 0.6 implies a fairly substantial attempt to hedge against inflation by holding goods. Thus, one of the costs of inflation is investment in inventories beyond the levels required by production needs. Among the uncertainty variables, only the one related to the *PLD EER* has a significantly non-zero coefficient. The long-run elasticity of −1.2 in this case implies a substantial reduction in inventory holding as uncertainty concerning the *PLD EER* increases. Under such conditions apparently the desire to hold foreign financial assets dominates over the greater incentive to hold more imports.

5.2. Foreign sector components of aggregate demand[13]

5.2.1. Imports

During the sample period imports averaged 10.3% of *GDP*. The available data permit the disaggregation of imports by final-demand components: consumption goods (32% of total imports in 1946–1965), investment goods (29%), intermediate goods (28%), and service imports (11%). Consumption goods are further subdivided into habitual goods (22%), durable goods (7%), and secondary goods (4%)[14]. Investment goods are disaggregated into machinery and

---

[13]Behrman (1975a and 1975b, chs. 6–8) provide extensive detail about the foreign sector variables.

[14]Habitual goods are essential mass-consumption items (especially food). Secondary goods are non-habitual, nondurable products.

equipment (19%) and transportation-related items (10%). Consumption imports averaged slightly less than 4% of total consumption. Investment imports averaged 28% of total investment[15].

The secular shift in the composition of imports during the first two postwar decades was from intermediate goods to capital goods and services, with consumption goods in between: transportation-related capital goods (a secular annual exponential growth rate of 14%), services (9.2%), machinery and equipment (8.8%), secondary consumer goods (5.8%), habitual consumer goods (4.5%), durable consumer goods (4.0%), and intermediate goods (15%).

The rapid increase in capital goods reflected increasing dependence on foreign machinery and equipment in development programs[16]. In substantial part, the emphasis on capital imports was due to the efforts of CORFO[17].

The rapid growth in service imports originated in the large increases in payments to foreign-owned factors and in foreign travel.

The moderate increase in consumption goods imports was due to the constraint by the exchange control system of rapidly raising demands for income-elastic durable and secondary goods, in combination with import desubstitution for the food component of habitual goods. The authorities apparently did not lose control of the system so that low-priority consumer imports expanded more rapidly than equipment imports as Huddle (1972) claims happened in Brazil.

The small rate of growth of intermediate goods imports is surprising. The ratios of *PLD EER*(*PI*)s in Behrman (1975b, table 5.1) suggest some secular upward trend for these goods. But the trend is not sufficiently large to imply that such items were in substantially increasing short supply, nor that protection for them rose greatly in this period of time. Behrman (1975b, section 5.2) does suggest an increase in *EPR*s for intermediate goods, but not before the mid-1960s. In any case, the growth of intermediate imports was

[15]For some sectors – especially mining and manufacturing – they accounted for a much higher proportion of investment goods (table 6.5).
[16]Over this same period the ratio of imported to total capital increased at a mean annual rate of 4.6%.
[17]CORFO was particularly important in the development of national steel (CAP), electrical (ENDESA), and petroleum (ENAP) enterprises, but also in many other developments which depended heavily on foreign capital goods.

much less than is suggested by the frequent characterization of import substitution for consumption goods leading to increased dependence on intermediate imports. Of course, this may only reflect that most of such import substitution took place before the post-Second World War decades (Behrman, 1975b, ch. 10).

Fluctuations around these secular trends have been considerable for some import categories. The ratio of the standard deviation from the secular trend of imports in a category to the mean for that category gives an index of the degree of relative variation. The ordering by this index (with the values of these ratios in parentheses) is intermediate goods (0.10), machinery and equipment (0.12), habitual consumer goods (0.20), durable consumer goods (0.20), secondary consumer goods (0.28), services (0.30), and transportation-related investment goods (0.52). The ranking by this index is the same as is indicated for the relative fluctuations in *PLD EER(PI)*s (Behrman, 1975b, section 5.1.2). This ranking implies that the government generally succeeded in its intention to curtail 'postponable' imports (i.e. primarily consumer and producer durables, but also secondary consumption goods) at times of foreign exchange shortages so that they had relatively large variations (except for consumer durables)[18]. The government also succeeded in limiting relative fluctuations in intermediate imports to lessen production disruptions.

5.2.1.1. Partial-equilibrium estimates of import functions
Table 5.2 presents single-equation estimates of import functions for 1947–1965. The disaggregation is to the same seven-category level used above.

On an overall level these results seem reasonably satisfactory. The point estimates have the anticipated signs. No undue problems of serial correlation are apparent (but see note a to the table). The corrected coefficients of determination indicate that the hypothesized determinants are consistent with from 83 to 97% of the variances in the dependent variables. Greater consistency is implied for investment goods and services than for consumption and intermediate imports.

---

[18]In contrast, the Instituto de Economía (1963, table 243) suggests that for the shorter period of their study (i.e. 1950–1959) variations in postponable imports exceeded those in non-postponable imports.

In the basic underlying model current real imports are hypothes-ized to depend on (1) relative price characteristics, (2) other demand characteristics, (3) the degree of policy restrictiveness, and (4) lagged imports.

(1) Relative price terms include the levels (or the inverses thereof) and standard deviations of *PLD NER*s, *PLD EER*s, and *PLD EER(PI)*s[19]. Since these different terms may capture somewhat different features of the regimes, more than one price term is allowed in each relation.

The estimates suggest significant and substantial responses to relative price levels among some imports. For example, the implied elasticities at the point of sample means for a change in the general *NER* are − 0.9 for secondary consumption goods, − 1.4 for trans-portation equipment, −0.3 for intermediate goods, and −0.8 for services[20,21]. For these four categories, therefore, price-related policies could have been used to enforce balance of payments discipline instead of using quantitative restrictions. Such a choice would have been preferable because it would have resulted in more flexibility, less fluctuations in the related *PLD EER(PI)*s as supply and demand curves shifted, and less income redistribution towards importers.

For these same four categories, the secular decline in the overall *PLD EER* caused a secular rise in the demand for imports. The 41% fall in the *PLD EER* for imported goods between 1946 and 1970 (Behrman, 1975b, table 5.1), and the above elasticities, for example, imply demand increases of 37, 57, and 12% for the first three respective categories, *ceteris paribus*. Likewise the 62% fall in the brokers' *PLD NER* between 1955 and 1972 induced an expansion of

---

[19]*PLD EER*s give the imported price relative to domestic alternatives for the importer if the appropriate domestic price is used as the deflator. Therefore they are the most appropriate of these relative prices for use in import functions. As Behrman (1975b, section 2.2, chs. 3 and 5) indicates, however, *PLD EER*s are very costly to estimate for Chilean disaggregates (as are the import premia – which also would be of interest in these functions). Alternative relative prices, hence, are utilized in some of these functions.

[20]These elasticities are based on the assumption that *EER*s change proportionately to the general *NER*. For transportation equipment the sign of the elasticity is negative despite the positive coefficients in table 5.2 because those coefficients are for the inverse of the levels.

[21]For services there also is a significant response (although only at the 15% level) to speculative pressures as represented by the ratio of the current to the lagged *PLD NER* for the black market in foreign exchange.

Table
Chilean real import functions for

Type of import	Relative prices			Other demand characteristics		
	Levels		Standard deviation	Relevant activity index	Total credit in real terms	Sector-specific variables
	1	2				
Consumption goods						
Habitual				$0.0344^{c,d}$ (6.0) [1.3]	0.0506 (3.4) [0.8]	$-369.^e$ $(1.7)^f$ [−1.2]
Durable				$0.0099^{c,d}$ (6.6) [0.8]	0.0296^d (5.0) [0.5]	
Secondary	$-15.6^{h,d}$ (2.5) [−0.9]			0.0019^c $(1.3)^k$ [0.7]		$189.^i$ (4.1) [4.7]
Investment goods Machinery and equipment			45.0^i $(1.2)^k$ [0.1]			
Transportation equipment	$182.^m$ (3.0) [1.1]	$59.0^{n,d}$ $(1.2)^k$ [0.3]				17.4^o (10.4) [1.3]
Intermediate goods	$-161.^r$ (2.4) [−0.3]				0.0182^d $(1.4)^f$ [0.1]	
Services	-43.7^s (2.5) [−0.8]	48.0^t $(1.2)^k$ [0.3]		0.105^u (11.7) [1.9]		

[a] Beneath the point estimates in parentheses are the absolute values of the *t*-statistics, each of which is significantly non-zero at the 5% level unless otherwise noted. Underneath the *t*-statistics in brackets are the long-run elasticities at the point of sample means. These elasticities are long-run in the sense that all adjustments due to the inclusion of lagged imports are assumed to have occurred. For such relationships in which the lagged import value is included, of course, the Durbin–Watson statistic is biased towards two. Appendix A gives data sources.

[b] Nominal value of exports divided by unit value of imports.

[c] Private consumption.

[d] Lagged one year.

[e] Ratio of current to lagged value of total inventory stock.

[f] Significantly non-zero at the 10% level.

[f] Ratio of black market *NER* to national accounts *NER*.

[h] *PLD EER* for secondary consumer imports under assumption that average tax and import deposit cost rates were applicable.

5.2
major uses of goods, 1947–1965[a].

Policy restrictiveness			Lagged imports	Constant	$\bar{R}^2$ SE	DW
Ffrench-Davis quantitative restrictions index	Export capacity to import[b]	Sector-specific variable				
−1207. (2.3) [−3.8]				1324. (2.4)	0.89 44.6	2.2
		−20.0[g] (4.8) [−0.2]	−0.532 (2.6)		0.87 11.4	2.2
−107. (2.8) [−3.5]		−13.6 (1.9) [−0.1]	0.418 (2.2)		0.83 8.3	1.9
−703. (2.6) [−7.4]	0.0779 (4.6) [2.1]		0.678 (7.6)	577. (2.2)	0.97 23.1	2.4
−1520. (4.1) [−9.1]	0.239[p,d] (3.0) [−0.0]	−1891.[q] (5.2) [−11.3]		2988. (8.0)	0.94 23.8	2.2
	0.113 (4.7) [0.4]		−0.322 (1.4)[f]	5549. (3.6)	0.80 34.0	2.8
−1503 (3.4) [−7.6]				1366 (3.1)	0.92 30.4	2.5

[i]Wage income relative to total income.
[j]Dummy variable with value 1.0 in 1962–1964 to represent the reversion to a very restrictive foreign sector regime in those years.
[k]Significantly non-zero at the 15% level.
[l]*PLD NER.*
[m]Inverse of *PLD EER* (PI) based on wholesale price indices.
[n]Inverse of *PLD EER* (PI).
[o]Time trend.
[p]Net foreign exchange reserves held by banking system relative to unit value of imports.
[q]Lagged Ffrench-Davis (1971) quantitative restrictions index.
[r]*PLD NER* calculated from unit value of imports relative to deflator for inventories.
[s]*PLD NER.*
[t]Ratio of current to lagged value for *PLD NER* in black market.
[u]Exports plus imports.

almost 50% in desired service imports, *ceteris paribus*. Such intensified demand pressures added substantially to the chronic post-Second World War foreign exchange problems.

For habitual and durable consumption goods and for machinery and equipment, in contrast, there is no evidence of a significant real import response to relative prices. For durable consumption goods and machinery and equipment, the extensive use of quantitative restrictions may obscure price responses. However, variables are included in the relations to represent policy restrictiveness (see below). Under the assumption that in fact they do so relatively well, significant coefficients for any important price responses should have been obtained even if quantitative restrictions were effective at times[22].

For the three import categories considered in the previous paragraph, therefore, price-related policies could not have been so easily substituted for quantitative restrictions to enforce balance of payments discipline. Likewise, the secular decline in the *PLD EER* did not generate substantial additional pressures for foreign exchange to use in these categories[23].

The standard deviation of relative price terms over the past three years is included in the basic model as a proxy for risk associated with future price movements. Table 5.2 includes almost no evidence of a risk-aversion response. Only for machinery and equipment is the relevant coefficient significantly non-zero even at the 15% level. Even for this category the implied extent of hedging against uncertainty by importing more when risks of future price changes are higher is very small.

(2) Other demand characteristics considered include relevant activity indices[24], total real credit, and the distribution of income between labor and other factors.

---

[22]Multicollinearity with other variables also might make such price responses difficult to identify. It does not appear to be a problem, however, in these cases.

[23]The difference in price responses across all six of the import categories, moreover, points to the difficulties of estimating Chilean import functions on even more aggregate levels, as Corbo (1974) and Ffrench-Davis (1971) have attempted. The relatively low price elasticities obtained by the latter apparently in part reflect the aggregation over a wide range of policies and over responses which vary across categories.

[24]That is, a time trend, the ratio of current to lagged stocks, consumption for categories of consumption imports, investment for categories of investment imports, *GDP* for intermediate imports, and exports plus imports for services. The inclusion of investment for investment imports might cause problems of interpretation if

Activity indices have significantly non-zero coefficients for consumption goods, transportation equipment, and services. (i) Total consumption enters into all three categories of consumption imports. The distribution of elasticities across these categories, however, is somewhat surprising. In contrast to usual Engle-curve patterns, the estimate for habitual goods is greater than unity, while that for durable goods is less than one. This inversion of the normal ordering may be due to the more extensive use of quantitative restrictions for the latter category. (ii) The state of inventory accumulation has a significantly non-zero, inverse relation to the level of habitual consumption imports. Apparently high inventory accumulation rates lessen the current demand for these imports, but there is no evidence of a significant impact on other categories. (iii) A time trend representing secular shifts in demand is significant for transportation equipment. (iv) Total trade is significant for the services because certain service imports (e.g. freight and insurance) depend upon it.

Total real credit is emphasized as an important variable by the Instituto de Economía (1963)[25]. It has significantly non-zero coefficients for habitual and durable consumption goods and for intermediate goods (with implied elasticities descending in the order of presentation). A very direct link, thus, exists between internal monetary policy and international economic flows. Note, however, that there is no evidence of this direct link between monetary policies and investment goods imports. This last result accurately reflects the predominately short-term nature of Chilean bank credit and the use of that credit.

Pinto (1962) hypothesizes that a shift in the distribution of income from non-labor factors to labor would reduce Chilean imports. Table 5.2 provides no support for this hypothesis. An income distribution variable is significantly non-zero only for secondary consumption imports. In that case the estimate implies an

---

Mamalakis (1971b) is correct that the level of investment depended on the level of such imports, and not vice versa. Table 6.5 indicates that some sectors – especially mining and manufacturing – imported high proportions of their investment goods. This activity index does not have a significantly non-zero coefficient, however, so it is not included in the results in table 5.2.

[25]Imports in fact are determined simultaneously with total credit. The latter depends indirectly on the size of foreign exchange reserves which, in turn, depends partially on imports. See section 3.2.

increase in imports as income shifts from non-labor factors to labor[26].

(3) Foreign sector policy restrictiveness is represented by five variables: (i) The Ffrench-Davis (1971) quantitative restrictions index; (ii) the export capacity to import; (iii) the net foreign exchange reserves held by the banking system deflated by the unit value of imports; (iv) the ratio of the black market *NER* to the national accounts *NER*; and (v) dummy variables for changes in the foreign sector regimes[27].

The results in table 6.3 indicate that significant and substantial responses to policy restrictiveness occurred for all types of imports. (i) The Ffrench-Davis quantitative restrictions index is significantly non-zero for all but consumption durables and intermediate goods. (ii) The export capacity to import has significantly non-zero coefficients for machinery and equipment and intermediate imports. (iii) The net foreign exchange reserves held by the banking system relative to the unit value of imports has a significant coefficient for transportation equipment. (iv) The black market *NER* relative to the national accounts *NER* has a significantly non-zero coefficient for durable consumption goods. (v) A dummy variable for the reversion to a more restrictive foreign sector regime in 1962–1964 has a significantly non-zero coefficient in the case of secondary consumption imports. This estimate implies a reduction on the average of 17% for those years.

Quantitative restrictions, therefore, had pervasive and substantial impacts. They apparently were the only effective policy instruments, in fact, for habitual and durable consumption goods and for machinery and equipment imports. Because several different indices of quantitative restrictions are used in the estimates, one cannot characterize the relative impact across categories of imports with complete confidence. However, the following ordering in respect to descending relative impact of such restrictions is suggested: trans-

[26]The increase in consumption imports which accompanied the redistribution of income favoring labor under the Allende government also may raise doubts about Pinto's hypothesis. At the same time, however, expectations were altered drastically in a way which might account for the import splurge.

[27]The second and third are included because restrictions were increased when reserves fell. Diaz-Alejandro (1976) uses the alternative hypothesis that restrictions were increased when reserves fell below some desired level. The more constant is the desired level, the more this hypothesis is like the one used here in regard to the implications for estimation.

portation equipment, services, machinery and equipment, habitual and secondary consumption goods (with the placement of durable consumption goods and intermediate goods not clear). Thus, these estimates seem to support the characterization of the use of quantitative restrictions as favoring consumption goods (at least of non-durable varieties) over investment goods and services.

(4) Lagged imports *a-priori* may have either positive or negative coefficients. A positive one reflects Houthakker–Taylor (1970) habit formation or the need for more than one year to adjust actual imports to desired levels[28]. A negative coefficient indicates a Houthakker–Taylor inventory effect. Stocks built up from previous imports diminish the demand for current imports[29].

The estimates in table 5.2 imply the dominance of the inventory effect for durable consumption goods and intermediate imports. They indicate the dominance of the adjustment or habit formation effects for secondary consumption goods and for machinery and equipment imports. For the other three categories the two effects tend to nullify each other. *A-priori*, such a pattern does not seem unreasonable.

One implication of this pattern is that, with liberalization, habitual and durable consumption imports, transportation imports and intermediate imports, and services all adjust rapidly to new levels. Secondary consumption goods and machinery and equipment adjust much more slowly. The result would seem to be more probable relative increases in *ERPs* for domestic production of the last-mentioned two categories than for the others, *ceteris paribus*, since competitive imports adjust slower than intermediate imports in these two cases.

5.2.2. *Exports*

During the sample period aggregate exports averaged 13.2% of *GDP*. Partly because of the conscious attempt to turn inward and

---

[28]Another necessary assumption is that the adjustment process is well represented by a geometric distributed lag.

[29]The Houthakker–Taylor inventory effect cannot be derived exactly from neoclassical theory. This should be intuitively clear from the lack of an interest rate in their formulation. The added precision from utilizing a theoretically somewhat more satisfactory formulation in this case, however, would be misleading because of the quality of the data. Therefore the original Houthakker–Taylor form is adopted.

partly because of the import response to overvaluation and to other policies, exports relative to *GDP* declined at an annual rate of − 1.6%. The extent of fluctuations around this secular trend were relatively larger than for any major component of aggregate demand (except for inventory changes), which is consistent with the structural characterization of exports as being quite volatile.

The available data permit the disaggregation of exports by sectors of origin: agriculture (8% of total exports in 1945–1965), mining (73%), manufacturing (7%), and services (11%). Mining is further divided between large-scale mining (62%) and small- and medium-scale mining (11%).

The secular shift in the composition of exports during the first two postwar decades was from agriculture and large-scale mining to small- and medium-scale mining, services, and manufacturing: agriculture (a mean growth rate of −1.3% in 1945–1965), large-scale mining (1.0%), small- and medium-scale mining (12.3%), industry (2.9%), and services (5.8%). These changes partially reflect the success of government policies which favored domestically owned small- and medium-scale mining and industry (Behrman, 1975b, chs. 3–5). The exact nature of these shifts, however, depends on the period considered because of fluctuations in the world copper price. For a somewhat longer period, for example, large-scale mining more than maintains its relative share due to the copper market booms of the late 1960s and early 1970s.

Fluctuations around the secular trends have been considerable for some export categories. The ratio of the standard deviation from the secular trend of exports in a category to the mean for that category provides an index of the degree of relative variation. The ordering by this index (with the values of the ratios in parentheses) for 1946–1965 is large-scale mining (0.13), services (0.20), agriculture (0.20), small- and medium-scale mining (0.29), and manufacturing (0.41).

The sectoral ordering of relative fluctuations in *PLD EER(PI)*s is agriculture (0.12), manufacturing (0.20) and mining (0.21) (Behrman, 1975b, table A8). There appears to be no particular relation between the degree of these variations and the degree of those in exports. Relative variations in exports have been smallest for large-scale mining because Chile has some market power in this case and because policies towards large-scale copper mining were relatively constant during the two post-Second World War decades, except for the Chilean sales monopoly in 1952–1953 and the enactment of the *Nuevo Trato* in 1955 (Behrman, 1975b, subsection 4.2.1). Variations also have been relatively small for agricultural exports, which is somewhat surprising because quantitative restrictions have been used more to limit exports from agriculture than from other sectors (Behrman, 1975b, subsection 4.2.2). Fluctuations have been by far the largest for manufacturing. Apparently this result reflects that Chile has been a marginal supplier of industrial goods in international markets, that policies affecting such exports have changed with relatively great frequency, and that the competition for domestic use of these exportables has varied considerably.

5.2.2.1. Partial-equilibrium estimates of export functions

Table 5.3 presents single-equation estimates of exports for 1947–1965. The disaggregation is into the same five production sectors and subsectors mentioned above.

On an overall level these results appear to be reasonably satisfactory. The point estimates generally are of the anticipated sign and problems of serial correlation are not apparent (but see note a). The corrected coefficients of determination indicate that variations in the hypothesized determinants are consistent with from 74 to 99% of the variations in the sectoral real exports. The ordering of sectors by such degrees of consistency is services, small- and medium-scale mining, large-scale mining alternative a, agriculture, large-scale mining alternative b, and industry. This pattern weakly suggests that the underlying model may be more consistent with variations in real exports from traditional than from non-traditional sectors[30].

The basic model hypothesizes that current real sectoral exports depend on (1) relative price characteristics, (2) quantitative supply considerations, (3) quantitative demand considerations, and (4) lagged real sectoral exports.

(1) Relative price terms include levels, first differences (to represent anticipations in the Harberger, 1963, accelerator sense), and

[30]This suggestion occurs if non-traditional exports are defined to be well represented by industrial exports and if the first alternative for large-scale mining is acceptable. However, industrial exports include traditional exports at least in the sense that many industrial commodities have been exported for decades; non-traditional exports certainly include some agricultural commodities and (depending on the definition used) perhaps some mining products; and the acceptability of the first estimate for large-scale mining is somewhat questionable. Therefore, such a distinction between traditional and non-traditional exports is weak.

Macroeconomic policy in a developing country

Table
Sectoral real export functions

Sector	Relative prices				Quantitative supply considerations	
	Levels			Standard deviation	1	2
	1	2	3			
Agriculture	39.2^b (9.1) [0.5]	6.72^c (2.6) [0.1]		-17.5^b (1.6) [−0.0]	49.8^d $(1.4)^g$ [0.4]	0.0531^e (2.3) [0.6]
Mining						
Large scale(a)	6.83^h (7.8) [0.2]	1.34^i (6.2) [0.1]		$-306.^j$ (4.1) [−0.1]	$-190.^k$ (3.6) [−0.0]	$-1454.^l$ (5.0) [−1.0]
Large scale (b)	7.99^h (5.6) [0.2]	1.58^i (4.4) [0.1]		$-332.^j$ (2.7) [−0.1]	$-218.^k$ (2.4) [−0.0]	
Small and medium scale	$0.992^{i,m}$ (5.8) [0.4]	$25.1^{j,m}$ $(1.5)^g$ [0.4]			0.106^n $(1.7)^g$ [0.0]	
Industry	$5271.^p$ (2.8) [1.0]	$117.1^{j,m}$ (4.2) [1.9]	$40.8^{c,m}$ (5.1) [4.4]	-48.8^c (2.6) [−0.2]	0.137^e (5.8) [2.0]	$-273.^q$ (1.9) [−1.3]
Services	23.3^r (5.1) [0.2]	11.5^s (4.9) [0.0]				

[a]Underneath the point estimates in parentheses are the absolute value of the *t*-statistics. All such *t*-statistics are significantly non-zero at the 5% level unless otherwise noted. Underneath the *t*-statistics in brackets are the long-run elasticities at the point of sample means. These elasticities are long-run in the sense that all adjustments due to the inclusion of lagged exports are assumed to have occurred. In such relationships, of course, the Durbin–Watson statistic is biased towards two due to the inclusion of the lagged dependent variable. Appendix A gives data sources.

[b]Unit value of sectoral exports times the exchange rate relative to the sectoral labor price including employers' social security contributions.

[c]Black market *PLD NER* minus the national accounts *PLD NER*.

[d]Sectoral output relative to sectoral output lagged.

[e]Sectoral *GDP*.

[f]Dummy variable for LAFTA (value of 1.0 in 1961 and thereafter).

[g]Significantly non-zero at the 10% level.

[h]United States producers' price for copper adjusted for direct tax rate on mining relative to the index of intermediate prices for mining adjusted for the *NER* for large-scale mining.

5.3
for Chile, 1947–1965[a].

Quantitative demand considerations				Lagged exports	Constant	$\bar{R}^2$ SE DW
1	2	3	4			
42.6[f] (5.5) [0.2]					−103. (2.1)	0.87 11.5 1.6
				−0.379 (3.8)	2737. (9.4)	0.91 46.9 1.8
				−0.557 (3.5)	1363. (8.6)	0.75 78.9 2.9
7.14° (3.2) [2.1]	11.5°,m (4.5) [3.2]				−1083. (11.2)	0.96 31.9 2.7
				0.363 (2.3)	−706. (2.8)	0.74 27.7 2.2
0.0261[t] (2.7) [0.3]	0.0567[t] (4.1) [0.6]	0.233[u] (4.1) [0.7]	65.2[f] (3.9) [0.1]	−0.600 (5.2)	−266. (7.6)	0.99 9.1 1.4

[i]United States producers' price for copper adjusted for direct tax rate on mining relative to price of labor in mining including employers' social security contributions.

[j]*PLD NER.*

[k]Post-Korean War Chilean sales monopoly dummy variable with value of 1.0 in 1953.

[l]Total *GDP* lagged one year relative to total *GDP* lagged two years.

[m]Lagged one year.

[n]First difference of sectoral *GDP*.

[o]Index of industrial activity in the United States.

[p]Unit value of sectoral exports times the exchange rate relative to domestic sectoral product price.

[q]Sectoral capacity utilization.

[r]*PLD NER.*

[s]Δ(*PLD NER*) to represent anticipations in the Harberger (1963) accelerator sense.

[t]The first two quantitative demand considerations for services are current and lagged total trade.

[u]*GDP* in Argentina.

standard deviations (as a crude proxy for uncertainty). The underlying price ratios themselves are of three types: (i) the ratio of the external price (or unit value) times the *NER* (adjusted for unit direct tax rates in the case of mining) to factor costs (intermediate or labor costs, the latter adjusted for employers' social security taxes); (ii) the ratio of the external price times the *NER* to the domestic market price; and (iii) ratios relating to various *PLD NER*s. The last group of ratios may be thought to be redundant because it is incorporated in the others. This third group, however, does seem to provide information about the most volatile element in the other ratios. In the cases in which the black market *NER* is involved, moreover, it provides a measure of an added incentive for exporting (perhaps accompanied by some such action as underinvoicing) beyond that captured by the other two types of ratios. Thus, more than one type of relative price ratio is allowed in the estimates.

The estimates in table 5.3 suggest that significant responses to both price levels and standard deviations are widespread. All three types of price ratios mentioned above are of relevance. The implied elasticities are fairly substantial for some sectors. For example, the elasticities with respect to the general *NER* are 2.9 for industry, 0.8 for small- and medium-scale mining, 0.5 for agriculture, 0.3 for large-scale mining and 0.2 for services[31]. Five features of these price responses merit mention.

(i) Price reactions were more pervasive for exports than for imports (see subsection 5.2.2).

(ii) The secular decline in the *PLD NER* caused substantial foreign exchange losses through reduced exports[32]. The above elasticities and the 63% drop in the overall *PLD NER* between 1946 and 1972, for example, *ceteris paribus* imply export drops of 100% from industry, 50% from small- and medium-scale mining, 32% from agriculture, 19% from large-scale mining, and 12% from services[33].

(iii) The non-traditional industrial exports are quite price responsive. The maintenance of a disequilibrium exchange rate system with an overvalued exchange rate, therefore, especially discouraged

[31] These elasticities refer only to changes in the ratio variables. They assume that the standard deviation and the difference between the *PLD NER* for the black market and the national accounts rate remain unchanged.
[32] For most export categories the *PLD EER* has moved closely with the *PLD NER*.
[33] Service exports are much less price responsive than service imports. The elasticity is only about one-fourth as large.

these exports[34]. In this manner the post-Second World War foreign sector regimes increased relative dependence on the traditional exports – despite the fact that one persistent underlying desire supposedly was to reduce their dominance. The export promotion programs started in the 1960s were not very effective because they only partially compensated for overvaluation.

(iv) The price response of large-scale mining exports, in contrast, was relatively small. As one result, the benefits to Chile of the more favorable treatment of this subsector initiated by the *Nuevo Trato* of 1955 probably were quite limited.

(v) For all sources except for small- and medium-scale mining and services[35], the estimates suggest a significant negative response to the standard deviation term. A policy to reduce uncertainty regarding future real returns from exports, thus would have a widespread pay-off in the form of increased exports. The sliding-peg *NER* of 1965–1970 was such a policy. Although the pay-off was widespread across sectors, however, the elasticities imply that it was limited in magnitude.

(2) Quantitative supply considerations include: (i) levels and indices of marginal changes of real sectoral outputs to investigate whether the availability of sectoral real product affects sectoral exports; (ii) sectoral capacity utilization rates and overall aggregate demand to see whether low demand facing a sector – and thus low sectoral capacity utilization – increases attempts to sell to external markets; (iii) the Ffrench-Davis (1971) quantitative restrictions index to explore whether such restrictions either on imported inputs or on explicit exports limit the levels of aggregate sectoral exports; and (iv) dummy variables such as one for the post-Korean War period of the Chilean sales monopoly in the case of mining.

The results support the existence of important reactions to these quantitative supply factors. Marginal changes in output cause significant and, in most cases, substantial responses in exports from agriculture, small- and medium-scale mining, and industry. The state of capacity utilization reinforces this effect in the last of these three sources. The continuance of the Chilean copper sales monopoly in the face of declining demand after the end of the Korean War was

[34]Sierra (1969) also emphasizes this point.
[35]For services, however, there is a significant reaction to a Harberger accelerator term. This term represents (naive) anticipations regarding future changes in the *PLD NER*.

associated with a fall of approximately 20% in the real value of large-scale mining exports.

Large-scale mining exports also seem to be significantly and strongly negatively related to the lagged rate of growth in overall *GDP*. Several interpretations of this relation are possible. (i) In periods of general stagnation inputs are more available for this subsector than otherwise. (ii) In recessions the government more vigorously pursues policies to induce expanded exports from large-scale mining in order to increase aggregate demand generally, and in order to obtain income to offset reduced tax revenues from the rest of the economy. (iii) In cyclical downturns the rate of inflation is less, *ceteris paribus*, so the *PLD EER* for such exports is more favorable. (iv) At such times competing demands for domestic uses are less, so a higher proportion of production was exported[36].

All of these rationales have some merit – although, in some cases, only if the hypothesized effect is not really better represented by another included variable which *a-priori* would seem more logical (e.g. the price ratios for the third possibility). That the total effect of such factors is as large as table 5.3 implies, however, is somewhat doubtful. Therefore, this table also presents an alternative relationship which is identical except for the exclusion of this one variable.

Despite widespread evidence regarding the importance of supply considerations, finally, no significant direct response to foreign sector quantitative restrictions is reported. This lack of statistical evidence does not definitely preclude the existence of a direct impact of quantitative restrictions on exports[37]. The effect of quotas and prohibitions, for example, may be obscured by aggregation, since such measures were applied only to a few specific products. Variations in the quantitative restrictions index, moreover, might not well represent possible negative effects on the competitiveness of Chilean exports. Inefficiencies may have been fostered by the generally high protective barriers, but may have varied quite slowly in response to changing quantitative restrictions.

(3) Quantitative demand considerations include a dummy variable

---

[36]In this case the variable might better be reclassified as representing quantitative demand characteristics.

[37]Simulation 8.3.2 suggests that the indirect impact of quantitative restrictions on exports is considerable.

for the impact of LAFTA and indices of demand in the most important destination countries[38].

The results indicate that only agricultural and service exports increased with the formation of LAFTA, but they rose 20 and 33%, respectively, of the mean real export values for the entire sample period.

The structuralist school (e.g. Sierra, 1969) has placed considerable emphasis on the role of fluctuations in the importing countries. Statistical support for this hypothesis is presented only for small- and medium-scale mining and services. The former was a relatively marginal supplier in the markets in which it participated and thus was more subject to demand fluctuations. Small- and medium-scale mining was a marginal supplier for two reasons: it lacked the intracorporation ties which large-scale mining had, and expanded its production capacities relatively quickly and had to find new buyers. For services, the Argentinian product is important because that neighboring country has long been the most important source of tourists visiting Chile, and such tourism is income sensitive. Service exports also respond to the overall trade level and the related demand for the Chilean provision of associated services (as is the case for service imports).

(4) Lagged exports are included to represent either the distributed lag adjustment of actual to desired real sectoral exports over several periods due to adjustment costs or an inventory effect (in the sense that large real sectoral exports one year result in inventory depletion and smaller exports in the subsequent year, *ceteris paribus*). The *a-priori* expected signs due to these two possibilities are opposite so that the two effects may cancel each other out partially or completely[39]. No attempt is made to identify these effects separately, however, in this study.

The estimates suggest that the inventory effect dominates for large-scale mining and the adjustment effect dominates for industry. Apparently, adjustment costs are relatively higher for the latter

---

[38]Incorporation of quantitative demand characteristics makes the results in table 5.3 for some sources more reduced-form, market-clearing relationships than export–supply functions.

[39]In respect to the difference between short- and long-run elasticities, the two effects have opposite implications. If the inventory effect is dominant, the short-run elasticity exceeds the long-run elasticity. The opposite is the case if the adjustment effect is prevalent.

sector. For agriculture and small- and medium-scale mining the two considerations neutralize each other. For service exports the estimates imply the dominance of an inventory effect. Although the existence of an inventory effect in respect to such service exports as those for tourists from neighboring countries does not seem unreasonable, the absolute magnitude of this coefficient is surprisingly large. The explanation probably is that the series for the dependent variable better reflects the payment of services (for which an inventory effect makes more sense) than the provision of services. Lags in payments also underlie the significance of the lagged trade term in addition to the current one for this sector.

5.2.3. Net factor income from abroad

During the sample period Chilean net factor payments from abroad primarily reflected payments to foreign-owned factors in large-scale mining. These net movements in absolute terms averaged 3.5% of the value of exports in 1945–1965. The determination of these movements is hypothesized to depend on flows related to large-scale mining: the prices of mining inputs (labor and intermediate), the real level of total or of mining exports, the price of mining products (or of copper in particular), the legal cost of production in large-scale mining, the employers' social security tax rate and the direct tax rate on large-scale mining, the *NER* for large-scale mining, and, possibly, foreign sector quantitative restrictions. This relationship is a somewhat *ad hoc* attempt to estimate the determinants of real factor income from abroad in response to composite variables constructed on the basis of such considerations:

$$NFIAB = 26.5V_1 - 0.840V_2 - 0.116V_3 + 0.377V_4 - 376.,$$
$$ (2.1) \quad (2.2) \quad (3.0) \quad (1.8) \quad (5.6)$$
$$ [-0.8] \quad [0.4] \quad [0.4] \quad [-0.7] \qquad (5.2)$$
$$\bar{R}^2 = 0.81, \quad SE = 31.4, \quad DW = 1.7, \quad 1947\text{–}1965,$$

where *NFIAB* is the net factor income from abroad in constant terms; V_1 is the real wage rate in mining, including employers' social security tax contributions; V_2 is the dollar value of mining exports after adjustment for direct taxes on large-scale mining relative to dollar cost of intermediate mining inputs at special *NER* for large-scale mining; V_3 is the export value with adjustment for direct taxes on large-scale mining relative to intermediate input index for mining with adjustment for ratio of national accounts to large-scale mining *NER*s (with all components lagged one year); and V_4 is the real value of the legal cost of production for large-scale mining at the large-scale mining *NER* (with all components lagged one year).

These factors are consistent with a considerable proportion of the variance in the dependent variable. The coefficients are of the anticipated signs. Judging from the *t*-statistics and the elasticities, government policies regarding the *NER*, the legal cost of production, and the tax rates for large-scale mining had particular important direct roles in determining variations in net factor payments from abroad.

Foreign sector quantitative restrictions[40], on the other hand, were not important because the Chilean government never limited the freedom of the large-scale mining companies in regard to the repatriation of after-tax earnings. In fact, the companies were not required either to return such earnings to Chile or to convert them into escudos.

Given a desire to limit factor payments abroad, finally, relation (5.2) supports the reluctance of Chilean governments to increase the *PLD NER* for large-scale mining. The export estimate for large-scale mining in table 5.2, however, implies that the limiting of foreign factor payments from this subsector was purchased at a price of reduced national command over foreign exchange from exports. It is not clear that awareness of this trade-off always existed.

---

[40]That is, quantitative restrictions beyond those which limited large-scale mining to a special *NER* for currency to pay for domestic inputs.

CHAPTER 6

Prices

Despite the existence of a small subsistence sector and of some direct quantitative allocations by the government, the Chilean economy is basically a market economy. Many of the policies discussed in ch. 3 have all or much of their impact through changing the absolute price level of relative prices[1]. Both supply and demand, as demonstrated in chs. 4 and 5, respond significantly to prices. Preoccupation with the considerable inflation, as described in ch. 2, has been a major feature of the postwar economy. Prices also play a major role in income distribution. For all of these reasons the question of what determines prices is of considerable interest.

This chapter addresses that question within a partial-equilibrium framework. Each of the sections considers the determinants of the rates of change of a group of prices: sectoral product prices, sectoral prices of labor, and other prices (i.e. intermediate input price indices, price of investment by destination, cost of capital by destination, national accounts deflators for major final demand components, wholesale and consumer price indices, and the black market exchange rate). Focus is on the rates of change of these prices because multicollinearity among the levels is so high due to the prolonged inflation[2].

---

[1]Hansen (1973) claims that government policies generally tend to work much more through altering relative prices in the developing countries than in the developed economies.

[2]One possible problem with utilizing the rates of change is that the estimates may pick up variations in the higher, but not the lower frequencies. Explanations with alternative formulations, however, do not reveal greater success in single-equation or complete model predictions.

6.1. Sectoral product prices[3]

Table 6.1 gives the mean rate of change and the ratio of the standard deviation from the secular trend to the mean for sectoral product prices during the 1945–1965 sample period. Column 1 indicates that for all but three sectors mean price increases were within 1.5% of the national average. Even among these sectors, however, fairly substantial changes in relative prices occurred in some cases because of the cumulative effect of maintaining slight discrepancies in growth rates for more than two decades. The three sectors with larger discrepancies from the national average are mining, construction, and housing. Mining had a relatively fast price increase because world market conditions changed from a fixed, below-equilibrium copper price in 1945 to the copper market boom of the mid-1960s (see Behrman, 1975b, subsections 4.2.1 and 7.1.2.3). Construction and housing had relatively low price increases, partially because of price controls on residential dwellings. On an overall basis, whether or not these three sectors are included, there is very little correlation between the sectoral price increases and growth in either sectoral real capacities or products (columns 2 and 14 in table 4.1). Of course, given differential supply and demand elasticities and shifts in supply and demand curves, there is no reason *a priori* to expect strong associations.

Column 2 of table 6.1 gives a measure of relative price stability around the overall inflationary trend. These variances have been particularly large for mining, and less so for manufacturing, but quite small for construction. This pattern suggests a positive association between the extent to which goods are tradable internationally and the degree of volatility. Of course, some of the variations for tradables originate in international fluctuations, especially for mining. The analysis in Behrman (1975a, 1975b), however, suggests that Chilean trade policy has contributed quite substantially to domestic price fluctuations.

[3]Behrman (1973c), Corbo (1971), García (1964), Harberger (1963) and Yver (1970) present earlier estimates of Chilean price determination (although generally on a more aggregate level than is used here).

Table 6.1
Characteristics of sector product and labor prices, 1945–1965[a].

Sectors	Product prices		Price of labor		
	Mean annual percentage increase	Standard deviation from trend as percentage of mean	Mean annual percentage increase	Standard deviation from trend as percentage of mean	Mean as percentage of overall mean
	1	2	3	4	5
Agriculture	30.1	20.7	36.4	19.4	50.7
Mining	33.9	30.6	31.9	17.4	186.4
Construction	27.0	11.9	34.1	25.3	145.2
Manufacturing	29.6	23.1	31.9	18.3	157.4
Transportation	30.8	19.1	35.0	41.7	131.6
Utilities	30.5	21.4	36.9	45.7	169.3
Housing	25.2	18.0			
Services	30.4	18.5	33.1	13.9	100.6
Government			31.9	24.4	47.0
Total	29.6	19.2	32.9	14.1	100.0

[a] Appendix A gives the underlying data sources.

6.1.1. Model of sectoral price change determinants and estimates

In a long-run, perfectly competitive equilibrium with no quantitative restrictions and no water in the tariff, the domestic producers price of internationally traded commodities would equal the cif price of the same commodities adjusted for price-related characteristics of the international economic regime. In such a situation the exchange rate and the prices of non-traded commodities also would have adjusted so that equilibrium existed in international payments and so that the domestic demand for real monetary balances equaled the supply of such assets.

Actual Chilean prices, of course, are not at long-run, perfectly competitive equilibrium levels. Instead, they are constantly adjusting the response to substantial shocks, especially in monetary policy and in the international economic regime (including varying degrees of use of quantitative restrictions in the latter). Thus, to estimate price determinants, sector-specific characteristics of the impact of relevant domestic and international variables and the sector-specific adjustment to those characteristics must be included.

The general specification adopted here reflects the assumption that the rate of change of prices in a particular product market is a function of the level and the rates of the excess demand in that market, which in turn depend upon the positions and rates of movement of the demand and supply curves for that market. Because of the unavailability of key data – in particular, sectoral inventory estimates – a somewhat eclectic quasi-reduced form is used. The dependent variable is the rate of change of prices because the high Chilean inflation rates in the sample period cause so much multicollinearity if levels are utilized that one cannot distinguish among competing hypotheses[4].

Table 6.2 presents estimates of the determinants of the rate of change of Chilean sectoral prices for 1945–1965. From an overall viewpoint these estimates appear quite satisfactory. The corrected coefficients of determination indicate that the specification is consistent with from 90 to 98% of the variance in the dependent variable over the sample period. No serious problems of serial correlation

---

[4]The adjustment processes are represented by the Hall–Sutch (1969) polynominal method (without a tail) over a six-year period for the rates of change of the money supply and real *GDP* and for expectations regarding the rate of change of the *NER*. Other adjustments are represented by the possibility of a geometric process for the dependent variable or by simple lags for other variables.

are obvious. The estimated coefficients generally have the *a-priori* anticipated signs.

For only three sectors – construction, transportation, and utilities – is the constant significantly non-zero at the 5% level. For two additional sectors – manufacturing and services – the constant is significantly nonzero at the 10% level. The estimated constants alone give the following ordering of secular sectoral growth rates in prices: utilities, manufacturing, construction, services, agriculture-mining–housing, and transportation. This ranking has little relation to that of actual growth rates of prices given in column 1 of table 6.1. The variables in the model modify considerably the relative growth patterns implied by the estimates of the constants.

These variables reflect the level and the movements in supply and demand due to both domestic and foreign sector conditions and to both general and sector-specific considerations. For discussion, they are considered in seven groups.

(1) Differentiation of the structural relations underlying the demand functions, including the demand for real money balances held as a function of income and of opportunity costs, and solution for the rate of change of prices suggests the first three general variables. The most important of these is the rate of change of the nominal money supply. In all sectors this variable has a substantial impact, either directly or indirectly through the rate of change of factor prices.

Such a result does not necessarily support the monetarist position in the monetarist–structuralist controversy over the cause of inflation. As discussed in section 3.2 above, in fact, the money supply is not completely an exogenous policy instrument, but is determined, in large part, endogenously. Therefore these results imply only that growth in the money supply is the proximate 'cause' of much of the Chilean inflation, not that it is the underlying fundamental source.

The lag patterns suggest very different timing of responses across sectors. That part of the pressure for price increases is transmitted through factor prices precludes a complete ordering of all the sectors in this respect. Nevertheless, manufacturing, construction, and utilities seem to respond relatively quickly, and services and housing relatively slowly. In disequilibrium these variances in adjustment result in some substantial relative price differentials.

These adjustment patterns also imply that not insignificant responses to changes in the money supply occur with a lag of several years. This result contrasts with the earlier work of Gregory (1967),

Table
Determinants of the rates of change of

Dependent variables: Rate of change of sectoral product prices	Domestic variables:				Economic
	Money supply[b]			Real product[c]	Current indicators index
Lags					0
Order of polynomial	1[b]	2	3	1[c]	2
Agriculture					
Mining					
Construction	−0.648[f] (4.2)	0.187 (3.3)	−0.0167 (3.0)	[f]	
Manufacturing	−1.24 (8.0)	0.433 (7.3)	−0.0414 (6.9)	0.250 (2.9)	
Transportation					0.634 (4.5)
Utilities	−0.621 (3.2)	0.163 (2.2)	−0.0128 (1.7)	0.566 (3.7)	0.338 (2.1)
Housing	−0.0465 (5.9)			1.814 (4.0)	−0.236 (3.6)
Services	−0.111[f] (2.2)	0.0128 (2.2)		[f]	

	Foreign sector variables:		
	Exchange rate[p]		Relative effective exchange rate for intermediate inputs
Lag			0
Order of polynomial	1	2	
Agriculture	−45.2 (1.5)[l]	5.43 (1.5)[l]	0.283[r] (2.9)
Mining			
Construction			0.191[m] (2.0)
Manufacturing			
Transportation			0.492 (3.8)

Chilean sectoral prices, 1945–1965ᵃ.

Rate of change in:

activity		Intermediate input prices	Labor variables		Average real labor productivity	Sector-specific variable
Alternative 1	Alternative 2		Unit real labor costs (including employer) SS tax			
0	1	0	0	1	0	
0.417ᵈ (2.2)	−0.715ᵉ (2.2)	0.890 (10.0)				
0.217ᵈ (2.4)			0.160 (3.9)			
1.21ᵍ (3.0)	0.378ᵍ (3.1)				−1.37 (3.8)	−0.515ʰ (5.1)
		0.478 (7.6)	0.191 (2.9)			−0.146ⁱ (4.6)
	−1.05ʲ (2.7)	0.357 (2.4)	0.0623 (1.3)ᵏ	0.0891 (1.5)ˡ	−0.870 (6.6)	
		0.298ᵐ (3.1)	0.145 (3.5)	0.298 (3.1)		
				0.125 (3.5)		1.12ⁿ (5.1)
		1.03 (8.7)	0.272 (4.3)		−0.776 (4.8)	−0.509ʰ (6.0)

Rate of change in:

Import deflator	Ffrench-Davis quantitative restrictions index	Prior depositsᑫ or sector specific	Constant	$\bar{R}^2$ / SE / DW
0	0	0		
				0.93 / 0.050 / 2.0
0.0854ᵐ (2.8)		0.749ˢ (15.6)		0.98 / 0.040 / 2.3
	−0.903 (1.8)	−1.04ᵗ (2.0)	0.0599 (1.8)	0.93 / 0.039 / 2.1
		−0.0091 (2.9)	0.128 (1.4)ˡ	0.98 / 0.033 / 2.6
0.470 (3.5)	0.992 (1.6)ˡ	−0.0015 (2.4)	−0.295 (3.8)	0.94 / 0.047 / 2.3

Table 6.2

Utilities

Housing -0.234^m
                                                                             (1.9)

Services

[a]Beneath the point estimates in parentheses are given the absolute values of the
t-statistics. All point estimates are significantly non-zero at the 5% level unless
otherwise indicated. Because the variables are in rate of change form, the point
estimates are elasticities. In those cases in which the lagged dependent variable is

Sector		
	-0	-1
Construction	0.770	0.290
Manufacturing	0.819	-0.034
Utilities	0.642	0.171
Housing	0.279	0.232
Services	0.203	0.105

[c]The Hall–Sutch (1969) polynomial method (without a tail) is used over a six-year

Sector		
	-0	-1
Manufacturing	-1.50	-1.25
Utilities	-3.40	-2.83
Housing	-2.37	-0.797

[d]Total real sectoral demand relative to real sectoral output.
[e]Total current inventory level relative to total *GDP*.
[f]The underlying variable is the money supply relative to real *GDP*.
[g]Sectoral capacity utilization.
[h]Lagged dependent variable.
[i]Stabilization dummy with value of 1.0 in 1956, 1957, 1959, 1960, 1961, 1965 and 0.0
otherwise.

Sector		
	-0	-1
Agriculture	0.0763	0.0364

[q]In this column are the coefficients of the prior deposit variables unless otherwise
indicated. The prior deposit variable is the change in the cost of prior deposits, not the
rate of change thereof.
[r]Domestic wholesale price index for agricultural products relative to United States
wholesale price index, all relative to the national accounts *EER*.

(continued)

0.204[u]		0.232	0.97	
(3.8)		(1.8)	0.036	
			2.6	
−0.325[v]			0.90	
(2.4)			0.062	
			2.3	
−1.66	−0.0041	0.0467	0.98	
(2.7)	(1.4)[l]	(1.5)[l]	0.036	
			3.0	

included the Durbin–Watson statistic is biased towards two. Appendix A gives the data sources.

[b]The Hall–Sutch (1969) polynomial method (without a tail) is used over a six-year period. The implied lag patterns are as follows:

Lags

−2	−3	−4	−5
0.088	0.056	0.098	0.113
−0.270	−0.136	0.119	0.247
−0.052	−0.103	−0.060	−0.000
0.186	0.139	0.093	0.046
0.033	−0.014	−0.035	−0.030

period. The implied lag patterns are as follows:

Lags

−2	−3	−4	−5
−1.00	−0.75	−0.50	−0.25
−2.26	−1.70	−1.13	−0.57
0.308	0.940	1.10	0.786

[j]Total inventory level relative to total *GDP*.
[k]Significantly non-zero at the 15% level.
[l]Significantly non-zero at the 10% level.
[m]This variable is lagged one year for this sector.
[n]Share of *GDP* originating in agriculture.
[p]The Hall–Sutch (1969) polynomial method (without a tail) is used over a six-year period. The implied lag patterns are as follows:

Lags

−2	−3	−4	−5
0.0073	−0.0104	−0.0181	−0.0145

[s]Unit value of mining exports times the national accounts *NER*.
[t]Lag of quantitative restrictions index.
[u]Black market *NER* relative to national accounts *NER*.
[v]Domestic *GDP* deflator relative to United States *GDP* deflator adjusted for the average import tax rate and the average prior-import-deposit rate.

Harberger (1963), and Ramos (1968) which suggest complete adjustment in the current year or after one more year. The substantially
greater lags found in this study obviously imply much greater
difficulties in eliminating inflation. The failures of four substantial
Chilean anti-inflationary programs in the last two decades attest to
those difficulties[5].

(2) The second variable implied by the differentiation of the
demand relations is the rate of change of real income. In construction, manufacturing, utilities, housing, and services this variable is a
significant determinant of sectoral price changes with the *a-priori*
anticipated negative sign due to the dominance of the positive effect
of higher real income on desired real balances (but see the fourth
variable below for discussion of an identification problem). The lag
patterns which are most consistent with variations in the dependent
variable once again extend over a number of years (and for
construction and services, in fact, are identical to those for the rate
of change of the money supply). Presumably these lags relate to
permanent income considerations in the demand functions.

(3) The third variable suggested by the differentiation of the
demand relations, or of the demand for real money balances in
particular, is the rate of change of the opportunity cost of holding
money. In an economy in which the major alternative to holding real
monetary balances is bonds, the rate of change of the bond rate
would be the appropriate variable. In Chile, however, the bond
market is very small, and goods represent the primary alternative to
holding money. Any variations in nominal interest rates, moreover,
have been swamped by fluctuations in the rate of inflation (section
3.2). Therefore the opportunity cost of holding real monetary
balances is best represented by the expected rate of inflation.
Differentiation leads to the first difference of the rate of inflation or
Harberger's (1963) accelerator variable. The addition of such a
variable to the relationships included in table 6.2 in no case results in
a significant coefficient. For manufacturing, however, the inclusion
of a dummy variable for the change in inflationary expectations at
the start of stabilization efforts does have a significant coefficient
which implies a drop of about 15% for price increases in that sector.

---

[5]The lag patterns also suggest some overshooting of the type discussed by Diz
(1966) and Behrman (1973c) – at least for manufacturing, utilities, and services. The
inclusion of a number of other correlated variables, however, precludes consideration
of the nature of these patterns in a partial-equilibrium context.

(4) The representation of the disequilibrium pressures between supply and demand is difficult because of the non-existence of time series for sectoral inventory data. In an attempt to represent demand pressures relative to supply, several variables are included in the price–change determination relationships: the inventory level relative to *GDP* and the rates of change of an *NBER*-type current economic indicators index, sectoral capacity utilization, and total demand facing a sector (including both intermediate and final components) relative to capacity. For all of the sectors except manufacturing, housing, and services at least one of these indices has a significant coefficient which implies a fairly substantial response to aggregate demand–supply conditions beyond that captured by the first three general variables.

(5) Further consideration of the supply side is provided by 'cost-push' type variables. These variables are pervasive in their impact. For every sector the rate of change of at least one of the following has a significant impact with the *a-priori* anticipated sign: intermediate input prices, unit labor costs (including employers' social security tax contributions), and average real labor productivity[6]. The results imply that rises in real labor productivity, for example, reduce price increases in all of the sectors except for agriculture. The general and often not-insubstantial impact of these cost-push variables contrasts sharply with the results of Harberger (1963). Only in his quarterly regression for the import price component (*sic*) of the wholesale price index does he present evidence of significant (at the 5% level) influence of labor costs on the rate of change of disaggregate prices. This difference between the present results and those of Harberger probably reflects his use of the rate of change of the government minimum wage (*sueldo vital*) instead of sector-specific wage and intermediate input cost data[7]. In any

[6]For transportation and services, both unit labor costs and average real labor productivity are included. *Prima facie* the inclusion of the latter variable in addition to the former may seem redundant. If the underlying technology is *CES* with elasticities of substitution unequal to one (see section 4.1) and the price is set so that the value of the marginal product of labor is equal to the wage, however, unit labor costs and real average labor productivity both enter into the relation:

$$\log P = \log ULC - [(1/\sigma) - 1] \log (V/L),$$

where P is the price, ULC is the unit labor cost, V/L is average labor productivity, and σ is the elasticity of substitution between capital and labor.

[7]The estimates discussed below in subsection 6.2.2 suggest that, in general, changes in the minimum wage do not accurately represent wage changes. See also Ramos (1968).

case, the results in respect to labor and intermediate costs in table
6.2 suggest a much larger role for cost-push factors in the determination of sectoral price changes than Harberger seems to allow. In
agreement with Harberger's interpretation, however, I see this role
as being one of transmitting overall pressures for price increases to
specific product prices. The determination of the rate of change of
wages, for example, apparently depends substantially on expectations as to the future rate of inflation, and such expectations
probably largely reflect recent experience (see section 6.2 below,
Behrman, 1971a, Behrman and García, 1973, and Ramos, 1968).

(6) Changes in sectoral and factoral income and product distribution variables might affect the relative rates of inflation in various
sectors because of their impact on the composition of demand. The
estimates in table 6.2 provide support for such a direct effect in only
one case. For the rate of change of housing prices, the change in the
share of *GDP* originating in agriculture has a significantly positive
coefficient. Even in this case, moreover, it is quite possible that the
downward trend in the share of *GDP* originating in agriculture is
only serving as a proxy for the downward pressure on the relative
price of housing through rent control. There is not much hard
evidence, thus, of the direct impact of distributional variables on
relative prices at the sectoral level in the Chilean experience, except
in so far as other variables discussed transmit such pressures.

(7) The international economic regime affects both demand and
supply factors. It has widespread impact in that some aspect of the
international economic regime apparently is a significantly non-zero
direct determinant of the rate of change of prices in every sector.

Price-related characteristics have significantly non-zero impact in
five of the eight sectors. These factors include expectational effects
of exchange rate changes[8], cost-push factors related to imported
intermediate inputs[9], and international prices[10]. The estimates imply
the highest relative responses to devaluation in the export-oriented
mining sector and in the relatively import-dependent transportation
sector.

[8]The *NER* changes may also represent a cost-push factor in that the local currency
cost of external indebtedness increases as the *NER* increases.

[9]The results suggest that the rate of growth of the price of services declines
relatively when these imported inputs increase relatively in price.

[10]For no sector is there evidence of significant response to rates of change of
import unit values times the *EER* or to sectoral imports relative to domestic
absorption.

Quantitative restrictions have significantly non-zero effects on price changes in five of the eight sectors[11]. The largest positive response is in transportation, which is consistent with the relatively large impact of quantitative restrictions on transportation imports, discussed in Behrman (1975b, subsection 6.2.1). However, negative responses are suggested for three non-tradable goods sectors. This might be rationalized as reflecting an inverse relationship between quantitative restrictions and the availability of inputs and credit to these sectors, although such an explanation seems somewhat forced. For services, the inverse response may be due to the considerable import-related trade margins included in this sector.

For industry, transportation, and services, finally, evidence exists of one further significantly non-zero direct link between the international economic policy regime and price changes. When prior import deposit requirements are increased (section 3.3), part of the banking system credit is absorbed and inflationary pressure is reduced – apparently especially in these sectors.

6.1.2. Implications of estimates

The estimates in table 6.2 support the proposition that major direct determinants of changes in sectoral prices have been the variables implied by the differentiation of the demand relations. Of particular significance is the rate of change of money supply. Four important aspects of these results, however, merit reiteration.

(1) The response is distributed over a much longer period of time than other studies have suggested. Therefore, breaking the inflationary pattern will be very difficult unless expectations are altered radically so that the legacy from the past no longer influences current price movements so much.

(2) The importance of changes in the money supply in this partial-equilibrium context does *not* mean that a lack of monetary discipline by the Central Bank is the underlying cause of Chilean inflation. The money supply, in fact, is an endogenous variable in the complete system (section 3.2). The Central Bank has only very limited control over its magnitude. Within the present institutional

---

[11]To the extent that changes in quantitative restrictions only change the premia going to traders with import licenses, of course, these changes do not affect sectoral prices.

framework, fiscal policies and foreign sector developments are much more important.

(3) In addition to the general variables affecting demand relations, other factors enter into the determination of prices. Proxies for demand relative to supply and for movements of the supply curve due to cost-push factors have significant and substantial impact in almost every sector. This result, once again, contrasts with earlier studies of the Chilean experience.

Not only general domestic considerations, but also those from the foreign sector are significant in a number of sectors. Both price-related and quantitative aspects of the international regime have effects. On the basis of these partial-equilibrium estimates, for example, devaluation would be accompanied by increased direct inflationary pressure – particularly for mining, transportation, and agricultural products.

(4) Sector-specific factors are pervasive in their impact: sectoral capacity utilization, domestic and international sectoral input prices, sectoral unit labor costs, and sectoral labor productivities. Chs. 4 and 5 give empirical evidence that significant responses to sectoral prices do occur in both short- and long-run Chilean allocation decisions (see also Behrman, 1972c and 1973a). The results in table 6.2 indicate that at least signals in the right directions are given for these allocation decisions. The price system apparently is playing to some degree a role that probably leads to greater efficiency. To ignore this role when conducting analysis and giving policy prescriptions may be costly in terms of foregoing the use of some policy tools and in terms of creating incentives for misallocations. Yet this role is ignored in much analysis and in many policy recommendations (see section 1.1).

A related point, finally, is that the responses are quite heterogeneous among sectors both in regard to lag patterns and to absolute magnitudes. As Hansen (1973) has emphasized, many of the interesting effects of government policies are on relative prices. These are lost with the greater level of aggregation used in previous studies (e.g. Gregory, 1967, Harberger, 1963, and Ramos, 1968). Ch. 8 below provides illustrations of these differential sectoral responses within a complete system framework.

6.2. Sectoral wages

The determinants of sectoral wages are of considerable interest for at least three reasons. (1) As indicated in section 6.1, wage changes play an important role in the determination of price changes (although perhaps only in the transmission of various pressures). (2) Factoral and sector income distribution is shaped in large part by sectoral wages. (3) Chs. 4 and 5 emphasize how wages affect both short- and long-run allocation decisions. The question remains to what extent do sectoral wages reflect productivity, unemployment, and other efficiency considerations.

Tables 4.1 (columns 3–6), and 6.1 (columns 3–5) and 6.3 provide information about various aspects of sectoral labor markets during the 1945–1965 sample period: the mean percentage distribution of the labor force across sectors, the mean percentage growth rates of sectoral labor forces, mean relative sectoral labor productivities, mean percentage growth rates in productivities, mean annual increases in sectoral wages, the volatility of sectoral wages as measured by the ratio of the standard deviation from the trend to the mean, the relative sectoral wages, and the correlation coefficients among the sectoral wage growth rates.

These data indicate substantial variance for the mean sectoral wage rates (column 5 in table 6.1). Mining has had the highest

Table 6.3
Correlation coefficients of annual rates of change of Chilean sectoral money wages, 1945–1965[a].

Sector	Correlation coefficients[b]							
	A	M	C	M	T	U	G	S
Agriculture	1.0							
Mining	0.65	1.0						
Construction	0.54	0.60	1.0					
Manufacturing	0.72	0.78	0.75	1.0				
Transportation	0.77	0.31	0.33	0.38	1.0			
Utilities	0.80	0.58	0.62	0.73	0.79	1.0		
Government	0.60	0.79	0.61	0.71	0.25	0.50	1.0	
Services	0.63	0.71	0.22	0.68	0.35	0.49	0.65	1.0

[a]Data sources are given in appendix A.
[b]A correlation coefficient of 0.42 or greater is significantly non-zero at the 5% level, and a correlation coefficient of 0.54 or greater is significantly non-zero at the 1% level.

average wage, which is not surprising since the large-scale copper miners long have been considered the aristocracy of Chilean laborers. The high wages in this sector reflect that labor is highly organized therein, foreign exchange regulations have often encouraged capital-intensive technology in this sector (see Behrman, 1975b, section 11.1), and the desire to avoid political problems led the foreign-owned companies to prefer a smaller, but higher-paid labor force than static maximization might have indicated.

The other above-average wage sectors generally are those which long have been encouraged by the government, especially by protective foreign sector and subsidized capital policies: utilities, manufacturing, and transportation. Construction also has had a mean wage above the last of these, but presumably not for the same reasons. The low-range sectors have been the government, agriculture, and perhaps services. These sectors generally have not benefited from the policies just mentioned.

Comparison of the mean relative wages (column 5 in table 6.1) with the mean labor productivities (column 5 in table 4.1) suggests a limited association. Of course, even under competitive conditions one would expect that wages would equal the marginal product of labor, not the average product. If the underlying technology were Cobb–Douglas, marginal products would be proportional to average products and the limited association between mean wages and average labor products might raise questions about any assumed neoclassical behavior. But the results of section 4.1 cast doubt upon the appropriateness of a Cobb–Douglas technology. If the more general CES technology is assumed, the marginal product of labor is proportional not to the average product, but to the average product raised to the power of one divided by the elasticity of substitution between capital and labor. In some cases (i.e. construction, utilities, and government) this proportionality, together with the estimates of the elasticity of substitution between capital and labor in tables 4.2 and 4.3, changes the relative rankings between average and marginal labor productivities so that the latter are more consistent with the sectoral ordering by mean wages.

Under the assumption that there is no systematic bias in the data for the rate of change of money wages and the rate of change for *GDP* deflators[12], real sectoral wages have increased from 2 to 7%

[12]Many observers think that the wage data used understates the *level* of actual wages systematically because there is an incentive to underreport wages in order to

per year. In every sector, except for mining, wage increases have been higher on the average than product price increases (columns 1 and 3 in table 6.1). Given that per capital real income increased at an annual rate of 1.4% over the sample period, the real income of wage earners probably increased relative to the national average. Given the position of wage earners in the distribution of income, disparities between lower-middle-class and upper-class incomes thus probably were reduced due to these real wage increases.

Sectoral wage movements have not been completely synchronized, however. The cross-sector correlations among rates of change of wages are significantly non-zero at the 5% level in 22 of the 28 cases, but in no case are greater than 0.80 (table 6.3). The ratios of the standard deviations from the trend to the means suggest that real wages have been much more volatile in utilities and transportation and, to a lesser extent, in construction and government[13], than in the other sectors (column 4 in table 6.1). The dispersion in this volatility has been much greater for wages than for product prices, with but limited association between the relative extent of variations in these two sets of prices (columns 1 and 4 in table 6.1).

Differing rates of growth wages across sectors have tended to

---

lessen employers' social security tax contributions and because of the existence of considerable non-wage benefits. The effects of such considerations on any bias in the *rate of change* of nominal wages, however, are not so clear. If employers have increased the extent of their underreporting because of the increases in the employers' social security tax rate (in the sample period such rates increased from 0.23 to 0.42), and/or if coverage within sectors has been expanded to include the lower-paying components thereof, the rate of increase of wages as estimated from the social security data would be biased downwards. If employers have been forced by the government to lessen the extent of underreporting and/or if employers have replaced non-wage benefits with wages, the rate of increase of wages as estimated from the social security data would be biased upwards. In my judgment all the tendencies suggested in the previous two sentences probably have occurred, but the net effect on the growth rates of money wages is not obvious and very little solid information is available with which to test for the net direction of the biases.

[13]The smallest overall standard deviation (not the standard deviation around the secular trend) is recorded for the government and mining (Behrman, 1971a). The relative stability by this measure of the rate of increase of nominal wages implied in the government sector may reflect the relative stability in legal minimum wage (*sueldo vital*) adjustments, and the relative stability implied in mining may reflect oligopsonistic behavior on the part of this heavily concentrated and foreign-controlled industry. Given the strong inflationary history, however, the measure used in the text seems more appropriate.

reduce real wage differentials among the goods-producing sectors of agriculture, mining, and manufacturing. For each of these cases above-average growth rates have been associated with below-average levels and vice versa (columns 3 and 5 in table 6.1). For the non-goods-producing sectors of transportation, utilities, services, and government, however, the opposite has been true. In these cases, differing rates of growing have tended to accentuate intersectoral wage discrepancies over time. The net effects on intersectoral wage levels depends upon what weights are attached to these opposing tendencies.

Comparison of the growth rates in sectoral wages (column 3 in table 6.1) with the growth rates in sectoral average labor productivities (column 6 in table 4.1) suggests no particular association. The adjustment discussed above for the relation between average and marginal labor productivities when the elasticity of substitution between capital and labor differs from one, however, in all cases but one (i.e. services) implies that the ranking by marginal labor productivities is more related to that for sector wages than is the ranking by average labor productivities.

One final question of interest about the sectoral wage changes is how are they associated with sectoral unemployment rates? Unfortunately, unemployment data are not available for most of the sample period. The mean capacity utilization rates (column 10 in table 4.1), however, are one available proxy. The secular growth rate of the labor force (column 4 in table 4.1) is another proxy under the assumption that the labor force has grown more quickly in sectors in which unemployment has been less. These seems to be almost no positive association between the ranking of sectors by these two sets of rates and by the growth rates in wages[14]. A simple comparison of the crude data, thus, does not support the hypothesis that wages have increased more rapidly in sectors in which the labor market has been tighter.

6.2.1. Model for the determination of the rates of change of sectoral wages

The specification of the model reflects the assumption that the rate of change of nominal wages in a particular labor market is a function

---

[14]For the labor force growth rates, in fact, if anything, the association is negative.

of the level and the rates of change of the excess demand for labor in that market, which in turn depend upon the positions and rates of movement of the demand and supply curves for that market. In the model specification the attempt is made to include the forces affecting both demand behavior and supply behavior. Although the data limitations are in some respects severe, the possibility seems to exist of representing (sometimes rather crudely) many of the major underlying considerations.

On the *demand side*, aspects of market behavior are represented by seven groups of variables.

(1) Simple economic theory of the firm suggests that changes in the marginal revenue product of labor should be important. To represent these considerations the rate of change of nominal and/or real average value added per laborer in the sector of interest are included. If the elasticity of substitution between capital and labor is significantly different from one, both of these variables may have significant coefficients, because under neoclassical behavior the response to changes in product prices may be different from the response to changes in average labor productivity[15]. If the elasticity of substitution between capital and labor is not significantly different from one, the rate of change of the nominal value added per laborer would seem to be more relevant unless the rate of change of the product price is being adequately represented by some other variable (e.g. expectations of the rate of change of consumer prices), in which case the rate of change of the real value added per worker instead might have a significant coefficient estimate. One particular factor in changing labor productivity is the stock of capital or capacity per laborer. Another factor which Harberger and Selowsky (1966) have argued has been very important in the Chilean experi-

---

[15]Under neoclassical behavior and an assumed CES production function with no technological change, labor L, value added V, the price of value added P, the wage of labor W, and the elasticity of substitution between capital and labor σ will be related as is indicated in the following expression (ignoring any stochastic elements):

$$W = \text{constant}(V_P/L)(V/L)(1/\sigma) - 1.$$

If the wage change determination relation discussed in the text can be considered to be a linear approximation to the relationship for the rate of change of wages derived from the above expression, and if σ is unequal to one, both the value of the average labor product and the average labor product may be included. For estimates of the elasticities of substitution between capital and labor for the sectors included in this study, see section 4.1 above.

ence is the change in the stock of human capital per capita[16]. Both of these variables are included in the model to see if they add any explanatory power to the rates of change of nominal and/or real average labor productivities.

(2) Representatives of Chilean enterprises argue that the level of credit availability is an important determinant of their ability to utilize productive capacity and thus maintain their labor force[17]. The rates of change of wages, therefore, may be affected by the rates of change of credit (relative to product) made available.

(3) The rate of change of subsidies relative to product would seem to play the same role as the rate of change of credit in the recipient sectors.

(4) The level of inventories relative to profits and the rates of change of profit levels and of the current economic index are related to current product market conditions and to expectations about future product market conditions and therefore possible changes in the demand for labor.

(5) The level and rate of change of capacity utilization are included in the model because enterprises are assumed to be more reluctant to allow money wage increases of a sufficient magnitude to offset expected inflation when they have more rather than less unutilized capacity[18]. The inclusion of this level variable obviously is related to the Phillips (1958) curve concern with representing excess demand in the labor market by the unemployment rate. Unfortunately, unemployment data is not available for the sample period, so the Phillips curve phenomenon cannot be included explicitly in the model by the unemployment rate[19], but the capacity utilization rate may serve the same purpose. Given the manner in which the capacity utilization rates are constructed, in fact, this variable may

[16]For the sample period neither this variable nor the next three (relative credit, relative subsidies, and relative profits) are available on a sector-specific basis, so aggregate representations are used.

[17]ODEPLAN (1968). The results in section 4.3 provide only marginal support for this claim. Given that the real rate of interest charged on loans over part of the sample period was negative, however, the inducement for enterprises to clamor for more credit at the same rates should be clear.

[18]Capacity is measured by the trend through the peaks method discussed in section 4.3. The sectoral variations in the degree of utilization of Chilean sectoral capacity so measured have been considerable.

[19]Behrman and García (1973) do include such a variable in their examination of the 1961–1967 period, but without clearcut success. The data are not available for most of the period of the present study.

have one advantage over the normal representation in that implicitly the effects of varying participation rates are included (Simler and Tella, 1968, alternatively attempt to adjust unemployment rates for varying participation rates). On the other hand, the capacity utilization rates used reflect phenomena other than the existence of excess demand in the labor market. The inclusion of the rate of change of capacity utilization can be justified in terms of expectations or in terms of Kuh's (1967) argument about the productivity determination of wage changes.

(6) In the case of mining, the few large foreign-controlled corporations which dominated this sector during the sample period apparently believed that it would have been impolitic to let their wage increases be out of line with those of the other large corporations in the economy[20]. For this sector, such large corporations (primarily in manufacturing) apparently played the role of pacesetters in respect to wage changes. Mining, in turn, apparently played the same role for the government sector. To see whether or not there is evidence that such phenomena were important, the rate of change of manufacturing wages is included in the model for mining and the rate of change of mining wages is included for the government.

(7) The employers' share of social security taxes increased steadily over the sample, from an average of 3.25% of total wages in 1945 to 8.79% in 1965. To the extent that increases in this tax were borne by laborers, the change in the effective tax rate should affect sectoral variations with a negative sign.

On the *supply side*, aspects of market behavior are represented by three groups of variables.

(1) Expectations of inflation presumably are very important in an economy with an inflationary experience such as Chile has had. To represent such expectations, on the supply side in the model are included lagged values of the rate of change of the deflator for consumer goods, the rate of change of the exchange rate[21], or the

---

[20]For the last half of the sample period, in fact, the Braden Copper Company conducted wage surveys among other large Chilean firms reputedly to be used as a basis for determining the changes in its wage payments. See Behrman (1975b, subsection 4.2.1) and Mamalakis (1967a) for detailed discussions of the relations between the copper companies and the Chilean government.

[21]Adjustments in the exchange rate are widely publicized. Moreover, several governments (including Alessandri in 1959–1961 and Allende in 1970–1971) have made exchange rate stability an important symbol of overall stability. For such reasons this variable has a not unimportant role in inflationary expectations.

rate of change of the minimum wage (the *sueldo vital,* which normally was adjusted annually in January or February)[22]. (Given that the correlation coefficient over the sample period between the rate of change of the consumer price deflator and the rate of change of the minimum wage is 0.90, variations in the latter variable would have served as a pretty good predictor of variations in the former in these years.) As is suggested above, of course, expectations of inflation enter into both sides of the market and because of substantial inflationary experience, expectations (or at least representations thereof) of rates of change of consumer goods prices. Therefore, it probably is not possible to distinguish empirically between expectations of product price changes (which are represented both directly and in the rate of change of the value of labor productivity) and the representations here discussed of expectations of consumer price changes.

(2) Following the suggestion by Ramos (1968) that past wage adjustments to *ex post* incorrect expectations of inflations have been corrected in subsequent wage changes, a representation of the error in the expectations of price changes held *ex ante* for the previous period is included in the model. This representation is simply the difference between the previous years *ex ante* expectations as represented as is discussed above and the actual rate of change of the relevant price index in the previous year. Note that in the case in which inflation expectations for a given year are represented by the lagged rate of change of the deflator for consumer goods, this variable is the negative of Harberger's (1963) accelerator variable. In the case of this second aspect of the supply-side considerations, again it is improbable that one can distinguish between supply and demand causes.

(3) At least for more developed countries Hines (1964, 1968) has argued that the wage determination process is being dominated more and more on the supply side by unions. In an attempt to see what evidence there is of an effect of union strength in the Chilean wage determination process, the level and the rate of change of the proportion of workers unionized are included in the model. Because

---

[22]For a discussion of the pattern of adjustments in the *sueldo vital* over the sample period, see Ramos (1968). A dummy variable is included for 1961–1962 because of the change in timing for the readjustment then. Dummy variables are also included for the institution of an agricultural minimum wage in 1953 and for the increase of that minimum wage to the industrial level in 1965.

of the nature of the available data, these variables can be constructed only for manufacturing and for all other sectors aggregated
together.

6.2.2. Estimates of the determinants of sectoral wage rate changes

Table 6.4 gives estimates of the model presented in subsection 6.2.1
for the eight relevant sectors. On an overall level the specification
appears to be reasonably successful. There is no indication of
serious problems of serial correlation. Examination of individual
residuals across data cells suggests that there is no excluded factor
which is systematically affecting a number of sectors simultaneously. The corrected coefficients of determination indicate that the
results are consistent with from 0.62 to 0.79 of the variance in the
dependent variable over the sample period. Although such a range
of corrected coefficients of determination is definitely lower than
those presented elsewhere in this chapter for product prices and
deflators, it is relatively high in comparison with other estimates of
the determinants of the rate of change of sectoral wages in developing countries[23].

The remainder of the characteristics of the model are most easily
discussed by considering again each of the aspects of the demand
and supply considerations discussed in subsection 6.2.1.

Consider first the *demand* variables.

(1) The rates of change of average and nominal labor productivities and related variables have significantly non-zero coefficients
only for utilities and services. Wage changes, therefore, apparently
do not, in general, accurately reflect productivity changes, which is
somewhat discouraging from the point of view of the question of the
efficiency of resource allocation and the appropriateness of the
signals given by wages. This result contrasts sharply with the
evidence presented in section 6.1 above that sectoral price changes
are quite responsive to productivity changes. The lack of significance of these terms in mining may reflect the reputed maintenance
of wage levels above market equilibrium levels in this sector due to
an attempt to limit nationalistic criticisms of the foreign dominance

---

[23]For earlier estimates of the determination of changes in Chilean wages, see
Behrman (1971a), Behrman and Garcá (1973), Corbo (1974), Gregory (1967), and
Ramos (1968).

Table
Determinants of the rates of change of

Dependent variable rate of change in sectoral wages	Rate of change in:					
	Leading price or wage[b]	Exchange rate	Accelerator[c]	Timing of minimum wage adjustment	Capacity utilization	Cyclical indicators[d]
Agriculture	0.416 (3.3)			1.52 (1.3)[f]		0.178 (2.3)
Mining	0.656 (3.7)	0.175 (1.4)[g]	0.404 (4.6)			
Construction		0.434 (3.0)	0.923 (3.6)			1.45 (4.3)
Manufacturing	0.482 (2.2)	0.328[h] (2.4)				0.209 (2.5)
Transportation			0.347 (1.9)		0.893 (2.8)	0.368 (4.5)
Utilities	0.982 (3.2)			2.40 (1.6)[g]	0.682[i] (1.9)	0.371 (1.2)[f]
Services	0.368 (2.3)					0.271 (2.4)
Government		0.232 (2.1)	0.343 (3.0)	1.14 (1.3)[f]		

[a]Beneath the point estimates in parentheses are the absolute values of the *t*-statistics. All point estimates are significantly non-zero at the 5% level otherwise noted. Because the variables are in rate of change form the point estimates are elasticities. In those cases in which the lagged dependent variable is included the Durbin–Watson statistic is biased towards two. Appendix A gives the data sources.

[b]The consumer price index for agriculture; the minimum wage (*sueldo vital*) for mining and utilities; the manufacturing product *GDP* deflator for manufacturing; and the lagged services *GDP* deflator for services.

[c]The accelerator, following Harberger (1963), is defined as the first difference (perhaps with a lag) of the rate of change of some indicator price or wage. For mining the industrial wage is used as such an indicator; for construction the lagged consumption deflator is used; for transportation the transportation *GDP* deflator is used; and for the government the mining wage is used.

[d]Lagged total profits for agriculture and transportation and the current indicator index for construction, manufacturing, utilities, and services (lagged in all but the last case).

6.4
Chilean sectoral wages, 1945–1965[a].

Effective employers' SS rate	Proportion of non-manufacturing labor force unionized	Sector specific[e]			Lagged dependent variable	Constant	$\bar{R}^2$ SE DW
		1	2	3			
−0.466 (1.8)	1.17 (3.1)	0.631 (3.4)					0.78 0.126 1.8
		0.233 (1.4)[g]					0.71 0.105 2.1
	−1.53 (2.8)	−1.96 (2.1)				−0.481 (3.0)	0.68 0.176 1.6
		0.482 (2.5)			−0.496 (3.2)		0.79 0.105 2.2
	1.89 (3.6)	0.229 (4.2)					0.67 0.176 1.4
		−2.09 (2.2)	0.718 (2.1)	0.718 (1.7)[g]		−0.794 (2.5)	0.71 0.160
−0.446 (1.9)		0.561 (3.1)			−0.211 (1.6)[g]		0.62 0.124 2.2
−0.526 (2.4)		0.238 (1.9)	0.481 (1.1)[f]			0.210 (5.4)	0.71 0.098 2.4

[e]The lagged consumption deflator for agriculture; the lagged consumer price index for mining; lagged total inventory relative to total *GDP* for construction; the lagged consumption deflator for manufacturing; the lagged level (*not* the rate of change) of capacity utilization for transportation; the lagged total inventory stock relative to total gross domestic product, the lagged sectoral capacity per laborer and lagged profits for utilities; average nominal labor productivity for services and the lagged exchange rate and an accelerator variable with the lagged rate of change in the consumption deflator minus the lagged rate of change in the minimum wage (*sueldo vital*).
[f]Significantly non-zero at the 15% level.
[g]Significantly non-zero at the 10% level.
[h]Black market exchange rate.
[i]Lagged one period.

therein. In the five other sectors, institutional considerations also may swamp any productivity considerations. Comparisons of the results presented here with those in Behrman (1971a), however, suggests the alternative explanation that multicollinearity with the current economic activity, capacity utilization, and sectoral price variables may be making it difficult to identify the productivity effects.

(2) For no sector is the coefficient of the rate of change of credit (private, public, or total) relative to product significantly non-zero even at the 15% level. In no case, therefore, is there evidence that wage changes are constrained by credit policy widespread assertions to the contrary.

(3) A similar result is obtained for the rate of change of subsidization.

(4) At least one of the three cyclical indicators variables (i.e. the rate of change of profits relative to product, the rate of change of the current indicators index, the level of inventories relative to product) is significantly non-zero in six of the eight sectors. For construction, the response is particularly large. The impact of general economic conditions (or of expectations concerning future developments in them) seems to be widespread. The two sectors which are exceptions are mining and government, neither of which one would expect to be particularly oriented towards general domestic market conditions[24].

(5) The coefficient estimates of the level of capacity utilization are significantly non-zero at the 5% level for transportation, but are not significantly non-zero even at the 25% level in any other sectors. Even for this sector, the estimates imply a relatively limited contribution to the overall variation in nominal wages in comparison to that of some of the other variables in the model (primarily of those related to price expectations). In general, thus, the results do not support the hypothesis that Phillips curve phenomena are widespread and relatively important in Chile. In only two sectors (i.e. transportation and utilities), moreover, are the coefficients of the rate of change of capacity utilization significantly non-zero. The results therefore provide but limited support for Kuh's (1967)

---

[24]Mining is oriented towards the world copper market. The government sector would not seem to respond in the same way as private sectors to these cyclical variables.

hypothesis that the rate of change, not the level of unemployment (or unutilized capacity), enters into the wage change determination process.

(6) The estimate of the coefficient of the rate of change of manufacturing wages is not significantly non-zero for the mining sector if the rate of change of the legal minimum wage is included in the model[25]. An accelerator variable based on manufacturing wages, however, does have a significant and substantial coefficient. That only this variable and the rate of change of the legal minimum wage have significantly non-zero coefficients at the 5% level in this sector provides some support for the hypothesis that the oligopsonistic foreign-controlled mining sector did attempt to keep its percentage wage changes in line with those of other large corporations and with changes in the legal minimum wage in order to limit political pressures. The results, however, do not really enable one to discriminate between the above hypothesis and the possibility that mining is a relatively small demander of the same labor as that which the much larger (in terms of employment) manufacturing sector uses and is basically a price-taker in this market.

For the government, the accelerator form of the rate of change of mining wages also has a significantly non-zero coefficient. The chain of responses to the wage adjustments in leading sectors thus well may go from large manufacturing corporations to large-scale mining to the government.

(7) The effective employers' social security tax rate has a significantly negative coefficient for agriculture, services, and government. In all three cases the point estimates suggest that about half of the increase in this effective tax rate is borne by the employees. For the other sectors there is no statistical evidence of a transfer of the incidence of this tax to the laborers.

The groups of *supply*-side variables are now considered.

(1) For every sector, except for transportation, the rate of change of the exchange rate, of the minimum wage, or of some product price represents inflationary expectations with significant coefficients. For transportation such expectations are probably incorporated into the rate of change of lagged profits[26].

---

[25]The two variables are quite collinear, however, so it is hard to identify their separate contributions.
[26]This same variable reinforces the effects of other representations in agriculture and utilities.

Only for agriculture, mining, and utilities, however, are there significant coefficient estimates for the variables specifically related to the *supply*-side expectations (i.e. the rates of change of the deflator of consumer goods and of the minimum wage). Only for the last two of these sectors is there evidence of a significant role of changes in the minimum wage[27]. The support for the hypothesis that the government minimum wage adjustments play a substantial role in the determination of the rates of change of nominal wages, therefore, seems at best to be quite limited (a result with which Ramos, 1968, concurs). Perhaps most surprising in this respect is the lack of evidence of a significant response in the rate of change of the government's own wages to the rate of change of the minimum wage (once again Ramos concurs), which may reflect in part the not unknown practice in government agencies of reclassifying employees and of giving bonuses in order to give higher effective rates of wage increases than are allowed by the minimum wage change laws.

For the other sectors the representation of inflationary pressures might well originate at least as much in the demand side as in the supply side. Whether these inflationary expectations are more important on the demand side or the supply side, the importance of many other variables in most sectors points to the conclusion that the expected rate of inflation plays a lesser role in the determination of money wage changes than Ramos (1968) and Behrman and García (1973) have reported in other studies[28]. Furthermore, the finding of very long lags entering into the formulation of expectations of the rate of change of prices which is reported in the latter study is not supported by the present investigation[29]. Apparently, the inclusion of

[27] In addition, for agriculture, utilities, and the government, there is marginal evidence of a response to the change in timing of the 1961–1962 minimum wage readjustments. The minimum wage also enters into the accelerator variable for the government.

[28] For six of the eight cells examined in Behrman and García (1973), coefficients of determination could not be increased significantly by adding other variables (i.e. the inverse of the unemployment rate, the change in the unemployment rate, the expectations of change in seasonal price patterns) to a representation of expected price changes. Ramos (1968) also presents results for manufacturing (1938–1966) and the overall wage level (1930–1967, 1940–1967) in which price change expectations alone are consistent with a considerable part of the variance in the rate of change of wages.

[29] In Behrman and García (1973) lags of up to ten years were found to enter into the expectations model which maximized the coefficient of determination. However, for most cells the weights are significantly not different from one after two years of

other variables in the model not only leads to the result that inflation expectations may be less important in Chilean wage-rate-change determination than has been previously suggested, but also that such expectations may be changed in a shorter period of time than has previously been suggested. This latter consideration is important in any evaluation of the prospects for reducing significantly the Chilean rate of inflation and is more optimistic in that respect than the conclusion which Behrman and García (1973) present[30].

(2) The second group of variables on the supply side (although once again the distinction between supply and demand pressures is tenuous) relate to Harberger's (1963) accelerator effect or to Ramos' (1968) hypothesized correction of errors in expectations held *ex ante* for the previous year in order to account for the *ex post* rate of increase of prices experienced in that year. For mining, construction, transportation, and government significant coefficients are obtained[31]. For construction and the government, the coefficients are not significantly different from one, which, for the Ramos hypothesis, implies complete correction of past errors in one period. For mining and transportation the implied corrections are significantly less than one[32]. Some support, thus, is provided for the Harberger and/or Ramos hypotheses[33].

(3) The rate of change of unionization does not have a significantly non-zero coefficient for manufacturing, the only case for which

---

adjustment and after ten years of adjustment, with the relatively small (in absolute terms) weights in between relating to the overshooting necessary to compensate for the lack of complete initial adjustment. The difference between the concentration of weights in the expectation model implied by Behrman and García and by the present results, thus, may not be as great as is suggested *prima facie*.

[30]The role of wage changes in transmitting inflationary pressures in Chile is emphasized in section 6.1 above and by Harberger (1963) and Behrman (1973c).

[31]The fairly widespread significance of these variables may be related to the lack of evidence of long lags in the formation of expectation of price changes, which is discussed above, since this variable serves a function related to that of the 'overshooting' of adjustment reported in Behrman and García (1973) by correcting for incomplete instantaneous adjustment.

[32]That the estimated corrections for these two sectors are significantly less than one, suggests that further lags of the relevant term might be included in order to allow several years for such adjustments to past errors. The addition of one further lag, however, does not result in a significant coefficient in either case.

[33]The support is more limited in these estimates, however, than appears to be the case in Behrman (1971a), apparently because of multicollinearity with changes in the current economic activity index and in the exchange rate.

sector-specific data are available[34]. The rate of change of non-manufacturing unionization, however, does have significantly non-zero coefficients in agriculture, construction, and transportation. In all three cases the estimated responses are elastic, but for construction the estimate is negative. This negative coefficient estimate may be plausible in that as increased unionization occurs elsewhere, non-construction employment opportunities may decrease relatively, and the resulting increased supply of applicants for construction work may reduce wages relatively in that sector. Despite this possible aberration, the estimates suggest that non-manufacturing unionization may have a substantial effect upon wage change determination in some sectors, thus supporting some generalization of Hines' (1964, 1968) emphasis on the role of trade unions to somewhat less developed economies. Given the limited extent of non-manufacturing unionization, however, these results seem to indicate a surprisingly strong influence of such unions. This area clearly merits further exploration in future studies.

6.2.3. Implications of wage rate change determination estimates

The results presented in table 6.4 allow a comparison with the numerous available studies of the wage determination processes in more developed countries, e.g. Hines (1964, 1968), Kuh (1967), Phillips (1958), Simler and Tella (1968), and Zaidi (1969). They suggest that the underlying model is somewhat less consistent with the variance in the rate of change of wages in the Chilean case than are the related models in the cases of the more developed countries. In part, this difference may reflect the absence of as satisfactory data as is available for more developed economies (e.g. sector-specific unemployment rates and profits), but in part it may reflect a greater role in Chile of factors other than those which are generally included in such a study. Despite the somewhat lesser success than in the cases of more developed economies, however, the model is consistent with a considerable proportion of the variance in the wage changes in Chilean sectors, which provides support for the

---

[34]For a different sample for this sector, Gregory (1967) presents results which somewhat more strongly suggest a role of trade unions in the wage determination process, but which are not very robust in respect to changes in the sample and in the specification. Therefore Gregory concludes that his results are 'inconclusive' in respect of the role of unionization on industrial wage changes.

hypothesis that the included considerations (primarily market pressures) do have a substantial role in wage change determination in this developing country. Moreover, the results provide some support for generalization to a somewhat different kind of economy: Kuh's (1967) emphasis on the role of productivity changes, Kaldor's (1959) emphasis on the role of general economic conditions as related to relative profit changes and other variables, Hines' (1964, 1968) emphasis on the role of unionization, and the fairly general emphasis on the role of price-change expectations in the wage change determination process.

Given that there exists evidence that wages do play a significant role in short- and long-run resource allocation and in price-change determination in Chile, whether or not wages are giving appropriate signals is another important question. In respect to both the allocation and the price determination questions, the fairly general response in wage changes to general economic conditions and the more limited response to utilization rates and productivity changes provide some support for the hypothesis that the wage changes do tend to give the correct signals. On the other hand, this support must be qualified because only for three sectors is there evidence of response to sector-specific considerations, because for mining[35] and the government there is no evidence of any of these responses and because the evidence of distortions due to unionization exists for three sectors. In respect to price-change determination, in addition, given that wages apparently do play an important transmitting role in sustaining inflation through inflationary expectations based on past experience, the suggestion from this study that such expectations depend primarily upon very recent experience, with some correction for the frustration of past expectations, rather than on the experience of a number of past years leads to a somewhat more optimistic appraisal of the possibility of lessening inflation at an acceptable cost than has been presented in Behrman and García (1973).

[35]The lack of such responses in the case of mining reflects distortions if wages are set above the equilibrium level in this sector by following minimum wage and manufacturing wage changes in order to limit political pressure. If, in contrast, the mining sector is a relatively small demander in the same market as is manufacturing, the lack of such responses may not reflect distortions, but only that this sector basically is a price-taker in the labor market. In my judgment, the former hypothesis is more probably correct, although the estimates presented in this study do not really permit one to distinguish between the two possibilities.

The effects of wage changes on the income distribution also are of interest. The available evidence suggests that over the sample period disparities between lower-middle-class and upper-class incomes probably have tended to be somewhat lessened by relative gains by wage earners in general, and by those in agriculture in particular. Given the substantial weight on a more equal income distribution in the apparent social welfare function of many recent governments, such tendencies are probably desirable[36]. To the extent that these tendencies reflect such changes as increased productivities due to increased investment in human capital, these movements in the income distribution probably do not conflict with efficiency considerations. To the extent that such factors as increased unionization played a role in these income distribution changes (especially in agriculture), moreover, the negative effects on allocation mentioned above *may* be offset by possibly positive effects on distribution. The apparently deteriorating position of the relatively poorly paid government workers, however, is probably a negative factor from the point of view of the assumed welfare function, and also may reflect some discrimination against publicly provided goods in the anti-inflation programs of the period. The partial-equilibrium estimates, together with those for price determination elsewhere in this chapter, furthermore, suggest that wages adjust less to exchange rate changes than do prices. Therefore, devaluation is likely to lead to a real income shift away from labor.

Finally, the frequently encountered assumption that wages are determined primarily by non-market (i.e. traditional or legal) forces is supported somewhat by the above-noted observations that the model is less consistent with the wage rate change in Chile than has been the case for results reported for more developed countries, and that productivity changes apparently are not widely important. On the other hand, for all sectors the model – which is based primarily on considerations of market pressures – is consistent with 60% or more of the variance in the sectoral rates of change of money wages, and there is not much evidence of an important role (even in the case of the government) for the change in the minimum wage which is widely assumed to be the major legal tool used by the government in

---

[36]Conceivably, however, these tendencies have resulted in increased disparities between lower-class and lower-middle-class incomes, which would not be desirable given the assumed social welfare function.

its wage policy[37]. Therefore, although non-market factors may be more important in Chilean wage-change determination than in the case of more developed economies, market forces apparently do play a substantial, if not dominant role.

6.3. Other prices

In addition to the price of products and the price of labor the complete model of Part III below includes a number of other prices. Table 6.5 presents the mean percentage increases and a measure of variance (i.e. the standard deviation from the trend as a percentage of the mean) over the 1945–1965 sample period for most of these prices.

6.3.1. Price indices for intermediate inputs, price indices for investment and cost of capital by sectors of destination

The sector-specific intermediate input price indices play important roles in the transmission of aggregate demand pressures (section 6.1) and in the determination of capacity utilization (section 4.3). The sector-specific costs of capital (and thus the price of investment goods) have considerable impact in the long-run capacity determination decisions (section 4.2).

The intermediate price indices are constructed on the basis of an appropriate aggregation of the 1962 Chilean input–output table [ODEPLAN (1970)], the sectoral product price indices, and the import price indices. The price indices for investment by destination are constructed from the mean sectoral sources of investment for the 1962–1966 period [Meza (1967)], the sectoral product price indices, and the import price indices. The cost of capital variables are based on these sector-specific investment goods prices and sector-specific information (when available) for depreciation rates, effective tax rates, and interest rates.

Table 6.6 gives the weights for the first two groups mentioned. The less are the elasticities of substitution among intermediate

[37]For mining, one of the two sectors for which this variable has a significantly non-zero coefficient estimate, however, my preferred interpretation of the estimates obtained in this study is that they do reflect non-market, basically political considerations by this foreign-dominated oligopolistic industry.

Table 6.5

Characteristics of indices for intermediate inputs, investments, cost of capital, wholesale and consumer prices and national income deflators and black market exchange rate, 1945–1965[a].

Deflator or index	Mean annual percentage change	Standard deviation from trend as percentage of mean
Price index for intermediate inputs		
Agriculture	29.9	20.1
Mining	29.5	27.3
Construction	29.9	24.7
Manufacturing	29.7	22.9
Transportation	29.5	25.6
Utilities	30.1	23.3
Price index for investment by destination		
Agriculture	30.2	19.0
Mining	31.2	35.3
Manufacturing	30.7	36.2
Transportation	31.7	35.5
Utilities	32.5	37.2
Housing	25.2	28.4
Cost of capital by destination		
Agriculture	33.1	29.0
Mining	33.9	35.3
Manufacturing	34.0	36.2
Transportation	35.3	35.6
Utilities	35.2	37.2
Housing	28.1	28.4
National accounts deflators		
Private consumption	29.7	19.2
Government	29.5	20.2
Investment	29.2	20.9
buildings	29.9	24.7
other construction	33.9	25.7
national machinery	29.4	26.1
Inventory change	29.9	24.3
Exports	33.4	28.9
Imports	29.8	27.3
Total	29.6	19.2
Wholesale price index		
Intermediate	33.1[b]	40.3
Total	29.2	25.2
Consumer price index		
Food	31.5	17.1
Housing	26.1	21.0
Clothing	30.8	24.6
Others	30.6	19.5
Total	30.7	18.3
Black market exchange rate	27.0	30.6

[a] Appendix A gives the underlying data sources.

[b] 1949–1965 only. If this index is assumed to have increased at the same rate as the total wholesale price index for 1945–1948, the average for 1945–1965 is 29.9%.

Table 6.6
Weights for sectoral intermediate input price indices and for sectoral investment price indices[a].

Index	Sectoral weights for sources of intermediate inputs							
	Agriculture	Mining	Construction	Manufacturing	Transportation	Utilities	Services	Imports
Intermediate price index for								
Agriculture	0.166	0.025	0.000	0.142	0.093	0.007	0.517	0.062
Mining	0.001	0.017	0.000	0.278	0.144	0.016	0.153	0.391
Construction	0.000	0.152	0.000	0.685	0.024	0.003	0.040	0.098
Manufacturing	0.194	0.030	0.000	0.342	0.033	0.013	0.245	0.138
Transportation	0.011	0.049	0.011	0.554	0.052	0.021	0.070	0.232
Utilities	0.000	0.187	0.018	0.158	0.034	0.389	0.064	0.154
Housing	0.000	0.000	0.909	0.000	0.000	0.000	0.092	0.000
Services and government	0.064	0.002	0.037	0.599	0.083	0.042	0.120	0.052

	Weights for sources of investment goods: gross investment in:			
	Buildings	Other construction	Domestic machinery	Imported machinery
Investment price index for:				
Agriculture	0.373	0.499	0.078	0.056
Mining	0.001	0.164	0.042	0.794
Manufacturing	0.050	0.000	0.215	0.735
Transportation	0.027	0.639	0.039	0.295
Utilities	0.001	0.771	0.011	0.217

[a]Weights for the sources of sectoral intermediate inputs are calculated from the 1962 input–output table in ODEPLAN (1970). Weights for the sources of investment are the means for 1962–1966 based on data in Meza (1967).

inputs and between intermediate and primary inputs, the more satisfactory are these weights. Theil and Tilanus (1966) and Balassa, Guisinger and Schydlowsky (1970) claim that the available empirical evidence reveals very low substitutibility on an aggregate level between intermediate and primary factors in other economies. The large number of non-zero entries suggest the existence of a considerable degree of inter-connectedness in the Chilean economy. For most sectors manufacturing is the most important domestic source of intermediate inputs, but the services sector is also a quite significant source (and is more important than manufacturing in the case of agriculture). Imported intermediate inputs are 39% of the total for mining[38] and 10% or more for transportation, utilities, manufacturing, and construction. Imported machinery accounts for over 70% of investment in mining and manufacturing, and over 20% in transportation and utilities. The dependence on the foreign sector, thus, is considerable and widespread.

These indices of intermediate input prices and capital costs, of course, are based on assumptions of a constant sectoral composition of intermediate inputs and capital goods by origin over the sample period. For the Chilean experience, unfortunately, there is almost no available information with which to test these assumptions[39]. Under the assumptions that the relevant substitution possibilities are indeed quite limited, however, these indices enable the complete model of Part III to incorporate the interindustry aspects of the economy much better than is usually the case for macroeconometric models[40].

Table 6.5 summarizes some of the characteristics of these groups of price indices over the sample for the sectors for which they are actually utilized in the complete model. The intermediate prices

[38]During the sample period large-scale mining companies were allowed to purchase foreign inputs without any currency regulation or control by the Chilean government. Much of the time, however, they were required to transfer dollars into domestic currency at very discriminatory exchange rates for any domestic purchases. Therefore, the high dependence of this sector on imported inputs in part may reflect a response to incentives created by government policy to use imported rather than domestic inputs. For more details, see Behrman (1975b, subsections 4.2.1, 7.1.2.3).

[39]Balassa (1971) cites some evidence about limited substitution among intermediate inputs for other economies.

[40]The sectoral total demand variables (which include intermediate demands facing each sector in addition to final demands) which enter into some of the capacity-utilization functions of section 4.3 also help to capture some of the interindustry aspects of the economy. The national accounts deflators, discussed in subsection 6.3.2, also capture some of the interindustry effects.

increased very much the same on the average across sectors, with mean annual percentage increases of from 29.5 to 30.1. Such a range implies a narrow band around the average of 29.6% for the overall *GDP* deflator. The smallness of this range is in contrast to the range of 27.0–33.9% for the product prices for the same six sectors (column 1 in table 6.1). Mean output–intermediate-input price ratios increased most in mining and least in construction, with the other four sectors in between. Mining also has had the greatest variability, however, in both product and intermediate input prices. These relatively great fluctuations apparently are due both to frequent changes in the world copper market and to alterations in the Chilean international economic regime (Behrman, 1975b, subsections 4.2.1, 7.1.2.3, 7.2).

In contrast to the growth rates in the indices for the price of intermediate inputs, those for the price of investment and the cost of capital have tended to vary more across sectors and – with the notable exception of housing – to be significantly higher than the mean increase in the overall *GDP* deflator. For each of the six included sectors, the mean growth in the cost of capital exceeds that in the price of investment goods, primarily because of the relatively rapid increases in the effective tax rates. For most sectors the mean increases in both of these variables has exceeded that in the sectoral product price index, although the pattern relative to the mean increases in the price of labor is mixed (columns 1 and 3 in table 6.1). Housing is an exception with regard to the comparison with the overall *GDP* deflator because construction, with its relatively low mean product price increase, has such a large weight among the sectoral sources of investment goods for this case (table 6.6). Even for housing, however, the mean increase in the cost of capital exceeds that in the product price. In a world without technological change and with substitution possibilities among capital, labor, and intermediate inputs, such patterns would set up inducements for substitution of intermediate inputs and, in some sectors (e.g. mining and manufacturing), labor for capital. The existence of quality changes, however, clouds the situation even if one is willing to assume substitution between primary and intermediate inputs.

One other aspect of the investment-price and capital-cost variables are the relative great variances around the secular trends[41]. The

[41]Although for transportation and utilities these fluctuations are not as great as those for the price of labor (columns 2 and 4 in table 6.1 and 2 in table 6.5).

major cause of this variance is the treatment of imported machinery and equipment as postponable during the frequent foreign exchange crisis (see Behrman 1975b, subsections 6.1.2, 6.2). For the same reason, the fluctuations for housing which depend primarily on home goods, have been smaller than those for most other sectors.

6.3.2. *Deflators for major components of the national accounts, wholesale price index, and consumer price index*

Table 6.5 suggests that the mean increases for the deflators of most of the major components of the national accounts and for the wholesale and consumer price indices have been bunched around that for the overall *GDP* deflator. The primary exception is the deflator for exports, which reflects the secular trend in the world copper price during the sample. The average change in the food component of the consumer price index also has been relatively high, although it is offset somewhat in the total consumer price index by the relatively low increase for housing. The price index for investment in other construction, finally, also has a relatively high growth rate during the sample.

Fluctuations around the secular trends have varied considerably across these deflators and indices. The most volatile ones by this measure have been the intermediate wholesale price index and the export and import deflators. The last two of these reflect, in part, the frequent alterations in the international economic regime which are mentioned above and discussed extensively in Behrman (1975b). The least volatile have been the food, miscellaneous, and total categories of the consumer price index and the private consumption and overall national accounts deflators. Since there is some cancelling out across subcategories, the more aggregate indices tend to have had lesser fluctuations than the less aggregate ones.

The basic underlying considerations for the general specification of models of the determinants of the rates of change of the deflators for the final demand components and of the wholesale and consumer price indices are the same as for the rates of change of the sectoral product prices in section 6.1. However, in the estimation of the determinants of the rates of change of these deflators (except for imports and exports) and indices, the rates of change of the sectoral product prices are included to incorporate the considerations summarized in the discussion of table 6.2. In addition, general and specific, domestic and international variables in rate of change form are tested to see if they add anything to the explanatory power of the rates of change of the sectoral prices.

Table 6.7 presents the results so obtained. On an overall basis these results are generally satisfactory. With the exception of the components of the investment deflators, the corrected coefficients of determination imply that the underlying specification is consistent with from 83 to 99.6% of the variances in the dependent variables over the sample period (and with at least 90% for 11 of the 13 series). No serious problem of serial correlation is evident. The significantly non-zero point estimates generally are of the *a-priori* anticipated sign. Adjustment to the variables directly included is estimated to be very quick with from 90 to 100% of the total adjustment occurring in the current period[42]. The indirect adjustments which occur primarily through the rates of changes in the sectoral prices of course are slower in many cases (see section 6.1).

Except for the export and import deflators, the major determinants appear to be weighted averages of the rates of change of various sectoral prices with estimated patterns of weights which seem reasonable in comparison to the sectoral composition of aggregates in the 1962 input–output table[43]. The rather substantial and fairly widespread impact of change in the service sector product price is particularly striking, but perhaps not surprising given the large role of services in *GDP* (column 3 in table 4.1). Other domestic variables with sighificantly non-zero coefficients are the rates of change of the white collar wage (*sueldo vital*) and of the government wage in the case of the deflator for government current expenditures (which, of course, are largely payments to labor) and the dummy variable for stabilization attempts in the case of the general wholesale price index.

Significantly non-zero coefficients for foreign sector determinants are obtained for all of the national accounts deflators and wholesale price indices except for the government deflator. The rates of

[42]Only for the private consumption deflator is there significant evidence at the 5% level of adjustment taking longer than the current year. For the inventory change and import deflators there are parallel estimates which are significantly non-zero at the 10% level.

[43]For the investment deflator and only for the investment deflator *a-priori* weights from the 1962 input–output table are more consistent with the variance in the dependent variable than are weights estimated from the sample period data.

Rate of change for deflator or index	Sectoral prices						Rate of
	Agri-culture	Construc-tion	Manufac-turing	Transpor-tation	Util-ities	Housing	
National accounts deflators							
Private consumption[a]	0.135		0.242	0.037			
	(3.6)		(6.2)	(1.6)[f]			
Government							
Investment[a]							
buildings		1.106					
		(16.0)					
other construction		1.161					
		(9.8)					
national machinery			1.028				
			(14.2)				
Inventory change[a]	0.337		0.407				
	(4.0)		(4.2)				
Exports[a]							
Imports[a] (1)							
(2)							
Wholesale price index							
Intermediate goods[a]							
Total[a]	0.189		0.340		0.112		
	(2.0)		(2.4)		(1.6)[f]		
Consumer price index							
Food	0.593						
	(7.3)						
Housing						0.832	
						(18.6)	
Clothing			0.710				
			(5.4)				
Miscellaneous			0.501	0.487			
			(4.4)	(4.4)			
Total	0.325		0.252			0.109	
	(4.6)		(2.7)			(2.2)	

[a]Beneath point estimates in parentheses are the absolute value of the t-statistics, each of which is significantly non-zero at the 5% level unless otherwise noted. Because the variables are in rate of change form the point estimates are elasticities. In those cases in which the lagged dependent variable is included the Durbin–Watson statistic is biased towards two. Appendix A gives the data sources.

[b]All unit values are adjusted for exchange rate, prior deposit cost rate and tariff rate changes. The particular unit values used are as follows: investment deflator – investment goods imports; inventory change deflator – import deflator; export deflator – weighted average of export unit values with weights which reflect export composition and the relevant exchange rates; imports deflator (1) – consumer goods imports, investment goods imports, and intermediate goods imports (the point estimates for the last two are included in the sector-specific columns); import deflator (2) – all imports; wholesale price index for intermediate goods – intermediate goods imports; and total wholesale price index – all imports.

[c]The Ffrench-Davis (1971) quantitative restrictions index is used for private consumption, inventory change and export deflators. For the investment deflator the ratio of the investment

6.7

demand components and in wholesale and consumer price indices, 1945–1965[a].

change in:						$\bar{R}^2$ SE	DW ρ
Services	Foreign unit values adjusted for trade policies[b]	Foreign-sector restrictions[c]	Sectoral specific[d] 1	Sectoral specific[d] 2	Lagged dependent variable		
0.463 (15.6)		0.228 (1.5)[f]			0.108 (4.6)	0.996 0.013	2.2
0.515 (6.9)			0.374 (3.3)	0.123 (2.0)		0.94 0.046	1.7
	0.363 (3.8)	0.655 (5.4)				0.90 0.068	2.6
						0.63 0.143	2.2 −0.530
						0.42 0.258	1.90 −0.619
						0.75 0.118	2.6
	0.189 (3.4)	0.795 (2.1)			0.084 (1.7)[f]	0.97 0.034	2.6
	1.104 (27.9)	−1.60 (2.1)				0.95 0.071	2.7
	0.430 (2.4)		0.313 (2.3)	0.169 (1.0)[g]	0.098 (1.4)[f]	0.92 0.082	2.4
	0.934 (14.0)	0.194 (1.3)[g]			0.100 (1.6)[f]	0.93 0.074	2.7
	0.416 (2.9)		0.841 (3.7)	−0.068 (1.2)[g]		0.85 0.128	2.1
0.127 (1.7)[f]	0.261 (4.6)		−0.057 (2.5)			0.97 0.034	1.9
0.446 (5.9)						0.96 0.044	2.0
0.153 (4.1)						0.96 0.035	2.0
0.324 (2.6)						0.90 0.072	1.5
						0.83 0.081	2.9
0.338 (6.6)						0.98 0.027	2.8

deflator to the United States investment deflator adjusted for the exchange rate, prior deposit cost rate, and tariff rate is used. For the import deflator (2) the ratio of the *GDP* deflator to the United States' *GDP* deflator adjusted for the exchange rate is used.

[d]The sector-specific variables are as follows: government deflator – white collar minimum wage (*sueldo vital*) and government wage; investment deflator – weighted average of sectoral deflators from agriculture, mining, construction, industry and imported capital goods with weights from the 1962 input–output table (respectively, 0.0406, 0.00697, 0.586, and 0.278); import deflator (1) – unit values for investment goods imports and intermediate goods imports, both adjusted as indicated in note b; wholesale price index for intermediate goods – total wholesale price index and constant term; total wholesale price index – dummy variable for stabilization attempts in 1956–1957, 1959–1961, and 1965.

[e]1948–1965.

[f]Significantly non-zero at 10% level.

[g]Significantly non-zero at 15% level.

change of unit values of exports or imports, adjusted for price-related characteristics of the international economic regime, have significantly non-zero coefficient estimates for investment, inventory change, export and import deflators, and for the intermediate goods and general wholesale price indices. The rates of change of foreign sector restrictions have significantly positive coefficient estimates for the deflators for private consumption, investment, inventory change and imports (the second alternative), but a significantly negative coefficient estimate for the deflator for exports, apparently because of the use of such restrictions to allow the continuance of an overvalued exchange rate. Thus for the final demand deflators and the wholesale price indices, once again there is evidence of a not inconsiderable direct impact of price-related and quantitative characteristics of the international economic regime.

6.3.3. Black market exchange rate [44]

The black market *NER* is the *EER* for marginal goods (of a non-bulk nature), services and capital transactions[45]. Over the sample the black market *NER* increased slightly slower on the average than the *GDP* deflator, but with greater variance from the secular trend because of changes in the restrictiveness of the foreign-sector regime (table 6.5, Behrman, 1975a, 1975b)[46]. The black market rate must be interpreted with care because this market is somewhat narrow[47] and may be affected by risk aversion due to its illegality[48]. Nevertheless, the *PLD NER* in this market – or the

---

[44]Other exchange rates are assumed to be exogenously determined by the government, at least in the short run (section 3.3).

[45]The black market rate approximates the *EER* and not the *NER* for such transactions because tariffs, taxes, and other charges generally are avoided in those cases in which the black market is the source of foreign exchange. There may be a cost due to risk, however, because of the illegality of dealing in this market (see note 48 below).

[46]The exact length of the sample period determines whether or not the black market rate increased relatively more or less than the overall *GDP* deflator. Because of the Frei stabilization attempt started in late 1964, in 1965 the *PLD NER*[BM] was relatively low and declining. For a period ending either a few years earlier or later, however, the opposite pattern would result.

[47]But information about this market seems to be widespread in the commercial centers of Santiago and Valparaiso.

[48]Risk aversion shifts both the demand and supply curves downward. The direction of the effect on the price of foreign exchange is uncertain. One might hypothesize that the supply curve shifts less than the demand curve since suppliers in this market are

discrepancy between it and the comparable legal rate – is one useful index of the extent to which demands for foreign exchange are not being satisfied in the legal market(s) because quantitative restrictions are being used to ration the available foreign exchange at the existing overvalued legal rate(s).

Regression (6.1) provides some support for this interpretation:

$$PLD\ NER^{BM} = 29.7QRFD + 0.113$$
$$\underset{[5.2]}{\overset{(3.8)}{}} \quad \underset{[0.1]}{\overset{(4.2)}{}}$$
$$\times \sum_{i=0}^{L} (PLD\ NER^{BM} - PLD\ NER^{NA}) - 23.5,$$
$$(3.2)$$

$$\bar{R}^2 = 0.84, \quad SE = 0.532, \quad DW = 1.3, \quad 1950\text{--}1965,$$

(6.1)

where BM refers to the black market (as a superscript); NA refers to the national accounts (as a superscript); $QRFD$ is the Ffrench-Davis (1971) quantitative restrictions index for the foreign sector; L is the first year of the last stabilization-cum-liberalization attempt (1956, 1959, 1965); and $PLD\ NER$ is the price-level deflated nominal exchange rate. The first right-hand-side variable is an index of quantitative restrictions in the foreign sector. Variations in it alone are consistent with 65% of the variance in the $PLD\ NER^{BM}$. The second right-hand-side variable is the sum of the difference between the $PLD\ NER$s for the black market and for the legal market(s) since the initiation of the last stabilization-cum-liberalization attempt. It represents the cumulative pressures for another liberalization attempt due to the disequilibrium system and, thus, motivation for speculative capital flight[49]. Together the two

---

largely foreigners for whom the penalties arising from convictions of operating in this market have been less than for nationals. On the other hand, the probability of arrest for black-market operations may be higher for the more visible foreigners than for nationals, which has a counteracting effect. In any case, attempts to surpress the black market in any manner (except for lessening the degree of overvaluation in the legal market) were very infrequent during the sample period.

[49] A somewhat different interpretation of relationship (6.1) is possible. The second right-hand-side term may be representing a distributed lag of the quantitative restrictions index. In such a case the entire right-hand side is a distributed lag of this index, which may represent expectations concerning future quantitative restrictions.

right-hand-side variables are consistent with 84% of the variance in the *PLD NER*[BM].[50] The inclusion of additional variables does not significantly increase this consistency[51].

[50]The elasticities, *prima facie*, may be misleading indicators of the relative contribution of the two right-hand-side variables because the coefficient of variation is much larger for the second than for the first of these variables.

[51]Other variables which were explored include dummy variables related to specific policies discussed in Part II of Behrman (1975b) and the *PLD NER*[NA]. If one thinks of foreign exchange obtained from the legal and illegal markets as being almost perfect substitutes, the lack of a stronger role for the last variable might be surprising. But if the black market primarily reflects excess demand in the legal market and if the degree of rationing in the legal market has varied considerably over time as section 1.4 and Part II of Behrman (1975b) suggest, there is no reason to expect a strong direct link between the two rates.

PART III

COMPLETE-MODEL ANALYSIS

CHAPTER 7

Complete model of the Chilean economy

Part II of this book presents and discusses many structural or quasi-reduced form relationships for the Chilean economy. The estimates of the parameters of these relationships are of considerable interest in themselves because of what they tell us about the structure of this economy. For analysis of changes in macroeconomic policies, or of changes in other macrovariables, however, examination of these relationships in isolation may be quite misleading. The *ceteris paribus* assumptions are very strong. There are important simultaneous and lagged interactions among the variables in the system. Adding up constraints – such as on government behavior or on the banking system – must be imposed.

Part III of this book, therefore, integrates these relationships into a general model of the Chilean economy[1]. This chapter gives an

---

[1]Several other quite competent general analyses of impacts of changes in Chilean economic policies are available. Cabezón (1969) and Clark and Foxley (1970) utilize linear-programming models for such studies. Black (1971) and Taylor and Black (1973) use a log–linear, Johansen-type model. For the purposes of the present investigation, however, these models have definite inadequacies. The linear-programming studies assume zero elasticities of factor substitution and proceed with the maximization of a global objective function which leads to the exploration of the question 'What *could* happen if socially optimal readjustment of the economy occurred in response to policy changes?', rather than 'What *would* happen if independent economic units which make up the economy followed their traditional behavioral patterns in response to such changes?' The Taylor–Black approach includes only one primary factor (labor), does not require consistency in the final demand and factor payments sides of the national accounts (i.e. relations linking factor payments, savings, and consumption are not included), and assumes short-run perfectly competitive behavior on the production side. More important, both of these approaches have substantial limitations for use in exploring the short- and medium-term impact of policy changes because immediate adjustments are assumed, the government policy tools incorporated in the analysis are few, and the entire fiscal–monetary–incomes–international policy–inflation nexus is ignored. Given the domi-

overview of the structure of the model, the solution procedure utilized, and the sample and immediate post-sample performance of the model. Ch. 8 explores a number of simulations related to changes in macroeconomic policy variables and in other exogenous variables.

7.1. Overview of the complete model

The model is composed of 72 exogenous variables and 172 endogenous variables (largely based on the relationships in Part II and necessary identities). Estimated relationships are generally based on data for the 1945–1965 period, with observations for earlier years used for some lagged values. This model includes a number of desirable features: (1) non-linear technological and behavioral responses of real variables to prices and to policies; (2) lags in adjustments and in the formation of expectations; (3) a wide range of government policy instruments and the interactions among them; (4) emphasis on the direct and indirect consequences of changes in the foreign sector; (5) adding-up constraints on fiscal and monetary behavior; (6) disaggregation to the nine-sector level to reflect sectoral heterogeneities; (7) the inclusion of input–output table-based intermediate demands and intermediate prices to link the sectors; and (8) simultaneous and lagged feedbacks.

The model has its roots in the Keynes–Tinbergen–Klein tradition. However, it is distinguished from that tradition by the following modifications in order better to reflect the structure and goals of the Chilean economy.

(1) Sectoral production capacities are determined within the model

---

nance of adjustment and cyclical problems in the Chilean economy, such deficiencies are very important ones.

Corbo (1971, 1974) presents an annual econometric model of Chile. His work is characterized by a number of inadequacies, however. The sample period is quite short (only three to five degrees of freedom in a number of estimated relationships). He ignores the impact of policy changes before the Frei administration. The level of aggregation (goods versus services) lumps together the behavior of quite heterogenous sectors such as agriculture, mining, and manufacturing. He cannot solve the model except by exogenizing important variables (e.g. the wage for labor involved in non-goods production, which is approximately 60% of the labor force), thus losing much of the simultaneous interaction in the system. For a review of Corbo's work, see Behrman (1976).

by physical investment and labor allocation decisions and by secular technological trends[2]. The implications of a set of policies for long-run growth thus can be investigated by examining changes in these capacities.

(2) Short-run output is *not* determined by final demand. Instead, sectoral capacity-utilization decisions determine real production in response to relative product – input prices (adjusted for the impact of fiscal policies), import and credit availabilities, and total demands. The difference between total production and (non-inventory) final demand determines the change in inventories, which feeds back on short-run capacity-utilization and balance of payments functions and on long-run capacity-creation decisions.

(3) The agricultural and services sectors absorb residual labor.

(4) The foreign sector is pervasive in its effects – not only through current prices and quantities, but also through expectations.

(5) The impact of inflation and of inflationary expectations is also very widespread because of the experience of very rapid price changes (e.g. an average annual increase of over 30% in the *GDP* deflator for the sample period).

(6) Substitution between domestic and foreign savings is incorporated. Increases in the command over foreign resources, therefore, go in part to increased current consumption.

(7) The specification of policies reflects the specific institutional constraints under which the government operates. Money supply basically responds passively to government deficits and changes in international reserves because of legal requirements to accept government debt and the lack of a developed open market. The effective internal monetary instruments are limited to average and marginal reserve rates, rediscount rates, bank interest rates, restrictions on the use of dollar bonds and deposits, credit ceilings and institutional changes such as the creation of the State Bank (Banco de Estado) in 1953. Tax revenues from a given activity depend not only on the level of that activity and legal tax rates, but also on the degree of inflation and expectations thereof. Government consumption is endogenous because of the limited short-run latitude of the government, given the annual legal determination of its wage structure. Government expenditure policy, therefore, operates

---

[2]Attempts to incorporate the effects of changing human capital on the basis of estimates by Harberger and Selowsky (1966) were not fruitful.

primarily through changes in public direct and indirect investment. Foreign sector policies include a multitude of both price-related and quantitative-based tools.

These seven features and the previous comments give much of the flavor of the model. However, some further detail with explicit reference to the estimates in Part II is useful. Therefore, subsection 7.1.1 lists the policy instruments in the model. Subsection 7.1.2 then reviews the nature of the model relationships.

7.1.1. Policy variables

The model includes the primary macroeconomic policy tools which the Chilean government used with a substantial degree of discretion in the sample period. In the long run, of course, not all of these instruments are independent[3]. To avoid redundancy with the discussion of constraints on Chilean policies in the last of the seven characteristics described above, the list of policy instruments included in the model is presented concisely. For more details see ch. 3 above.

7.1.1.1. Fiscal policies

Expenditure instruments include subsidies (either internal or for exports), current government consumption [but see the discussion in paragraph (7) above], and direct and indirect public financial investment (subsection 3.1.1).

Revenue instruments include legal tax rates (or proxies thereof) for 11 tax categories, import prior deposit rates, and the legal cost of production for large-scale mining (subsection 3.1.2). The last of these determines how many dollars the large-scale mining companies have to convert into escudos for local expenditures at a generally disadvantageous *NER*. The profits from the resale of those dollars at a higher exchange rate go to the government.

7.1.1.2. Internal monetary policies

The monetary base changes in large part because of internally financed government deficits and changes in international reserves.

---

[3]For example, long-run exchange rate and exchange control policies must be coordinated with internal fiscal and monetary policies because of effective limits on foreign debt accumulation. In the short run, however, there is often a substantial degree of independence among such policies.

The Central Bank shapes the impact of changes in the monetary base on the monetary supply by determining the marginal and average reserve requirements for time and demand deposits, the rediscount rate, the bank interest rate, quantitative restrictions on total credit and the requirements for dollar deposits. The nominal money supply is determined by these factors, together with behavioral relationships for the net free reserves held by the commercial banks and for the composition of assets held by the private sector. These behavioral relations depend upon expectations concerning inflation and devaluation, interest rates, and the relevant activity variables (section 3.2).

7.1.1.3. Foreign sector policies

The price-related tools included in the model are the average *ad valorem*-equivalent nominal tariff rate, the import prior deposit cost rate, a subsidy rate for non-traditional exports, three legal *NER*s (one for large-scale mining, another for services, and a third for other transactions)[4], and copper price and surtax policies (section 3.3). The last group of policies include the establishment of the Chilean sales monopoly in 1952–1954, the introduction of the Chilean producers' price in 1964, and the imposition of surtaxes in 1951 (all of which are discussed in detail in Behrman, 1975b, section 4.2.1).

Quantitative policies in the foreign sector are represented by the Ffrench-Davis quantitative restrictions index (variable 5.2.7.1 in table 2.1), ratios of aggregate internal prices to *EER*s[5], variables which relate to the short-run availability of foreign exchange (such as the export capacity to import and the net foreign exchange reserves of the banking system, variables 5.2.7.2–3 in table 2.1), the legal cost of production in large-scale mining and dummy variables for a number of particular policy changes which are discussed in detail in Behrman (1975b, Part Two).

7.1.1.4. Income policies

The minimum wage (*sueldo vital*) is the major direct tool in this area

---

[4]The black market *NER* also is included in the model – in part to represent the impact of quantitative restrictions (subsection 6.3.3).

[5]This ratio differs from one whenever the import premium rate is non-zero. However, the cause of a divergence from one may be adjustment lags instead of effective quantitative restrictions.

(section 3.4). Many other policies – such as taxes – obviously also affect income distribution.

7.1.2. Model relationships

For the most part, the model consists of a set of relationships for each of the nine sectors indicated above. In some cases, however, the lack of necessary data precludes estimation on the same level of disaggregation. A brief review of the nature of the included relations is now given. Part II above provides further interpretations of the estimated relationships.

7.1.2.1. Supply

Sectoral capacity for real GDP production. This is determined by a CES production function of the secular sectoral labor force and of the sectoral capital stock (section 4.1). The function has constant-returns-to-scale and Hicks-neutral technological change. The use of the secular sectoral labor force and of total capital stock makes possible the representation of production capacity instead of production. The estimated sectoral elasticities of substitution between capital and labor are significantly non-zero and substantial in some important sectors: agriculture (0.31), mining (0.51), manufacturing (0.76), utilities (0.32), and government (0.89).

Sectoral secular labor allocation. This is based on long-run, competitive-like adjustment to the expected ratio of the price of labor (including employers' social security taxes) to the product price (subsection 4.2.1). Agriculture and services absorb any excess labor, given the exogenous total supply.

Sectoral real physical capital investment. This consists of responses to replacement needs, changes in the desired stock of capital, the availability of government financial investment, and the availability of imported machinery and equipment (subsection 4.2.2). The desired stock of capital, in turn, depends on a neoclassical term, expected utilization rates, and price uncertainty.

Sectoral capacity utilization. This determines real sector *GDP* for a given sectoral capacity. Utilization rates depend on a number of domestic and foreign factors (section 4.3). Domestic determinants include relative product – input prices after adjustments for taxes, indices of the change in current economic activity, the relative availability of credit, natural conditions (e.g. the level of rainfall and the impact of earthquakes), the state of infrastructure development, the average indirect tax and subsidy rates, the rate of inflation, the real value of monetary balances, and a number of sector-specific considerations. Foreign determinants include the intermediate imports–product ratio, the competing imports–product ratio, quantitative restrictions indices, and sector-specific characteristics. Because of the lack of sector-specific data on unemployment fluctuations for the sample period, the sectoral capacity utilization rates are used as a proxy for such fluctuations within the model.

7.1.2.2. Demand
Real domestic savings–consumption relationships. These are included for the government, business, and households and non-profit institutions (subsection 5.1.1). Real savings depend on the relevant real net revenue variable (e.g. real disposable income for households) and real foreign savings[6]. In addition, private real savings respond to the level of real monetary balances, the means and standard deviations for expected inflation and exchange rate movements, and the sectoral and factoral distributions of income.

Inventory change. This is determined by the difference between aggregate supply and non-inventory components of aggregate demand (subsection 5.1.2).

Imports. These are included for seven categories. Imports depend on relative price characteristics, other demand characteristics, and the degree of policy restrictiveness (subsection 5.2.1). The relative prices are the levels and standard deviations (as a proxy for uncertainty) of *PLD EER(PI)*'s, *PLD EERs* and *PLD NERs*. The other demand characteristics include a relevant activity index (e.g. real consumption in the consumption import relations), total real credit, and variables related to the state of domestic inventories and to income distribution. The degree of policy restrictiveness is represented by the Ffrench-Davis quantitative restrictions index,

---

[6]The savings–consumption functions used in the simulations of the next chapter are the alternatives in table 5.1 which include real foreign savings.

the export capacity to import, the net foreign exchange reserves held by the banking system relative to the unit value of imports, and dummy variables to represent such events as the operation of the PL 480 food program.

Exports. These are determined for agriculture, large-scale mining, small- and medium-scale mining, industry, and services (subsection 5.2.2). Export determinants can be divided into three groups: (1) levels and standard deviations of relative prices (i.e. *EER*s relative to factor input costs or *PLD EER*s); (2) quantitative supply factors, including the effects of quantitative restrictions; and (3) quantitative demand considerations reflecting the level of activity in the countries of destination.

Net factor income from abroad. This primarily reflects flows related to large-scale mining (subsection 5.2.3).

7.1.2.3. Prices
Sectoral product prices. These reflect general and sector-specific factors from both the domestic and the international areas which underlie the levels of and movements in the supply and demand curves (section 6.1). General domestic considerations include the monetary supply, real *GDP*, indices of economic activity, indices of sectoral and factoral distributions, and dummy variables for the initiation of stabilization programs. Sector-specific domestic considerations are several measures of sectoral capacity utilization, sectoral intermediate input prices, sectoral unit labor costs (including the employers' social security tax contribution), and average real sectoral intermediate input prices, sectoral unit labor costs (including the employers' social security tax contribution), and average real sections, and prior deposit requirements on imports (which, when increased, absorb banking system credit and reduce inflationary pressures). Sector-specific international factors are the ratio of the *EER(PI)* for sectoral intermediate inputs to the general *NER*, *EER*s for sectoral imports or exports, and the level of sectoral imports relative to domestic absorption.

Sectoral wages. These primarily reflect domestic considerations which underlie the levels of and movements in the supply and demand curves: sectoral nominal and real average labor productivities; sectoral capacity per laborer; sectoral unionization; indices of sector-specific or general economic activity; the employers' social security rate; the institution and timing of minimum wages; and expectations for leading prices (and the Harberger, 1963, 'accelerator' variant). The international economic regime directly enters only through the expectational impact of legal and black market *NER*s (section 6.2).

Sectoral intermediate input prices. These are the prices which sectors must pay for domestic and imported intermediate inputs (subsection 6.3.1). These prices are weighted averages of all sectoral product prices and of imported intermediate goods prices. The weights are based on aggregation from the 1962 input–output table in ODEPLAN (1970c).

Prices for sectoral investment. These are weighted averages of sectoral product prices and of imported machinery and equipment prices (subsection 6.3.1). The weights are the average of the 1960–1966 estimates of the origin of sectoral investments by Meza (1967).

Deflators for final demand components, wholesale price indices, and consumer price indices. These are weighted averages of sectoral product prices and of relevant *EER*s, with an adjustment in the latter for the effects of quantitative restrictions (subsection 6.3.2).

7.1.2.4. Income distribution
Factoral income distribution depends on the production (or capacity utilization), labor allocation, product price and wage relationships mentioned above. Given the values calculated from these relationships and given government policies (especially of the tax variety), non-wage income is calculated as a residual.

7.1.2.5. Identities
Identities are of two types. (1) They are used to obtain total aggregates from the sectoral values (e.g. total *GDP* is the sum of sectoral *GDP*s, the total *GDP* deflator is a weighted average of the sectoral *GDP* deflators). (2) They are used to define residuals between two flows (e.g. the government deficit is the differences between government revenues and government expenditures, the balance on the current account is the difference between exports and imports). In all cases the standard definitions are utilized.

7.2. *Simulation procedure*

Chapter 8 uses the complete model of the Chilean economy to simulate the impact of changes in policies and in other exogenous variables. Eight important characteristics of the simulation procedure are now mentioned.

(1) The structure of the model outlined in the section 7.1 is assumed to be the true structure of the Chilean economy in the period of interest for these simulations. If biases exist in the estimated coefficients, such biases have an impact on the simulation results. Sensitivity analysis, of course, can be utilized to explore the effect of any such expected biases in specific parameter values or in particular relations in the model. Nevertheless, some possibly very important phenomena – such as changes in psychological and political attitudes or the effects of Krueger (1972) competitive rent-seeking – are not well incorporated into the model[7].

(2) The simulations presented in this study are all non-stochastic[8].

(3) All of the simulations used in this work are dynamic in that in the nth simulation period, simulation lagged endogenous values from the first $n-1$ simulation periods are used instead of actual lagged endogenous values. This procedure permits the tracing out of the time paths of the responses to a given change.

(4) For each simulation only an explicitly indicated alteration in policies or in other exogenous variables is explored. All other variables and parameters are fixed at their base simulation values in order not to confuse the impact of the change under examination with that of other changes.

(5) Because the model is non-linear, it cannot be solved by

---

[7]For example, the psychological and political impact of the nationalization of copper or of being a possibly unique experiment in the democratic transformation to socialism are very difficult to incorporate. However, the model can be used to give some insights about such effects. To the extent that psychological and political attitudes are related to collective consumption which should enter into the social maximand, the model can explore the trade-offs (if any) between such collective consumption and other arguments in the objective function. To the extent that such attitudes affect parameters such as those related to labor productivities, moreover, those parameters can be changed appropriately (although the direction of change is not obvious since the increased real income due to the collective consumption good may operate in the opposite direction from increased productivity due to increased pride).

[8]Young (1972) presents an interesting exploration of the impact on policy choices of including or excluding the stochastic aspects of a macroeconomic model.

simple matrix inversion. Instead a two-step Gauss–Seidel iterative procedure is utilized (with the two steps referring to iterations back and forth between the real and the monetary sectors, both of which also are solved iteratively).

(6) In some simulations, the indicated changes are for the initial year only. The results therefore give the time pattern of response to such once-and-for-all shocks. In other cases the indicated changes are maintained throughout the simulation period. The tables in ch. 8 identify which of these alternatives is used in each case.

(7) In most cases the important consequences of a particular one-time change occur before four or five years. Therefore ch. 8 generally includes the results for the first and the third year after the designated change. These two years are presented in order to include the short- and medium-term effects of the indicated change without the voluminous presentations which would be required if the year-by-year effects for a longer period were included. In the few cases in which two-year cycles or effects after the third year are important, such features are noted explicitly.

(8) Chapter 8 examines the effects of changes by focusing on each of the five major macro policy areas. For each change real trade-offs exist. The consequences are positive in at least one area and also are negative in at least one other realm. No particular change is uniformly beneficial[9].

7.3. Complete model performance in the sample and immediate post-sample periods

Chapter 8 utilizes the complete model of the Chilean economy to explore the impact of changes in policy instruments and in other exogenous variables. The impact of such changes is measured from a dynamic base simulation for 1962–1968. This time period includes the last four years of the sample and the first three years after the sample. This section discusses some of the characteristics of the base simulation.

Table 7.1 presents the percentage deviations between actual and

[9]Taylor (1973b) presents an interesting analysis, based in large part on the Chilean experience, of the difficulties in certain developing economies of pursuing stabilization, balance of payments, growth, and distributional objectives, even when all of the available major policy instruments are manipulated simultaneously.

Table 7.1

Percentage deviations and root-mean-squared percentage errors for variables related to major policy areas for dynamic base simulation, 1962–1967[a].

Variables relating to major areas of Chilean macroeconomic policy concern	Annual percentage deviations							Root-mean-squared percentage error
	1962	1963	1964	1965	1966	1967	1968	
1. Cyclical variables								
1.1. Nominal terms								
1.1.1. *GDP* deflator	-4.0	-0.1	-0.5	-0.6	-1.3	-10.9	0.3	4.4
1.1.2. Income velocity	0.7	9.7	9.0	7.7	-4.9	-13.4	-3.6	8.0
1.2. Real terms								
1.2.1. Capacity utilization for *GDP*	-0.3	5.3	2.5	7.4	0.5	2.3	5.4	4.2
1.3. Monetary policy–related variables								
1.3.1. Money supply deflator	-6.6	-7.9	-10.8	-6.7	-2.8	-1.8	1.5	6.3
1.3.2. Monetary base/deflator	-15.3	-6.6	-10.7	-4.2	-7.4	3.1	-5.6	8.5
1.3.3. Net Central Bank foreign reserves	-29.4	-7.4	-24.8	-22.6	-118.4	-83.0	-142.9	78.7
1.4. Fiscal policy related variables								
1.4.1. Government current expenditures	-6.2	5.8	1.4	-6.8	-10.0	-0.4	0.3	5.6
1.4.2. Government deficit	-5.8	28.0	2.5	11.3	60.8	64.6	15.8	36.0
2. Resource allocation and structural change								
2.1. Product/intermediate input price ratio								
2.1.1. Agriculture	8.4	12.7	-4.5	-6.2	11.1	28.4	68.1	28.9
2.1.2. Mining	5.1	3.2	-1.4	-3.0	-17.9	-4.9	-5.0	7.7
2.1.3. Industry	-2.5	-1.8	3.3	-0.1	-6.0	-21.7	-35.6	16.0

2.2. Labor force (secular movements)								
2.2.1. Agriculture	-0.5	-2.7	-3.8	-6.1	-7.5	-8.6	-10.1	6.5
2.2.2. Mining	-0.3	-0.5	-0.8	-1.1	-1.3	-1.5	-1.4	1.1
2.2.3. Industry	3.7	1.8	3.9	1.3	1.5	2.6	2.2	2.6
2.2.4. Services	0.5	-0.4	0.6	0.8	2.0	3.5	4.6	2.3
2.3. Capital stock								
2.3.1. Agriculture	2.3	3.1	2.2	0.9	0.5	-1.2	-4.0	2.4
2.3.2. Mining	3.1	2.5	2.0	0.1	3.3	10.2	16.9	7.8
2.3.3. Industry	2.1	3.9	3.4	2.7	2.9	1.7	1.5	2.7
2.4. Production capacity								
2.4.1. Agriculture	-14.5	-16.4	-17.6	-20.0	-21.5	-22.8	-25.5	20.1
2.4.2. Mining	-2.9	-5.4	-7.7	-8.7	-9.1	-8.7	-7.4	7.6
2.4.3. Industry	10.1	4.3	2.5	-3.1	-6.0	-6.9	-8.8	6.5
2.4.4. Services	-3.9	-5.4	-4.8	-3.2	-4.0	-3.9	-4.9	4.4
2.5. GDP								
2.5.1. Agriculture	-9.1	-4.4	-14.7	-13.1	-31.7	-37.6	-38.6	25.1
2.5.2. Mining	-8.8	-7.8	-11.5	-11.9	-17.4	0.1	3.9	10.2
2.5.3. Industry	1.4	8.5	-3.5	8.2	-11.6	-8.9	-2.8	7.3
2.5.4. Services	-1.3	-0.6	5.1	3.3	1.6	2.3	-2.8	-2.8
3. Distribution of income and resources								
3.1. Factoral								
3.1.1. Real wage	7.2	1.2	-4.5	-3.9	-6.7	10.3	-2.4	5.9
3.1.1.1. Agriculture	2.8	-2.5	5.8	-0.1	4.9	23.7	-2.2	9.6
3.1.1.2. Mining	5.0	-12.8	4.1	2.3	11.4	14.5	14.1	10.4
3.1.1.3. Industry	1.4	0.3	-1.6	10.1	4.4	16.3	-40.9	17.2
3.1.1.4. Services	-4.7	-4.8	-4.3	-5.3	-13.7	-11.3	-23.9	11.8
3.1.1.5. Government	-0.9	-0.2	3.4	15.9	16.8	41.1	36.4	22.5
3.1.2. Wage share in income	7.7	-1.4	12.9	1.5	12.3	21.9	14.5	12.4
3.2. International								
3.2.1. Net factor income from abroad	13.4	1.3	12.5	16.9	43.1	51.4	36.0	30.3

Table 7.1 (continued)

Variables relating to major areas of Chilean macroeconomic policy concern	Annual percentage deviations							Root-mean-squared percentage error
	1962	1963	1964	1965	1966	1967	1968	
3.3. Intertemporal	0.3	−3.0	−3.0	−2.4	2.0	2.1	2.2	2.2
3.3.1. Consumption/product								
3.4. Public versus private								
3.4.1. Taxes/deflator	−3.3	−3.0	−0.6	−4.6	−14.8	−4.9	−6.3	6.8
3.4.1.1. Indirect	−4.1	−3.2	0.7	0.1	−6.6	−2.8	−1.7	3.4
3.4.1.1.1. Sales	0.1	9.8	−2.1	−2.8	−6.6	−7.9	4.1	5.7
3.4.1.1.2. Import	−4.5	−29.6	2.4	10.2	13.0	44.3	16.2	22.0
3.4.1.2. Direct	−2.6	−2.9	−1.7	−8.2	−20.8	−6.7	−10.0	9.7
3.4.1.2.1. Large-scale mining	1.8	−13.0	−22.8	−19.6	−53.1	−28.8	−31.9	28.7
3.4.1.2.2. Other corporations	−9.6	−7.5	−30.9	−14.4	−51.1	−44.7	−41.9	33.1
3.4.1.2.3. Personal	3.7	−24.1	−21.9	−35.9	−46.7	−52.7	−60.1	39.5
3.4.2. Government consumption/*GDP*	−4.3	4.6	3.8	−7.8	−3.9	4.4	2.2	4.7
4. Economic growth related variables								
4.1. *GDP*	−2.0	1.1	−2.3	1.1	−6.3	−4.6	−2.4	3.3
4.1.1. Agriculture	−9.1	−4.4	−14.7	−13.1	−31.7	−37.6	−38.6	25.1
4.1.2. Mining	−8.8	−7.8	−11.5	−11.9	−17.4	0.1	3.9	10.2
4.1.3. Industry	1.4	8.5	−3.5	8.2	−11.6	−8.9	−2.8	7.3
4.2. Gross national savings	−24.5	20.4	141.9	24.8	123.8	162.3	134.1	107.8
4.2.1. Personal	−92.9	53.1	−113.7	21.2	−210.1	−363.6	−241.1	192.5
4.2.2. Business								
4.2.3. Government	39.1	−39.8	−3.7	−10.0	−29.8	−3.1	−6.3	24.4

4.3. Capacity	-1.7	-4.0	-4.7	-5.9	-6.8	-6.7	-7.4	5.6
4.3.1. Investment	5.3	8.5	-7.3	3.3	18.3	13.0	10.5	10.6
4.3.2. Capital Stock	0.5	1.2	0.5	0.7	1.3	1.0	0.4	0.9
5. Foreign sector								
5.1. Exports	-2.7	2.3	-3.1	7.1	-2.7	5.8	13.1	6.4
5.1.1. Agricultural	-9.5	-4.0	-21.2	2.6	NA	NA	NA	11.9
5.1.2. Mineral								
5.1.2.1. Large-scale	-1.8	1.0	-3.1	10.6	NA	NA	NA	5.6
5.1.2.2. Other	-4.5	-5.8	0.1	1.0	NA	NA	NA	3.7
5.1.3. Industrial	1.9	86.9	3.9	9.8	NA	NA	NA	43.8
5.1.4. Services	-2.3	-2.3	-2.4	5.6	13.2	10.3	37.3	15.7
5.2. Imports	4.0	-9.4	-2.2	4.4	-7.9	9.0	8.9	7.1
5.2.1. Consumption								
5.2.1.1. Habitual	-2.4	-18.2	-2.3	-1.7	NA	NA	NA	9.3
5.2.1.2. Durable	-7.9	29.5	19.0	0.8	NA	NA	NA	18.0
5.2.1.3. Secondary	19.0	-1.7	32.6	29.8	NA	NA	NA	24.0
5.2.2. Investment								
5.2.2.1. Machinery and equipment	-0.3	-5.9	-3.5	-0.9	NA	NA	NA	3.5
5.2.2.2. Transportation	5.5	-17.3	-2.6	5.3	NA	NA	NA	9.6
5.2.3. Intermediate	12.7	-5.1	-1.5	3.0	NA	NA	NA	7.1
5.2.4. Services	5.4	-18.5	-0.3	21.0	18.9	17.6	13.8	15.4
5.3. Surplus on current account	-28.9	71.3	-5.5	46.9	73.8	-22.7	27.8	46.1
5.4. Net bank international reserves	-19.5	-5.1	-17.1	-15.4	-85.9	-67.9	-157.5	73.4
5.5. Black market exchange rate	2.5	-4.6	-5.0	1.0	9.2	18.3	24.5	12.4

NA means not available because of a change in the foreign trade classification for the base data for 1966–1968.
ᵃAll variable definitions and sources are given in appendix A.

simulated values for each of the years of the base simulation and the root-mean-squared percentage errors over the seven years of the dynamic simulation. These statistics are given for important variables related to each of the five major areas of macroeconomic policy concern: cyclical fluctuations, resource allocation and structural change, the distribution of income and of resources, economic growth, and the foreign position. Five important characteristics of the results in table 7.1 merit emphasis.

(1) For the aggregate variables defined as levels, the seven-year dynamic simulation traces actual developments quite well. The root-mean-squared percentage errors for the most important aggregates are 3.3 for *GDP*, 4.4 for the *GDP* deflator, 4.2 for the capacity utilization rate, 5.6 for production capacity, 2.3 for the private consumption share of *GDP*, 4.7 for the government consumption share of *GDP*, 10.6 for investment, 0.9 for capital stock, 6.4 for exports, 7.1 for imports, 6.8 for real taxes, 9.6 for the real wage, and 6.3 for the real money supply. Given the large fluctuations in the Chilean economy, the high rate of inflation, and the general problems of modeling developing economies, these rates are quite satisfactory. For those aggregate variables defined as levels at least, the complete model seems to be a good tool for explaining the Chilean experience.

(2) For a number of aggregate variables defined as levels, moreover, the root mean percentage error would be much lower if it were not for specific identifiable events. In early 1967, for example, the government succeeded in applying considerable moral suasion, in addition to legal pressures, to keep wage increases down as one of the last effective measures in the Frei antiinflation program. For that year by far the largest discrepancy between actual and simulated values for the real wage occurs. The simulated value, 23.7% above the actual value (variable 3.1.1), suggests that the government transitorily succeeded in holding down this component of cost-push pressures. That this success was only temporary, however, is suggested by the quite small percentage discrepancy of 2.2% for this variable for 1968.

If the 1967 observation is excluded, the mean absolute percentage error drops to 3.1 for the real wage. Therefore, although the model does not accurately capture the impact of such policies as moral suasion, it seems to perform even better than the root-mean-squared percentage errors in table 7.1 indicate in tracing the effects of quantifiable government policies alone.

(3) For variables which are defined as the difference between two flows instead of levels (e.g. savings, net bank revenues, balance on current account, government deficit, net factor income from abroad) or which refer to a great degree of disaggregation, the root-mean-squared percentage errors are much greater. Most noticeable in the latter category are the variables related to agricultural production, for which sector the labor force, capacity, and *GDP* are systematically underestimated. Such results indicate that there may be a payoff to further work on the disaggregate relationships. Nevertheless, the sign of the percentage discrepancies between the base simulation values and the simulations in ch. 8 should at least be suggestive of the direction of the effects of changing various exogenous variables.

(4) The results do not suggest strongly that the model is less successful as the dynamic simulation period is lengthened or as consideration is extended to the immediate post-sample years[10]. The percentage errors do seem to be slightly larger for the last three years of the dynamic simulation than for the first four years for some important variables (e.g. *GDP*, variable 4.1). Even for most of these variables, however, the differentials are not large, and some significant counter examples exist (e.g. capacity utilization, variable 1.2.1).

(5) In the latter years of the base simulation, the model seems to succeed in picking up indications of the growing, but still partially latent, inflationary pressures which were to doom the Frei stabilization attempt and cause a resurgence of inflation beginning in late 1967. The persistent difference between the actual and simulated values of income velocity (variable 1.1.2), for example, points to this build-up in inflationary expectations and pressures.

---

[10]This is not to say that the model can be fruitfully utilized without revision for subsequent periods (such as in the 1970s) during which substantial structural changes are introduced.

CHAPTER 8

Policy simulations and multipliers with the complete model of the Chilean economy

The complete model of the Chilean economy described in section 7.1 is now utilized to explore the consequences of the various policies presented in chs. 2 and 3. The first four sections of this chapter are devoted, respectively, to fiscal policies, monetary policies, foreign sector policies and incomes and labor market policies. Section 8.5 summarizes the simulation results.

The simulation procedure is described in section 7.2. Each set of simulations posits some explicit deviation (e.g. the increase in all government expenditures, production, and employment in simulation 8.1.2) from the base simulation, which is described in section 7.3. In general, three alternative simulations have been run for each such deviation from the base simulation: (A) 10% increase in the first year only; (B) an increase equal to one standard deviation from the historical secular trend for the first year only; and (C) 10% increase above the base simulation for each year. Alternatives A and B thus give the impact of a one-time change. Alternative A, however, always assumes the same percentage change in the exogenous variable, while alternative B considers equally likely percentage changes for each exogenous variable. Alternative C considers the impact of a given percentage change which is maintained not only for the first year, but for each year of the simulation. Alternatives A and C have the advantage of having uniform percentage deviations in the relevant exogenous variables across simulations, so the discussion generally focuses on them. Nevertheless, at times the B alternatives are particularly interesting since they represent historically equally likely changes across simulations.

The four tables in this chapter present a number of these simulations. Space requirements preclude the presentation of each set of simulations or of each alternative in a given set, so only the most interesting ones are given[1]. For each simulation percentage deviations[2] are presented for a number of variables grouped in the same five major policy areas utilized in chs. 2 and 7: cyclical fluctuations, resource allocation and structural change, the distribution of income and of resources, economic growth, and the foreign sector position. For variables which are defined as the difference between flows (e.g. savings, net reserves, and deficits), the absolute value of the percentage deviation may be very high due to the small absolute value of the base difference relative to the magnitudes of the two underlying flows.

All of the simulations were run over the same seven-year period utilized for the base simulation in table 7.1. To save space and to preclude an inundation of numbers, however, the tables include the percentage deviations only for selected years. For simulations of type A, the values are presented at most for the first, second, and third years so that the immediate and medium-term impact of a given change can be seen. For simulations of type B, at most the first year is presented, since a comparison of this year with the first year of a type A simulation is sufficient to indicate the probable impact of historically likely changes. For simulations of type C the first year is identical to those for the type A in the same set. To have the medium- and longer-run impact of maintaining such changes instead of having a one-time change, therefore at most the third-, fifth-, and seventh-year results are included in the table. The year within the simulation period is given at the head of each column.

---

[1] Over 1200 simulation experiments have been conducted with the model.

[2] The sign of the percentage deviation indicates whether the variable of interest changes in the same (positive) or opposite (negative) *algebraic* direction as the exogenous variable(s) the value(s) of which is (are) altered for that simulation. For a variable the level of which is negative (as is the case for some of the variables which are defined as the difference between two flows), therefore, a positive percentage deviation implies that this variable increases algebraically (and decreases absolutely) in response to an increase in the exogenous variable(s) of interest.

8.1. Fiscal policies

Table 8.1 includes three sets of simulations relating to the impact of fiscal policy:

8.1.1. All of the endogenous tax and transfers functions (table 3.2) are multiplied by 1.10.

8.1.2. Real government expenditures (consumption, subsidies, and direct and indirect investment), government production, and government employment and increased.

8.1.3. Both the tax increases of simulation 8.1.1 and the government expenditure – production – employment increases of simulation 8.1.2 are implemented.

For each simulation the base simulation of section 7.3 is used as the point of comparison, except that in simulations 8.1.2 and 8.1.3 real government consumption expenditure is treated as an exogenous policy instrument instead of an endogenous variable in order to permit the maximum possible impact for government expenditure policies.

The simulation results are very rich. In order to facilitate digestion of them, major characteristics are discussed first. These features are common to most of the simulations presented in this chapter, not only those in table 8.1. Subsequently, the specific implications of the simulations in table 8.1 for the five major areas of Chilean macroeconomic policy concern are explored.

8.1.1. Major general characteristics of simulations

(1) *Substantial endogenous responses in governmental and bank behavior are induced.* Consider, for example, the first year of simulation 8.1.1A in which all tax functions are multiplied by 1.10. As a result, real taxes increase by 5.4% (variable 3.4.1). The added revenue, however, also induces an increase in real current government expenditures of 4.5% (variable 1.4.1), which offsets much of the aggregate demand impact of the increased taxes. The resulting reduced government deficit (variable 1.4.2) and reduced surplus on current account due to the decline in exports (variables 5.1 and 5.3), moreover, cause declines in net Central Bank international reserves, the monetary base, and the money supply (variables 1.3.1–3). That the money supply falls much less than the

Table
Fiscal policy simulations using complete

Variables relating to major areas of Chilean macroeconomic policy concern	Simulations 8.1.1 All tax functions increased by multiplication factor			
	A			C
	1	2	3	3
1. Cyclical variables				
1.1. Nominal terms				
1.1.1. *GDP* deflator	4.2	2.5	−0.2	5.0
1.1.2. Income velocity	7.7	6.7	1.8	11.9
1.2. Real terms				
1.2.1. Capacity utilization for *GDP*	−2.7	1.2	−1.3	−2.5
1.3. Monetary policy-related variables				
1.3.1. Money supply/deflator	−5.9	−3.0	−3.0	−8.3
1.3.2. Monetary base/deflator	−8.5	−0.8	−3.7	−9.8
1.3.3. Net Central Bank foreign reserves	−8.6	−0.9	−9.0	−12.6
1.4. Fiscal policy-related variables				
1.4.1. Government current expenditures	4.5	1.7	−0.3	6.3
1.4.2. Government deficit	−17.8	−3.1	−1.6	−25.1
2. Resource allocation and structural change				
2.1. Product/intermediate input price ratio				
2.1.1. Agriculture	1.5	1.9	−5.7	−2.1
2.1.2. Mining	−3.2	−0.8	−1.4	−4.2
2.1.3. Industry	0.5	−0.5	3.4	2.5
2.2. Labor force (secular movements)				
2.2.1. Agriculture	0.0	−0.4	−0.2	−0.3
2.2.1. Mining	0.0	0.0	0.0	0.0
2.2.3. Industry	−0.1	−1.5	−0.6	−1.0
2.2.4. Services	0.0	0.4	0.7	0.5
2.3. Capital stock				
2.3.1. Agriculture	−0.5	−0.2	−1.2	−1.2
2.3.2. Mining	−0.2	−0.5	−0.1	−2.7
2.3.3. Industry	−0.1	−0.1	−0.9	−0.9
2.4. Production capacity				
2.4.1. Agriculture	0.0	−0.4	−0.2	−0.3
2.4.2. Mining	0.0	0.0	0.0	0.0
2.4.3. Industry	−0.1	−1.3	−0.5	−0.9
2.4.4. Services	0.0	0.2	0.8	1.0
2.5. *GDP*				
2.5.1. Agriculture	−3.2	4.6	−1.4	0.1
2.5.2. Mining	−2.4	−2.6	−1.8	−6.0
2.5.3. Industry	−3.5	3.8	−4.9	−3.7
2.5.4. Services	−0.2	−1.0	2.1	1.2

8.1
model of Chilean economyᵃ.

	Simulations 8.1.2 All government expenditures, production, and employment increased			Simulations 8.1.3 All taxes, government expenditures, production, and employment increased					
A		B	C	A			C		
1	2	1	3	1	2	3	3	5	7
-2.7	0.3	-1.7	-6.4	2.0	3.9	-5.1	-1.2	0.9	-3.7
-5.1	-0.1	-2.7	-11.4	3.5	8.4	-8.5	-0.5	4.8	0.7
1.7	0.8	2.3	1.5	-1.2	2.0	-2.9	-1.7	-3.8	-2.4
3.2	2.1	3.1	7.6	-3.6	-1.3	0.6	-1.9	-6.8	-6.5
4.6	0.0	4.4	12.5	-5.0	-0.9	4.7	1.0	-4.4	3.8
3.3	1.6	4.8	10.4	-5.6	2.0	-2.3	-2.9	-20.5	-85.0
10.0	0.0	6.9	10.0	10.0	0.0	0.0	10.0	10.0	10.0
35.4	-0.7	51.6	40.0	9.4	-8.8	-1.2	-3.1	-15.6	6.8
3.7	2.9	4.7	2.1	3.6	3.1	-13.2	-4.1	-10.8	7.3
1.5	0.1	1.4	2.9	-2.2	-1.4	-0.6	-2.4	-4.4	0.3
0.0	-2.2	-2.3	0.2	0.8	-2.2	8.3	4.4	6.9	1.7
-1.6	0.1	-0.3	-2.3	-1.6	0.1	-1.9	-2.5	-2.2	-2.3
0.0	0.0	0.0	0.0	0.0	0.0	0.0	0.0	0.0	0.0
-4.8	0.7	-0.9	-6.9	-4.9	0.6	-5.8	-7.1	-6.2	-6.0
-1.6	2.0	-0.3	-0.5	-1.7	2.0	-0.1	-0.7	-0.3	-0.4
0.0	-0.1	0.6	0.4	-0.3	0.1	-2.5	-0.7	0.9	-0.1
-0.1	-0.3	-0.2	0.1	-0.3	-1.3	-1.7	-3.5	-7.7	-2.9
-0.7	-0.5	0.7	-2.4	-0.8	-0.4	-2.9	-3.1	-3.3	-3.6
-1.6	0.1	-0.3	-2.3	-1.6	0.1	-1.9	-2.5	-2.2	-2.3
0.0	0.0	0.0	0.0	0.0	0.0	0.0	0.0	0.0	-0.1
-4.2	0.5	-0.8	-6.2	-4.3	0.4	-5.1	-6.4	-5.9	-5.6
0.0	1.9	0.0	4.2	0.0	2.1	2.6	4.7	4.2	3.2
-2.6	1.6	0.6	-3.3	-5.5	7.6	-7.0	-3.6	-6.7	-13.2
0.0	-0.4	-0.6	0.2	-2.4	-3.3	-0.6	-5.8	-6.3	-5.0
-2.9	2.3	2.4	-5.9	-6.6	8.0	-14.4	-9.9	-13.4	-11.0
0.6	1.9	-0.2	5.2	0.2	0.6	5.3	6.1	4.4	3.9

Table 8.1
Fiscal policy simulations using complete

Variables relating to major areas of Chilean macroeconomic policy concern	Simulations 8.1.1 All tax functions increased by multiplication factor			
	A			C
	1	2	3	3
3. Distribution of income and resources				
3.1. Factoral				
3.1.1. Real wage	−6.9	−1.6	0.3	−5.6
3.1.1.1. Agriculture	−5.1	−1.2	1.7	−2.7
3.1.1.2. Mining	−4.9	0.8	3.3	−0.8
3.1.1.3. Industry	−3.0	−1.7	1.6	−2.0
3.1.1.4. Services	−1.8	−1.1	3.6	1.0
3.1.1.5. Government	−7.1	−0.5	−2.7	−6.8
3.1.2. Wage share in income	−0.5	−2.4	3.1	1.6
3.2. International				
3.2.1. Net factor income from abroad	−3.2	−1.2	1.7	0.2
3.3. Intertemporal				
3.3.1. Consumption/product	2.3	−1.8	−0.5	−0.2
3.4. Public versus private				
3.4.1. Taxes/deflator	5.4	0.4	−0.4	6.1
3.4.1.1. Indirect	7.1	0.8	−0.8	7.3
3.4.1.1.1. Sales	7.1	1.0	−1.1	7.5
3.4.1.1.2. Import	7.5	0.0	0.4	7.1
3.4.1.2. Direct	3.7	0.1	−0.1	5.1
3.4.1.2.1. Large-scale mining	1.9	−5.1	−2.9	−3.8
3.4.1.2.2. Other corporations	4.4	2.7	−9.6	−3.6
3.4.1.2.3. Personal	2.5	9.7	4.2	14.2
3.4.2. Government economic consumption/*GDP*	7.4	0.7	0.8	8.8
4. Economic growth-related variables				
4.1. *GDP*	−2.7	1.0	−1.1	−2.3
4.1.1. Agriculture	−3.2	4.6	−1.4	0.1
4.1.2. Mining	−2.4	−2.6	−1.8	−6.0
4.1.3. Industry	−3.5	3.8	−4.9	−3.7
4.2. Gross national savings				
4.2.1. Personal	−71.0	21.9	131.2	2.1
4.2.2. Business	70.8	27.1	−268.3	−69.4
4.2.3. Government	28.7	−1.3	2.3	21.3
4.3. Capacity	0.0	−0.2	0.2	0.2
4.3.1. Investment	1.0	−2.0	−4.2	−4.4
4.3.2. Capital stock	0.1	−0.1	−0.4	−0.4
5. Foreign sector				
5.1. Exports	−3.2	1.2	−4.6	−5.5
5.1.1. Agricultural	−2.2	4.8	−3.6	−1.1

(continued)
model of Chilean economy[a].

Simulations 8.1.2 All government expenditures, production, and employment increased				Simulations 8.1.3 All taxes, government expenditures, production, and employment increased					
A		B	C	A			C		
1	2	1	3	1	2	3	3	5	7
1.7	−1.5	0.6	5.3	−5.7	−3.6	6.0	−0.9	2.0	6.7
0.2	1.5	0.9	7.6	−5.3	−0.4	7.1	3.0	14.8	21.6
0.1	−1.0	0.4	1.6	−5.1	−0.1	7.7	1.2	62.5	−31.8
2.0	−1.3	0.5	6.8	−1.4	−3.7	8.8	4.2	6.2	8.1
1.6	−2.3	−0.3	5.2	−0.4	−3.7	11.8	6.6	9.6	9.6
1.5	0.8	2.1	4.7	−6.0	0.2	−2.2	−3.3	−6.0	−5.7
−0.1	−0.4	−1.4	6.0	−1.0	−3.7	12.0	6.9	20.9	−15.8
4.4	−0.6	2.2	10.2	0.3	−3.4	11.1	10.3	12.6	17.4
1.4	−1.0	0.1	0.2	3.0	−3.2	0.3	−0.2	−1.7	5.7
1.7	0.7	2.6	4.7	6.6	1.0	1.2	10.1	12.0	9.2
1.5	0.6	2.2	3.0	8.3	1.4	−0.5	9.9	8.3	13.3
0.7	1.7	2.1	1.8	7.6	3.0	−3.0	8.7	6.5	7.6
3.4	−4.2	2.4	7.0	10.2	−4.9	8.9	14.6	14.4	34.2
1.9	0.9	3.0	6.2	5.2	0.5	2.6	10.3	15.3	5.7
2.9	−0.9	1.1	7.4	4.1	−7.3	4.1	2.7	1.3	11.4
2.2	0.1	4.6	−10.5	7.1	4.0	−28.3	−14.1	−34.3	70.4
2.8	−2.5	4.3	7.1	4.8	7.4	8.5	21.2	15.1	40.2
9.2	−1.7	4.7	8.0	12.5	−2.9	3.1	11.3	13.6	12.5
0.7	1.7	2.1	1.8	−2.2	3.0	−3.0	−1.2	−3.2	−2.2
−2.6	1.6	0.6	−3.3	−5.5	7.6	−7.0	−3.6	−6.7	−13.2
0.0	−0.4	−0.6	0.2	−2.4	−3.3	−0.6	−5.8	−6.3	−5.0
−2.9	2.3	2.4	−5.9	−6.6	8.0	−14.4	−9.9	−13.4	−11.0
−7.8	26.4	6.6	275.7	−79.8	46.1	287.2	194.5	625.8	−456.2
−174.8	5.6	333.6	−458.4	100.8	43.1	−767.0	−433.2	−248.5	136.6
−93.7	0.5	−95.2	−15.7	−12.0	5.8	12.8	21.1	51.6	13.8
−1.0	0.9	−0.2	0.3	−1.0	1.0	−0.1	0.5	0.6	0.2
−0.7	2.1	5.8	−0.5	0.4	0.5	−10.6	−5.7	2.2	−4.1
−0.1	0.1	0.6	0.0	0.0	0.1	−0.8	−0.4	0.0	−0.1
−0.2	0.4	1.0	0.1	−3.4	2.0	−6.0	−6.1	−8.4	−7.6
−2.2	2.5	0.5	−2.6	−4.0	8.5	−10.7	−4.5	−22.4	−8.2

Table 8.1
Fiscal policy simulations using complete

Variables relating to major areas of Chilean macroeconomic policy concern	Simulations 8.1.1 All tax functions increased by multplication factor			
	A			C
	1	2	3	3
5.1.2. Mineral				
5.1.2.1. Large scale	−3.4	3.5	6.0	−5.8
5.1.2.2. Other	0.0	−1.6	−0.4	−1.5
5.1.3. Industrial	−23.4	−9.6	−12.3	−21.0
5.1.4. Services	−1.2	−1.3	−1.1	−2.3
5.2. Imports	0.4	−2.0	−2.7	−3.8
5.2.1. Consumption				
5.2.1.1. Habitual	4.1	−8.0	−4.8	−7.8
5.2.1.2. Durable	−1.2	−3.6	−1.6	−6.1
5.2.1.3. Secondary	−1.4	−5.5	4.3	0.9
5.2.2. Investment				
5.2.2.1. Machinery and equipment	0.4	−1.6	−0.6	−1.7
5.2.2.2. Transportation	1.3	0.1	0.8	2.5
5.2.3. Intermediate	−2.0	0.9	−3.7	−4.1
5.2.4. Services	0.0	0.7	−5.7	−5.0
5.3. Surplus on current account	−30.8	9.2	−12.5	−15.3
5.4. Net bank international reserves	−6.1	−0.7	−6.6	−9.3
5.5. Black market exchange rate	4.5	3.1	0.4	6.2

[a]The items in this table are the percentage deviations from the base simulation described in section 7.3 due to the exogenous changes indicated at the column heads. For simulations 8.1.2 and 8.1.3 government current consumption expenditures are exogenized in addition to the other assumptions of the base simulation. 'A' refers to a simulation in which there are 10% changes in the indicated exogenous variables in the first year, but no changes thereafter. 'B' refers to a simulation in which there are

(continued)
model of Chilean economy[a].

	Simulations 8.1.2 All government expenditures, production, and employment increased				Simulations 8.1.3 All taxes, government expenditures, production, and employment increased				
A		B	C	A			C		
1	2	1	3	1	2	3	3	5	7
0.7	−0.7	0.7	1.4	−2.5	3.4	−5.7	−5.2	−8.9	−10.9
0.0	0.6	0.0	0.3	0.0	−1.2	0.8	−1.4	−0.6	−0.6
−14.8	7.7	12.2	−6.8	−39.9	−0.5	−25.5	−30.1	−28.0	−17.2
0.6	0.0	0.6	1.0	−0.8	−1.6	−0.2	−1.7	−1.8	−0.9
0.5	0.2	0.6	0.4	0.6	−2.3	−2.6	−3.8	−3.1	−2.1
3.8	−1.6	2.6	2.5	6.3	−11.8	−2.0	−5.9	−2.9	12.5
0.8	2.2	0.5	4.1	−0.6	−2.4	−0.2	−2.4	−1.7	0.0
0.2	−1.1	−2.0	11.8	−2.1	−8.9	20.8	10.5	22.8	−20.0
−0.1	−0.3	−0.1	−0.6	0.1	−2.3	−1.3	−2.6	−3.6	−3.9
−0.5	0.4	−0.4	−3.3	0.9	1.0	−0.4	−0.3	3.2	1.4
−0.3	1.0	0.5	0.2	−2.3	2.1	−5.1	−4.6	−7.3	−8.1
−1.0	0.6	0.3	−2.6	−1.0	1.8	−9.0	−8.1	−7.4	−6.8
−1.3	0.8	5.0	2.9	−31.1	12.4	−18.1	−14.5	−35.0	−34.4
2.3	1.2	3.4	7.6	−4.0	1.5	−1.6	−2.0	−17.4	−69.9
−2.9	0.0	−1.8	−7.3	2.2	4.4	−5.0	−0.8	1.6	−2.0

changes equal to one standard deviation from the secular trend in the indicated exogenous variables in the first year, but no change thereafter. 'C' refers to a simulation in which there are 10% changes in the indicated exogenous variables in each year. The years within the dynamic simulation runs are indicated at the column heads. The first years of type C simulations are identical to that of the associated type A simulations and therefore are not presented.

monetary base (−5.9 versus −8.5%) reflects a reduction of −12.7% in net free reserves held by the commercial banking system, primarily in response to a decline in demand and time deposits.

(2) *The induced compositional changes may be quite considerable.* Although all of the tax functions are multiplied by 1.10 in simulation 8.1.1A, for example, the first-year increase in real tax collections vary from 1.9% for large-scale mining direct taxes to 7.5% for import taxes (variables 3.4.1.1.1–2 and 3.4.1.2.1–3). For this and for the other simulations, other examples of significant compositional changes are provided by the resource allocation and structural change variables (2.1–2.5), the real wage variables (3.1.1), the gross national savings variables (4.2), and the export and import variables (5.1 and 5.2).

(3) *The time patterns of responses vary considerably across variables, with much more than one year required for near to complete adjustment in many cases.* Most of the variables have their largest absolute percentage deviations in the first year, but a number of important exceptions exist in each of the simulations with shocks in the first year only. A few examples from simulation 8.1.1 are *GDP* in agriculture and in industry, the wage share in income, personal taxes, agricultural exports, and total imports (variables 2.5.1, 2.5.3, 3.1.2, 3.4.1.2.3, 5.1.1, and 5.2). In many cases, moreover, reversals in the sign of responses occur in the adjustment paths within the complete model context. Simulation 8.1.1A again provides examples such as the capacity utilization rate, the *GDP* from agriculture, the real wage in agriculture, real direct tax collections from large-scale mining, total *GDP*, total exports, and the surplus on current account (variables 1.2.1, 2.5.1, 2.5.1, 3.1.1.1, 3.4.1.2.1, 4.1, 5.1, and 5.3).

(4) *In substantial part because of capacity constraints, the model is quite non-linear so that simulations are not additive.* Table 8.1 provides some examples of these features. First, simulations 8.1.1 and 8.1.2 basically are combined in order to obtain simulations 8.1.3. The results for the last of these, however, cannot be obtained simply by summing the results from the first two. Second, the third year of type C simulations involves the combination of first-, second-, and third-year one-time or type A effects. The results from the first three years of type A simulations, however, cannot simply be summed to obtain the third year of the respective type C simulations. In fact, the latter are often smaller than the sums of

the former because of diminishing returns. Finally, although an example is not provided in table 8.1[3], if one multiplies all of the exogenous changes for a given simulation by a factor X the results change by proportions different from (and generally less than) X.

(5) *Feedbacks, both simultaneous and lagged, are often substantial.* The most important mechanism for these feedbacks is through the price and wage systems. Changes in real variables cause changes in the government deficit and in the surplus on current account. These result in a change in the money supply, with a lagged effect on prices throughout the system, which supplements the direct impact of real changes on prices and wages. The first year of simulation 8.1.1A again provides an illustration. Although all of the tax functions are multiplied by 1.10 in this simulation, total real taxes increase only by 5.4% (variable 3.4.1) and the increases across components of this aggregate vary considerably [see paragraph (2) above]. That there is not just a uniform increase of 10% in real taxes reflects the existence of considerable simultaneous feedbacks through the price system and though the differential effects on the relevant activity levels. Such results reinforce the claim that it is necessary to consider a complete system in the analysis of macroeconomic policies.

(6) *The combination of these characteristics means that simple traditional textbook macromodels are poor predictions of many of the effects within this model of exogenous changes.* Substantial feedbacks in a non-linear disaggregated model with endogenous government and banking system behavior and adjustment periods longer than a year, lead to results much different than those suggested by short-run equilibrium aggregate IS–LM textbook models. Feedbacks can be partially neutralizing, such as in the case of the indirect government current consumption response to increased taxes (see paragraph (1) above). Changes in sectoral composition and adjustment lags can lead to disequilibrium results which seem paradoxical within the traditional IS–LM curve framework. Once again, simulation 8.1.1A provides an example with the immediate increase in the *GDP* deflator (variables 1.1.1) when the tax functions are increased[4]. Only in the third period, in

---

[3] A comparison of simulations 8.3.1A and 8.3.1B in table 8.3 provides an illustration.
[4] Further discussion of these results is provided below in subsection 8.1.2.

fact, do the percentage deviations for this variable become negative.

(7) *Trade-offs among the degree of attainment of various policy goods are the norm.* Subsection 8.1.2 and sections 8.2–4 provide numerous illustrations in which macroeconomic policies which are successful in improving the economy in regard to one goal (e.g. dampening inflation) have negative effects in at least one other major area of concern (e.g. capacity utilization, growth, foreign position, and distribution of control over income and resources).

8.1.2. The simulated impact of fiscal policy on five major areas of macroeconomic policy concern

8.1.2.1. Cyclical concerns

The variables related to *nominal stability*, as is noted above, provide an example of how the results differ from those predicted by simple IS–LM curve models because of disequilibrium adjustments and compositional changes. For the first year of the tax increase case (simulation 8.1.1A), the monetary base and the money supply both decrease due to a reduction in the surplus on current account (originating in a fall in exports) and in the government deficit (variables 1.3.1–2, 1.4.2, 5.1, and 5.3). The negative impact of the decline in the money supply on the price level is initially outweighed by positive effects due to bottlenecks in shifting the structure of production to accommodate demand shifts and direct impacts of taxes (especially indirect taxes, such as on imports) on prices. Therefore, the *GDP* deflator actually increases for the first two years, and the income velocity rises by even a larger percentage (variables 1.1.1–2). When the exogenous increase in the tax functions is maintained for a number of years, moreover, these adjustment effects last even longer (simulation 8.1.1C).

For the case of increases in government expenditures, production, and employment, the pattern is reversed, although by the second year after a one-time change the impact on the *GDP* deflator is positive (simulations 8.1.2). When taxes and government expenditures–production–employment all are increased, initially the pressure for price increases dominate despite a reduction in the money supply (simulation 8.1.3A). This is *not* the price impact of the traditional 'balanced budget' effect (note that output actually initially declines), but the dominance of the adjustment–composition change processes described above. Because of differing patterns of adjustment, subsequently sign reverses occur both for one-time changes and maintained changes (simulations 8.1.3A and 8.1.3C).

The variables related to *real stability* behave more closely, although not identically to the predictions of the traditional IS–LM curve model. In the first year capacity utilization falls -2.7% due to tax increases, and rises 1.5% due to government expenditure–production–employment increases (variable 1.2.1). The direction of these changes is the same as predicted by the traditional model, but the magnitudes are quite small. The implied impact multipliers, for example, are about 1.4 and 0.9, respectively. That the initial effect of the tax change is larger in absolute value than the effect of the expenditure–production–employment change, moreover, is in contrast to the spirit of the traditional 'balanced budget' analysis. When all of the exogenous changes are combined in simulation 8.1.3C, therefore, in the first year capacity utilization falls (although it cycles somewhat thereafter).

8.1.2.2. *Resource allocation and structural change*
In all of the simulations the impact is proportionately much greater for the sectoral product to intermediate price ratios and sectoral *GDP*s than for the sectoral labor force, capital stock and capacity distributions (although some fairly significant shifts of labor out of manufacturing do occur in the last two simulations). Such a result is plausible since the latter group of variables are real stocks for which, in general, only relatively small changes at the margin can occur within a year or two. The first-year impact in all three sets of simulations seems to be to move resources out of the goods-producing sectors (especially manufacturing and agriculture) into services (see especially variables 2.4.1–4). Subsequently, this tendency is less strong (i.e. there is some cycling for agriculture and manufacturing in the type A simulations), but still persists. One final interesting feature is that in a number of cases the sectoral product–intermediate input price ratio moves in the opposite direction from product and/or capacity variables. This result raises questions about the tremendous emphasis in the international trade

literature of the past decade on various measures of resource allocation incentives which are generally based on sectoral product to intermediate input price ratios (e.g. effective protection rates).

8.1.2.3. *Distributions of income and resources*

In the *factoral* dimension, all three simulations initially have a negative effect from the point of view of labor. The real wage does increase in the first two years when government expenditure–production–employment are increased (simulation 8.1.2A), but declines in the other two cases and the wage share in income falls in all three type A simulations (variables 3.1.1–2). Among laborers, the initial redistribution tends to be regressive, with a relative shift from low-wage services, government, and agriculture to high-wage mining and manufacturing (variables 3.1.1–5). In the third year in all three type A simulations, however, both the real wage and the wage share in income improve. In the medium run in the type C simulations in which the increase in government expenditure–product–employment are maintained, moreover, by both of these indices, the position of labor is improved (although the opposite is true in the case in which tax functions are increased). But even in the longer run, among laborers the more highly paid workers benefit relatively more. In summary, thus, labor – at least in the aggregate – benefits in the medium run from greater government expenditure–production–employment, but the lags in wage adjustment cause an initial deterioration.

In the *international* dimension of distribution, the most important variable in the model is the net factor income from abroad (variable 3.2.1)[5]. The simulation results suggest that increased taxes tend to reduce that inflow, increased government expenditures–production–employment tend to increase it, and – at least after the first two years – the latter tends to dominate when all of the exogenous changes are made simultaneously.

In the *intertemporal* dimension of distribution, the share of current consumption in product (variable 3.3.1) implies that the initial impact of increased taxes or of expenditure–production–employment, or of both, is to favor current over future generations. Subsequently, the direction of this effect is sometimes reversed, especially when taxes are increased.

[5]Capital movements are not endogenous in the model.

Finally, in the *public versus private* dimension, the results tend to imply a relative increase in the public sector position for increases in either taxes or government expenditure–production– employment. When both are increased, for example, in the first year the value of real taxes rises 6.6% and the share of government consumption in *GDP* rises 12.5% (variables 3.4.1–2). Given the nature of the simulated exogenous changes, of course, such shifts towards the public sector are hardly surprising. One might usefully note again, however, that the simultaneous feedback causes such shifts to be different in real terms than in nominal terms. Because of these feedbacks and because of lags, government policy cannot easily fine tune the public–private split of the command over resources.

8.1.2.4. Economic growth

As noted above, the initial impact on *GDP* due to an increase in taxes or an increase in government expenditure–production–em- ployment is in the direction indicated by simple traditional IS–LM curve macromodels: a decrease in the annual growth rate of -2.7% in the former case and an increase of 0.7% in the later case (variable 4.1)[6]. When both changes are considered simultaneously, however, in contrast to the traditional model the tax change dominates so that the growth rate falls by -2.2%. On a more disaggregate level, the tax increases causes industry and services to grow relatively quickly in the first year, and the expenditure– production–employment increase causes mining and services to grow relatively quickly (variable 4.1.1.3).

The magnitude of such changes is not small compared to the historical growth record (variable 4.1 in table 2.1). They imply that the historical growth rate could almost be doubled in a given year by a 10% tax cut or an increase of one standard deviation in government expenditure, production, and employment. But these changes are more of a short-run than of a long-run nature, reflec- ting variations in capacity utilization more than in capacity itself. As the simulation indicates, they are often reversed in subsequent years.

---

[6]Note that the increase in the latter case is bigger at 2.1% when government expenditures–production–employment are increased by one standard deviation in simulation 8.1.2B.

Of more interest from the point of view of growth are changes in capacity brought about by the saving and investment processes. The simulations suggest that large compositional changes in gross national savings occur, with that for the government varying in predictable ways (i.e. directly with taxes, inversely with expenditures), but with that from business having even larger percentage changes (variables 4.2.1–3). But these changes are basically compositional. Total savings and investment are affected much less. The tax increases have an immediate positive impact on investment (and capital stock and capacity basically reflect investment decisions, although the latter also depends on labor force movements), but larger negative effects follow (variables 4.3 and 4.3.1–2). For government expenditure–production–employment increases, the pattern is reversed with more of a suggestion of cycling. For simultaneous increases in taxes, expenditures, production, and employment, the impact is positive for the first two years, but larger and negative in the third year, with some evidence of subsequent cycling.

In summary, these results suggest that fiscal policy can have significant impact on capacity. Perhaps most promising are tax cuts (particularly in direct corporate taxes, although a simulation for this case alone is not presented here). Even in this case the inducement to invest because of the lower cost of capital is effective only with a lag of a year.

8.1.2.5. Foreign economic position

For both increased taxes and increased government expenditures–production–employment (and for all of these increased together) exports follow a cyclical pattern of first decreasing, then increasing, and then falling again, although the long-run impact is clearly more negative when taxes are increased (variable 5.1). On a disaggregate level, most strongly affected in a proportional sense are industrial exports, with a change of −23.4% in the first year when taxes are increased, and a fall of −39.9% in the first year when taxes, expenditure, production, and employment all are increased (variables 5.1.1–4).

Aggregate imports rise in the first year of the simulations with increased taxes and in all years of the simulations for increased expenditure–income–employment, but fall in subsequent years when taxes are increased (variable 5.2). When taxes are increased, of course, the decline in aggregate activity reinforces the reduced import incentive due to higher import taxes. On a disaggregate level, the responses are varied in sign and magnitude (variables 5.2.1–4). Most affected are non-durable consumer goods imports and intermediate imports.

The net impact on the surplus on current account is predominately negative (although not in the second year of any of the three simulations, nor in the first year of simulation 8.1.2B, nor in the third year of simulation 8.1.2C). The impact is much greater when taxes are increased: a fall of −30.8% in the first year (variable 5.3). As a result of the drop in the current account surplus when taxes are increased, net bank international reserves tend to fall and pessimistic expectations about the foreign position are developed, which combine with the inflation to drive up the black market exchange rate (variables 5.4 and 5.5). The conclusion that increased taxes worsen the foreign position through their greater negative impact on exports (largely through indirect links) than on imports, reflects, of course, the imposition of a uniform general tax increase. With selective increases focused on imports, the surplus on current account could be improved.

8.2. Monetary policies

Section 3.2 above describes the treatment of monetary policy within the model. The money supply is *not* assumed to be an exogenous policy instrument. It is determined by policy decisions (e.g. marginal and average reserve rates) together with behavioral relations for the portfolio composition of the private sector and for net free reserves of the commercial banks and with international reserve movements and government deficit financing obligations which modify the monetary base. In the simulations discussed elsewhere in this chapter, therefore, the monetary base and the money supply both vary substantially although monetary policy variables are held fixed (variables 1.3.1 and 1.3.2 in tables 8.1, 8.3, and 8.4).

This section focuses on the impact of varying the variable

Table
Monetary policy simulations using complete

Variables relating to major areas of Chilean macroeconomic policy concern	Simulation 8.2.1 All average and marginal required reserve ratios increased			Simulation 8.2.2 Central bank loans to commercial banks and to private sector increased				
	A		B	A			B	C
	1	2	1	1	2	3	1	3
1. Cyclical variables								
1.1. Nominal terms								
1.1.1. *GDP* deflator	−0.1	−0.3	−0.8	3.1	−1.5	0.3	14.5	2.2
1.1.2. Income policy	0.0	−0.3	−0.7	2.9	−0.8	0.1	16.9	2.4
1.2. Real terms								
1.2.1. Capacity utilization for *GDP*	0.0	0.0	−0.1	−0.3	−0.3	0.9	−0.8	0.1
1.3. Monetary policy-related variables								
1.3.1. Money supply/deflator	−0.1	0.0	−0.2	−0.9	−1.1	−0.2	−2.9	0.0
1.3.2. Monetary base/deflator	0.4	1.0	2.3	−1.0	−0.4	−1.5	−3.1	−0.4
1.3.3. Net Central Bank foreign reserves	0.5	1.2	2.7	−9.8	−6.4	−6.3	−44.0	−16.4
1.4. Fiscal policy-related variables								
1.4.1. Government current expenditures	0.0	0.0	0.0	−0.3	0.9	0.2	−1.3	0.5
1.4.2. Government deficit	0.1	0.2	0.3	−0.3	−1.3	3.1	−1.0	−1.5
2. Resource allocation and structural change								
2.1. Product/intermediate input price ratio								
2.1.1. Agriculture	0.0	0.0	−0.1	0.7	−0.4	2.8	3.0	0.7
2.1.2. Mining	0.1	0.1	0.4	−1.3	0.3	0.1	−5.8	−1.3
2.1.3. Industry	0.0	0.0	0.1	−0.3	−0.8	−1.9	−1.1	−0.2
2.2. Labor force (secular movements)								
2.2.1. Agriculture	0.0	0.0	0.0	0.0	−0.2	−0.1	−0.1	−0.2
2.2.2. Mining	0.0	0.0	0.0	0.0	0.0	0.0	0.0	0.0
2.2.3. Industry	0.0	0.0	0.0	−0.1	−0.6	−0.5	−0.3	−0.7
2.2.4. Services	0.0	0.0	0.0	0.0	0.2	0.3	−0.2	0.2
2.3. Capital stock								
2.3.1. Agriculture	0.0	0.0	0.0	−0.1	−0.1	0.5	−0.5	−0.1
2.3.2. Mining	0.0	0.0	0.0	0.1	0.1	2.2	0.5	−0.1
2.3.3. Industry	0.0	0.0	0.0	−0.1	−0.4	−0.2	−0.2	−0.5
2.4. Production capacity								
2.4.1. Agriculture	0.0	0.0	0.0	0.0	−0.2	−0.1	−0.1	−0.2
2.4.2. Mining	0.0	0.0	0.0	0.0	0.0	0.0	0.0	0.0
2.4.3. Industry	0.0	0.0	0.0	−0.1	−0.6	−0.5	−0.3	−0.6
2.4.4. Services	0.0	0.0	0.0	0.0	0.2	0.2	−0.1	0.4
2.5. *GDP*								
2.5.1. Agriculture	0.0	0.0	−0.1	0.1	−0.6	0.9	0.4	0.8
2.5.2. Mining	0.1	0.1	0.3	−0.7	−0.6	0.3	−3.2	−0.9
2.5.3. Industry	−0.1	0.0	−0.3	0.1	−1.4	1.5	0.7	0.5
2.5.4. Services	0.0	0.0	0.0	−0.9	0.6	0.3	−3.7	0.2
3. Distribution of income and resources								
3.1. Factoral	0.1	0.1	0.6	−2.5	2.8	−2.3	−10.6	−1.7
3.1.1. Real wage	0.1	0.0	0.4	−1.8	2.3	−3.1	−7.5	−1.5
3.1.1.1. Agriculture	0.1	0.0	0.4	−1.4	3.0	−4.7	−6.0	−1.0
3.1.1.2. Mining	0.1	0.2	0.7	−2.7	2.6	−2.8	−11.2	−2.7
3.1.1.3. Industry	0.1	0.0	0.5	−2.0	3.3	−3.4	−8.5	−1.3
3.1.1.4. Services	0.0	0.0	0.0	−0.9	0.0	−0.3	−3.9	−0.3
3.1.1.5. Government	0.2	0.0	0.6	−1.7	2.8	−4.4	−7.2	−1.8
3.1.2. Wage share in income								
3.2. International								
3.2.1. Net factor income from abroad	0.2	0.3	1.2	−5.0	3.5	−1.6	−22.6	−3.1
3.3. Intertemporal								
3.3.1. Consumption/product	0.0	0.0	0.0	0.4	−0.2	0.0	1.7	0.2

8.2
model of Chilean economy[a].

	Simulation 8.2.3 Bank interest rate increased			Simulation 8.2.4 Contractionary monetary policy. All required reserve rates and interest rates increased Central Bank loans to private sector decreased					Simulation 8.2.5 Contractionary fiscal and monetary policy	
	A		C	A			C		A	
	1	2	3	1	2	3	3	5	1	2
	5.1	−8.1	4.7	−6.6	−1.6	3.3	−2.8	−3.0	1.4	1.0
	4.5	−8.1	4.2	−6.6	−1.5	2.3	−0.6	−0.7	8.2	6.1
	0.7	−1.7	2.5	−0.4	0.8	−0.2	−0.9	−0.4	−5.0	1.0
	0.8	−1.8	3.0	−0.4	0.8	0.0	−3.3	−3.0	−10.1	−4.5
	−13.2	10.1	−13.7	−16.4	13.7	−6.7	−15.6	−11.2	−30.2	13.0
	−15.9	−4.4	−24.4	18.3	23.9	4.6	33.8	91.1	4.9	21.5
	0.0	1.8	1.0	0.2	−1.5	−1.4	−2.4	−1.3	−10.0	0.0
	−1.5	0.8	4.3	3.0	5.9	−2.5	4.9	5.1	−56.9	1.8
	0.8	−2.5	5.9	−0.6	1.6	−2.0	−0.2	0.9	−4.6	−1.2
	−2.4	2.6	−1.8	3.6	1.4	−1.6	2.5	1.7	−2.2	0.3
	−0.5	2.7	−3.7	0.4	−1.7	2.0	−0.3	−0.3	1.6	1.1
	0.0	−0.1	−0.1	0.0	0.2	0.2	0.2	−0.2	1.6	−0.4
	0.0	0.0	0.0	0.0	0.0	0.0	0.0	0.0	0.0	0.0
	0.0	−0.5	−0.4	0.1	1.0	0.9	1.0	−0.1	4.7	−1.2
	0.0	0.3	0.3	0.0	−0.4	−0.5	−0.4	−0.8	1.6	−1.9
	−0.1	−0.1	1.0	0.1	0.1	−0.3	0.2	0.7	−0.4	0.3
	0.1	1.6	2.5	0.0	0.0	0.8	1.7	3.9	−0.3	−1.1
	−0.2	−0.8	−0.2	−0.2	0.4	0.6	0.6	0.8	0.4	0.7
	0.0	−0.1	−0.1	0.0	0.2	0.2	0.2	−0.2	1.6	−0.4
	0.0	0.0	0.0	0.0	0.0	0.0	0.0	0.0	0.0	0.0
	0.0	−0.5	−0.5	0.0	0.8	0.9	0.9	0.1	4.1	−1.0
	0.0	0.2	0.2	0.0	−0.3	−0.7	−0.9	−0.5	0.0	−1.9
	0.9	−3.6	2.6	−1.0	1.9	−1.0	−0.6	0.3	−1.4	5.2
	−1.7	0.6	−0.7	−0.3	1.9	−1.8	−0.5	−0.7	−2.7	−0.6
	1.7	−5.4	5.6	−1.7	3.2	−1.6	−1.6	−1.0	−3.1	4.7
	−0.4	2.0	0.1	0.5	−1.2	−1.2	−2.3	−1.2	−0.4	−3.9
	−4.0	9.9	−7.2	5.6	−2.2	−1.0	1.5	0.6	−4.3	−2.1
	−2.5	−7.6	−7.4	3.6	−2.8	2.4	1.8	1.0	−2.8	−5.7
	−2.3	7.9	−9.2	3.3	−4.8	5.9	1.9	4.7	−2.7	−2.6
	4.3	10.3	−8.4	6.2	−1.6	0.8	4.0	1.6	0.0	−1.9
	−3.3	10.9	−8.3	4.6	−4.3	1.0	0.4	−0.7	0.5	−2.5
	−0.1	−0.7	0.0	0.3	0.1	−1.0	1.4	−1.2	−9.0	−2.0
	−3.6	10.1	−10.3	4.5	−3.7	3.9	3.2	2.3	3.3	−5.8
	−7.9	15.4	−8.1	10.6	−0.2	−2.5	2.8	3.2	1.1	−1.4
	0.2	0.3	0.2	0.1	−0.2	−0.2	−0.4	−0.1	0.1	−1.1

Table 8.2

Variables relating to major areas of Chilean macroeconomic policy concern	Simulation 8.2.1 All average and marginal required reserve ratios increased			Simulation 8.2.2 Central bank loans to commercial banks and to private sector increased				
	A		B	A			B	C
	1	2	1	1	2	3	1	3
3.4. Public versus private								
3.4.1. Taxes/deflator	0.0	0.1	0.2	−1.5	1.1	−0.2	−6.2	−0.6
3.4.1.1. Indirect	0.0	0.0	0.1	−1.1	0.7	0.2	−4.7	0.1
3.4.1.1.1. Sales	0.0	0.0	−0.1	−0.3	−0.4	0.9	−0.9	0.3
3.4.1.1.2. Import	0.1	0.2	0.7	−3.3	5.4	−2.4	−14.3	−1.4
3.4.1.2. Direct	0.0	0.1	0.3	−1.8	1.5	−0.6	−7.5	−1.0
3.4.1.2.1. Large-scale mining	0.2	0.4	1.2	−4.0	0.9	−0.5	−16.6	−3.5
3.4.1.2.2. Other corporations	−0.1	0.1	−0.5	0.7	−2.9	10.6	3.2	3.0
3.4.1.2.3. Personal	0.0	0.2	0.3	−2.2	5.6	−1.0	−10.0	0.8
3.4.2. Government consumption/*GDP*	0.0	0.0	0.1	0.0	1.3	−0.7	−0.4	0.3
4. Economic growth-related variables								
4.1. *GDP*	0.0	0.0	−0.1	−0.3	−0.4	0.9	−0.9	0.2
4.1.1. Agriculture	0.0	0.0	−0.1	−0.1	−0.6	0.9	0.4	0.8
4.1.2. Mining	0.1	0.1	0.3	−0.7	−0.6	0.3	−3.2	−0.9
4.1.3. Industry	−0.0	0.0	−0.3	0.1	−1.4	1.5	0.7	0.5
4.2. Gross national savings								
4.2.1. Personal	0.7	0.8	4.3	−25.9	36.7	−139.0	−114.0	−57.7
4.2.2. Business	−20.4	−0.4	−108.1	345.1	−20.8	433.6	457.5	205.4
4.2.3. Government	0.3	0.4	2.1	−9.4	9.6	−4.7	−40.3	−3.2
4.3. Capacity	0.0	0.0	0.0	0.0	−0.1	0.0	−0.1	0.1
4.3.1. Investment	0.0	0.0	−0.1	0.5	−1.2	2.4	2.4	−0.4
4.3.2. Capital stock	0.0	0.0	0.0	0.1	−0.1	0.1	0.2	0.0
5. Foreign factor								
5.1. Exports	0.0	0.1	0.2	−1.1	1.0	0.2	−5.2	−1.0
5.1.1. Agricultural	0.0	0.1	0.0	−0.1	−1.2	3.1	−0.3	1.2
5.1.2. Mineral								
5.1.2.1. Large-scale	0.0	0.0	0.3	−1.1	−0.3	−0.4	−5.8	−0.2
5.1.2.2. Other	0.0	0.0	0.0	0.0	−0.8	0.3	0.0	−0.5
5.1.3. Industrial	0.2	0.7	1.1	−8.2	−8.2	2.1	−33.7	−7.4
5.1.4. Services	0.0	0.1	0.2	−0.7	−0.2	−0.7	−3.2	−1.0
5.2. Imports	0.0	0.0	−0.1	0.0	−0.9	−0.3	0.0	−1.2
5.2.1. Consumption								
5.2.1.1. Habitual	0.0	0.0	0.0	−0.4	−0.3	−0.2	−1.4	−2.2
5.2.1.2. Durable	0.0	0.0	0.2	−0.9	−1.4	0.8	−4.1	−2.1
5.2.1.3. Secondary	0.2	0.1	1.0	−3.0	4.8	−7.2	−12.7	−3.1
5.2.2. Investment								
5.2.2.1. Machinery and equipment	0.0	0.1	−0.1	0.3	0.1	−0.2	1.6	−1.0
5.2.2.2. Transportation	−0.1	−0.1	−0.5	1.3	−2.9	−1.9	6.1	−1.5
5.2.3. Intermediate	0.0	0.0	0.0	−0.3	−1.3	0.6	−1.6	−0.4
5.2.4. Services	0.0	−0.1	−0.4	0.7	−2.3	0.1	2.3	−0.7
5.3. Surplus on current account	0.5	0.5	3.3	−11.7	0.3	2.6	−53.6	−0.3
5.4. Net bank international reserves	0.3	0.9	1.9	−7.1	−4.6	−4.6	−31.7	−12.1
5.5. Black market exchange rate	−0.1	−0.3	−0.6	3.4	−1.4	0.5	15.7	2.9

[a]The items in this table are the percentage deviations from the base simulation described in section 7.3 due to the exogenous changes indicated at the column heads. For simulation 8.2.5 government current consumption expenditures are exogenized in addition to the other assumptions of the base simulation. 'A' refers to a simulation in which there are 10% changes in the indicated exogenous variables in the first year, but no change thereafter. 'B' refers to a simulation in which there are changes equal to one

(continued)

Simulation 8.2.3 Bank interest rate increased			Simulation 8.2.4 Contractionary monetary policy. All required reserve rates and interest rates increased. Central Bank loans to private sector decreased					Simulation 8.2.5 Contractionary fiscal and monetary policy	
A		C	A			C		A	
1	2	3	1	2	3	3	5	1	2
−1.6	3.9	−1.3	2.4	−0.5	−1.9	−0.6	−0.1	5.0	−0.8
−1.0	2.0	0.1	1.7	−0.5	−2.1	−1.5	−0.6	6.6	−0.2
0.7	−1.7	2.5	−0.4	0.9	−1.1	−1.1	−0.7	5.4	0.0
−5.2	17.2	−8.7	7.0	−6.6	−5.9	−3.0	−0.5	9.6	−1.2
−2.1	5.6	−2.6	3.0	−0.4	−1.7	0.1	0.3	3.6	−1.3
−7.1	9.2	−6.1	6.6	3.5	−5.0	2.3	1.9	4.3	−1.2
2.9	−9.7	22.4	−5.1	5.4	−13.9	−7.9	−6.2	−2.8	8.5
−2.3	14.1	−5.3	3.4	−6.4	−7.7	−6.4	−2.8	2.0	7.3
−0.7	3.6	−1.5	0.6	−2.4	−0.7	−1.3	−0.6	−6.2	0.0
0.7	−1.7	2.5	−0.4	0.9	−1.1	−1.1	−0.7	−4.1	0.0
0.9	−3.6	2.6	−1.0	1.9	−1.0	−0.6	0.3	−1.4	5.2
−1.7	0.6	−0.7	−0.3	1.9	−1.8	−0.5	−0.7	−2.7	−0.6
1.7	−5.4	5.6	−1.7	3.2	−1.6	−1.6	−1.0	−3.1	4.7
−36.3	106.0	−349.5	38.0	−41.9	127.8	112.4	41.0	−28.8	−46.2
671.6	−81.5	1035.6	−868.8	27.2	−359.0	−290.0	−30.9	−772.6	49.8
−12.8	31.7	−15.8	16.7	−10.1	−4.2	0.1	0.6	192.5	−6.8
0.0	0.0	0.0	0.0	0.1	−0.1	−0.2	−0.3	1.0	−1.0
0.0	−2.1	5.3	−1.6	2.3	1.3	2.3	0.8	0.2	−2.7
0.0	−0.2	0.3	−0.2	0.1	0.2	0.1	0.3	0.0	−0.2
−1.6	−2.8	0.4	1.4	2.5	−2.6	1.0	0.4	−1.6	3.2
0.7	−4.7	6.5	−0.7	3.8	−5.3	−2.3	−2.1	−0.4	5.9
−2.0	−2.7	−0.2	1.2	0.4	−5.1	−1.6	−2.1	−2.3	5.4
−1.5	2.2	0.6	0.0	1.3	0.8	1.5	0.6	0.0	−1.1
−8.3	−11.0	2.6	14.9	23.4	1.3	15.4	8.0	−2.5	0.1
−1.2	0.9	−1.6	1.5	1.1	0.1	1.4	1.5	−0.6	−0.4
0.0	−0.9	0.0	−0.1	1.0	0.9	1.2	0.8	−0.6	−1.8
−0.5	2.8	0.8	0.8	−0.5	−0.6	−0.5	−1.9	−0.7	−8.1
−1.5	2.6	−0.8	1.9	0.3	−1.6	−0.8	−1.6	−0.4	−6.5
−6.0	18.7	−17.2	8.1	−5.0	5.7	4.7	4.1	5.1	−10.2
0.5	1.3	−0.5	0.1	1.1	2.9	3.3	3.4	0.1	−0.9
2.0	−8.4	−1.7	−2.6	2.8	8.6	5.7	7.7	−0.5	2.4
−0.4	−3.0	1.8	0.0	1.7	−1.9	−0.4	−0.7	−1.6	1.4
1.1	−7.5	2.3	−2.3	2.0	0.1	0.4	−0.2	−0.9	1.9
−18.2	−1.1	−0.5	20.7	6.8	−22.9	0.9	0.8	−8.8	16.5
−11.4	−3.2	−18.0	13.2	17.1	3.4	24.8	77.6	3.5	15.4
5.5	−8.3	5.3	−7.2	−2.3	2.7	−4.2	−3.6	1.5	1.2

standard deviation from the secular trend in the indicated exogenous variables in the first year, but no change thereafter. 'C' refers to a simulation in which there are 10% changes in the indicated exogenous variables in each year. The years within the dynamic simulation runs are indicated at the column heads. The first years of type C simulations are identical to that of the associated type A simulations and therefore are not presented.

monetary policy tools. Table 8.2 presents five sets of simulations of interest:

8.2.1. All bank reserve rates (i.e. average and marginal rates on time and demand deposits) are increased.

8.2.2. Central Bank loans to commercial banks and to the private sector are increased.

8.2.3. The bank interest rate is increased.

8.2.4. All bank reserve rates and the bank interest rate are increased; all Central Bank loans (except to cover the government deficit) are reduced.

8.2.5. All bank reserve rates, the bank interest rate, and all tax functions are increased; all Central Bank loans (except to cover the government deficit) and government expenditures, production, and employment are reduced.

For simulations 8.2.5 government current consumption expenditures are exogenously decreased by 10%. In all other respects all of these simulations are identical to the base simulation presented in section 7.3 except as is noted above.

These simulation results, like those of section 8.1, are very rich. Examples of the major general characteristics discussed in subsection 8.1.1 can all be found in table 8.2, but to point them out explicitly would be unnecessarily repetitive. However, one might note that in the simulations with only monetary policy changes, the disequilibrium features do not lead to immediate price changes in the opposite direction of those predicted by the textbook IS–LM curve model, as occurred with fiscal policy in section 8.1 (variable 1.1.1). When deflationary fiscal policies are added to deflationary monetary policies, nevertheless, in the first year the disequilibrium aspect of the former dominate so that the *GDP* deflator increases by 1.4% (simulation 8.2.5A).

The simulations suggest that manipulating the internal monetary policy instruments under the control of the Central Bank can have substantial effects – even if control over the money supply is far from complete for the reasons discussed at the start of this section. The first three sets of simulations in table 8.2 illustrate the impact of changes in three groups of Central Bank policies, one at a time, and the fourth simulation illustrates the effects of making all of these changes simultaneously. Note that for the first two groups of policies – concerning required reserve rates and Central Bank loans to commercial banks and to the public – the hypothesized 10% changes for the type A simulations are much smaller than the one standard deviation from the secular trend utilized in the type B simulations[7]. The remainder of this section explores the effects of these monetary policies on the five major areas of macroeconomic policy interest.

8.2.1. Cyclical concerns

The variables related to *nominal stability*, as is noted above, generally move immediately in the directions suggested by partial-equilibrium analysis when monetary tools alone altered. Although there are some subsequent cyclical fluctuations, in the longer run if monetary policy changes are sustained they also tend to move in such a direction (type C simulations).

The most important indicator of nominal stability is the *GDP* deflator (variable 1.1.1). When all three groups of monetary tools are changed by 10% in contractionary directions, the *GDP* deflator drops by −6.6% (simulation 8.2.4A). If such policy changes are sustained over a longer period of time, the impact is about −3.0% (simulation 8.2.4C). Because of the effect of actual price changes on inflationary expectations, the income velocity moves in the same direction as the *GDP* deflator, with an immediate decline of −6.6% and a sustained drop of about −0.6% (variable 1.1.2). Note that for both of these variables the combined effects of the three changes made simultaneously are less than the sum of the three absolute effects of making the changes individually. Also, the sustained impacts are substantially less than the immediate effects. Apparently interactions and non-linearities are quite important.

When only Central Bank loans to commercial banks and to the private sector are increased (simulation 8.2.2) or when fiscal policies are added to monetary policies (simulation 8.2.5), other price determinants outweigh changes in the money supply in the first year so that the *GDP* deflator moves in the opposite direction from the money supply (variables 1.1.1 and 1.3.1). When required reserve rates are changed (simulations 8.2.1), when bank interest

---

[7]For the third group of policies a one standard deviation change has almost the same impact as a 10% change, so to conserve space the type B results are not included in table 8.2.

rates are changed (simulations 8.2.3), or when all three groups of monetary policy tools are changed (simulations 8.2.4), prices generally move in the same direction as the money supply. Even in these last three simulations, however, the money supply does not necessarily move in the same direction as the monetary base (variables 1.3.1–2). When required reserve rates are increased (simulations 8.2.1), for example, in the first year the monetary base increases because the impact of the induced surplus on the current account outweighs that of the increased government deficit (variables 1.3.2–3, 1.4.2, and 5.3). The increased required reserves, nevertheless, result in a reduced money supply. The amount of the reduction, of course, is much less than partial-equilibrium analysis might suggest because of the large and partially canceling feedback of this policy change on the monetary base.

The first year of simulations 8.2.3, when interest rates are increased, provides another interesting illustration of how the money supply changes in response to policies. Because the drop in the surplus on the current account outweighs the reduction in the government deficit, the monetary base falls −13.2% (variables 1.3.2–3, 1.4.2, and 5.3). Due to the behavioral response of commercial banks induced by the higher interest rates, nevertheless, net free reserves fall enough so that the money supply actually increases.

The monetary policy changes illustrated also have significant effects on *real stability*. Capacity utilization falls in the first or second year in each of the five sets of simulations (variable 1.2.1). When all three monetary changes are made in contractionary directions (simulation 8.2.4), capacity utilization drops −0.4% in the first year and then cycles, with the sustained effect somewhat larger in magnitude. When contractionary fiscal policies are added, the immediate drop is −5.0%, again with subsequent cycling. The hypothesized changes in monetary policy, thus, do affect capacity utilization, but their impact is much smaller than that of the fiscal policies considered.

8.2.2. Resource allocation and structural change

Once again, because of the difference between flows and slowly changing stocks, in all the simulations the effects tend to be proportionately larger for the sectoral product–intermediate price ratios and for the sectoral *GDP*s than for the sectoral stocks of capital, labor, and production capacity. Once again, the changes in product to intermediate prices do not provide a very good guide for short- or long-run resource shifts.

When all three groups of monetary tools are made more con-tractionary (simulation 8.2.4A), the first-year effect is to shift production away from manufacturing and agriculture to services (variables 2.5.1–4). Subsequently, there is some cycling. When these changes are sustained (simulation 8.2.4C), however, the shift is out of services and out of industry. The shift out of services partially reflects lowered capacity due to a reduced labor force (variables 2.2.4 and 2.4.4). The shift out of industry reflects lowered utilization of an increased capacity due to positive increments of both capital and labor (variables 2.2.3, 2.3.3, and 2.4.3). Thus, the largest longer-run declines in *GDP* occur in the sectors which experience the largest absolute changes in capacity, but these capacity changes are opposite in direction!

When contractionary fiscal policy is added (simulation 8.2.5A), the absolute magnitude of the effects are, in general, increased significantly. In the first year, *GDP* drops relatively in manufac-turing and mining (variables 2.5.1–4). For industry, once again, the drop is due to a fall not in capacity (which actually increases initially with an infusion of labor), but in capacity utilization (variables 2.2.3, 2.3.3, and 2.4.3).

8.2.3. Distribution of income and resources

In the *factoral* dimension, the increase in required reserve ratios tends to have a positive impact on labor's position in the aggregate, but the increases in Central Bank loans to the commercial banks and to the private sector or in the bank interest rate, tend to have a negative immediate and sustained impact, albeit with some cycling (variables 3.1.1–2, simulations 8.2.1–3).

When all three policies are contractionary (simulations 8.2.4), the aggregate real wage increases 5.6% immediately and on the order of magnitude of 1.0% on a sustained basis (variable 3.1.1). Like-wise, the wage share income increases 4.5% immediately, and on the order of magnitude of 3.0% on a sustained basis (variable 3.1.2). Despite some cycling, this, labor in the aggregate seems to benefit from contractionary monetary policies because of the

stickiness of wages relative to prices. The addition of fiscal policies
with their opposite effect on prices leads to much less (perhaps no)
clearcut benefits for labor (simulation 8.2.5) since the real wage
falls and the labor share in income drops after the first year
(variables 3.1.1–2).

On a more disaggregate level, the contractionary monetary policies taken together, whether or not supplemented by contractionary fiscal policies, lead to regressive changes among laborers.
The relatively high-wage sectors, mining and manufacturing, improve their relative positions (variables 3.1.1.1–5).

In the *international* dimension of distribution when all monetary
policies are contractionary (simulation 8.2.4A), the immediate
impact is an increase of 10.6% in the net factor payments from
abroad (variable 3.2.1). In the subsequent years declines much
smaller in absolute value occur, but the sustained result is a rise on
the order of magnitude of 3.0% (simulation 8.2.4C). When contractionary fiscal policies are added (simulation 8.2.5A), the
benefits are substantially less positive from the point of view of
Chile.

In the *intertemporal* dimension, the first-year impact of each of
the three monetary policies considered separately or of all of them
taken together in a contractionary move (with or without associated fiscal policies) is to increase the share of consumption in
the present (variable 3.3.1). With contractionary policies, whether
of a once-and-for-all or a sustained kind, however, subsequently
the shift is away from the present.

Finally, in the *private versus public* dimension, contractionary
monetary policy, with or without associated fiscal policies, increases both the real value of tax collections and the share of
government consumption in *GDP* immediately, but lowers them
subsequently and on a sustained basis (variables 3.1–2). The differential effects on different taxes are quite striking, due to the
variance in the changes among the underlying activity levels
(variables 3.1.1–2).

8.2.4. Economic growth

The combination of all three contractionary monetary policies
leads to an immediate drop of −0.4% in the growth of *GDP* and a
sustained drop on the order of magnitude of −1.0%, although there

is some evidence of cycling after the first year (variable 4.1). The addition of contractionary fiscal policies increases substantially the first year impact to −4.1%, reflecting the greater effect on aggregate output of the fiscal policies considered than of the monetary policies explored.

The composition of gross national savings are altered substantially by the policies considered. Contractionary monetary policies, with or without contractionary fiscal policies, shift savings away from businesses – although there is some cycling (variables 4.2.1–3). The initial impact on aggregate savings – investment of the contractionary monetary policies alone is − 1.6%, which is not surprising given the immediate increases in the cost of capital (variable 4.3.1). Over time, however, relative price changes and compositional effects lead to an increase in investment. If contractionary fiscal policy is added, this pattern is reversed. In any case, the total impact on capacity is neither very large, nor sustained over time (variable 4.3). Only when contractionary fiscal policy is added is the absolute value of the percentage deviation of capacity even 1.0%, and in that case there is a reversal in the sign between the first and second years.

8.2.5. Foreign economic position

With all contractionary monetary policies, aggregate exports increase in the first two years and in the longer run if such policies are sustained (variable 5.1). Industrial exports tend to increase by relatively large proportions, but service exports and small- and medium-scale mining exports also tend to increase systematically (variables 5.1.1–4). In substantial part, these changes reflect responses in the export functions (table 5.3) to altered relative prices due to the internal deflation. When contractionary fiscal policies are added and relative domestic to foreign prices vary in the opposite direction, exports decline in the first year.

In the short run, imports are affected less than exports in response to the contractionary monetary policies (variable 5.2). After a small initial decline, they increase and remain about 1.0% above the base simulation. Some fairly significant compositional changes occur, with tendencies to shift towards secondary consumption goods and investment goods (variables 5.2.1–4). When contractionary fiscal policies are added, the initial decline on aggregate imports is enlarged and extended at least over two years due to the lessened over all economic activity.

The net impact of contractionary monetary policies on the surplus in the current account is a 20.7% increase in the first year, a 6.8% increase in the second year, but a decline of −22.9% in the third year (variable 5.3). For a sustained set of such policies, the impact is slightly positive. As a result net bank international reserves increase, which – together with the initially lowered price – causes the black market exchange rate to tend to decline (variables 5.4–5). With the addition of contractionary fiscal policies, a number of these signs are reversed because of the different price impact.

8.3. Foreign sector policies

A large number of foreign sector policy instruments have been utilized during the past four decades in Chile. Section 3.3 provides a brief summary of these policies. Behrman (1975 and 1975b) provide detailed presentations and analyses. Table 8.3 presents six sets of simulations related to foreign sector policy changes:

8.3.1. All exchange rates are increased.

8.3.2. All foreign sector quantitative restrictions are increased.

8.3.3. All exchange rates are increased and all foreign sector quantitative restrictions are reduced simultaneously as part of an overall liberalization program.

8.3.4. All policies specific to large scale mining (*i.e.* special exchange rate, legal costs of production, and direct taxes), are increased.

8.3.5. All mining exports are increased exogeneously under the assumption that the price elasticity of demand facing Chile is −4.0[8] and the prices which Chile receives for these exports adjusts accordingly.

8.3.6. Agricultural and manufacturing exports are subsidized.

For all of these simulations the model is identical to the base

[8]The price elasticity of demand for Chilean copper exports commonly is assumed to be about −4.0 on the basis of Chile's share in the world market and estimates of price elasticities on the world market level of aggregation. For example, see Bacha and Taylor (1973) or de Castro and de la Cuadra (1971, p. 17).

simulation of section 7.3 except as is noted in the simulation descriptions.

Once again, the major general characteristics discussed in subsection 8.1.1 hold for these simulations. To avoid redundancy, explicit examples are not given here.

However, it is useful to point out how the first three simulations in table 8.3 illustrate the difference between the type A (10% increase) and type B (one standard deviation from the secular trend increase) assumptions. Simulations 8.3.1 increase all exchange rates, for which variables the standard deviations from the secular trend are larger than 10%. Simulations 8.3.2 increase all the foreign sector quantitative restrictions, for which the standard deviations from the secular trend are smaller than 10%. Therefore, the type A simulation understates the impact of equally likely changes in exchange rates relative to those in quantitative restrictions. When both exchange rates are increased and quantitative restrictions are reduced in simulations 8.3.3, as a result, the type A estimates are different in sign from the type B ones in the case of some important variables (e.g. the *GDP* deflator). Even though the type B estimates in a sense represent more likely alternatives, however, the discussion in this section will continue to focus on the type A results because the equal changes in exogenous variables lead to easier understanding of the experiments being conducted.

Before turning to the impact of changes in foreign sector policies on each of the five major areas of macroeconomic concern, one further observation is warranted. In part because Chile is a relatively small economy, changes in the domestic and foreign sectors have many strong links. Tables 8.1 and 8.2 illustrate how variations in domestic policies can indirectly cause rather substantial responses in the foreign sector. Table 8.3 also provides a number of examples of how alterations in foreign sector policies can substantially affect variables of interest throughout the domestic economy.

8.3.1. Cyclical concerns

Changes in foreign sector policies have substantial effects on *nominal stability*. The sensitivity of Chilean policymakers to the inflationary impact of foreign sector changes seems well justified.

Table
Foreign sector policy simulations using

Variables relating to major areas of Chilean macroeconomic policy concern	Simulation 8.3.1 All exchange rates increased					Simulation 8.3.2 All foreign-sector quantitative restrictions increased				
	A			B	C	A			B	C
	1	2	3	1	3	1	2	3	1	3
1. Cyclical variables										
1.1. Nominal terms										
1.1.1. *GDP* deflator	6.1	0.0	3.3	15.8	8.9	17.1	−0.4	14.4	3.2	63.3
1.1.2. Income velocity	11.1	0.5	4.1	27.5	12.4	26.2	−7.4	10.4	4.5	64.9
1.2. Real terms										
1.2.1. Capacity utilization for *GDP*	−0.4	−0.8	1.1	−0.5	0.1	1.1	−1.0	−2.1	0.2	2.9
1.3. Monetary policy-related variables										
1.3.1. Money supply/deflator	−4.9	−1.5	0.4	−9.7	−2.9	−6.2	6.4	6.3	−1.0	1.2
1.3.2. Monetary base/deflator	−7.0	4.3	−4.2	−13.9	−4.4	−8.5	21.9	−8.8	−1.3	−11.9
1.3.3. Net Central Bank foreign reserves	0.8	8.4	1.9	5.7	9.3	12.9	35.1	18.5	3.3	87.6
1.4. Fiscal policy-related variables										
1.4.1. Government current expenditures	0.2	0.1	−0.6	0.1	−0.1	−4.1	−3.2	−7.9	−1.1	−15.7
1.4.2. Government	−6.2	−0.2	−0.5	−2.5	−13.9	−11.8	−24.1	−14.1	−2.0	−70.3
2. Resource allocation and structural change										
2.1. Product/intermediate input price ratio										
2.1.1. Agriculture	−0.9	−1.3	2.3	−1.5	−0.3	3.9	−17.7	−4.7	0.3	−1.4
2.1.2. Mining	1.4	−0.2	−1.5	2.5	−0.4	−8.2	1.8	−7.3	−1.9	−25.1
2.1.3. Industry	−0.8	1.8	−1.6	−2.0	−0.1	−5.8	17.7	−0.8	−1.1	−1.4
2.2. Labor force (secular movements)										
2.2.1. Agriculture	0.0	−0.4	−0.2	−0.1	−0.4	0.0	1.1	3.1	0.0	3.6
2.2.2. Mining	0.0	0.0	0.0	0.0	0.0	0.0	0.0	0.0	0.0	0.0
2.2.3. Industry	−0.1	−1.4	−0.8	−0.3	−1.4	−0.1	3.7	9.3	0.0	10.8
2.2.4. Services	−0.1	0.3	0.5	−0.1	0.3	0.1	−0.2	−1.6	0.0	−1.2
2.3. Capital stock										
2.3.1. Agriculture	−0.2	−0.1	0.6	−0.4	−0.2	−0.7	−2.7	−3.5	−0.2	−2.2
2.3.2. Mining	0.1	0.3	0.6	0.4	1.9	0.3	−0.2	13.3	0.0	−3.1
2.3.3. Industry	−0.3	−0.7	−0.4	−0.6	−1.3	−0.4	−1.9	−0.7	−0.1	2.9
2.4. Production capacity										
2.4.1. Agriculture	0.0	−0.4	−0.2	−0.1	−0.4	0.0	1.1	3.1	0.0	3.6
2.4.2. Mining	0.0	0.0	0.0	0.0	0.0	0.0	0.0	0.0	0.0	0.0
2.4.3. Industry	−0.1	−1.3	−0.8	−0.2	−1.3	−0.1	3.2	7.8	0.0	9.3
2.4.4. Services	−0.0	0.3	0.6	−0.1	0.9	0.0	−2.1	−5.4	0.0	−6.9
2.5. *GDP*										
2.5.1. Agriculture	0.1	−0.7	1.8	0.9	2.0	10.6	3.7	7.3	2.4	20.4
2.5.2. Mining	0.9	1.0	−0.9	2.8	1.6	−5.4	−30.8	16.4	−0.8	−30.7
2.5.3. Industry	−0.5	−2.4	2.3	−0.1	0.2	8.4	0.1	15.4	1.6	31.1
2.5.4. Services	−1.6	0.1	0.5	−3.9	−0.5	−4.7	3.9	−7.1	−1.0	−8.8

8.3
complete model of Chilean economy[a].

	Simulation 8.3.3 All exchange rates increased and all quantitative reductions decreased				Simulation 8.3.4 Exchange rate, legal costs of production and taxes for large-scale mining increased			Simulation 8.3.5 Mining exports increased with price elasticity of demand of −4.0			Simulation 8.3.6 Agricultural and manufacturing exports subsidized		
	A			B	A			A			A		
	1	2	3	1	1	2	3	1	2	3	1	2	3
	−18.1	−16.0	−15.0	11.9	2.9	0.0	0.7	5.6	1.4	0.4	1.0	1.3	1.3
	−23.8	−15.3	−14.3	22.5	3.5	0.5	1.4	6.9	1.8	1.3	1.3	1.4	0.8
	−0.3	2.9	−1.8	−0.8	−0.2	−0.6	0.9	0.1	−1.8	1.5	0.0	−0.2	0.0
	7.3	2.5	−1.8	−9.5	−0.8	−1.2	0.2	−1.1	−2.3	0.7	−0.3	−0.3	0.3
	7.9	−2.9	4.9	−13.8	−0.9	−0.7	−0.5	−1.1	−1.9	−0.4	−0.3	−0.2	0.5
	−16.0	−29.0	−26.6	1.0	3.6	0.5	1.4	8.0	2.4	2.9	1.2	2.0	3.8
	6.8	7.2	18.1	1.3	−0.1	0.2	0.5	−0.5	−1.1	0.3	0.0	−0.2	+0.1
	6.2	43.5	−26.1	−0.5	6.0	−2.2	1.0	−4.1	−6.9	−0.8	1.8	1.7	2.3
	−3.3	10.0	−34.8	−1.7	0.6	−0.5	2.0	1.2	−1.7	2.7	0.3	0.0	0.0
	12.8	7.0	12.4	4.6	−0.8	−0.1	−0.1	−2.4	−1.5	−0.6	0.4	−0.4	0.1
	6.3	−11.7	12.6	−1.1	−0.4	0.9	−1.3	−1.3	2.2	−1.8	−0.3	0.1	0.1
	0.1	−0.3	−0.5	−0.1	0.0	−0.2	−0.1	−0.1	−0.3	−0.2	0.0	0.0	−0.1
	0.0	0.0	0.0	0.0	0.0	0.0	0.0	0.0	0.0	0.0	0.0	0.0	0.0
	0.3	−1.1	−1.5	−0.3	−0.1	−0.6	−0.5	−0.1	−1.1	−0.7	0.0	−0.2	−0.4
	0.2	0.3	0.2	−0.1	0.0	0.2	0.2	−0.1	0.3	0.4	0.0	0.1	0.0
	0.1	−0.5	−4.4	−0.3	−0.1	0.0	0.4	−0.1	−0.1	0.7	0.0	0.0	0.0
	3.0	16.5	23.8	0.5	0.0	0.2	1.0	0.6	1.0	1.6	0.1	0.1	−0.2
	−0.2	−1.7	−3.2	−0.6	−0.1	−0.4	−0.3	−0.2	−0.9	−0.7	0.0	−0.1	−0.0
	0.1	−0.3	−0.5	−0.1	0.0	−0.2	−0.1	−0.1	−0.3	−0.2	0.0	0.0	−0.0
	0.0	0.0	0.0	0.0	0.0	0.0	0.0	0.0	0.0	0.0	0.0	0.0	0.0
	0.3	−1.0	−1.5	−0.2	−0.1	−0.5	−0.5	−0.1	−1.0	−0.8	0.0	−0.2	−0.8
	0.1	1.9	3.2	0.0	0.0	0.1	0.3	0.0	0.3	0.6	0.0	0.0	0.2
	−10.2	−0.2	2.7	−1.6	0.3	−0.8	1.3	1.3	−2.4	3.1	0.2	−0.1	0.4
	4.4	39.3	−0.4	3.5	−0.6	−1.4	0.2	1.2	−2.0	−0.2	0.7	0.2	0.5
	−7.5	3.4	−9.0	−1.8	0.3	−1.8	1.8	1.8	−4.9	3.9	0.3	−0.4	0.1
	7.0	−0.9	6.2	−2.9	−0.8	0.3	0.2	−1.7	0.4	0.6	−0.3	−0.2	−0.1

Table 8.3
Foreign sector policy simulations using

Variables relating to major areas of Chilean macroeconomic policy concern	Simulation 8.3.1 All exchange rates increased					Simulation 8.3.2 All foreign-sector quantitative restrictions increased				
	A			B	C	A			B	C
	1	2	3	1	3	1	2	3	1	3
3. Distribution of income and resources										
3.1. Factoral										
3.1.1. Real wage	−3.3	3.6	−5.5	−8.3	−3.6	−13.8	14.2	−29.9	−3.3	−37.2
3.1.1.1. Agriculture	−3.1	2.5	−5.2	−7.5	−4.6	−10.4	20.1	−27.9	−2.5	−23.7
3.1.1.2. Mining	−3.9	4.8	−6.2	−9.0	−4.1	−8.6	19.2	−17.2	−2.3	−12.7
3.1.1.3. Industry	−2.9	2.1	−5.8	−7.7	−6.2	−15.0	22.2	−42.4	−3.6	−44.2
3.1.1.4. Services	−3.2	4.1	−5.3	−7.9	−4.1	−13.2	47.9	−35.1	−3.1	−17.8
3.1.1.5. Government	−3.0	−0.3	−0.6	−6.3	−2.7	−4.8	−2.5	−8.7	−1.1	−12.0
3.1.2. Wage share in income	−3.1	3.6	−7.0	−7.6	−5.1	−11.8	22.0	−28.5	−2.4	−25.9
3.2. International										
3.2.1. Net factor income from abroad	−11.1	2.3	−6.7	−37.1	−13.7	−26.9	24.1	−42.3	−4.9	−96.2
3.3. Intertemporal										
3.3.1. Consumption/product	0.2	−0.4	0.0	0.1	−0.5	−0.4	−5.3	2.5	−0.3	−4.1
3.4. Public versus private										
3.4.1. Taxes/deflator	−1.0	1.0	−1.2	−2.6	−1.0	−8.9	1.0	−5.4	−2.0	−18.1
3.4.1.1. Indirect	−1.5	0.7	−0.2	−3.6	−0.9	−10.4	−0.9	−2.7	−2.4	−13.8
3.4.1.1.1. Sales	−0.4	−0.9	1.2	−0.6	0.2	1.1	−1.1	2.6	0.2	2.2
3.4.1.1.2. Import	−4.7	7.5	−5.3	−11.9	−5.1	−36.9	0.7	−21.2	−8.4	−66.2
3.4.1.2. Direct	−0.5	1.4	−2.1	−1.8	−1.1	−7.6	2.7	−7.7	−1.5	−21.7
3.4.1.2.1. Large-scale mining	2.4	2.6	−5.1	5.5	1.3	−20.8	−34.7	9.9	−4.2	−63.5
3.4.1.2.2. Other corporations	5.5	−3.0	14.8	13.2	12.6	11.2	−48.8	77.3	2.3	25.2
3.4.1.2.3. Personal	−4.5	6.7	−2.4	−11.2	−3.2	−8.7	18.4	−14.7	−1.4	−37.3
3.4.2. Government consumption/GDP	0.6	1.1	−1.8	0.7	−1.1	−5.1	−2.1	−10.2	−1.3	−17.5
4. Economic growth-related variables										
4.1. *GDP*										
4.1.1. Agriculture	−0.4	−1.0	1.2	−0.6	0.2	1.1	−1.1	2.6	0.2	2.2
4.1.2. Mining	0.1	−0.7	1.8	0.9	2.0	10.6	3.7	7.3	2.4	20.4
4.1.3. Industry	0.9	1.0	−0.9	2.8	1.6	−5.4	−31.8	16.4	−0.8	−30.7
4.2. Gross national savings	−0.5	−2.4	2.3	−0.1	0.2	8.4	0.1	15.4	1.6	31.1
4.2.1. Personal	−33.3	51.0	−228.1	−78.0	−137.7	−176.0	397.1	−1607.5	−40.3	−1030.3
4.2.2. Business	612.5	−28.4	714.5	1535.6	524.7	2749.4	−152.5	2788.2	545.1	3178.5
4.2.3. Government	−4.8	18.2	−6.9	−13.9	0.5	−21.4	62.3	−9.4	−5.5	−0.1
4.3. Capacity	0.0	−0.2	0.1	−0.1	0.1	0.0	−0.1	−0.5	0.0	−0.7
4.3.1. Investment	0.1	−1.9	1.7	0.6	−1.1	−12.6	−19.3	5.7	−3.2	−13.6
4.3.2. Capital stock	0.0	−0.2	0.0	0.1	−0.2	−1.2	−2.9	−2.3	−0.3	−4.2
5. Foreign sector										
5.1. Exports	1.6	−0.3	−0.4	6.2	0.9	−7.6	−6.0	−3.0	−1.5	−6.4
5.1.1. Agricultural	2.7	−1.8	4.3	6.4	3.7	25.0	−3.6	12.8	5.7	31.3

(continued)
complete model of Chilean economy[a].

Simulation 8.3.3 All exchange rates increased and all quantitative reductions decreased				Simulation 8.3.4 Exchange rate, legal costs of production and taxes for large-scale mining increased			Simulation 8.3.5 Mining exports increased with price elasticity of demand of −4.0			Simulation 8.3.6 Agricultural and manufacturing exports subsidized		
A			B	A			A			A		
1	2	3	1	1	2	3	1	2	3	1	2	3
20.8	−1.5	24.5	−5.0	−2.3	1.4	−1.8	−4.3	1.8	−2.5	−0.8	−0.6	−0.7
14.4	−9.8	50.5	−5.1	−1.6	1.4	2.5	−2.9	2.5	−4.3	−0.5	−0.1	−0.6
9.9	−11.8	88.8	−6.9	−1.3	2.3	−3.2	−2.5	4.2	−4.6	−0.4	0.4	−0.2
25.7	−7.1	46.1	−4.1	−2.5	1.3	−2.6	−4.8	1.7	−4.5	−0.9	−0.6	−1.1
20.9	−31.9	29.0	−4.9	−1.9	2.3	−2.6	−4.0	4.4	−4.4	−0.7	0.0	−0.4
11.9	2.0	2.1	−5.4	−0.6	−0.5	0.0	−0.5	1.4	0.5	−0.1	−0.3	0.0
15.8	−10.9	55.7	−5.0	−1.7	2.1	−3.6	−3.3	4.7	−6.1	−0.6	0.1	−0.6
32.6	15.6	47.9	−30.4	−9.0	0.1	−1.7	−12.6	−4.2	−2.5	−2.1	−2.7	−3.0
2.1	4.8	−9.0	0.5	0.1	0.1	−0.3	−0.4	0.1	−0.2	0.0	−0.1	−0.1
14.7	8.2	22.3	−0.6	−0.9	0.1	0.0	−1.6	0.6	0.6	−0.2	−0.4	−0.1
13.7	5.5	−0.4	−1.4	−0.9	0.1	0.5	−0.9	−0.5	1.4	−0.2	−0.2	0.1
−0.2	3.4	−1.0	−0.9	−0.2	−0.7	0.9	0.1	−1.9	1.6	0.0	−0.2	0.0
46.1	11.9	−0.3	−3.8	−2.5	3.3	−1.0	−3.4	5.5	0.8	−0.5	0.1	0.4
15.5	10.6	41.7	0.0	−0.9	0.2	−0.3	−2.2	−0.7	−0.1	−0.2	−0.5	−0.3
36.2	72.4	35.7	10.0	1.4	−1.6	−0.5	−3.3	−4.2	−1.7	1.3	−0.5	1.0
−9.6	47.8	−14.5	11.4	3.8	−3.5	9.1	4.5	−8.7	15.5	2.0	−0.3	2.3
7.7	−0.4	−7.9	−9.2	−2.0	3.0	0.4	−3.3	3.1	3.6	−0.6	−0.7	0.1
7.0	3.8	19.3	2.2	0.1	0.9	−0.4	−0.6	0.8	−1.3	0.0	0.0	0.0
−0.2	3.3	−1.0	−0.9	−0.2	−0.7	0.9	0.1	−1.9	1.6	0.0	−0.2	0.0
−10.2	−0.2	2.7	−1.6	0.3	−0.8	1.3	1.3	−2.4	3.1	0.2	−0.1	0.4
4.4	39.3	−0.4	3.5	−0.6	−1.4	0.2	1.2	−2.0	−0.2	0.7	0.2	0.5
−7.5	3.4	−9.0	−1.8	0.3	−1.8	1.8	1.8	−4.9	3.9	0.3	−0.4	0.1
180.0	−282.4	2759.3	−40.8	−21.2	20.9	−106.9	−27.0	38.3	−197.6	−5.4	1.4	−18.5
3651.0	49.6	−5634.2	982.9	325.5	−15.6	360.2	730.3	−33.8	601.9	126.5	0.4	62.4
59.5	−39.0	74.8	−7.4	−4.5	5.8	−2.8	−8.0	13.9	0.1	−0.4	0.6	1.4
0.1	0.4	0.8	−0.1	0.0	−0.1	0.0	0.0	−0.1	0.1	0.0	0.0	0.0
11.5	12.5	−0.4	3.5	0.4	−1.0	1.1	0.9	−2.1	0.2	0.2	−0.1	−0.4
1.1	2.2	1.9	0.3	0.0	−0.1	0.0	0.1	−0.1	−0.1	0.0	0.0	0.0
−1.9	1.7	−4.9	7.0	1.0	−1.6	0.4	7.4	−1.5	−0.1	1.1	1.0	1.0
−22.4	8.7	−21.3	0.7	0.1	−1.5	3.0	1.1	−4.1	6.3	4.2	2.6	4.1

Table 8.3
Foreign sector policy simulations using

Variables relating to major areas of Chilean macroeconomic policy concern	Simulation 8.3.1 All exchange rates increased					Simulations 8.3.2 All foreign-sector quantitative restrictions increased				
	A			B	C	A			B	C
	1	2	3	1	3	1	2	3	1	3
5.1.2. Mineral										
5.1.2.1. Large-scale	1.5	−0.5	−0.8	8.0	0.3	−7.4	−4.4	−5.0	−1.3	−15.9
5.1.2.2. Other	0.0	1.0	0.0	0.0	0.9	0.0	−4.5	−5.8	0.0	−10.4
5.1.3. Industrial	10.0	0.1	−1.5	19.7	4.1	−95.5	−12.0	5.5	−21.7	48.5
5.1.4. Services	0.8	−0.2	−1.1	2.3	−0.7	−8.6	−13.8	−4.5	−1.8	−20.6
5.2. Imports	−0.7	−1.0	−0.4	−0.5	−1.7	−24.2	−16.9	−2.5	−5.3	−40.4
5.2.1. Consumption										
5.2.1.1. Habitual	−0.7	−2.2	−2.7	−2.2	−6.7	−30.5	−18.1	−1.8	−7.2	−49.7
5.2.1.2. Durable	1.0	−4.3	−1.3	1.6	4.3	−24.1	−1.2	−17.7	−4.6	−64.9
5.2.1.3. Secondary	−5.5	3.2	−12.7	−13.7	−12.1	−32.6	30.7	−44.8	−6.9	−67.5
5.2.2. Investment										
5.2.2.1. Machinery and equipment	−0.1	0.8	0.8	0.1	1.5	−14.0	−11.5	−8.7	−3.2	−32.9
5.2.2.2. Transportation	−1.0	−0.7	3.6	−1.5	0.5	−41.5	−92.6	21.1	−9.3	−99.5
5.2.3. Intermediate	−0.2	−1.1	0.1	1.7	−0.1	−3.9	−5.0	0.9	−0.3	−0.7
5.2.4. Services	−1.1	−1.0	0.8	1.1	−1.0	−46.3	−23.5	1.4	−10.1	−62.7
5.3. Surplus on current account	6.7	2.3	−2.3	25.1	10.0	102.2	33.6	−12.4	23.5	169.1
5.4. Net bank international reserves	0.6	6.0	1.4	4.1	6.8	9.2	25.1	13.6	2.4	64.3
5.5. Black market exchange rate	5.8	−0.4	3.2	15.3	8.1	91.5	8.3	26.0	17.6	187.5

[a]The items in this table are the percentage deviations from the base simulation described in section 7.3 due to the exogenous changes indicated at the column heads. 'A' refers to a simulation in which there are 10% changes in the indicated exogenous variables in the first year, but no change thereafter. 'B' refers to a simulation in which there are changes equal to one standard deviation from the secular trend in the

(continued)
complete model of Chilean economy[a].

Simulation 8.3.3 All exchange rates increased and all quantitative reductions decreased				Simulation 8.3.4 Exchange rate, legal costs of production and taxes for large-scale mining increased			Simulation 8.3.5 Mining exports increased with price elasticity of demand of −4.0			Simulation 8.3.6 Agricultural and manufacturing exports subsidized		
A			B	A			A			A		
1	2	3	1	1	2	3	1	2	3	1	2	3
−2.8	−2.1	−7.3	8.1	2.2	−1.2	0.8	10.0	0.0	0.0	0.1	0.1	0.4
0.0	8.0	11.6	0.0	0.0	−0.8	−0.2	10.0	0.0	0.0	0.0	0.0	−0.4
−3.8	−7.0	−30.4	43.0	−6.5	−10.1	−0.5	−7.4	−21.9	−2.0	18.8	9.4	6.5
10.0	13.0	4.1	4.1	−0.2	0.2	−1.1	0.8	2.6	−2.3	0.1	0.6	0.4
21.6	19.8	0.3	4.5	0.5	−0.5	−0.2	2.4	0.1	−0.4	0.5	0.5	0.6
34.9	19.4	−17.7	4.9	−0.5	−0.6	−1.2	−1.4	−1.4	−3.6	−0.3	−0.5	−1.3
19.4	13.8	24.0	5.8	−0.8	−1.8	−0.2	−1.6	−3.7	−1.2	−0.3	−0.9	−1.3
40.6	−8.3	100.8	−6.8	−2.9	3.4	−5.9	−6.1	7.3	−9.0	−1.1	−0.3	−1.0
20.0	15.8	12.2	3.8	0.2	1.0	−0.2	0.5	4.8	2.1	0.1	1.0	1.3
39.6	84.8	−13.8	7.6	1.2	1.9	0.4	2.1	5.0	0.8	0.4	1.5	1.6
−3.7	3.5	−4.2	1.5	1.0	−1.8	0.8	5.2	−3.1	0.7	1.3	0.4	1.1
28.8	32.1	−11.4	10.2	2.4	−1.7	0.4	9.3	−0.5	−0.2	1.6	1.8	1.8
−136.9	−45.6	−19.9	−1.0	−1.1	−4.1	2.9	24.7	−6.5	1.7	2.1	1.0	1.9
−11.5	−20.7	−19.5	0.7	2.6	0.3	1.0	5.8	1.7	2.1	0.9	1.5	2.8
−71.3	−25.8	−26.6	−4.1	3.2	0.3	1.0	6.0	1.9	1.0	1.1	1.5	1.6

indicated exogenous variables in the first year, but no change thereafter. 'C' refers to a simulation in which there are 10% changes in the indicated exogenous variables in each year. The years within the dynamic simulation runs are indicated at the column heads. The first years of type C simulation are identical to that of the associated type A simulations and therefore are not presented.

Increases in exchange rates, foreign sector quantitative restrictions, large-scale mining policies, mining exports, and subsidies to agricultural and manufacturing exports all result in immediate and sustained price and income velocity increases (variables 1.1.1–2). The links are directly through cost-push connections between domestic and foreign prices (table 6.2) and indirectly through changes in aggregate demand and in the money supply induced by variations in the balance of payments, the government deficit and other behavioral responses (variables 1.3.1–3, 1.4.1–2, 4.1, and 5.3).

The changes in money supply are powerful, but they do not overwhelm all of the other effects. For some years in each of the simulations in table 8.3, in fact, the change in the *GDP* deflator is in the opposite direction from that of the money supply.

When a liberalization package with increased exchange rates and reduced quantitative restrictions is applied for 10% variations in all exogenous variables, the impact of the reduction in quantitative restrictions dominates in respect to price and the *GDP* deflator falls substantially (simulation 8.3.3A). If equally likely variations in all of the exogenous exchange rates and quantitative restrictions are imposed, however, the exchange rate effects dominate and the impact on the *GDP* deflator is reversed (simulation 8.3.3B). To reduce inflation, thus, these results suggest liberalization should focus on a reduction in quantitative restrictions relative to the increase in exchange rates. Such a policy package in fact was attempted by the Alessandri government, with substantial transitory success regarding inflation (section 2.2). Eventually, however, the accompanying drain on foreign reserves due to the maintenance of an overvalued exchange rate necessitated an abrupt shift in policy at the end of 1961. The tremendous decline in the surplus on current account in simulations 8.3.3 reflects the buildup of these same pressures (variable 5.3).

Changes in foreign sector policies also have significant impact on *real stability*. The first-year effect of increased exchange rates (whether or not accompanied by reduced quantitative restrictions) and of upward changes in policies for large-scale mining (simulations 8.3.1, 8.3.3, and 8.3.4) is to reduce capacity utilization, while the first-year impact of intensified quantitative restrictions (simulation 8.3.2) is to increase it (variable 1.2.1). These immediate tendencies support part of the reluctance of many Chilean policy makers and structuralists regarding liberalization of the foreign sector because of the fear of resulting stagnation. Subsequently, however, the signs of these effects are reversed. Increased exchange rates lead to a rise in capacity utilization of 1.1% in the third year and to a small positive sustained increase, for example, while intensified quantitative restrictions cause declines of −1.0 and −2.1% in the second and third years (although not on a sustained basis). The aversion to liberalization because of fear of stagnation, thus, may be justified only if the appropriate discount rate is quite high.

8.3.2. Resource allocation and structural change

Increased exchange rates (simulations 8.3.1) cause the share of capacity and of product originating in agriculture and mining to increase relative to that from manufacturing and services (variables 2.5.1–4). Increased quantitative restrictions (simulations 8.3.2) tend to increase the share of capacity and of *GDP* originating in manufacturing and, perhaps to a lesser extent, agriculture and discriminate mostly against mining. Liberalization (simulations 8.3.3) tends to favor mining most clearly. Such results are not very surprising. The maintenance of the disequilibrium overvalued exchange rate system through quantitative restrictions always had as one of its motivations the shifting of resources away from foreign-controlled mining (and, to a lesser extent, from agriculture, the base of the traditional elite) to manufacturing and to services, including the government. The simulations in table 8.3 suggest that foreign sector policies have tended to be successful in these respects.

Two other features of the impact of foreign sector policy changes on resource allocation and structural change also merit mention. First, once again the movements in the product–intermediate input price ratios are far from perfectly correlated with the changes in either *GDP*s or in capacities. Such a result is not surprising, given the multitude of determinants of capacity changes and capacity utilization (ch. 4). The limited association merits reiteration at this point, however, because of the substantial emphasis on final product to intermediate price ratios (or on related measures) as indicators of inducements for resource movements in the literature on international economics of the past decade.

Second, the indirect effects often are very strong and even offset the direct effects at times. The last three simulations in table 8.3 provide examples. The first two of these refer to exogenous changes with direct impact on mining, while the last has direct effects on agriculture and manufacturing. In all three cases for some years there is the suggestion of larger proportional induced changes on sectors other than those affected directly.

8.3.3. Distribution of income and resources

In the aggregate in the *factoral* dimension, both increases in exchange rates (simulations 8.3.1) and in quantitative restrictions (simulations 8.3.2) lower the real wage and the labor share in income immediately and on a sustained basis, although there is some cycling (variables 3.1.1–2). With liberalization (simulations 8.3.3) the impact depends on the relative magnitude of the reductions in quantitative restrictions versus rises in exchange rates, with the results being more favorable to labor the larger in absolute value is the former relative to the latter. For the last three simulations in table 8.3, each with changes affecting the exports of specific sectors, the impact on the factoral distribution of income is smaller, but still negative from the point of view of labor (and still with cycling). What these results all reflect basically is the relative stickiness of wages. When prices increase (decrease) nominal wages lag behind so real wages fall (rise) accordingly. On a disaggregate level, nominal wages tend to adjust somewhat more quickly in the high-wage sectors of mining and manufacturing, so when prices increase (fall) the distribution among laborers tends to become more (less) regressive.

In the *international* dimension, all of the policies considered individually in table 8.3 (simulations 8.3.1–2, 8.3.4–6) led to immediate declines in net factor income abroad, albeit with subsequent cycling (variable 3.2.1). With liberalization (simulations 8.3.3) the direction of the impact depends upon the relative size of exchange rate versus quantitative restriction movement. As consideration of relationships (5.3) shows, in large part those changes reflect the direct impact of the exogenous variations on the real wage and the real value of the legal cost of production in large-scale mining. Through these links, the larger is the price increase and the less are net factor payments from abroad in real terms.

In the *intertemporal* dimension of distribution, all of the policies considered individually in table 8.3 (simulations 8.3.1–2, 8.3.4–6) tend to favor future generations over the present generation, although not in the first year for exchange rate increases, nor without cycling (variable 3.3.1). With liberalization (simulations 8.3.3), in contrast, for both of the combinations of exchange rate and quantitative restriction movements considered, the immediate effect is four to favor present over future consumption. These results reflect the complex interaction of a number of factors within the simultaneous system.

Finally, in the *private versus public* dimension, the impact of increases in exchange rates (simulations 8.3.1) is somewhat mixed. The prevalent tendency seems to be a shift from the public sector, although increases are recorded in real taxes for the second year and in the share of government consumption in *GDP* for the first and second years (variables 3.4.1–2). The effects of increasing foreign sector quantitative restrictions (simulations 8.3.2) are more clearly to shift resources away from the public sector, although with some cycling. When increased exchange rates are combined with reduced quantitative restrictions in a liberalization program (simulations 8.3.3), a fairly substantial shift occurs towards the public sector.

These results, as well as those of smaller magnitude of the other three simulations in table 8.3, reflect changes in the underlying activity levels in real terms and in the price levels. Taxes from imports, for example, are fairly substantially affected by the foreign sector policy changes because of the induced changes in real imports (variables 3.4.1.1.2 and 5.2). More important than the changes in real activity levels, however, are the changes in prices. Aggregate tax collections simply adjust slowly to price changes. When inflation increases, taxes in real terms tend to decline, which causes a reduction in current real government expenditures.

8.3.4. Economic growth

Exchange rate increases (simulations 8.3.1) reduce the growth rate by −0.4 and −1.0% in the first two years, although in the third year there is a 1.2% gain for a one-time change and a 0.2% increase for a sustained change (variable 4.1). Capacity cycles somewhat, with a very small positive immediate and sustained increase (variable 4.3). The intensification of quantitative restrictions (simulations 8.3.2) in contrast, tends to increase *GDP*, although capacity is slightly reduced (variables 4.1 and 4.3). When liberalization combines changes in both exchange rates and quantitative restrictions (simulations 8.3.3), the growth rate of *GDP* tends to decline (although a 3.3% increase is recorded in the second year) despite a slight rise in capacity.

These results and those for the other three simulations are quite mixed. They do provide some support for those who question the supposedly great growth benefits to be gained from liberalization (as claimed for example, *ex ante* by the proponents of the Ibañez–Klein–Saks and Alessandri stabilization–liberalization programs). But they do not suggest that increased restrictionism has substantial or unequivocal growth benefits.

8.3.5. Foreign economic position

The simulations in table 8.3 suggest that immediate increases in aggregate exports result from higher exchange rates, lessened quantitative restrictions, increases in all large-scale mining policy tools, and subsidies for agricultural and manufacturing exports (variable 5.1). In some cases subsequent cycling occurs. The rather large inverse relationship between quantitative restrictions and aggregate exports in simulations 8.3.2 merits emphasis because it reflects indirect links through production decisions and prices, not the imposition of quantitative limitations directly on exports.

On a disaggregate level, industrial exports continue to be most responsive to changes in the system (variable 5.1.3). Immediate increases of 19.7 and 18.8%, respectively, result from a rise of one standard deviation in the exchange rate and a 10% export subsidy (simulations 8.3.1B and 8.3.6). The same policies also cause immediate responses of 6.4 and 4.2%, respectively for agricultural exports. Such an increase in the exchange rate, moreover, induces a 8.0% increase in the exports from large-scale mining. This last result raises doubts about the wisdom of the maintenance of a highly overvalued exchange rate policy for large-scale mining for a number of years before the *Nuevo Trato* of 1955. The responses of agricultural and manufacturing exports also raise questions about the wisdom of more generally maintaining overvalued exchange rates with quantitative restrictions if, as was claimed, expansion of non-traditional exports was desired.

Aggregate imports (variable 5.2) drops when either exchange rates or quantitative restrictions are increased (simulations 8.3.1 and 8.3.2). Within the complete system, however, the responses to a 10% devaluation are quite small – implying an elasticity of −0.1 or less – and in contrast to the larger partial-equilibrium elasticities presented in table 5.2. The feedback effects of devaluation on domestic prices make partial-equilibrium elasticities very poor guides to behavior within the complete system and also justify the elasticity pessimism prevalent in Chile.

The aggregate import response to a 10% increase in quantitative restrictions, in contrast, is quite substantial within the complete system. The first-year drop is −24.2%, and the fall after such a change if sustained three years is −40.4%. Feedback effects do occur here also and again offset part of the direct effect of the policy change. Within the complete model, however, the impact on imports of variations in quantitative restrictions seems to be damped by these feedbacks less than is that of exchange rate changes (i.e. compare variable 5.2 for simulations 8.3.1B and 8.3.2B). When both policies are combined with 10% changes in a liberalization attempt (simulations 8.3.3), therefore, imports still expand considerably. It is also interesting to note that the other three simulations in table 8.3, although they are related to policy changes affecting only exports directly, all result in immediate increases in aggregate imports.

On a disaggregate level, simulations 8.3.1 suggest that devaluation leads to a shift in the composition of imports away from consumer imports, especially those characterized as secondary (variables 5.1.1–4)[9]. The ordering of the impact of intensified quantitative restrictions of imports is transportation-related investment goods, services, secondary consumer goods, durable and habitual consumer goods, machinery and equipment investment goods, and intermediate goods. Such restrictions thus apparently favor intermediate goods, as has been the announced intention (in order not to lower domestic production). They do not limit 'postponable imports' (i.e. transportation-related and machinery and equipment investment goods, durable consumer goods) relative to habitual and secondary consumer goods as much as has been the supposed aim.

[9]The export policies explored in the last three simulations of table 8.3 also lead to a shift away from consumer imports.

Finally, note that services are treated as postponable relative to most goods imports.

The impact of policy changes on the surplus on current account once again simply reflects the combination of the changes in aggregate exports and in aggregate imports. Both devaluations and intensified quantitative restrictions, therefore, lead to an improvement in the surplus on current account (variable 5.3). An 18% devaluation (simulations 8.3.1) leads to an immediate 6.7% increase and a 10.0% augmentation in the third year if the devaluation is sustained. A 10% intensification of quantitative restrictions (simulations 8.3.2) induces a 102.2% immediate increase and a 169.1% rise in the third year if the intensification in restrictions is sustained. When 10% changes in both policies are combined in a liberalization package (simulations 8.3.3), the immediate impact is a −136.9% deterioration in the surplus on current account.

One should not conclude from these figures that quantitative restrictions are more powerful tools than exchange rates, nor that liberalization has a disastrous impact on the surplus on current account. As is noted above, increased quantitative restrictions have more of an impact on imports than does devaluation, but the former also has a negative effect on exports while the latter induces an exports expansion. Since, historically, exchange rates have varied much more from the secular trend than have quantitative restrictions, in comparing the force of the two sets of policies the type B simulations are of primary relevance. For such simulations, the surplus on the current account is immediately increased by 25.1% for devaluation and 23.5% for intensified quantitative restrictions and falls by −1.0% for the liberalization package. In terms of the impact of historically equally likely changes on the surplus on current account, therefore, the two sets of policies are about equally effective and liberalization has, on net, very little effect.

The other three simulations in table 8.3 suggest that the immediate impact of a 10% exogenous increase in mineral exports is to improve the surplus on current account by 24.7% (simulation 8.3.5), the immediate impact of a 10% subsidy for agricultural and manufacturing exports is to increase the surplus on current account by 2.1% (simulation 8.3.6), and that the immediate effect of a 10% increase in all large-scale mining policies is to cause a −1.1% deterioration in this account (simulation 8.3.4). All three of these simulations reveal the possibility of significant impacts on the surplus on current account, but of substantially less magnitude than those resulting from devaluations or alterations in quantitative restrictions.

Finally, for all six simulations, of course, the movements in net bank international reserves (variable 5.4) follow the movements in the surplus on current account (since the capital accounts are being held fixed exogenously). Also, the black market exchange rate (variable 5.5) basically follows the movement of domestic prices, with some modifications due to variations in exchange rates and quantitative restrictions.

8.4. Incomes and labor market policies

Sections 8.1, 8.2, and 8.3 indicate that fiscal, monetary, and foreign sector policies all have substantial effects on the distribution of income and resources. Perhaps the major characteristics of these results is that both the position of labor and that of the public sector tend to adjust relatively slowly to inflation, so increased price changes cause shifts away from these two groups.

Table 8.4 presents five additional simulations in which the effects of exogenous changes directly in the labor market are explored:

8.4.1. The minimum wage (*sueldo vital*) is increased.

8.4.2. Non-manufacturing unionization is increased.

8.4.3. Labor mobility among sectors is restrained by limiting for each sector the absolute values of the percentage changes in the sectoral labor force to the mean of the absolute values of such percentage changes for the four immediate presimulation years (1958–1961).

8.4.4. The total labor force is endogeneously determined by the sum of the sectoral labor forces.

8.4.5. Manufacturing, instead of agriculture and services, absorbs any surplus labor given the exogenous total supply.

Except as is noted in these simulation descriptions, all of these simulations use a model identical to the base model of section 7.3.

These simulations again reflect the general characteristics discussed in subsection 8.1.1. Interested readers can identify illustrations of almost all of those features in table 8.4.

Table
Incomes and labor market policy simulations

Variables relating to major areas of Chilean macroeconomic policy concern	Simulations 8.4.1 Minimum wage (*sueldo vital*) increased					Simulations 8.4.2 Non-manufacturing unionization increased			
	A			B	C	A			C
	1	2	3	1	3	1	2	3	3
1. Cyclical variables									
1.1. Nominal terms									
1.1.1. *GDP* deflator	0.3	−0.3	−0.2	0.7	−0.1	0.1	−0.1	−0.3	−0.3
1.1.2. Income velocity	0.7	−0.1	0.0	1.5	0.4	0.4	0.1	−0.4	−0.2
1.2. Real terms									
1.2.1. Capacity utilization for *GDP*	−0.3	0.0	0.0	−0.7	−0.3	−0.1	0.1	0.0	0.0
1.3. Monetary policy-related variables									
1.3.1. Money supply/deflator	−0.7	−0.2	−0.2	−1.5	−0.8	−0.4	−0.1	0.2	−0.1
1.3.2. Monetary base/deflator	−1.0	0.1	−0.4	−2.2	−1.0	−0.5	0.1	0.4	0.1
1.3.3. Net Central Bank foreign reserves	−1.3	−0.7	−1.4	−2.7	−2.6	−0.9	−0.3	−0.1	−0.9
1.4. Fiscal policy-related variables									
1.4.1. Government current expenditures	−2.2	0.0	−0.4	−4.6	−2.1	0.0	0.0	0.0	0.2
1.4.2. Government deficit	4.1	0.3	1.1	9.1	4.2	−0.5	0.4	0.2	−0.2
2. Resource allocation and structural change									
2.1. Product/intermediate input price ratio									
2.1.1. Agriculture	−0.7	−0.2	−0.4	−1.5	−0.5	−0.8	−0.1	−0.4	−0.5
2.1.2. Mining	1.0	0.5	0.2	2.3	1.5	−0.2	0.0	0.0	0.0
2.1.3. Industry	0.2	0.2	0.1	0.4	0.2	0.1	0.0	0.0	−0.1
2.2. Labor force (secular movements)									
2.2.1. Agriculture	0.0	0.0	0.0	0.0	0.0	0.0	0.0	0.0	0.0
2.2.2. Mining	0.0	0.0	0.0	0.0	0.0	0.0	0.0	0.0	0.0
2.2.3. Industry	0.0	−0.1	−0.1	0.0	−0.1	0.0	0.0	0.0	0.0
2.2.4. Services	0.0	0.0	0.0	0.0	0.0	0.0	0.0	0.0	0.0
2.3. Capital stock									
2.3.1. Agriculture	0.1	0.1	0.1	0.2	0.1	0.1	0.1	0.0	0.1
2.3.2. Mining	−0.4	−0.6	−0.3	−0.8	−0.7	0.0	0.0	0.1	0.1
2.3.3. Industry	0.0	0.0	0.0	0.0	0.0	0.0	0.0	0.0	0.0
2.4. Production capacity									
2.4.1. Agriculture	0.0	0.0	0.0	0.0	0.0	0.0	0.0	0.0	0.0
2.4.2. Mining	0.0	0.0	0.0	0.0	0.0	0.0	0.0	0.0	0.0
2.4.3. Industry	0.0	−0.1	−0.1	0.0	−0.1	0.0	0.0	0.0	0.0
2.4.4. Services	0.0	0.0	0.0	0.0	0.1	0.0	0.0	0.0	0.0
2.5. *GDP*									
2.5.1. Agriculture	−0.1	0.1	−0.1	−0.2	−0.1	0.0	0.0	−0.1	−0.1
2.5.2. Mining	−1.6	−1.5	−0.3	−3.3	−2.9	0.0	0.0	0.0	0.1
2.5.3. Industry	−0.4	0.2	−0.2	−0.9	−0.3	−0.2	0.2	−0.1	0.0
2.5.4. Services	0.0	0.0	0.1	0.0	0.2	0.0	0.0	0.1	0.1

8.4
using complete model of Chilean economy[a].

Simulation 8.4.3 Annual percentage change in sectoral labor force limited to pre-simulation period average			Simulation 8.4.4 Total labor force endogenously determined as sum of sectoral labor forces			Simulation 8.4.5 Manufacturing absorbs surplus labor in given labor force		
C			C			C		
1	2	3	1	2	3	1	2	3
−0.1	0.4	−0.1	−1.0	1.3	−1.2	−0.7	1.5	−0.9
−0.3	0.5	−0.4	−2.2	2.0	−1.1	−1.8	1.8	−2.7
0.0	0.2	−0.2	−0.1	0.7	−0.9	0.0	0.5	−1.1
0.1	0.2	0.1	0.4	−0.9	−2.2	1.0	0.4	0.8
0.1	0.0	0.4	0.6	−3.0	−1.0	1.5	−0.9	2.8
0.0	0.5	0.7	−0.7	−2.7	−4.4	1.3	1.5	3.7
0.0	0.0	−0.2	−0.1	−0.3	−0.4	0.2	−0.1	−0.1
0.2	0.0	−0.6	1.2	1.7	1.4	0.1	−0.7	−3.1
−0.3	−0.2	−1.1	0.0	1.3	−2.8	0.8	1.8	−1.3
0.1	−0.1	−0.1	0.3	−0.5	−0.2	0.2	−0.6	−0.1
0.3	−0.1	0.5	1.4	−0.4	2.8	0.5	−1.1	1.7
0.3	1.2	2.1	−1.2	−0.7	−1.3	−1.2	−0.7	−1.3
0.1	0.2	0.3	0.0	0.0	0.0	0.0	0.0	0.0
−0.8	0.5	1.3	−3.4	−1.5	−3.4	0.0	2.1	3.0
−0.2	0.1	−0.5	−1.1	−1.0	−1.6	−1.2	−1.0	−1.6
0.0	0.0	−0.2	0.0	0.0	−0.6	0.0	0.2	−0.6
0.0	−0.1	−0.3	0.0	−0.2	−0.9	0.0	−0.3	−1.0
−0.2	0.1	0.4	−0.7	−0.8	−1.7	0.1	1.4	1.8
0.3	1.2	2.1	−1.2	−0.7	−1.3	−1.2	−0.7	−1.3
0.0	0.0	0.1	0.0	0.0	0.0	0.0	0.0	0.0
−0.7	0.4	1.2	−3.0	−1.4	−3.0	0.0	4.3	3.6
0.0	−0.3	−0.8	0.0	−1.4	−1.1	0.0	−1.3	−1.1
0.3	2.0	2.2	−2.5	0.1	−3.0	−1.6	0.2	−3.0
0.1	−0.3	−0.2	0.4	0.3	0.3	0.2	−0.2	0.1
−0.8	1.1	0.4	−4.0	0.3	−5.8	0.0	5.8	0.6
0.1	−0.4	−1.0	0.6	−1.7	−0.7	0.2	−2.0	−1.1

Table 8.4
Incomes and labor market policy simulations

Variables relating to major areas of Chilean macroeconomic policy concern	Simulations 8.4.1 Minimum wage (*sueldo vital*) increased					Simulations 8.4.2 Non-manufacturing unionization increased			
	A			B	C	A			C
	1	2	3	1	3	1	2	3	3
3. Distribution of income and resources									
3.1. Factoral	1.9	−4.5	0.3	4.2	−2.9	0.1	0.1	0.2	0.2
3.1.1. Real wage	0.6	−0.4	0.1	1.3	0.1	1.5	−0.7	0.1	0.9
3.1.1.1. Agriculture	−0.1	−0.2	0.5	−0.1	0.1	9.3	−1.0	1.4	9.9
3.1.1.2. Mining	6.2	1.1	1.0	13.8	6.4	0.0	0.0	0.3	0.3
3.1.1.3. Industry	0.0	0.2	0.0	0.1	0.0	0.1	0.0	0.2	0.1
3.1.1.4. Services	−0.2	0.0	−0.2	−0.5	−0.3	−0.1	0.0	0.0	−0.1
3.1.1.5. Government	0.7	−0.4	0.0	1.6	0.2	1.5	−0.8	0.1	0.9
3.1.2. Wage share in income									
3.2. International									
3.2.1. Net factor income from abroad	5.7	0.3	0.5	12.6	3.1	0.0	0.4	0.5	0.7
3.3. Intertemporal									
3.3.1. Consumption/product	−0.2	0.2	0.0	−0.3	0.1	−0.2	0.2	0.1	0.1
3.4. Public versus private									
3.4.1. Taxes/deflator	−0.4	0.0	0.0	−0.7	−0.3	0.0	0.0	0.1	0.2
3.4.1.1. Indirect	−0.3	0.2	−0.1	−0.7	−0.2	−0.1	0.1	0.1	0.1
3.4.1.1.1. Sales	−0.3	0.0	0.0	−0.7	−0.3	−0.1	0.1	0.0	0.0
3.4.1.1.2. Import	−0.4	0.9	−0.2	−0.8	0.0	−0.2	0.2	0.3	0.3
3.4.1.2. Direct	−0.4	−0.1	0.0	−0.8	−0.4	0.1	−0.1	0.2	0.4
3.4.1.2.1. Large-scale mining	−1.0	−1.4	−0.2	−1.7	−2.3	−0.1	0.2	0.3	0.4
3.4.1.2.2. Other corporations	−2.1	0.0	−0.2	−4.4	−2.0	−3.0	1.3	0.0	−1.9
3.4.1.2.3. Personal	−0.6	0.9	−0.2	−1.3	−0.2	−0.3	0.4	0.2	0.2
3.4.2. Government consumption/ GDP	−1.9	0.0	−0.4	−3.9	−1.8	0.1	−0.1	0.0	0.2
4. Economic growth-related variables									
4.1. *GDP*	−0.3	0.0	0.0	−0.7	−0.3	−0.1	0.1	0.0	0.0
4.1.1. Agriculture	−0.1	0.1	−0.1	−0.2	−0.1	0.0	0.0	−0.1	−0.1
4.1.2. Mining	−1.6	−1.5	−0.3	−3.3	−2.9	0.0	0.0	0.0	0.1
4.1.3. Industry	−0.4	0.2	−0.2	−0.9	−0.3	−0.2	0.2	−0.1	0.0
4.2. Gross national savings									
4.2.1. Personal	10.9	−8.2	3.1	24.0	1.3	21.6	−16.3	2.1	31.4
4.2.2. Business	−105.2	3.2	1.1	−231.9	−2.9	−240.9	5.9	−11.8	−77.4
4.2.3. Government	−10.9	−0.2	−1.1	−23.7	−5.2	1.0	−0.8	0.3	0.9
4.3. Capacity	0.0	0.0	0.0	0.0	0.0	0.0	0.0	0.0	0.0
4.3.1. Investment	0.0	−0.2	0.0	−0.1	−0.2	0.0	−0.2	−0.2	0.0
4.3.2. Capital stock	0.0	0.0	0.0	0.0	0.0	0.0	0.0	0.0	0.0
5. Foreign sector									
5.1. Exports	−0.2	0.1	−0.3	−0.4	−0.2	−0.3	0.0	−0.1	−0.2
5.1.1. Agricultural	−0.1	0.3	−0.3	−0.2	−0.1	−3.6	0.0	−0.9	−2.9
5.1.2. Mineral									
5.1.2.1. Large-scale	−0.1	0.4	−0.6	−0.2	−0.1	−0.1	0.1	−0.2	−0.1

Policy simulations and multipliers   295

(continued)
using complete model of Chilean economy[a].

Simulation 8.4.3 Annual percentage change in sectoral labor force limited to pre-simulation period average			Simulation 8.4.4 Total labor force endogenously determined as sum of sectoral labor forces			Simulation 8.4.5 Manufacturing absorbs surplus labor in given labor force		
C			C			C		
1	2	3	1	2	3	1	2	3
0.2	−0.5	0.5	0.9	−2.0	2.5	0.5	−2.0	2.1
−0.1	−0.4	0.5	0.0	−1.6	2.5	0.7	−0.1	3.1
0.0	−0.1	1.3	0.5	−0.1	5.3	1.0	0.5	4.7
0.3	−0.5	0.6	1.2	−2.2	3.1	0.7	−2.1	2.5
0.3	−0.6	0.9	1.4	−2.4	3.8	0.7	−2.2	3.4
0.0	−0.1	−0.2	−0.1	−0.9	−0.8	0.5	−0.4	−0.1
0.1	−0.7	0.8	0.4	−2.4	3.8	0.4	−1.1	4.6
0.3	−0.7	0.4	2.0	−2.5	3.6	1.4	−2.5	2.2
0.1	−0.2	−0.1	0.7	0.1	0.4	0.1	−0.6	−0.1
−0.1	−0.1	0.0	−0.3	−1.2	−0.7	0.3	−0.2	0.4
−0.1	0.1	−0.1	−0.3	−0.7	−1.1	0.2	0.0	0.0
−0.1	0.3	−0.2	−0.8	−0.1	−2.1	−0.1	0.7	−0.9
0.2	−0.9	0.6	1.1	−3.2	2.4	0.9	−2.7	3.5
−0.1	−0.2	0.0	−0.3	−1.5	−0.3	0.3	−0.5	0.8
0.2	−0.7	0.0	1.5	−1.0	1.8	1.0	−1.6	1.5
0.0	0.8	−2.1	−0.2	2.6	−8.9	−0.2	0.8	−10.6
−0.1	−0.4	0.3	−0.3	−3.2	0.5	0.4	−2.3	1.6
0.1	−0.3	0.0	0.7	−0.1	1.7	0.3	−0.8	0.9
−0.1	0.3	−0.2	−0.8	−0.2	−2.1	−0.1	0.7	−1.0
0.3	2.0	2.2	−2.5	0.1	−3.0	−1.6	0.2	−3.0
0.1	0.3	−0.2	0.4	0.3	0.3	0.2	0.2	−0.1
−0.8	1.1	0.4	−4.0	0.3	−5.8	0.0	5.8	0.8
−0.8	−2.1	29.9	−13.4	−36.1	67.0	−0.1	−5.0	134.3
−17.1	6.2	−78.6	−136.0	19.5	−364.6	−109.7	11.0	−446.6
0.1	−1.7	1.0	0.5	−9.9	1.0	2.4	−4.0	6.1
−0.1	0.1	0.0	−0.7	−0.9	−1.2	−0.1	0.2	0.1
−0.4	0.8	0.9	−1.8	0.3	−4.0	0.0	3.3	0.3
0.0	0.0	0.1	−0.2	−0.1	−0.4	0.0	0.3	0.3
−0.1	0.3	−0.1	−0.8	0.3	−2.0	0.0	1.3	0.2
0.3	1.7	1.1	−2.5	0.7	−4.7	−1.9	0.2	−4.5
0.0	0.2	−0.5	0.2	1.1	−0.7	0.1	0.3	−0.4

Table 8.4
Incomes and labor market policy simulations

Variables relating to major areas of Chilean macroeconomic policy concern	Simulations 8.4.1 Minimum wage (*sueldo vital*) increased					Simulations 8.4.2 Non-manufacturing unionization increased			
	A			B	C	A			C
	1	2	3	1	3	1	2	3	3
5.1.2.2. Other	0.0	−0.6	0.1	0.0	−0.3	0.0	0.0	0.0	0.0
5.1.3. Industrial	−2.3	−0.5	0.1	−4.8	−0.6	−0.6	0.3	0.4	0.6
5.1.4. Services	−0.1	0.0	0.0	−0.2	0.0	−0.1	0.1	0.1	0.0
5.2. Imports	0.0	0.0	0.0	−0.1	0.0	−0.1	0.0	0.0	0.0
5.2.1. Consumption									
5.2.1.1. Habitual	−0.4	0.2	0.1	−0.9	0.1	−0.5	0.3	0.4	0.3
5.2.1.2. Durable	−0.1	−0.3	0.5	−0.2	0.2	0.0	−0.3	0.7	0.5
5.2.1.3. Secondary	1.2	0.0	−0.1	2.8	0.7	2.6	−0.1	0.1	2.6
5.2.2. Investment									
5.2.2.1. Machinery and equipment	0.0	0.0	0.1	0.0	0.0	0.0	−0.2	−0.1	−0.2
5.2.2.2. Transportation	0.1	−0.3	−0.3	0.3	−0.3	−0.1	−0.4	−0.3	−0.6
5.2.3. Intermediate	−0.1	0.0	−0.2	−0.2	−0.2	−0.2	0.1	−0.1	−0.1
5.2.4. Services	0.0	−0.1	−0.3	0.0	−0.2	0.3	0.0	−0.1	−0.2
5.3. Surplus on current account	−1.2	0.6	−1.1	−2.8	−0.7	−1.5	0.3	−0.3	−0.7
5.4. Net bank international reserves	−0.9	−0.5	−1.1	−1.9	−1.9	−0.6	−0.2	−0.1	−0.7
5.5. Black market exchange rate	0.3	−0.3	−0.2	0.7	−0.1	0.1	−0.1	−0.3	−0.4

ªThe items in this table are the percentage deviations from the base simulation described in section 7.3 due to the exogenous changes indicated at the column heads. 'A' refers to a simulation in which there are 10% changes in the indicated exogenous variables in the first year, but no change thereafter. 'B' refers to a simulation in which there are changes equal to one standard deviation from the secular trend in the indicated exogenous variables in the first year, but no change

(continued)
using complete model of Chilean economy[a].

Simulation 8.4.3 Annual percentage change in sectoral labor force limited to pre-simulation period average			Simulation 8.4.4 Total labor force endogenously determined as sum of sectoral labor forces			Simulation 8.4.5 Manufacturing absorbs surplus labor in given labor force		
C			C			C		
1	2	3	1	2	3	1	2	3
0.0	0.0	−0.2	0.0	0.3	−0.3	0.0	0.2	−0.4
−4.5	1.3	1.5	−20.8	−5.2	−14.0	0.3	14.9	6.8
0.0	−0.1	0.1	0.1	−0.5	0.0	0.2	0.0	0.9
0.0	−0.1	0.0	0.1	0.1	−0.8	0.1	0.4	0.4
0.2	−0.3	0.3	1.5	0.2	−0.2	0.5	−0.5	0.4
0.0	0.0	−0.1	0.3	0.2	−0.4	0.2	0.1	−0.5
0.0	−1.5	1.1	0.7	−5.1	5.7	0.7	−2.1	8.6
0.0	−0.2	0.0	−0.1	−0.8	−0.6	0.0	−0.3	0.2
0.0	0.2	0.2	−0.1	0.9	−0.1	−0.1	1.5	0.7
−0.1	−0.1	−0.4	−0.5	0.4	−1.7	0.0	0.9	−0.3
−0.1	0.4	−0.1	−1.0	1.0	−2.6	−0.3	2.2	0.0
−0.6	1.3	−0.3	−4.5	0.1	−6.6	0.4	2.2	−0.5
0.0	0.4	0.5	−0.5	−1.9	−3.2	1.0	1.1	2.7
−0.2	0.4	−0.1	−1.1	1.3	−1.2	−0.8	1.6	−0.9

thereafter. 'C' refers to a simulation in which there are 10% changes in the indicated exogenous variables in each year. The years within the dynamic simulation runs are indicated at the column heads. The first years of type C simulation are identical to that of the associated type A simulations and therefore are not presented in cases in which the type A first year results are presented.

The remainder of this section, parallel to those above, is organized around the impact of the simulation on the five major areas of macroeconomic policy interest.

8.4.1. Cyclical concerns

The exogenous changes explored in table 8.4 have quite limited effects on *nominal stability*. The increase in the minimum wage (simulations 8.4.1) and the increase in non-manufacturing unionization (simulations 8.4.2) both increase the *GDP* deflator in the first year, but cause a reduction subsequently (variable 1.1.1). The three alternatives concerning labor mobility and surplus labor absorption (simulations 8.4.3–5) all result in an initial decline in the *GDP* deflator, but with a two-year cycle thereafter. Only in the case of there being no sector to absorb surplus labor (simulation 8.4.4) or in the second year when manufacturing absorbs surplus labor (simulation 8.4.5), however, are the absolute values of the deviations in the *GDP* deflator even as large as 1.0%.

These quite limited effects reflect that those exogenous changes do not have a very substantial impact on wages (see below) and, thus, on cost-push aspects of price determination. That the cost-push facets of price determination are relatively important in these simulations in comparison to other factors is reflected in the relatively high correlation between price and real wage movements (variables 1.1.1 and 3.1.1). In contrast, movements between prices and the money supply are often inverse (variables 1.1.1 and 1.3.1).

For similar reasons, the impact on *real stability* also is quite limited. A 10% increase in the minimum wage (simulations 8.4.1) results in an immediate decline in capacity utilization of −0.3%, with the same fall experienced in the third year if the increase is sustained (variable 1.2.1). A 10% increase in non-manufacturing unionization (simulations 8.4.2) causes an immediate decline in capacity utilization of −0.1%, followed by an equal increase in the second year. The other three simulations also imply relatively small cyclical changes in capacity utilization, with an absolute value of the deviation as large as 1.0% only in the third year of a sustained change in which industry absorbs surplus labor.

One implication of the relatively limited impact of these labor market changes on cyclical variation is that the labor policies can be used to affect income distribution somewhat without much of a negative effect on the cyclical variables. An illustration of this point is provided by adding a 10% increase in the minimum wage to the contractionary monetary and fiscal policies of simulation 8.2.5[10]. As a result, in the first year the *GDP* deflator increases an additional 0.2% and the capacity utilization rate falls an additional 0.1%. Associated with these quite small negative changes are relatively larger improvements in the position of labor: an increase of 0.7% in the real wage and of 0.9% in the labor share of income.

8.4.2. *Resource allocation and structural change*

A higher minimum wage (simulations 8.4.1) causes reductions in *GDP* relatively in mining and manufacturing due to variations in capacity utilization rates (variables 2.5.1–4). The only discernible effect on capacity is small reduction in manufacturing due to a fall in the labor force therein, although the capital stock in mining also drops measurably (variables 2.2–4). Increased non-manufacturing unionization (simulations 8.4.2) has little impact on resource allocation, although some small cyclical movements do result for the *GDP* from manufacturing.

The resource allocation effects of the last three simulations tend to be larger than those of the first two. They are somewhat difficult to summarize, however, because considerable fluctuations occur. Nevertheless, some systematic tendencies are apparent. The limitation on intersectoral labor mobility of simulation 8.4.3, for example, tends to cause both capacity and current production shifts from services and mining to agriculture and manufacturing (variables 2.4–5). The ceilings on labor movements basically keep more labor in agriculture and, to a lesser extent, after the first year in manufacturing than occurs in the base simulation.

When agriculture and services no longer absorb surplus labor (simulation 8.4.4), they both tend to lose labor, capacity, and production relative to the base simulation (variables 2.2–5). Of greater surprise are the somewhat larger losses experienced by manufacturing due to indirect effects. When manufacturing absorbs the surplus labor (simulation 8.4.5), this last outcome is reversed with additions to the labor force, capacity, and *GDP* of manufacturing.

[10]The full results of this simulation are not presented here due to space limitations.

8.4.3. Distribution of income and resources

In the aggregate in the *factoral* dimension, the 10% rise in the minimum wage (simulations 8.4.1) causes immediate increments of 0.6% in the real wage and of 0.7% in the labor share (variables 3.1.1–2). However, the small price changes which are set in motion, given the stickiness of wages, result in a decline in both of these variables in the second year, although both increase in the third year of a sustained change. On a more disaggregate level, the highest-wage sector, mining, benefits most, so such a policy has some regressive implications related to the distribution of income among laborers (variables 3.1.1.1–5).

Increases of 10% in non-manufacturing unionization (simulations 8.4.2) cause immediate increases of 1.5% for both real wages and the labor share in income (variables 3.1.1–2). Both cycle somewhat, but are 0.9% higher in the third year of a sustained change. On a more disaggregate level, by far the largest immediate and sustained increase is enjoyed by the highest-wage sector, mining, once again (variables 3.1.1.1–5).

The other three simulations in table 8.4 tend to result in smaller immediate changes of a positive nature from the viewpoint of labor, followed by cyclical fluctuations with a two-year period. On a more disaggregate level, the largest absolute changes do not seem to be concentrated particularly in the sectors directly affected by the exogenous changes of simulations 8.4.4 and 8.4.5. Apparently, indirect effects and feedbacks are relatively important.

In the *international* dimension, the increase in minimum wages (simulations 8.4.1) results in a 5.7% immediate increase in net factor payments from abroad and a 3.1% augmentation in the third year of a sustained policy change (variable 3.2). This result primarily reflects the lowering of factor payments from abroad. For similar reasons the last three simulations have an immediate increase in this variable but with subsequent fluctuations.

In the *intertemporal* dimension of distribution, the absolute value of the percentage deviations in the consumption share of product are small – in no case as large as 1.0% (variable 3.3.1). When there is no sector to absorb surplus labor, present consumption systematically increases (simulation 8.4.4). In the other simulations, there are frequent sign reversals over time. Then, the impact on this dimension of distribution generally seems small, and not very clear in direction.

Finally, in the *private versus public* dimension, the increase in minimum wages (simulations 8.4.1) results in a shift away from the public sector, whether measured by the real value of taxes or the government consumption share of *GDP* (variables 3.4.1–2). The increase in non-manufacturing unionization (simulations 8.4.2) causes a small shift towards the government. For the other three simulations in table 8.4, the results are mixed, both because of cycling and because of opposing movements in the two indicators. Generally, price movements are important in transmitting the impact of the exogenous changes to these variables, but many other factors also enter into their determination within the simultaneous system. In any case, the changes induced in this dimension of distribution are relatively small.

8.4.4. Economic growth

All of the exogenous changes considered in table 8.4 result in an initial decline in the growth rate of *GDP* (variable 4.1). The absolute value of the magnitudes of these declines are not very large, however – from −0.1 to −0.8%. Moreover, cycling occurs subsequently in three of the five cases. Furthermore, the induced changes in capacity are not larger than 0.2% in absolute value in four of the five cases (variable 4.3). The exception is when there is no sector to absorb the surplus labor (simulation 8.4.4), which results in lessened capacity primarily because of the smaller labor force employed (reinforced by a slight decline in the capital stock). With this possible exception, the implications of these simulations for growth seem to be sparse.

8.4.5. Foreign economic position

The first four simulations in table 8.4 all show an immediate decline in aggregate exports, followed by cycles of two years' duration (variable 5.1). The case in which industry absorbs surplus labor (simulation 8.4.5) shows a slight increase after a lag of one year. For all five simulations the major movement on a more disaggregated level is in manufacturing exports (variable 5.1.3), substantially because of responses to relative price movements. Because the induced movements in imports are very small, the variations in the surplus on current account and in net bank international reserves basically follow the pattern of the exports (variables 5.3–4). Thus, the first four simulations result in decreases, although with some cycling, and the fifth has increases. Finally, the black market exchange rate varies slightly, primarily in response to the price movements,

8.5. *Summary comments*

The complete model results are very rich in their implications. Subsection 8.1.1 discusses in detail some general conclusions. Substantial endogenous responses in government and bank behavior are induced. Compositional changes can be quite considerable. The time patterns of responses vary considerably across variables, with much more than one year required for near-to-complete adjustment in many cases. In substantial part because of capacity constraints, the model is quite non-linear so simulations are not additive. Feedbacks, both simultaneous and lagged, are often substantial. The combination of these characteristics means that simple textbook macromodels are poor predictors of many of the effects of exogenous changes. Trade-offs among the degree of attained policy goals often are substantial.

Considerations of the details of the simulations lead to further generalizations. Fiscal, monetary, and foreign sector policies can have quite substantial effects on most areas of policy concern, although relatively less so on capacity expansion. Incomes policies have less potency. Fiscal policies have larger impacts on real capacity utilization than do the other alternatives. In all cases the complete model results often imply considerably different results than do the partial-equilibrium estimates of Part II because of the substantial feedbacks and indirect effects within the complete system. Also, the lags and indirect effects mean that it is almost impossible for the government to successfully fine-tune the economy.

In some respects the complete model simulations support some of the prevailing beliefs conditioning Chilean policy choices. Despite fairly high price elasticities under *ceteris paribus* conditions, for example, within the complete model the balance of payments responses to devaluation are quite limited. Prices are increased significantly, not only with inflationary implications, but also with largely neutralizing effects on trade movements. Because of the stickiness of wages and tax collections, resources are shifted away from labor and from the government when inflation occurs, whether due to devaluation or to some other cause. The immediate impact of liberalization is stagnating, although subsequent reversals occur. Overvaluation does seem to have the effects desired by various governments of shifting resources from agriculture and mining to manufacturing. For balance of payments reasons alone, quantitative restrictions seem to be more effective policy instruments than exchange rate adjustments.

In other respects, however, the simulations point out ways in which historical policies have caused results opposite to those intended. Foreign sector policies tend to discourage most of all, for example, the non-traditional exports which various governments have claimed they want to expand. The highly discriminatory exchange rate policy for large-scale mining discouraged exports from that sector substantially, even within the complete model context. The intensification of quantitative restrictions not only does not limit primarily the 'postponable' durable imports, but also has substantial negative effects on exports – which exacerbates the foreign exchange shortage. Policies designed to improve the income distribution from the point of view of labor have often increased the regressiveness of distribution among laborers.

The simulation results also question the value of some of the important modes of analysis widely used by economists. Disequilibrium lags in adjustment, endogenous government responses, and compositional changes – as is noted above – vitiate many of the predictions of the traditional IS–LM curve macroeconomic models. Despite the considerable effort in the last decade to measure final–intermediate product price ratio related concepts in order to capture inducements for resource shifts, for another example, such price ratios often have no relation to either short- or long-run resource movements in the complete model. For periods of significant duration, moreover, movements in production may even be opposite in direction from movements in capacity – thus raising questions about the widespread tendency to ignore the determinants of capacity utilization. Along the same lines, compositional changes often are quite large – thus raising questions about more aggregate analysis.

In closing, it is necessary to emphasize that in this chapter the complete model of the Chilean economy is discussed as if it represents the Chilean economy. Part II of the book reports on the considerable care taken in establishing the components of this model. Despite such care, however, questions remain considering the data base and the model specification. Some of the assumptions are quite *ad hoc*. Alternative judgments and decisions may have been made by other investigators, perhaps with some significantly different results. Econometric modeling remains an art as well as a science. Hopefully, others who work in this field, even if they come to substantially different judgments about some aspects of the modeling procedure, will benefit from the considerations and reflections presented in this book. Their conclusions then may contradict, but also may reinforce, some of those presented here.

References

Adelman, I. and E. Thorbecke (eds.), (1966). The Theory and Design of Economic Development (Johns Hopkins University Press: Baltimore).

Albertelli, O. (1967). A macroeconometric model of Mexico (International Monetary Fund: Washington), mimeo.

Allende, S. (1971). La via Chilena, el primer mensaje del Presidente Allende al Congreso Pleno, 21 de Mayo 1971 (Santiago).

Arrow, K. J., H. B. Chenery, B. S. Minhas, and R. M. Solow (1961). Capital–labor substitution and economic efficiency, Review of Economics and Statistics, 45: 225–250.

Bacha, E. and L. Taylor (1973). Growth and trade distortions in Chile and their implications in calculating the shadow price of foreign exchange, in: Eckaus, R. S. and P. N. Rosenstein-Rodan (eds.), Analysis of Development Problems: Studies of the Chilean Economy (North-Holland: Amsterdam), pp. 121–146.

Baer, W. (1967). The inflation controversy in Latin America: a survey, Latin American Research Review (Winter).

Baerresen, D. (1966). The multiple exchange rate system of Chile: 1931–1955, Latin American Essay Series, No. 2 (University of Wisconsin: Milwaukee).

Balassa, B. and Associates (1971). The structure of Protection in Developing Countries. Published for the International Bank for Reconstruction and Development and the Inter-American Development Bank. (Johns Hopkins University Press: Baltimore).

Balassa, B., S. E. Guisinger, and D. M. Schydlowsky (1970). The effective rate of protection and the question of labor protection in the United States: a comment, Journal of Political Economy, 78: 1150–1162.

Ballesteros, M. and T. Davis (1963). The growth of output and employment in basic sectors of the Chilean economy, 1908–1957, Economic Development and Cultural Change, 11(2): 152–176.

Banco Central (1953–1973). Boletín Mensuales (Santiago).

Banco de México (1970). A system of short run projections (mimeo).

Barraza-Allande, L.E. (1968). A three-sector model of growth for Mexico, Ph.D. dissertation (University of Wisconsin: Madison).

Barraza-Allande, L. E. and L. Solis (1974). Tecpatl I, short run econometric model of Mexico (Banco de México: Mexico City), mimeo.

Behrman, J. (1970). Forecasting properties and prototype simulations of a model of the copper market, Report to the General Services Administration (Philadelphia).

Behrman, J.R. (1971a). The determinants of the annual rates of change of sectoral money wages in a developing economy, International Economic Review, 12:3, 431–447 (Oct.). Spanish transl. in Cuadernos de Economía (1972), 9(26): 70–88 (Apr.).

Behrman, J.R. (1971b). Review article: trade prospects and capital needs of developing countries, International Economic Review, 12(3): 519–525 (Oct.).

Behrman, J. R. (1972a). Sectoral elasticities of substitution between capital and labor in a developing economy: time series analysis in the case of Chile, Econometrica, 40(2): 311–327. (Spanish transl. in Cuadernos de Economá, 9(26): 70–88.)

Behrman, J.R. (1972b). Sectoral investment determination in a developing economy, American Economic Review, 62(5): 825–841 (Dec.).

Behrman, J.R. (1972c). Short run flexibility in a developing economy: the postwar Chilean experience, Journal of Political Economy, 80(2): 292–313 (Mar.–Apr.).

Behrman, J.R. (1973a). Aggregative market response in developing agriculture: the postwar Chilean experience, in: Eckaus, R. and P. Rosenstein-Rodan (eds.), Analysis of Development Problems: Studies of the Chilean Economy (North-Holland: Amsterdam), pp. 229–250.

Behrman, J.R. (1973b). Cyclical sectoral capacity utilization in a developing economy, in: Eckaus, R. and P. Rosenstein-Rodan (eds.), Analysis of Development Problems: Studies of the Chilean Economy (North-Holland: Amsterdam), pp. 251–268.

Behrman, J.R. (1973c). Price determination in an inflationary economy, the dynamics of Chilean inflation revisited, in: R. Eckaus and P. N. Rosenstein-Rodan (eds.), Analysis of Development Problems: Studies of the Chilean Economy (North-Holland: Amsterdam), pp. 369–398.

Behrman, J. R. (1975a). Foreign-sector regimes and economic development in Chile, paper presented at ECLA-NBER conference, Bogota.

Behrman, J. R. (1975b). Foreign Trade Regimes and Economic Development: Chile, Vol. VII of National Bureau of Economic Research Special Conference Series on Foreign Trade Regimes, and Economic Development (Columbia University Press: New York).

Behrman, J. R. (1975c). Modeling stabilization policy for the LDC's in an international setting, in: A. Ando, R. Herring, and R. Marston (eds.), International aspects of stabilization policy, Proceedings of ISPE–Boston Federal Reserve Bank Conference (Federal Reserve Bank: Boston), pp. 421–449.

Behrman, J.R. (1975d). Econometric modeling of national income determination in Latin America, with special reference to the Chilean experience, Annals of Economic and Social Measurement 4(4): 461–488 (Spanish translation in Demografía y Economía (Feb. 1976)).

Behrman, J.R. (1975e). Proposed specification of quarterly Panamanian econometric model, ILPES – Ministerio de Planificación y Política Económica Project Working Paper No. 3, Panamanian volume (University of Pennsylvania: Philadelphia), mimeo.

Behrman, J.R. (1976). Review of Corbo (1974) in Journal of Development Economics.

Behrman, J.R. and J.M. García (1973). A study of quarterly nominal wage change determinants in an inflationary developing economy, in: R. Eckaus and P. Rosenstein-Rodan (eds.), Analysis of Development Problems: Studies of the Chilean Economy (North-Holland: Amsterdam), pp. 339–416.

Behrman, J.R. and J. Hanson (1975). The use of econometric models in developing countries (Philadelphia and Santiago), mimeo. Revised version in Behrman and Hanson (1976).

Behrman, J. R. and J. Hanson (eds.), (1976). Short Term Macroeconomic Policy in Latin America. IPLES–NBER–Minister of Planning of Panama Conference volume, English and Spanish.

Behrman, J.R. and L.R. Klein (1970). Econometric growth models for the developing economy, in: M.F.G. Scott and J.N. Wolfe (eds.), Induction, Growth and Trade (Oxford University Press: Oxford).

Behrman, J.R. and P. Taubman (1975). Nature and nurture in the determination of earnings and occupational status (University of Pennsylvania: Philadelphia), mimeo.

Behrman, J.R. and P. Taubman (1976a). Intergenerational transmission of income and wealth, American Economic Review, Proceedings, 66.

Behrman, J.R. and P. Taubman (1976b). Nature and nurture in the determination of earnings and occupational status (tentative title).

Bello, P. (1969). A simple macroeconomic model for the Chilean economy, Ph.D. dissertation, University of Southern California.

Beltran del Rio, A. (1973). A macroeconomic forecasting model for Mexico: specification and simulations, Ph.D. dissertation (University of Pennsylvania: Philadelphia).

Beltran del Rio, A. (1974). Statistical regularities in macroeconometric models of developing economies, paper presented at seminar on Economic Models of Emerging Nations, Tel-Aviv (University of Pennsylvania: Philadelphia), mimeo.

Beltran del Rio, A.B. and L.R. Klein (1974). Macroeconometric model building in Latin America: the Mexican case, in: N. Ruggles (ed.), The Role of the Computer in Economic and Social Research in Latin America (Columbia University Press: New York), pp. 161–190.

Bischoff, C.W. (1969). Hypothesis testing and the demand for capital goods, Review of Economics and Statistics, 51: 354–368.

Bischoff, C.W. (1971). The effect of alternative lag distributions, in: G. Fromm (ed.), Tax Incentives and Capital Spending (The Brookings Institute: Washington), pp. 61–130.

Black, S. (1971). A multi-sectoral study of comparative advantage in the Chilean Economy. B.A. Thesis presented to Department of Economics, Harvard College, April.

Blitzer, C.R., P. Clark, and L. Taylor (eds.), (1975). Economy-Wide Models and Development Planning (Oxford University Press: London).

Bradford, C.J., Jr. (1970). Economic planning and structural change in Chile (Overseas Development Council: Washington), mimeo.

Brown, M. (1966). On the Theory and Measurement of Technological Change (Cambridge).

Brown, M. (1967). The theory and empirical analysis of production, National Bureau of Economic Research, Studies in Income and Wealth, vol. 31 (New York).

Cabezón, Pedro (1969). An evaluation of commercial policy in the Chilean economy, Ph.D. dissertation (University of Wisconsin: Madison).

Campos de Olivereira, R. (1964). Economic development and inflation with special reference to Latin America, in: OECD, Development Plans and Programmes (OECD Development Center: Paris).

Carter, N.G. (1970). A macro-economic model of Jamaica, 1959–1966, Social and Economic Studies, 19: 178–201.

Causa, J. (1970). Stabilization policy – The Chilean case, Journal of Political Economy, 78: 4-II (July–August), 815–825.

Causa, J. (1972). Short term economic theory and policy: The Chilean case 1964–1972 (Cambridge), mimeo.

Cerboni, C. (1975). A macroeconometric model of Venezuela (University of Pennsylvania, WEFA: Philadelphia), mimeo.

Chenery, H. and A. Strout (1966). Foreign assistance and economic development, American Economic Review, 56: 679–733.

Chenery, H. and L. Taylor (1968). Development patterns among countries and over time, Review of Economics and Statistics, 50: 391–416.

CIAP, Subcommittee on Chile, Domestic efforts and the needs for external financing for the development of Chile, appendix A to chapter 10 (General Secretariat of the Organization of American States: Washington), CIAP/46, add. 2, mimeo.

Clague, C.K. (1969). Capital–labor substitution in manufacturing in underdeveloped countries, Econometrica, 37: 528–537.

Clark, P. and A. Foxley (1970). Sub-optimal growth: the social cost of make-work employment policies, paper presented at Second World Congress of the Econometric Society (Cambridge, England) mimeo.

Clark, P. and A. Foxley (1973). Target shooting with a multisectoral model, in: R.S. Eckaus and P.N. Rosenstein-Rodan (eds.), Analysis of Development Problems: Studies of the Chilean Economy (North-Holland: Amsterdam), pp. 341–368.

Coen, R.M. (1968). Effects of tax policy on investment in manufacturing, American Economic Review Proceedings, 58: 200–211.

Coen, R.M. (1969). Tax policy and investment behavior: comment, American Economic Review, 59: 370–379.

Coen, R.M. (1971). The effect of cash flow on the speed of adjustment, in: G. Fromm (ed.), Tax Incentives and Capital Spending (The Brookings Institute: Washington), pp. 131–196.

Cohen, A. (1960). Economic Change in Chile, 1929–1959 (University of Florida Press: Gainsville).

Condos, A. (1966). The application of macroeconomic models to development planning: Peru (Iowa State University).

Corbo Lioi, V. (1971). An econometric study of Chilean inflation, Ph.D. dissertation (MIT: Cambridge, Mass.).

Corbo Lioi, V. (1974). Inflation in Developing Countries: An Econometric Study of Chilean Inflation (North-Holland: Amsterdam).

CORFO (1963). El Programa Nacional de Desarrollo Económico 1961–1970, Breve Descripción sobre su Contenido, Experiencias sobre su Aplicación y Cumplimiento de las Metas (Santiago).

CORFO (1968). Financiamiento Exterior, Santiago: CORFO.

CORFO (1970). Chile economic notes, New York: CORFO.

Council of Economic Advisors (1972). Annual Report (United States Government Printing Office: Washington).

Crosson, P.R. (1970). Agricultural Development and Productivity: Lessons from the Chilean Experience (Johns Hopkins University Press: Baltimore), published for Resources for the Future, Inc.

David, P.A. and T. van de Klundert (1965). Biased efficiency growth and capital–labor substitution in the U.S., American Economic Review 55: 357–394.

Davila, O. (1966). A small econometric model of Ecuador, in: Essays in Economics (Quito, Ecuador).

de Castro, S. and S. de la Cuadra (1971). Towards a new trade policy for Chile (AID: Santiago), mimeo.

de la Cruz, S. (1967). Actualización del Texto Oficial Elaborado en 1965 por el Ministerio de Relaciones Exteriores Relativo a los bases Juridicos y Aministrativos de los Restricciones a las Importaciones de Chile, Boletín Mensual del Banco Central (September).

Deprano, M.E. and J.B. Nugent (1966). A global financial model of Ecuador (Junta Nacional de Planificación: Quito), mimeo.

Diaz-Alejandro, C. (1976). Foreign Trade Regimes and Economic Development: Colombia (Columbia University Press: New York).

Diz, A.C. (1966). Money and prices in Argentina, 1935–1962, Ph.D. dissertation (University of Chicago: Chicago).

Durán Downing, L. and J. F. Solís (1975). Proyecto de un modelo econométrico para Nicaragua (Banco Central: Managa), mimeo.

Dutta, M. and V. Su (1969). An econometric model of Puerto Rico, Review of Economics and Statistics, 26: 319–334.

Eckaus, R.S. (1955). The factor-proportions problem in underdeveloped areas, American Economic Review, 45: 539–565.

Eckaus, R.S. (1967a). Notes on some features of the Chilean national income accounts (ODEPLAN: Santiago), mimeo.

Eckaus, R.S. (1967b). Questions concerning the Chilean national income accounts (ODEPLAN: Santiago), mimeo.

Eckaus, R.S. and K.S. Parikh (1968). Planning for growth: multisectoral, intertemporal models applied to India (MIT: Cambridge, Mass.).

ECLA (1970). Economic Survey of Latin America (New York: United Nations).

Edel, M. (1969). Food Supply and Inflation in Latin America (Praeger: New York).

Eisner, R. (1960). A distributed lag investment function, Econometrica, 28: 1–29.

Eisner, R. (1967). A permanent income theory for investment: some empirical explorations, American Economic Review, 57: 363–390 (June).

Eisner, R. (1969a). Investment and the frustrations of econometricians, American Economic Review Proceedings, 59: 50–64.

Eisner, R. (1969b). Tax policy and investment behavior: comment, American Economic Review, 59: 379–388.

Eisner, R. and M.I. Nadiri (1968). Investment behavior and neo-classical theory, Review of Economics and Statistics, 50: 368–382.

Eisner, R. and R.H. Strotz (1963). Determinants of business investment, in: Commission on Money and Credit, Impacts of Monetary Policy (Prentice-Hall: Englewood Cliffs) pp. 59–337.

Ellsworth, P.T. (1945). Chile: An Economy in Transition (Macmillan: New York).

Escuela Nacional de Economía (1970). Un modelo de política económica para México (Universidad Nacional Autónoma de México: Mexico City).

Evans, M.K. (1969). An agricultural submodel for the U.S. economy, in: Essays in Industrial Econometrics, 2 (Economics Research Unit, University of Pennsylvania: Philadelphia), pp. 63–146.

Fei, J.D. and G. Ranis (1964). Development of the Labor Surplus Economy: Theory and Policy (Irwin: Homewood, Illinois).

Ffrench-Davis, R. and Camilo C. (1969). Chile: Cuatro Anos de Experiencia con una Nueva Política de Tipo de Cambio, Boletín Mensual de Banco Central 498 (August).

Ffrench-Davis, Ricardo (1971). Economic policies and stabilization programs: Chile, 1952–1969, Ph.D. dissertation (University of Chicago: Chicago).

Fisher, F. M. (1969). The existence of aggregate production functions, Econometrica, 37: 533–577 (Oct.).

Fisher, F.M. (1971). Discussion, in: G. Fromm (ed.), Tax Incentives and Capital Spending (The Brookings Institute: Washington), pp. 243–255.

Fletcher, L. P. (1965). Some aspects of economic development in Trinidad, 1951 to 1959, Ph.D. dissertation (Brown University).

Friedman, M. (1974). Monetary policy in developing countries, in: Paul A. David and Melvin W. Reed (eds.), Nations and Households in Economic Growth: Essays in Honor of Moses Abramovitz (Academic Press: New York), pp. 265–278.

Fukuchi, T. (1973). An econometric model for the Indonesian economy (Department of Economics, International Christian University), mimeo.

García, E. (1964). Inflation in Chile: a quantitative analysis, Ph.D. dissertation (MIT: Cambridge, Mass.).

Geithmann, D.T. (1964). Money and income in Columbia, 1950–1960, Ph.D. dissertation (University of Florida).

Goldfeld, S.M., R.E. Quandt and H.F. Trotter (1966). Maximization by quadratic hill-climbing, Econometrica, 34: 541–551.

Gomez, J. (1968). Trade projections for Agrentina (UNCTAD), mimeo.

Gregory, P. (1967). Industrial Wages in Chile (Cornell University, New York State School of Industrial and Labor Relations: Ithaca).

Griffin, K. (1964). Underdevelopment in Spanish America: An Interpretation (MIT: Cambridge).

Gunder-Frank, A. (1972). La política económica en Chile – del frente popular a la unidad popular, Punto Final, 153.

Gupta, S. (1974). Econometric model for Argentina (IBRD: Washington), mimeo.

Haberler, G. (1961). The terms of trade and economic development, in: H. Ellis and H. Wallich (eds.), Economic Development for Latin America (St. Martin's: New York), pp. 275–307.

Hachette, D. (1966). Efectos de la sobrevaluación del escudo en la distribución del ingreso en Chile, Cuadernos de Economía, 3.

Hall, R.E. and D.W. Jorgenson (1967). Tax policy and investment behavior, American Economic Review, 57: 391–414.

Hall, R.E. and D.W. Jorgenson (1969). Tax policy and investment behavior: reply and further results, American Economic Review, 59: 388–401 (June).

Hall, R.E. and D.W. Jorgenson (1971). Application of the theory of optimum capital accumulation, in: G. Fromm (ed.), Tax Incentives and Capital Spending (The Brookings Institute: Washington), pp. 9–60.

Hall, R.E. and R.C. Sutch (1969). A flexible infinite distributed lag (University of California: Berkeley), mimeo.

Hansen, B. (1973). Simulation of fiscal, monetary and exchange policy in a primitive economy: Afghanistan, in: H.C. Bos, H. Linneman and P. deWolff (eds.), Economic Structure and Development (North-Holland: Amsterdam), pp. 215–237.

Harberger, A. (1963). The dynamics of inflation in Chile, in: C. Christ (ed.), Measurements in Economics (Stanford University Press: Stanford).

Harberger, A.C. and M. Selowsky (1966). Key factors in the economic growth of Chile: an analysis of the sources of past growth and of prospects for 1965–1970, paper presented at conference on The Next Decade of Latin American Economic Development.

Harris, D.J. (1970). Saving and foreign trade as constraints in economic growth: a study of Jamaica, Social and Economic Studies, 19: 147–177.

Helliwell, J. (1971). Aggregate investment equations: a survey of issues (Monash University: Melbourne), seminar paper No. 9.

Hernandez, R. (1974). National-regional macroeconometric model for Argentina, paper presented to the NBER-Colegio de Mexico conference (Mexico City).

Hines, A.G. (1964). Trade unions and wage inflation in the United Kingdom, 1893–1961, Review of Economic Studies, 31: 221–252 (Oct.).

Hines, A.G. (1968). Unemployment and the rate of change of money wages in the United Kingdom: a reappraisal, Review of Economics and Statistics, 40: 60–67 (Feb.).

Hirschman, A.O. (1962). Development Projects Observed (The Brookings Institute: Washington).

Hirschman, A.O. (1963). Journeys Toward Progress: Studies of Economic Policy-Making in Latin America, ch. 3, Inflation in Chile (Columbia University Press: New York), 159–223.

Hobsbaum, E.J. (1971). A special supplement: Chile: Year one, New York Review of Books (September), pp. 23–32.

Houthakker, H.S. and L.D. Taylor (1970). Consumer Demand in the United States: Analysis and Projections (Harvard University Press: Cambridge), 2nd ed.

Huddle, D. L. (1972). Disequilibrium foreign exchange systems and the generation of industrialization and inflation in Brazil, Economia Internazionale, 25: 1–22.

Humuel Tleel, C. (1969). El sector público Chileno entre 1830 y 1930 (Universidad de Chile, Facultad de Ciencias Económicas: Santiago), memoria.

Hurtado Ruiz-Tagle, C. (1966). Population concentration and economic development: the Chilean case, Ph.D. dissertation (Harvard University: Cambridge).

IMF and IBRD (1953–1972). Direction of Trade (Washington). Before 1957 entitled Direction of International Trade by UN, IMF, and IBRD.

IMF (1950b–1972b). Exchange Restrictions Report (Washington).

Inada, Ken-ichi (1968). Development in monocultural economies (Stanford University, Institute for Mathematical Studies in the Social Sciences: Stanford).

Instituto de Economía (1958–1971). Encuesta Trimestral de Cesantía (Universidad de Chile: Santiago).

Instituto de Economía (1956). Desarrollo Económico de Chile, 1940–1956 (Instituto de Economía, Universidad de Chile: Santiago).

Instituto de Economía (1963). La Economía de Chile en el Periodo 1950–1963 (Instituto de Economía, Universidad de Chile: Santiago).

Iton, J.W. (1968). Economic development and the external sector (with reference to post-war Brazil), Ph.D. dissertation (Johns Hopkins University: Baltimore).

Jeanneret, T. (1971). The structure of protection in Chile, in: B. Balassa et al., The Structure of Protection in Developing Countries (Johns Hopkins University Press: Baltimore), pp. 103–136.

Johnson, L.J. (1967). Problems of import substitution: The Chilean automobile industry, Economic Development and Cultural Change, 15: 2 (January), 202–216.

Johnston, J. (1963). Econometric Methods (McGraw-Hill: New York).

Joo Arredondo, S. (1970). Distribucíon sectoral del crédito en moneda corriente y extranjera (Banco Central: Santiago), mimeo.

Jorgenson, D.W. (1963). Capital theory and investment behavior, American Economic Review Proceedings, 53: 247–259.

Jorgenson, D.W. (1965). Anticipation and investment behavior, in: J.S. Duesenberry et al. (eds.), The Brookings Quarterly Econometric Model of the United States (Chicago), pp. 35–92.

Jorgenson, D. (1971). Econometric studies of investment behavior: a survey, Journal of Economic Literature, 9(4): 1111–1147.

Jorgenson, D.W. and C.D. Siebert (1968). A comparison of alternative theories of corporate investment behavior, American Economic Review, 59: 681–712.

Jorgenson, D.W. and J.A. Stephenson (1967a). Investment behavior in U.S. manufacturing, 1947–1960, Econometrica, 35: 169–220.

Jorgenson, D.W. and J.A. Stephenson (1967b). The time structure of investment behavior in U.S. manufacturing, 1947–1960, Review of Economics and Statistics, 49: 16–27.

Jul, L. A. (1969). Diversificación de exportaciones: el caso Chileno (Universidad de Chile: Santiago), memoria.

Kaldor, N. (1959). Economic growth and the problem of inflation – part II, Economica 26: 287–298.

Katz, J.M. (1969). Production Functions, Foreign Investment and Growth: A study based on the Argentine Manufacturing Sector, 1946–1961 (North-Holland: Amsterdam) (Contributions to Economic Analysis No. 58).

Kelso, C.M., Jr. (1973). An econometric study of the Peruvian economy (mimeo.).

Khan, M.S. (1974). Experiments with a monetary model for the Venezuelan economy, International Monetary Fund Staff Papers, 21: 389–413.

Kindleberger, C.P. (1956). The Terms of Trade (Wiley: New York).

Klein, L.R. (1960). Some theoretical issues in the measurement of capacity, Econometrica, 28: 274.

Klein, L.R. (1974). Issues in econometric studies of investment behavior, Journal of Economic Literature, 43–49.

Klein, L.R. and R. Summers (1966). The Wharton Index of Capacity Utilization (Economics Research Unit, University of Pennsylvania: Philadelphia).

Klein, L.R. and P. Taubman (1971). Estimating effects within a complete econometric model, in: G. Fromm (ed.), Tax Incentives and Capital Spending (The Brookings Institute: Washington), pp. 197–242.

Krueger, A.O. (1972). The political economy of the rent-seeking society (University of Minnesota: Minneapolis), mimeo.

Kuh, E. (1967). A productivity theory of wage levels – an alternative to the Phillips curve, Review of Economic Studies, 34: 333–362.

Kuznets, S. (1966). Modern Economic Growth: Rate, Structure and Spread (Yale University Press: New Haven).

Lagos Escobar, R. (1966). La Industria en Chile: Antecedentes Estructurales (Universidad de Chile, Instituto de Economía: Santiago).

Lau, Lawrence (1975). A bibliography of macroeconomic models of developing economics (Stanford: Palo Alto), mimeo.

Lawrsen, K. (1967). Macroeconomic relationships in Columbia (Bogota), mimeo.

Lawrsen, K. and L.D. Taylor (1968). Unemployment, productivity and growth in Columbia (Bogota), mimeo.

Leftwich, R.H. (1966). Exchange rate policies, balance of payments, and trade restrictions in Chile, Economic Development and Cultural Change, 14: 400–413 (Feb.).

Leibenstein, H. (1957). Economic Backwardness and Economic Growth: Studies in the Theory of Economic Development (Wiley: New York).

Levinson, J. and J. de Onís (1970). The alliance that lost its way: A critical report on the Alliance for Progress (Quadrangle-20th Century Fund).

Lewis, W.A. (1954). Economic development with unlimited supplies of labor, The Manchester School, 22: 139–191 (May).

Líbano, D. (1970). El Tipo de Cambio en Chile desde 1948, Boletín Mensual de Banco Central, 722–734.

Lira, Ricardo (1975). Un modelo macroeconometrico de Corto Plazo y de dos sectores para la economía Chilena, Cuadernos de Economía, 12: 63–94.

Liu, J.C. and B.A. De-Vries (1969). An econometric model of inflation and growth in Brazil, paper presented at Econometric Society N.Y. (mimeo).

Luders, R. (1970). Historia monetaria de Chile, 1925–1958, Cuadernos de Economía, 20.

McCabe, J.L. (1970). Two non-linear planning models of Turkey, Ph.D. dissertation (University of Pennsylvania: Philadelphia).

Mamalakis, M. (1965). Public policy and sectoral development: a case study of Chile, 1940–1958, in: M. Mamalakis and C. Reynolds (eds.), Essays on the Chilean Economy (Irwin: Homewood, Illinois), pp. 1–203.

Mamalakis, M. (1967a). The American copper companies and the Chilean government, 1920–1967: profile of an export sector (Yale University, Economic Growth Center: New Haven).

Mamalakis, M. (1967b). Negative personal saving in the Chilean national accounts: an artifact or reality? (Yale University, Economic Growth Center: New Haven), Discussion Paper No. 36 (mimeo).

Mamalakis, M. (1967c). Historical Statistics of Chile (Economic Growth Center, Yale University: New Haven), mimeo.

Mamalakis, M. (1969). An analysis of the financial and investment activities of the Chilean development corporation: 1939–1964, Journal of Development Studies 5(2): 118–137 (Jan.).

Mamalakis, M. (1971a). Contribution of copper to Chilean economic development, 1920–1967: profile of a foreign-owned export sector, in: R. Mikesell (ed.), Foreign Investment in the Petroleum and Mineral Industries: Case Studies of Investor–Host Country Relations (Johns Hopkins University Press, published for Resources for the Future: Baltimore).

Mamalakis, M. (1971b). The Growth and Structure of the Chilean Economy (Yale University, Economic Growth Center: New Haven), mimeo.

Maneshi, A. and C.W. Reynolds (1964). The effect of import substitution on foreign exchange needs, savings rates and growth in Latin America (Yale University, Economic Growth Center: New Haven), Discussion Paper No. 18.

Manhertz, H. (1971). An exploratory econometric model for Jamaica, Social and Economic Studies, 20: 198–226.

Manne, A.S. (1974). Multi-sector models for development planning: a survey, Journal of Development Economics 1(1): 43–70 (June).

Marshall, S.J. (1967). Inflation and economic development, a case study: the Chilean experience 1937–1950, Ph.D. thesis (Harvard University: Cambridge, Mass).

Marwah, K. (1969). An econometric model of Colombia: a prototype devaluation view, Econometrica, 37: 228–251.

Marzouk, M.S.H. (1969). The predictability of predetermined variables in macro-econometric models for developing economies, Ph.D. dissertation (University of Pennsylvania: Philadelphia).

Maynard, G. and W. von Rijckeghem (1965). Stabilization policy in an inflationary economy, in: G. Papanek (ed.), Development Policy: Theory and Practice (Harvard University Press: Cambridge, Mass.).

Merrill, W.C., L.B. Fletcher, R. Hoffman and M. Applegate (1975). Panama's Economic Development: The Role of Agriculture (Iowa State University Press: Ames).

Meza, W. (1967). La inversión geográfica bruta en capital fijo por sectores de destino, periodo 1962–1966 (ODEPLAN: Santiago), mimeo.

Mikesell, R.F. (1971). Conflict and accommodation in Chilean copper, in: R.F. Mikesell (ed.), Foreign Investment in the Petroleum and Mineral Industries: Case Studies of Investor–Host Country Relations (Johns Hopkins University Press, published for Resources for the Future: Baltimore), pp. 369–386.

Ministerio de Relaciones Exteriors (1970). Acuerdo de integración subregional, antecedentes texto documentacion (Santiago, Secretaria Ejecutiva Alalc-Chile, Publicación No. 18.

Molina, C. and P. Mellor (1974). A shortrun macroeconomic model of the Chilean economy (Catholic University: Santiago), mimeo.

Montemayor, R. (1974). An econometric model of the financial sector: the case of Mexico, Ph.D. dissertation (University of Pennsylvania: Philadelphia).

Monterio, J.V. (1971). Uma análise de macromodele da economia Brasileirá, PUC-RJ (Catholic University: Rio de Janeiro).

Moran, T.H. (1970). The multinational corporation and the politics of development: the case of copper in Chile, 1945–1970, Ph.D. thesis (Harvard University: Cambridge, Mass.).

Morawetz, D. (1974). Employment implications of industrialization in developing countries: a survey, The Economic Journal.

Morgan, T. (1959). The long-run terms of trade between agriculture and manufacturing, Economic Development and Cultural Change, 1–23.

Muñoz, G., Oscar (1968). Crecimiento Industrial de Chile 1914–1965 (Universidad de Chile, Instituto de Economía y Planificación: Santiago).

Naranjo-Villalobos, F.E. (1970). Un modelo macroeconométrico de política fiscal para Costa Rica (San José: Costa Rica), mimeo.

Naranjo-Villalobos, F.E. (1972). Macroeconomic policy in Costa Rica, Ph.D. dissertation (University of Pennsylvania: Philadelphia).

Naranjo-Villalobos, F.E. (1974). An econometric model for Honduras (San José: Costa Rica), mimeo.

Naylor, T.H., M. Shubik, M. Fioravante and I.A.S. Ibrahim (1974). A simulation model of the economy of Brazil, in: N. Ruggles (ed.), The Role of the Computer in Economic and Social Research in Latin America (Columbia University Press: New York), pp. 151–160.

Nerlove, M. (1967). Recent empirical studies of the CES and related production functions, in: The Theory and Empirical Analysis of Production (National Bureau of Economic Research, Studies in Income and Wealth: New York), vol. 31.

Nugent, J.B. (1965). Country study: Argentina (Agency for International Development, Summer Research Report Series: Washington), mimeo.

Nugent, J.B. (1974). Economic Integration in Central America: Empirical Investigations (Johns Hopkins University Press: Baltimore).

ODEPLAN (1968). Capacidad utilizada de la industria manufacturera, 1964–1965–1966 (ODEPLAN: Santiago), mimeo.

ODEPLAN (1970a). Cuentas Nacionales de Chile, 1960–1969 (ODEPLAN: Santiago).

ODEPLAN (1970b). Macro de referencia cuantitativo preliminar para la elaboración del programa 1970–1980 (ODEPLAN: Santiago).

ODEPLAN (1970c). Cuadro de Transacciones Intersectoriales para la Economía Chileno, 1962 (ODEPLAN: Santiago).

ODEPLAN (1975). Cuentos Nacionales de Chile, 1965–1973 (ODEPLAN: Santiago).

Okun, A.M. (1962). Potential GNP: its measurement and significance, Proceedings of the Business and Economics Section of the American Statistical Association.

Oury, B. (1966). A Production Model for Wheat and Feedgrains in France (North-Holland: Amsterdam).

Pandit, V. (1971). Sources of inflation in developing economies: case studies of Colombia, India, Korea and Taiwan, Ph.D. dissertation (University of Pennsylvania: Philadelphia).

Papanek, G.F. (1973). Aid, foreign private investment, savings, and growth in less developed countries, Journal of Political Economy, 81: 120–130.

Papanek, G.F. (1972). The effect of aid and other resource transfers on savings and growth in less developed countries, Economic Journal, 327.

Pazos, F. (1972). Chronic Inflation in Latin America, trans. Ernesto Cuesta (Praeger: New York).

Perez-Castillo, J.P., et al. (1963). Dynamic Models for Simulating the Venezuelan Economy (Simulmatics Corporation: Washington).

Phillips, A. (1958). The relation between unemployment and the rate of change of money wage rates in the United Kingdom, 1861–1957, Economica, New Series, 25: 283–299.

Phillips, A. (1963). An appraisal of measures of capacity, American Economic Review, 53: 275–292.

Picks' Currency Yearbook, 1960–1972 (New York).

Pinto Santa Cruz, A. (1960). Ni Estabilidad ni Desarrollo: La Política del Fundo Monetaria (Editorial del Pacifico: Santiago).

Pinto Santa Cruz, A. (1962). Chile, un caso de desarrollo frustrado, 2nd ed. (Editorial Universitario: Santiago).

Pisciotta, J.L. (1971). Development policy, inflation and politics in Chile, 1938–1958: an essay in political economy, Ph.D. dissertation (University of Texas: Austin).

Prebisch, R. (1959). Commercial policy in the underdeveloped countries, American Economic Review 44 (May), 251–273.

Prebisch, R. (1961). Economic development or monetary stability: the false dilemma, Economic Bulletin for Latin America, 4.

Pujol, J.P. (1969). An econometric model of Argentina (University of Pennsylvania: Philadelphia), mimeo.

Ramos, J. (1968). Políticas de remuneraciones en Chile (Universidad de Chile, Instituto de Economía y Planificación: Santiago), mimeo.

Rao, V.K. (1952). Investment, income and the multiplier in an underdeveloped economy, The Indian Economic Review; reprinted in: A. Agarwala and S. Singh (eds.) (1963). The Economics of Underdevelopment (Oxford: New York).

Reinafarje, W. and M. Yepez (1972). An econometric model of Peru (University of Pennsylvania: Philadelphia), mimeo.

Reynolds, C.W. (1965). Development problems of an export economy: the case of Chile and copper, in: M. Mamalakis and A.W. Reynolds (eds.), Essays on the Chilean Economy (Irwin: Homewood, Illinois), pp. 203–393.

Rosenstein-Rodan, P.N. (1961). Notes on the theory of the 'Big Push', in: H.S. Ellis (ed.), Economic Development for Latin America (St. Martin's Press: New York).

Seers, D. (1963). A theory of inflation and growth in underdeveloped countries based on the experience of Latin America, Oxford Economic Papers, 192–195.

Selowsky, M. (1970). Política cambiaria y asignación de recurso (Center of Economic Investigation, Catholic University of Chile: Santiago).

Senado, Oficina de Informaciones (1971). Cobre: Antecedents Económics y Estadisticas Relacionades con la Gran Minería del Cobre, Boletín de Información Economica No. 208 (Santiago).

SIECA (Secretaria Permanente del Trátado General de Intergración Económica Centroamericana) (1973). Evolución 1960–1970, perspectivas y 1970–1980, El Desarrollo Integrado de Centroamérica en la Presente Decada, vol. 2, anexo 1.

Sierra, E. (1969). Tres Ensayos de Estabilización en Chile: Las Politicas Aplicadas en el Decenio 1956–1956 (Editorial Universitaria: Santiago).

Simler, N.J. and A. Tella (1968). Labor reserves and the Phillips curve, Review of Economics and Statistics, 40: 32–49.

Slooten, R.V. (1968). A macroeconomic analysis of the medium-term economic development prospects of Peru, Ph.D. dissertation (Iowa State University: Ames).

Stahl, J.E. (1965). An application of a Klein growth model to Puerto Rico, 1947–61, Economic Development and Cultural Change, 13: 463–471.

Stavrou, J. and Arboleda, H. (1975). An econometric model of the Panamanian economy (Wharton Econometric Forecasting Associates Inc.: Philadelphia), mimeo.

Steed, L.D. (1969). The nature of economic fluctuations in Argentina: an econometric study, Ph.D. dissertation (Columbia University: New York).

Stewart, G.T. (1966). The economic development of Uruguay, 1936–1961, Ph.D. dissertation (University of Alabama: Tuscaloosa).

Summers, R. (1968). Further results in the measurement of capacity utilization, Proceedings of the Business and Economics Section of the American Statistical Association, 26–29.

Sunkel, O. (1963). El fracaso de las politicas de estabilización en el contexto Latino Americano, Trimestre Económico, 30.

Sunkel, O. (1967). Polítics nacional de desarrollo y dependencia externa, Estudios Internacionales (May).

Sutton, D.S. (1968). A model of self-generating inflation, The Argentina case, Ph.D. dissertation (Michigan State University).

Taubman, P. (1975). The determinants of earnings: genetics, family and other environments – a study of white male twins (University of Pennsylvania), mimeo.

Taylor, L.D. (1969a). A small econometric model of Colombia (Bogota), mimeo.

Taylor, L.D. (1969b). Macroeconomics and fiscal policy in an import constrained underdeveloped country: the case of Colombia, Revista de Planeación y Desarrolo, 1: 1–30.

Taylor, L. (1974). Short-term policy in open developing economies: the narrow limits of the possible, Journal of Development Economies, 1: 85–104.

Taylor, L. and S.L. Black (1973). Practical general equilibrium estimation of resource pulls under trade liberation, Journal of International Economics 3.

The Economist Intelligence Unit (1960–1972). Quarterly Economic Review of Chile.

Theil, H. and C.B. Tilamus. The demand for production factors and the price sensitivity of input–output coefficients, International Economic Review, 7: 258–273.

Thorbecke, E. (1969). Structure and performance of the Guatemalan economy, 1950–1966 (mimeo.).

Thorbecke, E. and A. Condos (1966). Macroeconomic growth and development models of the Peruvian economy, in: I. Adelman and A. Thorbecke (eds.), The Theory and Design of Economic Development (Johns Hopkins University Press: Baltimore), pp. 181–209.

Tintner, G., I. Consigliere and J.T.M. Carneiro (1970). Un modélo econometrico aplicado à economia brasileira, Revista Brasileira de Economia, 24: 5–29.

Tintner, G., W. Den Hertog, P. Bello and M.T. Carrino (1970). Un modelo econometrico aplicado a la economia mexicana (mimeo.).

Torres, T.C. (1969). Analisis evaluativo de los indices de comercio exterior calculados en Chile, Analisis Serie B.

United Nations (1964). Studies in Long-Term Economic Projections for the World Economy: Aggregate Models, UN Doc. ST/ECA/80.

UNCTAD (1968). Trade Prospects and Capital Needs of Developing Countries, UN Doc. TD/34/Rev. 1.

UNCTAD (1972). Developing countries in project LINK (Argentina, Brazil, India, Mexico, Venezuala, regional).

UNCTAD (1973). Models for developing countries, in: R.J. Ball (ed.), the International Linkage of National Economic Models (North-Holland: Amsterdam), pp. 109–176.

United Nations, Economic Commission for Asia and the Far East (UNECAFE) (1960). Programming Techniques for Economic Development (United Nations: Bangkok).

United Nations, Industrial Development Organization (UNIDO) (1969). Conference on excess capacity in the developing countries (mimeo.).

Von Rijckeghem, W. (1965a). A model of inflation in the Argentine economy, 1950–1963 (Consejo Nacional de Desarrollo–Harvard Development Advisory Service: Buenos Aires).

Von Rijckeghem, W. (1965b). A stabilization model for the Argentine economy (Consejo Nacional de Desarrollo–Harvard Development Advisory Service: Buenos Aires).

Von Rijckeghem, W. (1969). An econometric model of a dual economy in the case of Puerto Rico, paper presented to the European meeting of the Econometric Society (Brussels).

Vuskovic, P. (1971). La presencia de Chile en el CIAP, presented to CIAP subcommittee on Chile in February 1971 and reprinted in Banco Central, Boletín Mensual, pp. 385–399.

Wachter, S. (1974). Latin American structural and monetarist inflation theories: an application to Chile, Ph.D. dissertation (Boston College: Chesnut Hill).

Weisskopf, T.E. (1972). An econometric test of alternative constraints in the growth of underdeveloped countries, The Review of Economics and Statistics, 54: 67–78.

Winston, G.C. (1969). Capacity utilization in economic development (Williams College: Williamstown, Mass.), mimeo.

Yoon, Y. (1974). Skilled labor as a factor of production and its implications for international trade, Ph.D. dissertation (Bryn Mawr College: Bryn Mawr).

Young, R.M. (1972). Macro-decision making under uncertainty: some theoretical and simulation results, Ph.D. dissertation (University of Pennsylvania: Philadelphia).

Yver, R.E. (1970). Dinámica del ajuste de la tasa de inflación: el caso Chileno (Centro de Investigaciones Económicas, Universidad Católica de Chile: Santiago), mimeo.

Zaidi, M.A. (1969). The Determination of money wage rate change and unemployment – inflation 'Trade-off' in Canada, International Economic Review, 10: 207–219.

Zorilla, A. (1970). Exposición Sobre la Política Económica del Goberno y del Estado de la Hacienda Pública, Minister of Finance, presented to the Joint Budget Commission, 27 November 1970 and printed in Banco Central, Boletin Mensual, pp. 1477–1492.

APPENDIX

Data for the macroeconometric model

The model includes 72 exogenous variables and 172 endogenous variables. Space limitations preclude the reproduction here of all of these data. Most of the sources, however, are standard Chilean publications. In addition, most of the basic national income accounts data, as well as many other useful Chilean historical data, are in Mamalakis (1967a). Furthermore, the text of the present book provides substantial examination of important secular tendencies and deviations from those tendencies for the basic data and for important ratios. For critiques of the basic data, see Ballesteros and Davis (1963), Behrman (1973b, 1975b), Corbo (1971, 1974), Eckaus (1967a, 1967b), Ffrench-Davis (1971), García (1964), Hurtado (1966), Instituto de Economía (1956, 1963), Lagos (1966), Mamalakis (1967b, 1967c), Marshall (1957), ODEPLAN (1970a, 1970c, 1975), Pinto (1962), Ramos (1968), Sierra (1969), and Wachter (1974).

This appendix is divided into three sections. Section A.1 gives the sources, definitions, units, and some summary statistics. Section A.2 considers the relations between the CORFO and ODEPLAN national accounts. Section A.3 discusses alternative calculations of the deflators for value added.

A.1. Definitions, sources, and units

Table A.1 lists the variables, sources, units of measurement and some additional summary statistics for the sample period. The 72 exogenous variables are divided into seven groups: government domestic fiscal policies (8 variables), domestic monetary policies

Table
Variables, sources, units and some additional summary

Variables[a]	Sources[b]

EXOGENOUS
Government domestic fiscal policies
   1. Total net subsidies
   2. Government *GDP*
   3. Government consumption[e]
   4. Direct and indirect government investment[g]   Instituto de Economía (1963), Mamalakis (1971b),[b]
   5. Amortization of government debt[g]   h
   6. Interest paid on government debt[g]
   7. Direct taxes on large-scale mining[g,e]
   8. Legal cost of production in large-scale mining[g]
Domestic monetary policies
   9. Marginal reserve rate, demand deposits   h
 10. Marginal reserve rate, time deposits   h
 11. Average reserve rate, demand deposits   h
 12. Average reserve rate, time deposits   h
 13. Rediscount dummy (1.0 in 1945–1955)
 14. Bank rate of interest   h
 15. Central Bank loans to banks and private sector[g]   h
 16. Central Bank loans to government[g]   h
 17. Central Bank loans to private sector[g]   h
 18. Residual change in monetary base[g,i]   h
International sector policies
 19. Quantitative restrictions index, total imports   Ffrench-Davis (1971)
 20. Quantitative restrictions index, *GDP*[j]   Behrman (1975b)
 21. Quantitative restrictions, investment   Behrman (1975b)
 22. Quantitative restrictions, wholesale   Behrman (1975b)
 23. Prior deposit rate on imports   Ffrench-Davis (1971)/nominal imports
 24. Exchange rate, general
 25. Exchange rate, large-scale mining   h
 26. Exchange rate, services   h
 27. Trade policy adjustment, consumer goods[k]
 28. Trade policy adjustment, intermediate goods
 29. Trade policy adjustment, capital goods
 30. Transfers to government from abroad[g]
Income policies
 31. Minimum wage (*sueldo vital*)   h
 32. Secular government employment[e]   Spottke (1965)
International market conditions
 33. Import unit values, total   Behrman (1975b), h
 34. Import unit values, consumer goods   Behrman (1975b), h
 35. Import unit values, capital goods   Behrman (1975b), h
 36. Import unit values, intermediate goods   Behrman (1975b), h
 37. Import unit values, habitual consumer goods   Behrman (1975b), h
 38. Import unit values, secondary consumer goods   Behrman (1975b), h
 39. Import unit values, machinery and equipment goods   Behrman (1975b), h
 40. Import unit values, other intermediate goods   Behrman (1975b), h
 41. Import unit values, other capital goods   Behrman (1975b), h
 42. Import unit values, primary materials   Behrman (1975b), h

A.1
statistics for data in Chilean macroeconometric model.

Units[e]	Summary statistics for 1946–1965		
	Mean	Standard deviation from secular trends as percentage of mean	Exponential annual average growth rate
	221	27.6	11.3
	1215	11.2	4.3
	1409	6.9	4.6
	183	28.5	32.4
	126	15.8	26.5
	8	72.4	27.4
	69	29.5	31.4
10⁶ US dollars	78	14.9	4.2
unitless	0.339	51.6	8.0
unitless	0.231	95.1	14.2
unitless			
unitless			
unitless	0.132	8.9	2.9
	142	46.9	26.7
	281	97.5	35.4
	173	61.9	27.0
	− 123	−223.9	−12.6
	0.956	2.2	−0.0
	0.959	17.4	−1.6
	0.923	11.7	−1.8
	0.937	15.5	−1.1
unitless	0.016	38.1	−10.3
escudo/dollar	0.700	22.9	27.2
escudo/dollar	0.707	39.3	33.4
escudo/dollar	0.947	24.5	25.3
unitless			
unitless			
unitless			
	13	41.7	−19.9
escudo/month			26.4
	194	1.9	2.9
	1.03	7.0	0.0
	0.924	8.2	−0.0
	0.886	7.9	2.5
	1.30	13.0	−1.6
1965 = 100	30.7	12.6	−1.9
	1.28	14.8	−2.2
1965 = 100	22.1	6.5	2.7
1965 = 100	33.2	13.4	−1.3
1965 = 100	125	7.9	2.5
	1.25	12.8	−1.8

Table A.1
Variables, sources, units and some additional summary

Variables[a]	Sources[b]
43. Export unit values, total	Behrman (1975b), h
44. Export unit values, agriculture	Behrman (1975b), h
45. Export unit values, mining	Behrman (1975b), h
46. Export unit values, large-scale mining	Behrman (1975b), h
47. Export unit values, other mining	Behrman (1975b), h
48. Export unit values, industrial	Behrman (1975b), h
49. Spot copper price, London Metal Exchange	Behrman (1975b), h
50. Spot copper price, United States	Behrman (1975b), h
51. United States wholesale price index, total	Economic Report of the President (1972)
52. United States wholesale price index, farm products	Economic Report of the President (1972)
53. United States industrial production index	Economic Report of the President (1972)
54. Argentinian *GDP* index	United Nations (1963, 1970)
55. Adjustment for variation in terms of trade	
56. Transfers from abroad	
57. Net transfers on current account	
58. Residual balance of payments items	
59. Other Central Bank international reserves	h
Domestic variables not under Government control	
60. Total labor force[e]	Spottke (1965)
61. Non-industrial union membership	
62. Gross investment, services and construction[e]	m
63. Gross investment, mining[e]	Zaldivar (1967)
64. Interest paid on private debt[g]	
65. Loans of banks to government	h
66. Population	h
Other	
67. Time (1945 = 1)	
68. Statistical discrepancy, disposable income[g]	n
69. Statistical discrepancy, government account[g]	n
70. Statistical discrepancy, national income[g]	n
71. Statistical discrepancy, *GDP*[g]	n
72. Statistical discrepancy, stock change	n
ENDOGENOUS	
GDP capacity	o
1. A	
2. M	
3. C	
4. I	
5. T	
6. E	
7. H	
8. S	
9. G	
10. Total	p
GDP	q
11. A	
12. M	

(continued)
statistics for data in Chilean macroeconometric model.

Units[c]	Summary statistics for 1946–1965		
	Mean	Standard deviation from secular trends as percentage of mean	Exponential annual average growth rate
	0.845	16.2	2.1
	1.24	12.8	−1.8
1965 = 100	25.0	18.6	2.8
	0.819	18.6	2.7
	0.648	22.6	3.6
	1.16	9.5	−1.8
cents/pound	30.3	26.0	3.5
cents/pound	27.7	18.3	3.3
	0.914	4.9	1.4
	1.04	7.4	−0.7
1965 = 100	60.3	4.9	4.1
	878	5.4	2.1
	−296	−68.4	11.9
	12	119.1	12.6
	17	640.5	4.8
	−376	−35.2	−8.2
10^6 US dollars	−373	−34.7	−8.2
	2322	0.8	1.5
	121	11.3	0.5
	121	168.2	4.3
	46	104.5	2.3
	11	39.4	30.7
	−113	−204.3	−13.0
10^6 people	7.04	0.4	2.4
unitless			
	−8	−149.2	−6.7
	0.48	12445.3	2.5
	−11	−433.8	−4.6
	33	712.6	2.0
	−18	−246.2	−3.7
	1912	5.0	2.6
	1106	7.5	1.6
	410	7.8	6.2
	3084	5.9	3.5
	1196	7.5	3.2
	221	15.8	5.2
	1160	10.1	6.2
	5389	3.0	3.8
	1327	7.2	4.5
	15700	2.4	3.8
	1782	7.4	2.1
	943	21.8	2.1

Variables[a]	Sources[b]

13. C
14. I
15. T
16. E
17. H
18. S
19. G
20. Total

GDP deflators

21. A	r
22. M	s
23. C	t
24. I	r
25. T	u
26. E	v
27. H	w
28. S, G	x
29. Total	

Secular tendency in labor force — Spottke (1965)

30. A
31. M
32. C
33. I
34. T
35. E
36. S
37. G
38. Total

Price of labor — y

39. A
40. M
41. C
42. I
43. T
44. E
45. S
46. G

| 47. Total | z |

Price of intermediate inputs — aa

48. A
49. M
50. C
51. I
52. I
53. E

Gross domestic fixed capital investment

| 54. A | bb |
| 55. M | Zaldivar (1965) |

(continued)

statistics for data in Chilean macroeconometric model.

Units[c]	Summary statistics for 1946–1965		
	Mean	Standard deviation from secular trends as percentage of mean	Exponential annual average growth rate
	381	11.2	6.5
	2906	8.4	3.4
	1059	11.4	4.2
	180	23.3	3.3
	1049	12.6	5.9
	5069	6.0	3.7
	1215	11.2	4.3
	14531	2.6	3.8
1965 = 100	20.9	20.7	27.2
1965 = 100	20.9	30.6	29.7
1965 = 100	21.5	11.9	26.2
1965 = 100	21.8	23.1	27.1
1965 = 100	20.9	19.1	28.1
1965 = 100	18.5	21.4	29.2
1965 = 100	23.5	18.0	24.8
1965 = 100	21.9	18.5	28.5
1965 = 100	0.217	19.2	27.8
	0.537	19.4	32.4
	1.70	17.4	30.2
	1.20	25.3	28.8
	1.26	18.3	28.1
	1.12	41.7	29.3
	1.79	45.7	32.6
	0.91	13.9	30.1
	0.37	9.1	28.3
	0.898	14.1	29.8
1965 = 100	22.1	20.1	27.9
1965 = 100	23.2	27.3	26.9
1965 = 100	22.1	24.7	27.3
1965 = 100	22.0	22.9	27.3
1965 = 100	22.6	25.6	27.0
1965 = 100	21.1	23.3	28.0
	78	21.4	7.4
	46	104.5	2.3

Table A.1
Variables, sources, units and some additional summary

Variables[a]	Sources[b]
56. C + S + G	m
57. I	Lazzerini (1968), ODEPLAN (1969d)
58. T	cc
59. E	dd
60. H	
61. Total	
Capital stock	
62. A	
63. M	
64. C + S + G	
65. I	
66. T	
67. E	
68. H	
69. Total	
Price index for investment	ff
70. A	
71. M	
72. I	
73. T	
74. E	
75. H	
Cost of capital	gg
76. A	
77. M	
78. I	
79. T	
80. E	
81. H	
Exports	
82. A	
83. M, large-scale	
84. M, other	
85. I	
86. S	
87. Non-commercial	
88. Total	
Imports	hh
89. Consumer goods, habitual	
90. Consumer goods, durables	
91. Consumer goods, secondary	
92. Capital goods, machinery and equipment	
93. Capital goods, transportation equipment	
94. Intermediate goods	
95. Services	
96. Total	
Other final demand components	
97. Consumption	

(continued)
statistics for data in Chilean macroeconometric model.

Units[c]	Summary statistics for 1946–1965		
	Mean	Standard deviation from secular trends as percentage of mean	Exponential annual average growth rate
	121	168.2	4.3
	327	26.5	3.9
	348	16.7	8.8
	128	18.9	8.6
	510	22.8	0.8
	1607	11.4	4.9
	621	14.9	12.2
	1333	4.1	−2.7
	1932	12.2	7.2
	4201	6.3	6.4
	4007	3.9	5.2
	1001	5.3	11.8
	7059	3.2	3.6
	19309	5.4	5.9
	0.204	19.0	28.0
	0.218	27.3	29.3
	0.217	26.3	29.1
	0.217	25.1	28.8
	0.218	25.5	28.7
	0.235	18.0	24.8
	0.040	29.0	30.5
	0.053	35.4	31.2
	0.040	36.2	31.4
	0.044	35.6	31.0
	0.041	37.2	31.1
	0.046	28.4	27.0
	150	19.9	−1.3
	1138	13.3	1.0
	189	29.0	12.3
	125	40.7	2.9
	194	19.7	5.8
	4	57.8	−2.0
	1831	12.5	2.3
	288	19.9	6.4
	91	20.3	3.2
	48	28.3	5.2
	272	11.8	6.2
	148	51.8	3.8
	492	9.6	2.7
	184	29.6	9.0
	1536	10.9	5.8
	12815	2.7	3.9

Variables[a]	Sources[b]

98. Consumption, private
99. Consumption, government
100. Domestic savings[g]
101. Domestic savings, business[g]
102. Domestic savings, personal[g]
103. Domestic savings, government[g]
104. Depreciation
105. Investment in construction
106. Investment in buildings
107. Investment in machinery and equipment
108. Inventory change
Income
109. Disposable[g]
110. Personal[g]
111. Net domestic[g]
112. Wages and salaries[g]   ii
113. Nonwages[g]   jj
Other final demand deflators
114. Private consumption
115. Government consumption
116. Fixed investment
117. Fixed investment, construction
118. Fixed investment, buildings
119. Fixed investment, other construction
120. Fixed investment, national machinery
121. Inventory changes
122. Exports
123. Imports
Other price indices   h
124. Wholesale
125. Wholesale, intermediate goods
126. Consumer
127. Consumer, food
128. Consumer, housing
129. Consumer, clothing
130. Consumer, other
Taxes and transfers
131. Total taxes[g]
132. Direct taxes[g]
133. Direct taxes, business[g]
134. Direct taxes, business, large-scale mining[g]
135. Direct taxes, business, other[g]
136. Direct taxes, personal[g]
137. Social security, paid by employees[g]
138. Social security, paid by employers[g]
139. Indirect taxes[g]
140. Indirect taxes, imports[g]
141. Indirect taxes, production[g]

(continued)
statistics for data in Chilean macroeconometric model.

Units[c]	Summary statistics for 1946–1965		
	Mean	Standard deviation from secular trends as percentage of mean	Exponential annual average growth rate
	11407	2.8	3.8
	1409	6.9	4.6
	379	43.1	30.1
	140	81.3	31.6
	−195	78.1	−11.6
	83	113.3	32.8
	336	33.8	31.2
	743	23.8	3.5
	97	33.3	27.9
	709	15.8	8.5
	−33	−873.5	4.3
	2914	15.1	31.3
	3245	15.3	31.6
	3321	16.5	31.3
	2496	14.2	31.6
	815	27.7	30.6
	0.219	19.2	27.8
	0.219	20.2	27.8
	0.209	20.9	28.1
	0.197	18.4	27.0
	0.180	24.7	27.1
	0.217	25.7	28.6
	0.222	26.1	28.0
	0.210	24.3	27.4
	0.204	28.9	29.3
	0.216	27.3	27.1
1965 = 100	22.7	25.2	27.4
1965 = 100	30.2	40.3	29.0
1965 = 100	21.3	18.4	28.0
1965 = 100	20.5	17.1	29.2
1965 = 100	23.9	21.0	25.7
1965 = 100	23.1	24.6	27.2
1965 = 100	21.7	19.5	27.9
	841	20.1	34.0
	457	22.3	34.2
	127	26.0	33.1
	69	29.5	31.4
	58	30.3	36.0
	43	88.4	30.8
	78	20.8	33.9
	211	26.5	36.5
	383	19.5	33.8
	87	25.2	31.4
	26	26.9	22.8

Table A.1
Variables, sources, units and some additional summary

Variables[a]	Sources[b]

142. Indirect taxes, sales[g]
143. Indirect taxes, legal acts[g]
144. Indirect taxes, services[g]
145. Indirect taxes, others[g]
146. Net transfers from government[g]
147. Private transfers to government[g]
Other foreign sector variables
148. Black market exchange rate   Picks (1960–1972)
149. Net factor income from abroad[g]
150. Surplus on current account
Monetary sector
151. Net international reserves, Central Bank[g]   h
152. Net international reserves, all banks[g]   h, Ffrench-Davis (1971)
153. Monetary base[g]   Corbo (1971)
154. Bank reserves[g]   h
155. Net free reserves   kk
156. Net free reserves, including time deposit   kk
157. Money supply (year-end)[g]   h
158. Money supply (mid-year)[g]   h
159. Currency[g]   h
160. Demand deposits[g]   h
161. Time deposits[g]   h
162. Credit   h
163. Credit, to public sector   h
164. Credit, to private sector   h
165. Commercial bank credit to private   h
Other variables
166. Inventories (year-end)   mm
167. Government deficit on fiscal account   Corbo (1971)
168. Government income from enterprises & property[g]
169. Goods/services
170. *GDP* capacity for C + S + G
171–2. Summary measures for simulation results

[a]All monetary quantities are real (i.e. measured in terms of 1965 escudos) unless explicitly noted as nominal. For sectoral designations, the following first letters are used: agriculture (A), mining (M), construction (C), manufacturing (I), transportation (T), electricity, gas and water (E), housing services (H), other private services (S), government (G).

[b]Unless otherwise indicated, all data for 1940–1957 are from CORFO (1963b), all data for 1958–1963 are from CORFO (1964), and all data for 1964–1965 are from ODEPLAN (1966). These data are defined in terms of the CORFO definitions. Data for 1960–1973 in terms of the ODEPLAN definitions are from ODEPLAN (1970a, 1975). See section A.2 for a comparison of data from these two sources.

[c]Unless otherwise noted, all nominal quantities are measured in 10^6 escudos, all real quantities are measured in 10^6 1965 escudos, all labor numbers are measured in

(continued)
statistics for data in Chilean macroeconometric model.

Units[c]	Summary statistics for 1946–1965		
	Mean	Standard deviation from secular trends as percentage of mean	Exponential annual average growth rate
	190	96.5	53.4
	28	54.5	36.4
	35	42.8	29.5
	61	17.8	34.8
	296	43.4	37.2
	4	60.9	32.6
escudo/dollar	1.08	30.6	26.3
	−83.0	−151.1	−8.9
	140	146.2	10.1
10^6 US dollars	−12.6	−8.5	−12.8
10^6 US dollars	−25.3	−695.5	−15.6
	216	20.6	31.2
	32	240.2	16.7
	−2.6	−1642.9	3.4
	−8.1	−466.5	−0.0
	313	22.5	29.5
	320	19.4	28.8
	167	19.8	28.9
	146	26.5	30.2
	30	78.3	36.7
	2262	32.8	2.7
	602	44.4	14.0
	1650	25.6	−0.8
	165	43.8	27.1
	4529	3.6	1.3
	126	26.4	30.3
	37	48.1	35.5
	0.655	6.2	−1.8
	7039	2.3	3.8

10^3 people, all price and unit value and quantitative restrictions, indices and deflators have a value of 1.00 in 1965, and all prices of labor are measured in 10^3 escudos per laborer per year.

[d]Estimated from least squares regressions of natural logarithms of variable on time trend. The rates are in percentage terms.

[e]This variable may be exogenous or endogenous, depending upon the desired assumptions for a given simulation.

[f]Deflated by overall investment deflator (endogenous variable).

[g]In nominal (i.e. current) terms.

[h]Banco Central (1953–1973).

[i]This variable includes the change in the monetary base *not* due to changes in the Central Bank's holdings of international reserves, nor due to government deficits.

[j]Represents that part of the domestic to international price ratio not accounted for by movements in exchange rates, import taxes, and prior deposits on imports.

[k]Multiplicative adjustments to differentiate impact of trade policies on types of goods.

[l]Unpublished data from Dirección General de Trabajo (1969) made available to the author by Stephen Sinding.

[m]Calculated as residual, given total and other sectoral investment estimates.

[n]Calculated as residual to balance both sides of accounts.

[o]Sectoral values are defined as trend through peaks in sectoral *GDP*. See Klein and Summers (1966) and Behrman (1973b).

[p]Sum of sectoral totals.

[q]Nominal values from national accounts deflated by sectoral product price indices defined below.

[r]Sectoral component of wholesale price index in Banco Central (1953–1973).

[s]Unpublished ODEPLAN estimate on basis of unit value of mineral exports in Banco Central (1945–1969b) and the national accounts exchange rate (exogenous variable 24).

[t]Value of a square meter of construction in the private sector on the basis of projected construction in 13 to 16 communities from Banco Central (1953–1973).

[u]1940–1961: On the basis of weights for value added in 1960 from ODEPLAN (1969a), weighted average of (a) index of average railroad tariff for passengers and cargo from FF. CC. de Estado (1940–1961) and (b) index of urban autobus fares (Dirección de Estadística y Census). 1960–1965: Index of the average tariff for transportation from ODEPLAN (1969a).

[v]Based on index of average tariff of KWH from CHILECTRA (1945–1966).

[w]1940–1957, housing services component of index of cost of living, 1958–1965, housing services component of index of consumer prices; both from Banco Central (1953–1973).

[x]Calculated as a residual from the above information and the aggregate *GDP* deflator.

[y]1944–1946 and 1948–1951 from Caja de Seguro Obligatorio (1944–1951); 1952–1965, Servicio de Seguro Social (1957–1968); 1940–1943, 1947 (and all pre-1951 years

for transportation and utilities) from regression estimates between above data and 1940–1952 data from CORFO (1954).

^{z}Weighted average of sectoral values.

^{aa}Price index with base of 1965 = 100 for inputs used by indicated sectors on basis of sectoral price deflators, import deflator, and weights implied by 1962 input–output table (ODEPLAN (1970c)).

^{bb}Sum of real gross agricultural investment in machinery and equipment in ODEPLAN (1968b) and real gross investment in public irrigation works (1940–1953 from Controlería (1953–1965) 1954–1965 from MOP (1953–1965)).

^{cc}Real gross investment in vehicles (1950–1965 from ODEPLAN (1968c)) plus real gross investment in infrastructure (1950–1952 from ODEPLAN (1968d) and 1953–1965 from MOP (1953–1965)).

^{dd}Real gross investment in electricity (1945–1965 from CHILECTRA (1945–1966), 1945–1960 from ENDESA (1945–1960), 1961–1965 from ODEPLAN (1968c)) plus real gross investment in sanitary services (1940–1952 from Controlería (1953–1965) and 1953–1965 from MOP (1953–1965)).

^{ee}Calculated from sectoral gross domestic investment, sectoral depreciation, estimates from the División de Programación Global in ODEPLAN (i.e. A = 0.0333, M = 0.0796, I = 0.0222, T = 0.0385, E = 0.0263, H = 0.0367), and maximum likelihood estimates of initial capital stocks (see ch. 4).

^{ff}Weighted average of sectoral deflators and imported prices, with weights from Meza (1967).

^{gg}Calculated as in Jorgenson and Siebert (1968) from sectoral price indices for investment, product price indices, depreciation rates, and the interest and indirect business tax rates.

^{hh}Breakdown of national accounts proportional to breakdown given in Banco Central (1945–1969b).

^{ii}Calculated from wage and labor force data.

^{jj}Residual from subtracting wages and salaries from net domestic income.

^{kk}Calculated from total reserves, required average and marginal reserve rates, and deposits.

^{mm}Calculated from ODEPLAN (1969b) and change in stock estimates.

(10 variables), international sector policies (12 variables), income policies (2 variables), international market conditions (27 variables), domestic variables not under government control (7 variables), and other (6 variables). This listing points to the incorporation of a large number of policy variables in the model (a total of 32) and to the importance of international market conditions.

The 172 endogenous variables reflect the attempt to specify the model as much as is possible on the nine-sector production level (i.e. agriculture, mining, construction, manufacturing, transportation and storage, utilities, housing, other private services and government) and to include details about the endogenous functioning of fiscal, monetary, foreign-sector and income policies and their impact on the major areas of macroeconomic concern which are emphasized in the text. These variables are grouped into 20 categories: *GDP* capacities, *GDP*'s, *GDP* deflators, secular tendencies in the labor force, prices of labor, prices of intermediate inputs, gross domestic fixed capital investments, capital stocks, price indices for investment, costs of capital, exports, imports, other final demand components, incomes, other final demand deflators, other price indices, taxes and transfers, other foreign-sector variables, monetary sector, and other variables.

A.2.   Relations between CORFO and ODEPLAN national accounts

CORFO national accounts are available for 1940–1965. ODEPLAN national accounts are available starting in 1960. In order to have a reasonable number of degrees of freedom, in this study the former are utilized. However, the relation between the two sets of accounts is of interest because the latter now is commonly used and because of the desire to perform some post-sample simulations and to compare them with actual experience (see ch. 8).

Therefore, over 200 regressions between the individual variables in the ODEPLAN and CORFO national accounts have been run for the overlapping years. Space limitations preclude the presentation of all of these. However, table A.2 presents some of the most important of them for the real quantities and deflators for *GDP* by production sectors and for the major components of final demand.

Table A.2
Regressions of ODEPLAN national accounts data on CORFO national accounts data, 1960–1965[a].

Variables	Real quantities						Deflators					
	Coefficient of CORFO variable	Constant	$\bar{R}^2$	SE	DW	F	Coefficient of CORFO variable	Constant	$\bar{R}^2$	SE	DW	F
GDP by product sectors												
Agriculture	0.85 (60.5)		0.24	69	1.2	1.2	0.98 (128.3)		0.999	0.01	1.8	5.0
Mining	1.26 (32.3)		0.43	121	1.9	2.2	0.98 (90.5)		0.997	0.01	1.3	5.0
							1.02 (60.6)	−0.023 (2.4)	0.999	0.01	2.3	3671
Construction	1.55 (31.6)		0.64	71	2.3	3.2	0.90 (18.7)		0.94	0.07	1.2	4.7
	1.07 (4.3)	291 (2.0)	0.77	57	2.3	18	1.08 (11.9)	−0.120 (2.1)	0.97	0.06	2.6	142
Manufacturing	1.12 (46.8)		0.83	206	0.5	4.2	1.00 (187.7)		0.999	0.008	1.2	5.0
	1.70 (8.1)	−2035 (2.8)	0.93	135	2.2	66						
Transportation	0.44 (24.0)		0.82	64	1.4	4.1	1.12 (14.1)		0.70	0.12	0.4	3.5
	0.58 (5.2)	−189 (1.2)	0.84	61	2.4	27	0.76 (14.1)	0.239 (7.5)	0.97	0.03	2.2	198
Utilities	1.18 (66.2)		0.94	9	1.8	4.7	0.970 (66.6)		0.995	0.02	1.4	5.0
	1.00 (11.4)	37 (2.1)	0.96	7	2.6	131						

Table A.2 (continued)

Regressions of ODEPLAN national accounts data on CORFO national accounts data, 1960–1965ᵃ.

Variables	Real quantities						Deflators					
	Coefficient of CORFO variable	Constant	R̄²	SE	DW	F	Coefficient of CORFO variable	Constant	R̄²	SE	DW	F
Housing	0.40 (38.1)		−0.06	38	1.5		1.08 (34.6)		0.95	0.05	1.0	4.8
	0.20 (2.6)	306 (2.7)	0.53	25	0.5	6.7	0.92 (18.3)	0.108 (3.6)	0.98	0.03	2.2	334
Commerce	0.52 (67.6)		0.71	124	2.7		0.98 (64.9)		0.99	0.02	2.4	5.0
Banks, insurance, and real estate	0.06 (20.0)		−0.23	48	2.7		0.95 (39.5)		0.98	0.04	1.6	4.9
Services	0.28 (74.4)		0.76	60	2.2		0.97 (49.4)		0.99	0.03	2.0	4.9
Public administration and defense	0.53 (39.1)		−0.01	52	2.3		0.92 (25.5)		0.96	0.05	1.9	4.1
	0.26 (2.1)	419 (2.1)	0.40	40	1.1	4.4						
Aggregate demand												
Private consumption	0.79 (99.6)		0.90	282	1.2	4.5	1.00 (170.7)		0.999	0.01	1.6	5.0
	0.97 (7.6)	−2532 (1.4)	0.92	260	2.0	58						
Government consumption	0.94 (43.3)		0.30	101	2.4	1.5	0.95 (45.1)		0.99	0.03	1.9	4.9
	0.54 (3.1)	771 (2.3)	0.63	74	1.1	9.4						

Variable	Coefficient	Constant	$\bar{R}^2$	SE	DW	F
Fixed capital investment	1.12 (69.4)		0.88	93	2.1	4.4
	0.98 (86.3)		0.997	0.02	1.9	5.0
Inventory change	2.99 (2.9)		−0.84	155	2.3	
	1.03 (47.6)		0.99	0.03	2.1	4.9
Exports of goods and services	0.95 (76.7)		0.90	70	2.0	4.5
	1.02 (96.7)		0.997	0.01	1.2	5.0
	99 (54.9)	0.020 (2.0)	0.998	0.01	1.6	3019
Imports of goods and services	0.96 (62.8)		0.43	87	2.5	2.1
	1.03 (36.7)		0.98	0.04	2.0	4.9
Adjustment for variations in the terms of trade	1.12 (4.7)	−116 (1.4)	0.01	114	2.1	
	0.61 (1.4)	−4529 (1.8)	0.17	105	2.0	
GDP at market prices	0.70 (63.6)		0.87	497	1.1	4.4
	0.94 (7.4)		0.91	409	2.4	54.4
	0.985 (117.0)		0.998	0.01	2.8	5.0
Net factor income from abroad	0.95 (23.4)		0.76		1.9	
GNP at market prices	0.85 (143.4)		0.97	266	1.0	
	0.99 (16.9)	−2595 (2.4)	0.98	189	2.9	287

[a]The data sources are given in the previous section. For each variable one regression is presented with the constant supressed. If the constant is significantly nonzero at the 25% level when not supressed, another regression is presented with the constant. $\bar{R}^2$ is the coefficient of determination corrected for degrees of freedom, SE is the standard error of estimate, DW is the Durbin–Watson statistic and F is the F statistic. Beneath the point estimates in parentheses are presented the absolute values of the t statistics.

The estimated coefficients of the real quantity variables imply a number of different compositional shifts. For production, the ODEPLAN estimates are significantly below the CORFO ones for agriculture, transportation, housing, and the various private and public service subsectors, but significantly above the CORFO ones for mining and manufacturing. For final demand, the ODEPLAN estimates are significantly below the CORFO ones for government consumption and the adjustment due to variations in the terms of trade, but significantly above the CORFO ones for fixed capital and inventory investment. In about half the cases the marginal estimates differ from the average ones if a nonzero constant is allowed.[1] However, only in about half of the cases in which a significantly nonzero constant is obtained does its inclusion lead to a coefficient estimate closer to one. For the most aggregate measures (i.e. *GDP* and *GNP*), finally, despite the compositional changes noted above, the marginal estimates do not differ significantly between the two sets of accounts, although the averages are less in the ODEPLAN case.

The estimated coefficients of the deflators imply much less in the way of compositional shifts. Only for transportation is there a significant marginal shift – downward, in this case. Also, evidence of a significant difference between the average and marginal relations is about half as common as for the real quantity relations.

The degree to which the variations in the two sets of data coincide varies substantially for the quantity data. For production in banks, insurance, and real estate and for inventory changes there is no evidence of a significant association. For production in agriculture, mining, and public administration and defence and for imports of goods and services and the adjustment for variations in the terms of trade, one set of data is consistent with less than half of the variance in the other. For the other two thirds of the variables the consistency is greater than half. In over half of the total number of variables it is greater than 0.75 and in a third of the cases it is greater than 0.87. Included in this last group are the total *GDP* and *GNP* variables. Apparently, a number of the sources of

---

[1]The comments about the relative size of the ODEPLAN versus the CORFO estimates above and about the consistency between the variances in the two sets of data below always refer to the estimates with constants included in cases in which such constants are significantly nonzero.

differences on a more disaggregate level cancel out with aggregation.

The two sets of data are much more consistent with respect to
variations in the deflators. If differences are allowed between
average and marginal relations, in no case is the degree of consistency less than 97%. If the average and marginal relations are
forced to be the same, only for *GDP* in transportation is the degree
of consistency less than 94%. The general high degree of correlation between the two sets of deflators, of course, reflects the
incorporation of the general inflationary trend in all of these
indices, which predominates even if the construction of a particular
deflator differs substantially in the two cases.

A.3. Alternative deflators for sectoral value added

The CORFO national accounts do not have separate sectoral *GDP*
deflators. Instead, the overall deflator is constructed as a weighted
average of the deflator for the components of final demand. This
overall deflator is used for each of the production sectors which
ignores the impact of possible relative price changes.

Ideally, one would like to use the double deflation method to
obtain sectoral real value added estimates from the CORFO
nominal value added estimates. That is, one would like to subtract
from the value of sectoral gross product (deflated by an index
reflecting movements in the product price) the value of intermediate input purchases by that sector (deflated by the appropriate
weighted index for the intermediate inputs) in order to obtain
sectoral real value added. The annual input–output flow matrices
required for this procedure, however, are not available. Therefore,
some approximation must be adopted.

The alternative which is used in this study is to assume that the
sectoral gross price index is an appropriate deflator for the sectoral
value added. This approach involves the assumption that expenditures on sectoral intermediate inputs are a constant share of
sectoral gross value for a given sector over time. This assumption
is consistent with an elasticity of substitution of one among
intermediate inputs or constant relative prices and fixed coefficients
among intermediate inputs (for elaboration, see Jul (1972)).

Another alternative would be to use the existing input–output

coefficients for 1962 from ODEPLAN (1970c), assume that they
are constant in physical terms throughout the sample, and use them
to weight the intermediate input prices. Of course, this procedure is
consistent with the assumption of an elasticity of substitution of
zero among the intermediate inputs.

Jul (1972) has examined the implications of using alternative
sectoral value added deflators for the Chilean experience over the
sample period. She considers the CORFO procedure, the procedure adopted in this study, and the procedure outlined in the
previous paragraph. She compares the time patterns of the alternative deflators, of their rates of change, and of their implications for the sectoral composition of total product.

Of course without information about the time patterns of actual
value added, she cannot conclusively decide that a particular
alternative is preferable. However, she tentatively decides that the
method used in the present study is preferable for the following
reasons: (1) relative prices have varied considerably over the
sample, which raises questions about the CORFO procedure; (2)
the last method leads to erratic changes in the deflators and in the
sectoral composition of product which do not seem plausible (e.g.
large negative rates of change in a number of sectoral deflators
early in the sample, although overall inflation then was considerable), apparently because of an inappropriate assumption of a fixed
coefficient technology; and (3) the last method is more difficult
computationally than the other two. Her conclusion, qualified
though it need be, is somewhat reassuring for the present study.